To Kajsa

System, Structure, and Contradiction

The Evolution
of "Asiatic" Social Formations

Second Edition

Jonathan Friedman

ALTAMIRA
PRESS

A Division of Sage Publications, Inc.
Walnut Creek • London • New Delhi

For information address:

AltaMira Press
A Division of Sage Publications, Inc.
1630 North Main Street, Suite 367
Walnut Creek, CA 94596
explore@altamira.sagepub.com
http://www.altamirapress.com

DS
528.2
.K3
F74
1998

SAGE Publications Ltd.
6 Bonhill Street
London EC2A 4PU
United Kingdom

SAGE Publications India Pvt. Ltd.
M-32 Market
Greater Kailash 1
New Delhi 110 048

PRINTED IN THE UNITED STATES OF AMERICA

Library of Congress Cataloging-in-Publication Data

Friedman, Jonathan.
    System, structure, and contradiction : the evolution of "Asiatic" social formations / by Jonathan Friedman. – 2nd ed.
        p. cm.
    A revision of the author's thesis, Columbia, 1972.
    Includes bibliographic references.
    ISBN 0-7619-8933-1. – ISBN 0-7619-8934-X (pbk.)
    1.   Kachin (Asian people)—Social conditions. 2. Kachin (Asian people)—Economic conditions. 3. Social structure—Burma.
4. Social change—Burma. 5. Asiatic mode of production—Burma.
6. Marxist anthropology—Burma. 7. Burma—Social conditions.
I. Title
DS528.2.K3F74   1998
306'.09591—dc21   98-5914
                                                                        CIP

Credits: Maps from *Rainfall in Burma*, by R. Huke, courtesy of the author. Maps from *Political Systems*, by E. R. Leach, courtesy of Athlone Press. Maps from *Southeast Asia*, by C. A. Fisher, courtesy of Metheun Press.

Production: Janice Sellers
Editorial Services: David Feathestone
Editorial Management: Jennifer R. Collier
Cover Design: Joanna Ebenstein

Contents

Acknowledgments

The stimulus for my original thesis owes much to seminars on exchange structures held by Professors Abraham Rosman, Paula Rubel, and Harvey Pitkin at Columbia University. I owe a great deal of thanks to Professors Rosman and Rubel, who advised and criticized me on the original manuscript and who have been encouraging throughout. Without the help of Professor Lehman of the University of Illinois the thesis might never have been written. His many enlightening letters and my long discussions with him were very important in the formulation of my ideas, and his extensive familiarity with the Southeast Asian material was an essential ingredient in the initial stages of my research. My studies in Paris in 1967–1968 were clearly important in my theoretical development, especially through the works and lectures of Levi-Strauss and the early work of Godelier. The single most powerful theoretical influence, however, was probably that of Lynn Marcus, especially his then-unpublished manuscript *Dialectical Economics*.

As I say in the introduction, my theoretical outlook has changed considerably since 1972. The original manuscript was kicked about for several years by friends in Sweden and later Denmark, where it was presented in seminars. A great deal of thanks is due to all those who were involved in those discussions. I would like, finally, to acknowledge the fundamental inspiration that I have received from my association with Kajsa Ekholm over the past six years, which is largely responsible for my theoretical development since 1972.

Preface to the 1998 Edition

It is arguable that this book ought not to be republished. After all, the structuralist Marxism it represents is no longer explicitly practiced in anthropology. On the other hand, the global anthropology that developed—very much as a reaction to the closed nature of the Marxist model (Ekholm 1973, First introduction to this book 1979)—did so to a large extent out of the work that went into this approach, one which stressed the existence of cycles of growth and decline, a structural transformation generated by processes of social reproduction, and of a systemic approach to structural historical process. The macrohistorical nature of the models developed in this book may account for their use among archaeologists. There are, to be sure, a number of archaeologists who, over the years, have attempted to apply some of these models in their analyses of European prehistory (Kristiansen 1982, Hedeager 1987) or of the development of Polynesian chiefdoms (Kirch 1984). In the fields of anthropology, history, and archaeology a rather broad literature has emerged on growth and collapse that has made use of either my work or similar approaches. Even Colin Renfrew (1978, 1984), in his experimentation with catastrophe theory and in his critique of my work, has, in fact, come close in a very general sense to the basic formulations offered here. All this is certainly gratifying to me, but I have often been skeptical, or at least uneasy, as to the applicability of such models to other times and places.

I wrote the first preface introducing the first edition eight years after the completion of the original manuscript. Attempts at early publication were unsuccessful. The late Sir Edmund Leach vowed that he would quit his position at Cambridge University Press if the manuscript was accepted, and he circulated widely a rather long and personal attack on both an early article and the manuscript itself. He even managed to insert a nasty reference in the last introduction to his *Political Systems of Highland Burma*, a book that inspired me enormously as a student and to which I paid great respect in this volume. By the time this was finally published, I was already engaged in another perspective, one that is now referred to as "global anthropology."[1]

In the 1979 introduction, I attempted to place my earlier work in a larger framework in order to understand the regional position of the highlands of northern Southeast Asia in relation to the lowland states and to the interregional

---

[1] This should not be confused with the current and rather faddish literature on globalization in anthropology, which came more than a decade after Kajsa Ekholm Friedman first wrote about global systems and which lacks any clear theoretical structure other than the "discovery" that the world has become increasingly interconnected.

and international trade that had traversed the area for the past millennia. Here I received a great deal of inspiration from discussions with F. K. Lehman and Maran LaRaw. My self-criticism gave way to a reformulation of the transformation of these societies, but also to a reaffirmation of the value of the previous analysis. A recent study has lent some support to the general thesis of my book, especially the idea that a devolutionary process might account for some of the "egalitarian" social forms that I discussed (Satyawadhna 1990).[2] I cannot complain about the reception of the book, as most of the reviews were favorable, some in the extreme (Schwimmer 1981). In the first introduction, I went to some length to reply to criticism of the original manuscript and related articles. I have continued in this vein by devoting some time to a quite elaborate argument developed by Luc de Heusch (1981) as an appendix to his earlier article on the Kachin, which I discussed in the previous edition of this book. I have done so out of respect, not only for those who have taken the time to argue with me, but for the principle of the public arena, which declined so markedly among anthropologists as well as other academics during the eighties. One review of the book (Claessen 1980), in fact, wondered why I was so concerned with self-criticism. I can only reply that I feel that any intellectual product must be open to continuous scrutiny, criticism, and reformulation if it is to maintain any value as part of a process of the development of knowledge. All the criticism that has been directed to the content of what I have written, and not merely to labeling and its consequences, is valuable for my own rethinking and understanding of the world. Several critical reviews by specialists in the area have led me to rethink much of what I have attempted to do.

Critical Rethinking
One very long and intricate analysis that has not been published (Hedén 1979) tried to develop some of the models of the original thesis before its publication. Hedén made some very trenchant criticism of the way I dealt with some of the empirical material, not least the material on the Naga. First, while I had tended to assume a rather strict devolutionary model of the Kachin-type

---

[2]) Cholthira Satyawadhna, who has done extensive research among the Lua, the Laveue and the Wa of Thailand and Yunnan, argues for structural relations of variations among the different groups and for the thesis of devolution.

> In the case of the Wa of Yunnan, my field investigation and analysis of the available body of information argue for the validity of his theoretical contribution. (1990:98)
> She uses a regional model concerning the relation between position in the larger political system and local political organization, from the emergence predatory dynamic polities to peripheralized communities.
> Between such centre-periphery structures, the Mon-Khmer communities, including the Lua of Nan, were those that were constrained by their position within the larger system....(Friedman 1979:13) (1990:96)

system, he suggested that the model would be more adequate if it could account for the emergence of chiefly structures such as those that are found among the Konyak Naga and which seem to be based on another kind of accumulation process. He suggests the following long cycle, in which the last developments are the result of warfare among "egalitarian" polities, resulting in a new kind of hierarchy (see Fig. 1).

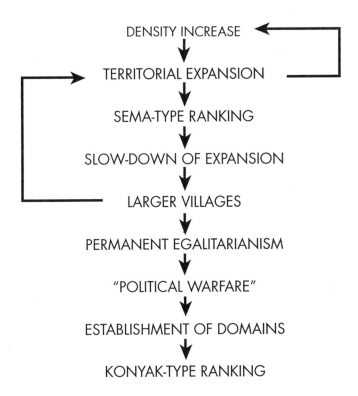

Figure 1. A Naga Cycle of Hierarchization.

The chiefly structures of the Konyak Naga are very different from those of the Kachin, and it might be that this is a better explanation of those variations that I did not consider in the original work. Part of the reason for this is that the ethnography of the area was rather thin and that perhaps there was a lack of clear understanding of how these societies functioned.

Mark Woodward (1989) has also discussed my book with reference to the historical and ethnographic material on the Naga. His critique is also powerful, but it is directed toward the more general properties of the model proposed in the book. His argument is essentially that one of the Naga groups, the Ao, has neither the population density nor the ecological degradation that I associate with a tendency toward dualism and egalitarianism. But his interpretation of my model is somewhat simplified.

> He treats ideology as a constant, arguing that variant social forma-
> tions are determined by a calculus of ecological variables including
> soil fertility, rainfall and population density. He associates rich
> environments with hiearchical political systems and degraded envi-
> ronments with egalitarian systems." (1989:132)

But this is not really how I have put it. I have argued that it is the social system itself that is the driving force in these changes, and that the transformation of the environment resulting from a socially organized overintensification leads in its turn to the transformation of the social structure, but not in a direct causal relation since it is the social actors, in their specific social conditions, that react to material changes that they have themselves generated. In my discussion, there is in fact room for the Ao case, but it must be contextualized carefully and hypothetically. In my approach, the larger transformation that generates the particular set of Naga configurations cannot be reduced to man–environment relations because the emergent social structure becomes an organizational force in Naga society. Much of my discussion of the social structure of clan strategies is an attempt to show the dominance of transformed social relations; but this is not the same as assuming that there are cultural differences that in themselves, without reference to historical process, account for social differences in strategies and practices. Thus, I would disagree with Woodward's conclusion:

> The Ao are "egalitarian" not because they cannot afford to have
> chiefs, but because their cosmological system does not allow any
> individual or social group to monopolize the available sources of
> magical potency. (135)

My argument assumes that it is precisely the transformation of the cosmology that is instrumental in the other changes. This does not imply that the structures of the cosmology have no material effects. On the contrary, the latter are embedded in the social practices of reproduction (see discussion of Sahlins below), in the strategies of prestige accumulation, and in their immediate institutional conditions of prestige accumulation. I would, however, argue somewhat differently than Woodward, who seems to rely on an ahistorical assumption that the Ao Naga, unlike most of the other Naga, have a cosmology that eliminates the possibility of hierarchization. On the contrary, it is the general transformation of Naga social structure that may account for the specific combination among the Ao of high productivity without chiefdom development. The explanation in the model suggested by Hedén, in which a strategy of accumulation via production is replaced by a strategy based on conquest, may be the key to understanding this problem. In my model, increasing population density, which is driven by a social dynamic and not by ecological considerations, as suggested by Woodward (1989:125, 135), leads to a threshold after which a certain implosion occurs—the formation of larger defensive villages, an intensification of agriculture, and an increase and systematization of warfare.[3] This process leads, in turn, to a restructuring of social relations that I discuss in detail in the chapters on "devolution."

What I missed in my analysis was the possibility and apparent existence of a new trajectory based on this transformation, and it is this trajectory that Hedén points out so well. Ao society, as Woodward himself states, is not egalitarian, in spite of his quote above. It is quite elaborately ranked, but not like the Kachin. Instead, there is a system of "merit" that is expressed in the institutionalization of prestige ranks, and there is a clear aristocratic ideology. It is interesting that the Ao associate themselves with, and are neighbors of, the Konyak, who are much more hierarchical. The latter, according to Hedén, base their chiefly organization on the way warfare is institutionalized into hierarchy. And it is the case that the Ao "*pongen* phratry corresponds with, and is the 'brother' of, the Konyak *ang*, or aristocratic clan." (Woodward 1989:125). This might imply that both the Ao and the Konyak represent different phases in a new trajectory, one based on the more general transformation of a former Kachin-type of structure.

Last But Not Least: The State as Historical Revolution

Luc de Heusch, a structuralist and symbolic anthropologist, has vigorously attacked an earlier article (Friedman 1975) summarizing much of the argument of this book (de Heusch 1981). He appreciates my suggestion that it is the relation to the ancestors that represents a primary operator in the dynamics of Kachin expansion, but he falls back, strangely for a structuralist, on straightforward mechanical materialism and questions the power of mystification by which a chief might emerge by converting productivity into rank. It is as if I had suggested that it was a question of cunning and trickery, of fooling others into becoming followers because of the symbolic power of generosity. That does not work in Melanesia, he claims, and he refers to Sahlins's early work. But it does work in Melanesia up to a certain threshold, after which it collapses—not because ordinary people cease to be lured by the symbolism of feasting, but because the cycle of indebtedness leads to increasing conflicts in a situation of overintensification and most likely declining returns to

---

[3]) Schwimmer is quite clear about my relation to cultural ecology.

Dans les écrits ultérieurs de Friedman, Marx l'emportera largement sur Lévi-Strauss, mais les duex maîtres se côtoient . . . dont la bête noire (combattue par l'invocation conjointe de deux maîtres) est l'écologie culturelle. (Schwimmer 1981:223)

productive effort. In any case, my argument was that Kachin-type systems were quite different from classical Big-man systems because prestige was converted into rank via matrimonial exchange (i.e. bride price inflation). The latter system is an example of the way in which generalized exchange can become hierarchical. De Heusch never discusses this absolutely central argument. I do not argue that hierarchization depends upon "belief." I invoke the notion of fetishism precisely in order to stress that what might appear to the observer as mystification is simultaneously an immediately lived reality, a logical set of meaningful relations that organize a world. De Heusch's own argument, based on changes in relations of land tenure, makes the false assumption that there is lineage property in the sense of alienable title to land. In order to account for the process of alienation, he assumes that matrilocal marriages made by immigrant lineages create clientship relations to landowners that are the basis for political hierarchy. In the conclusion to chapter seven of this book, I went to some length to demonstrate why this argument is both inconsistent and empirically unfounded, since what appeared as land title was a secondary, "ideological" product of the political hierarchization process itself, in which control over village or territorial spirit ancestors could be equated with control of their land. While it is certainly the case that my early article might seem to dwell too much on the model rather than on the ethnographic and historical data, my book musters substantial material in favor of the same arguments.

In a more general critique, de Heusch claims that I use the ecosystem concept in the same way that vulgar materialists use other "last instances." I find this difficult to understand, as I argue for exactly the contrary, i.e., for a contradictory relation between the dominant social strategies and their ecological conditions of existence. He is also skeptical of, and rightly so as an Africanist, a model of social practice that is predicated on the conversion of increasing agricultural yields into a process of political hierarchization. Nowhere do I suggest that political hierarchization depends *in general* upon agricultural intensification. In fact, in the book's original appendix, I argue that in systems organized in terms of the accumulation of prestige-goods, hierarchy is dependent upon control over the regional exchange of specific goods. In such systems, agricultural intensification need play no significant role at all, except as a response to increasing population densities at central places. I refer explicitly to Central Africa and to Tonga in this respect.

Finally, Luc de Heusch is not at all pleased with my suggestion that, in proper conditions, Kachin-type systems can develop into the kind of state-class structures that I refer to as "Asiatic" since he believes, along with both evolutionists and primitivists (e.g. Clastres 1977), that the state marks a break, or even a revolution, in world history that can never be accounted for in terms of "imperceptible" changes. I can only say that I beg to differ and that I devote quite some space to this argument. His absolutist distinction between state and nonstate is, I would argue, very much a nineteenth-century, or better a seventeenth-century European dichotomy, based on an emergent "modern" identity rather than a rational-empirical investigation into actual historical processes.

It belongs to the neoevolutionist tradition in anthropology as well as that of Clastres[4] and anarchism, for which I feel sympathy however absurd it is in empirical terms. I would like to thank de Heusch for his concise remarks and the time he took to criticize my article, but I do feel that his argument is more a product of his own vision of Leach's publications and a very limited vision of the Marxism I proposed than an objective analysis of my own work.

Structuralist Marxism and Historical Structuralism

I would like, not merely for the sake of surprise, to argue that the specific combination of structuralism and Marxism represented here cannot be dismissed as outmoded, antiquated, nineteenth-century, or some other wand-waving, fashion-conscious term of rejection. While terminology is often heavy-handed, especially in its Althusserian versions, and while its reductionist determinism is a fatal weakness, one that many of us criticized, the approach had the advantages of a framework in which power, history, and social dynamics were central. This framework is certainly not dead, even if internal critique and an external shift in general ideological orientations has led to the abandonment of much of its discourse. On the contrary, it is alive and well in many quarters—clothed in different and sometimes less precise terms and often with weaker assumptions—but still strongly informed by the issues raised by the framework.

Certainly the most significant and indeed powerful form in which this framework is reproduced is in the later work of Marshall Sahlins. I feel an especially strong affinity for his project, which sprang from a critique of materialist reductionism yet maintained a dialectically historical and structuralist approach to the understanding of social life. Let me note some parallels. In 1974, I published an article on the problem of fetishism in Marxist analysis in which I tried to demonstrate the way the social forms of capitalist reproduction, based on the commodity form itself and especially on the domination of "real-abstract" relations such as money-capital, exemplified the way in which imaginary relations were the organizational force of material realities. The tradition of historical materialism, however, had reduced, if not eliminated, the notion of fetishism by making it a secondary, and therefore nonoperational form, a mere representation. This kind of argument exists in Marx's own work, even in his analysis in volume one of *Capital*, where commodity fetishism can be interpreted as a misrepresentation of already-existent relations of exploitation rather

---

[4]) It should not be forgotten that Clastres, while attacking the notion that "primitive" societies evolved into states, argues himself that the historical circumstances that led to the State revolution, i.e., the usurpation of power, were increasing population density and warfare. Thus both the idea that the state emerges as a form of usurpation (Rappaport 1977) and that its development is driven by population pressure (Harris 1981, Harner 1970) are well-established neoevolutionary arguments.

than the organization of those relations. In other works, however, but especially in volume three of *Capital*, the crucial role of capital as fictitious capital, as abstract wealth that structures the entire economic process, is made clear. And the accumulation of this "real-abstract" wealth becomes the dynamic, as well as the source, of the contradiction in the larger system.

I argued that the fetishized nature of those social relations that dominate the processes of social reproduction are the source of both the misrepresentation of reality, viewed from the outside, and the actual lived reality of the participants on the inside. This implies a distinction between fetishism and ideology. The latter refers to representations of lived reality, but the former refers to the *very organization of that reality*, the fact that the real is a lived fantasy. In simple terms, this could account for why "fictitious" capital accumulation might seem perfectly reasonable as a strategy at the same time that it undermines the conditions for further accumulation by making the system as a whole too expensive for its own reproduction . . . i.e., the basis of liquidity crises. When this work was published, most Marxists did not agree with this approach because, from their point of view, representations are always a question of ideology, i.e., of secondary forms—faithful reflections or equally faithful inversions of the real world—that move in parallel with reality and thus have no organizing power.

In 1975, Sahlins published his *Culture and Practical Reason*, which made some of the same kinds of arguments but in a much more general way. Instead of fetish he used the concept of culture, a much broader but also much more vague concept. His purpose here was different than my own. He was making an argument within anthropology about the use of the concept in two traditions that he traced from Morgan, on one hand, and Boas, on the other. While the arguments against practical reason, including the ambivalences of Marx's own writings, were most welcome, there was little sustained discussion of the area in which Marx's notion of fetishism was most applicable, the concept of money-capital. Instead, the culture of capitalism was taken from Baudrillardian- (Jean Baudrilard) and Barthian- (Roland Barthes) inspired analyses of consumption. Distinctions in clothing, for example, were seen as capitalist culture, "the savage mind gone wild." But this felicitous phrase ought not to be understood as referring to an autonomous cultural process, since it is closely linked to a market-driven process of product differentiation, the linking of the imagination of difference to the necessity of capitalist survival. Sahlins's notion of culture alluded to code and paradigm rather than to the fetishized relations that were central to my own approach. This accounts for the difficulty in comprehending why distinctions can be replaced ad infinitum since the dress code is an ever-changing product, rather than a *producer*, of market processes.

In my argument, the dominant fetishism lay in the structure of capital itself and not in the more Boasian cultural codes invoked by Sahlins. Now capital is a "real abstraction," a social form of wealth whose properties are socially material, but not, of course, natural. It is in the social materiality of capital that its organizational force is located. But what is the meaning the "socially" material? It is often easy to confuse the material with the physical and the natural. A book is a cultural construction, a product that is generated in its form and content within a specific social context, constructed on the basis of a specific, i.e., cultural, plan. A book is also a material entity in its entirety, but the semantic content conveyed by the words printed on paper is not the same as the printed words themselves. The latter have material properties, in this case physical properties, that are not reducible to the cultural construction of the book. Even if the shape and size of the book are socially organized products, the fact that it has weight and occupies space—the fact that I can throw it and hit someone who can be hurt by it—are related to noncultural properties of the book.

A business cycle is also material, but in a different way. It is an unintended product of individual strategies in a world organized by the meaningful structures of capital as abstract wealth in a market system of a particular kind. But the business cycle itself is not an organizational feature of the capitalist market. It is a nonintentional, yet structured, product of its functioning. The materiality of the business cycle lies in its structuration within a complex of social conditions that regulate the distribution of wealth and buying power over time. This is not the materiality of the physical, but a "social" materiality constituted in two moments. First, money, fictitious in itself, is provided with the social power to appropriate the world via its systemic constitution as capital. Second, the distribution of money over time is structured by the basic social forms in which capital is reproduced. It is the fetishized nature of capital that is the key to its materiality; the imaginary is realized in the control over people, their time, and their products.

This argument is similar to that made by Sahlins in his insistence on the social content of the material, but the kinds of abstraction involved in the analysis are different. Sahlins, as I indicate above, tended to use a notion of culture as a symbolic code that, abstracted from its social context, enables the kind of semiotic analysis suggested by Barthes. This makes it possible to separate the order of meaning from the order of practice, the former being the source of the latter. I suggested that the material properties of social relations were crucial to understanding the interface between fetishized social realities and their conditions of existence. The concept of fetishism, I argued, should not be understood in terms of the misrepresentation of reality, as if it were generated as a transformation of that reality, but as the very form of lived reality itself whose representational properties are simply incommensurate with that to which they refer. The origin of fetishized relations was argued to be the result of historical transformation of previous fetishized relations. The culture concept is far too indifferent to this problem of incompatibility. The general thrust of *Culture and Practical Reason* was the argument for the primacy of culture as a system of meaning in the organization of material existence. Sahlins expresses this in his attempt to amplify the claims of structuralism beyond those of Lévi-Strauss, who claimed that conceptual schemes "merely" mediated between praxis and practices (Lévi-Strauss 1966:130–31).

> This (conceptual) scheme is the very organization of material pro-
> duction . . . Its presence there dissolves the classic antinomies of
> infrastructure and superstructure, the one considered "material" the
> other "conceptual." Of course, it does not dissolve the "material" as
> such. But the so-called material causes must be, in that capacity, the
> product of a symbolic system whose character it is our task to inves-
> tigate. (Sahlins 1976:56–7)

The organization of a workplace is certainly the result of the imposition of a plan, a conceptual scheme; but the capacity to impose such plans depends upon social relations that encompass and dominate the organization of the workplace and which determine largely what kind of organization shall be cho- sen. There is no symbolic structure of capitalism that is applied as a whole to the organization of reality. Nor is there a symbolic structure of a Kachin uni- verse that is applied to the organization of Kachin social relations. Over time, the practice of capitalist relations leads to the formation of a certain world of production, social structures, and secondary representations. The primary or- ganizational relations are always-already imaginary in their content; they are constituted of representations, but representations that are self-referential, i.e., they are not symbolic in the sense of referring to something external to them- selves. This is the difference between the flag and real money. The imaginary is a ubiquitous component of behavior, except for behaviorists; but symbolic structures are generated by a practice of structuring, and thus by the structural properties of social relations. The difference between infrastructure and su- perstructure is not one of material versus conceptual structures. It is a differ- ence between the direct organization of social reproduction and the discourses and "material" practices that are predicated on that organization. These con- stitute a hierarchy of structures connected to material reproduction, both prac- tices that are organized in representations, and representations that are also practices. But, as it is said of some proverbial turtles on which the world rests, it's "concepts" all the way down.

In a reply to my review of *Islands of History* (1985), Sahlins claims that "cul- tural" is anything that is ordered or configured by the human symbolic faculty, anything whose mode of existence is thus symbolically constituted . . . other- wise there is no such thing as a domestic horse" (1988:46). But is a "domestic horse" constituted by a cultural scheme, or is it constituted in a social relation between man and animal, in which the "natural" properties of the animal are ever–present? The only thing that is symbolically constituted is the symbol itself—the category, the definition, the name—not the reality that it denotes or connotes. While Sahlins's critique was certainly successful against the prac- tical reason of certain anthropological approaches, it tended to abstract the meaningful aspect of social life and transform it into an autonomous deter- minant of the reality from which it was abstracted. My own argument against a certain materialism matched that of Sahlins, but there is apparently a misunderstanding with respect to what I interpreted as a cultural determinist argument.

In the next phase of Sahlins's work, this cultural determinism was linked to the problem of historical change via a dialectic between "the practice of structure" and the "structure of practice." I have suggested elsewhere (1987) that this model, too, is a culturalist form of the kind of approach employed in this book. Sahlins has indicated his total disagreement with my characterization of his work in terms of culturalism or cultural determinism, so I shall, in all good faith, try to clarify my argument. In my usage, cultural determinism refers to Sahlins's explicit acceptance and refinement of the "Boasian" model of the relation between categories and practice, expressed precisely in expressions such as "the practice of structure" and "mythopraxis." Such terms imply a relation of code to action on the order of *script* to *performance* and of *grammar* to *speech*. Speech events, just as social events, are the product of linguistic and/or cultural structures. This relation is absolutely explicit in Sahlins's work, and it is with this that I have taken issue. While I have often written of the fetish as the organizer of "material" relations, I do not make use of the concept of culture in such discussions; and I do not partition social action into script and performance, or code and practice. On the contrary, the fetishized aspect of the social is always embedded in the social relations themselves and has no independent existence as a pure representation to be applied to the organization of action. The latter can only be the product of an abstraction, after the fact so to speak, that occurs in discourses about reality, but does not create it.

It is true, of course, that cultural forms can exist autonomously, that they can be institutionalized and highly systematized so as to take the form of a code, rule book, or recipe. But they are, as such, social products rather than the primary determinants of social action. The code is always the product of a codification, i.e., a *specific social practice*. Even where the code is employed to organize practice, as in social movements, rituals and socialization, or the domestication of horses, it is the social use of the code that is the valence of its power, rather than the code itself. Thus, *cultural determinism is always a form of social power, a social determinism*. This argument has been made cogently in linguistics as part of a general critique of the Saussurian notion of *langue* that is Sahlins's conscious model for culture. In contemporary discussions, it is argued that grammar is a social institution and part of an organization both of power and of the authority of socialization rather than an abstract mental structure (Rommetveit 1983, Labov 1972, Bourdieu 1982).

In Sahlins, the fundamental contradiction is one between a cultural structure and the conditions of its realization as social practice. The practice of a structure leads to its modification because it occurs in a context where outside forces, e.g., other cultural practices and interests, intervene in such a way as to modify its outcome. In the model suggested here, social relations harbor strategies that produce a dynamic that leads to contradictions in the larger system, contradictions that arise because of the incompatibility between different structures that constitute, and thus coexist in, the process of social reproduction.

That relationship, which in Sahlins belongs to the external context of the practice of culture, is internal to the notion of social reproduction suggested here. In fact, all the nonintentional properties of the reproductive process are internal in this approach; the cycles and long-term trends, the processes of hierarchization and devolution. In Sahlins, the dialectic is constructed on the basis of a contradiction between culture and practice. In my own approach, the dialectic is constructed on the basis of a contradiction between practice and its conditions of existence. I do not divide praxis into cultural structure and practice, but see the latter as a unity that cannot be so divided (see Fig. 2). Culture as code is a mere abstraction and a textualization of the structural properties of practice. But representing such properties as a Saussurian system of signs is a false abstraction, unless the latter actually exists for those subjects. In such a case I would argue that culture has been institutionalized, elaborated, and used—socially—to organize behavior. Where this does not occur then, culture refers only to the specificity of practice, and not to the mode of its organization.

This critique is applicable to my own arguments concerning fetishized social relations wherever I implied that imaginary constructions are realized as social form. My suggestion that social relations are fetishized because fetishes become social relations (Friedman 1974) is part of a larger argument that the

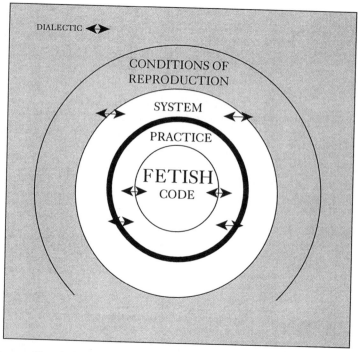

Figure 2. Structure/Practice/System Dialectics

historical transformation of social relations is simultaneously the transformation of their fetishized properties. Thus the historical metamorphosis of sacred chiefs into gods that is discussed in this book results from a reduction of the distance between superior ancestor-gods and their living representatives that occurs as an aspect of the increase in real power that follows the intensification of accumulation. The way in which this transformation occurs depends upon the internal logic of the representation itself. This logic is a structure of interpretation in which the wealth of a person is identical to a relatively closer genealogical relation to the highest deities. Is this the cultural code of power among the Kachin? Yes, there is an implicit set of highly structured semantic connections here, but these connections do not organize practice as such. Rather they are embedded in a structure of practice that unites generalized exchange and feasting in a process of political hierarchization, and to which they endow a specific, i.e., cultural, form—an immediate and implicit interpretation. The advantage of using the concept of fetishism here is that it refers specifically to the imaginary aspect of a material social reality and to the internal incommensurability between the properties of the imaginary and the social reality in which it is embedded. This is a difference between Weber's and Geertz's notion of culture as a "web of significance" and the qualification, as Ingmar Bergman would have it, that life is a "tissue of lies."

In sum, while the differences between the historical structuralist framework espoused by Sahlins and the structuralist Marxist frame espoused by myself share much in common, I think the differences are significant enough to warrant this discussion. The differences are by no means easy to delineate, but they can be said to relate to the way social reality is dissected. For Sahlins, as I understand him, the primary division is between the cultural as a symbolic structure and the social practices from which such a structure is, in my terms, abstracted. The problem as I see it is that such structures cannot be adequately understood outside of their social contexts unless they become institutionalized as "official" strategies, rules, ritual organizations, etc. To say that practice is culturally constituted is not to say that it is constituted *by* a cultural structure with a prior existence. It is to say that it is constituted *of* culture, in the sense that meaning is always embedded in the intentionality of practice. Recent suggestions by Bruce Kapferer, which make use of Husserl's concept of *intentionality*, might be a solution to the problem as I see it. In Husserl's phenomenology, and this has a longer tradition, *intentionality* is the movement of the subject into the world, a movement from a center to an external social arena where it assimilates the latter to itself. *Intentionality* harbors power, the power to organize the world in a way that is at once emotionally powerful and meaningful. The specificity of this in any particular time and place is its *cultural* specificity. In this understanding, meaning is a ubiquitous quality, or property, of intentionality, and the latter is, in turn, the content of social practice. There may well be a dialectical relation between meaning and practice, but it must be understood as a relation within the confines of human practice as an *intentional* unity. In this book I suggest that the transformation from chiefs to antichiefs, from feasting to headhunting, from hierarchy to competitive equality, from generalized to restricted exchange, and from a cosmology of expansive fertility and generosity to a cosmology of scarcity, warfare, and witchcraft is a transformation in which interpretations of the world become inverted in the very practices within which those interpretations are embedded. The contradiction that provokes this historical change is, in my argument, one that emerges between an entire reproductive process and its conditions of existence, between the practice and its conditions of reproduction. There is, on the other hand, a dialectic between cosmological interpretations and the transformation of the larger social system, one that is organized via the contradictions of practice, via the impossibility of maintaining a particular interpretation of the world. I argue that the new resulting interpretations are logically deducible from the old ones, which is why I use the term *transformation*.

Confession

There is no question that structuralist Marxism was full of jargon and neologisms, especially for the unsuspecting anthropologist with his own storeroom of jargon. This was the result of the excessive theoreticism of the period. The conceptual baggage developed as a result of attempts to find ways of describing a certain number of processes more precisely. The fact that they made use of unfortunate old terms, such as *"Asiatic" social formation* and *mode of production*, may seem amusing to proponents of *theater states* (Geertz 1980) and *sinking status patterns* (Geertz 1980:30–1), but they did a certain job in clarifying the issues. Other terms, such as *theocratic regimes*, that I employ in the discussion also have both advantages and disadvantages. The argument of the time was that a certain kind of social order, or social formation, could be so characterized, and that it was not localized geographically but represented a very general type. I have maintained the term here because the language of the thesis is very much anchored in the history of a discussion harking back to Marx.

Another and more serious criticism that I would level at this work is its exclusive focus on structures and processes, and the total lack of interest in the nature of personal agency, the constitution of personal experience and motivation, and the relation between agency and structure. Agency is, of course, implied in the text. In the central section on the "political economy of the local lineage," I outline the properties of the strategy implemented by competing potential chiefs in their rise to power. My arguments concerning the relations between production and the "work of the gods" is an attempt to provide an explanation for the way in which the strategy of accumulation is lived as an immediate experience, i.e., as an immediate and unquestioned interpretation of reality. Here again, the notion of fetishism is itself an inadequate attempt to account for the experienced reality of the imaginary, the life of the illusion. I have made some suggestions in this direction (Friedman 1992), but I do not think that such analysis could be carried out given the nature of the ethnographic and historical material that was available to me. Nor was I interested in such problems, since, like many of today's culturalists, I was more concerned with charting the specificities of action and the logic of practice and institutions, than with the constitution of experience. The interest for culturalists, who did seem to appreciate my work in that period, seems to have lain in my attempt to reveal a logic in the representation of the lineage and alliance relation that implied a specific form of theocratic hierarchy. I imagine that this interest, which came most clearly from certain quarters in Oxford, stemmed from the fact that I had criticized both American cultural materialism and French structural Marxism for their purely materialist "operators," and had stressed the importance of culturally specific forms as "operators" in the process of social reproduction. What was clearly misconstrued, perhaps even by myself, was the degree to which such culturally specific forms had any independent existence or whether cultural specificity referred merely to an aspect, i.e., the form, of dominant social relations. I would insist here that this misunderstanding is real, and that it may have been based on my own opposition to "vulgar materialism" and to all forms of functionalist "last instance" explanations.

Genre

This book was written almost exclusively in the third person singular and plural. It represents an extreme form of ethnographic "realism," so extreme that the genuinely ethnographic practically disappears as such, represented only by material selected by the argument to be pursued. The language takes the standard form: "The x do such and such; the system has x and y tendencies," etc. This was not so unusual for the period. *Political Systems* is framed in very similar language, as are many other monographs concerning Southeast Asia and elsewhere. If my own work is somewhat different and more extreme, it is because of the explicit model building and theorizing to which it is dedicated. This is the reason that the concepts became so readily and even dangerously applicable to more general issues in the study of social transformation and "evolution." This book can hardly be considered an ethnographic monograph in today's usage. But in this social context, I do recall the help and even encouragement that I got from a high-ranking Kachin, Maran La Raw, himself a student of Chomsky and quite a brilliant man, who was dismissed by Leach (1969) as a Kachin schoolteacher. His criticisms of my original manuscript were purely historical-ethnographic and theoretical, but he accepted the abstract and ethnographically "authoritarian" way in which I wrote about his people. He was, of course, even more formal-minded than I. It might be added that while ethnographic authority was indeed taken for granted, something that very much disappeared in the 1980s' revolt was theoretical debate. In the late 1960s and 1970s, there was a clear distinction between ethnography and theory, and as a theoretician, Maran La Raw greatly aided the development of my model of the origins of *gumlao* society by offering me valuable material and insights relating to nineteenth-century trade and the concrete process of *gumsa* expansion and its conditions of reproduction (200–201). The assumed transparency of the ethnographic data was always subject to interpretive debate, and since, in my circles at least, we assumed that all ethnography was already interpreted, the latter was always suspect and susceptible to reformulation.

Perhaps because of the explicitness of the theorizing, applications of this work have been essentially limited to the models of "tribal" reproduction themselves. When applied to the "evolution" of Polynesian chiefdoms, or to the rise and fall of European Bronze Age political hierarchies, these studies have been inspiring for my own interest in these areas. Especially with respect to Oceania, I have tried to develop and combine these models in various ways, not least with regard to processes of transformation between structures resembling those that I posited for Southeast Asia and the prestige good systems (a model first developed by Kajsa Ekholm Friedman 1972, 1977) that are also found there (especially in Indonesia), as well as in parts of Melanesia and Western Polynesia (Friedman 1981, 1982).

There is, however, a more serious cautionary note to be made regarding the effects of the implicit authoritarianism of this work. While, in the first introduction, I do attempt to place the highlands of Burma, Assam, and Yunnan in a regional and global context, I fail utterly to place them in a specific historical context. It is only in the article reproduced in this new edition as appendix two that I am explicitly concrete and historical, and this is also to make a theoretical point. The historical, as well as the global, models offered in the body of the work are abstract models in which the ethnography is more an illustration than a problem. I do not take into account, except occasionally and again for the sake of illustration, the processes or the results of the concrete history of this area—the pacification and opening of tea plantations in Assam, the British annexation of Burma, the wars, and the colonial period itself. I must note that Leach, in his excellent and powerful Ph.D. thesis, discussed the colonial period in some detail, but excluded this very important material from his published work. I cannot correct this serious lack here, for it would require another kind of work, a concrete analysis of the real populations of the region in their historically specific circumstances. I hope such work will be forthcoming. The Kachin, Chin, Naga, Lisu, Wa, and other groups in the vicinity of one of the world's largest trade and contraband routes, where numerous wars have occurred and continue to occur, and where local populations struggle to preserve their existence and their ways of life in an increasingly difficult world, deserve a dedicated dialogical ethnography and history, one that they might produce largely on their own given the formidable intellectual resources that they have so often displayed.

References to 1998 Preface

Bourdieu, P.
  1982   *Ce que parler veut dire: l'économie des échanges linguistiques.*
              Paris: Fayard.

Claessen, H. J. M.
1981   Review of *System, Structure and Contradiction*, by Jonathan
            Friedman. *American Anthropologist* 83:161–2.

Clastres, P.
1977   *Society Against the State*. Oxford: Blackwell.

Ekholm, K.
1972   *Power and Prestige: The Rise and Fall of the Kongo Kingdom.*
            Uppsala: Skrivservice.
1977   "External Exchange and the Transformation of Central
            African Social Systems." In Friedman, J., and Rowlands,
            M. J. (eds.), *The Evolution of Social Systems.* London:
            Duckworth.
1975   "On the Limits of Civilization: The Dynamics of Global
            Systems," *Dialectical Anthropology* 5:155–66.

Friedman, J.
1974   "The Place of Fetishism and the Problem of Materialist
            Interpretations," *Critique of Anthropology* 1.
1975   "Tribes States and Transformations." In Bloch, M.(ed.),
            Marxist Analyses and Social Anthropology. London.
1979   *System, Structure and Contradiction in the Evolution of
            "Asiatic" Social Formations.* Copenhagen: National
            Museum of Copenhagen.
1981   "Notes on Structure and History in Oceania," *Folk* 23. In
            memoriam volume for Johannes Nicolaiesen.
1982   "Catastrophe and Continuity in Social Evolution." In
            Renfrew, C., Rowlands, M. J., and Segraves, B. A. (eds.),
            Theory and Explanation in Archaeology. London: Academic
            Press.
1985   "Captain Cook, Culture and the World System," *Journal
            of Pacific History* 20.
1987   "No History Is an Island: On Sahlins, *Islands of History,"
            History and Theory* XXVI, 1.
1992   "Religion, the Subject and the State." In Bax, M., Kloos,
            P., and Koster, A. (eds.), *Faith and Polity: Essays on
            Religion and Politics.* VU University Press.

Geertz, C.
1980   *Negara: The Theater State in Nineteenth Century Bali.*
            Princeton: Princeton University Press.

Harner, M.
1970   "Population Pressure and the Social Evolution of Agri-
            culturalists," *Southwest Journal of Anthropology* 26.

Hedeager, L.
1987   "Empire, Frontier and the Barbarian Hinterland. Rome and Northern Europe from A.D. 1–400." In Rowlands, M., Larsen, M. T., and Kristiansen, K. (eds.), *Center and Periphery in the Ancient World*. Cambridge: Cambridge University Press.

Hedén, T.
1979   "The Evolution of Naga Society: A Development of a Hypothesis Outlined by Jonathan Friedman." (Unpublished manuscript, Department of Social Anthropology, University of Stockholm.)

Heusch, Luc de
1981   *Why Marry Her.* Cambridge: Cambridge University Press.

Kirch, P. V.
1984   *The Evolution of the Polynesian Chiefdoms.* Cambridge: Cambridge University Press.

Kristiansen, K.
1982   "The Formation of Tribal Systems in European History." In Renfrew, C., Rowlands, M., and Segraves, B. (eds.), *Theory and Explanation in Archaeology*. New York: Academic Press.

Labov, W.
1972   "The Study of Language in its Social Context." In *Sociolinguistic Patters*. Philadelphia: University of Pennsylvania Press.

Leach, E.
1969   "Kachin and Haka Chin: A Rejoinder to Lévi-Strauss," *Man* 69.

Lehman, F. K.
1989   "Internal Inflationary Pressures in the Prestige Economy of the Feast of Merit Complex: The Chin and Kachin Cases from Upper Burma." In Russell, S. (ed.), *Ritual, Power, and Economy: Upland-Lowland Contrasts in Mainland Southeast Asia*. Occasional Paper 14. Chicago: Center for Southeast Asian Studies.

1993   "Kachin." In Hockings, P. (ed.), *Encyclopedia of World Cultures*, vol. V: *East and Southeast Asia*. Boston: G. K. Hall.

Lévi-Strauss, C.
1966   *The Savage Mind*. Chicago: University of Chicago Press.

Rappaport, R.
1977   "Maladaptation in Social Systems." In Friedman, J., and
                Rowlands, M. J. (eds.), *The Evolution of Social Systems*.
                London: Duckworth.

Renfrew, C.
1978   "Trajectory Discontinuity and Morphogensis. The
                Application of Catastrophe Theory in Archaeology,"
                American Antiquity 43:203–22.
1984   *Approaches to Social Archaeology*. Edinburgh: Edinburgh
                University Press.

Rommetveit, R.
1983   "In Search of a Truly Interdisciplinary Semantics."
                Journal of Semantics 2:1–27.

Sahlins, M.
1976   *Culture and Practical Reason*. Chicago: Chicago University
                Press.
1988   "Deserted Islands of History: A Reply to Jonathan
                Friedman," *Critique of Anthropology* 8:3.

Satyawadhna, C.
1990   "A Comparative Study: Structure and Contradiction in
                the Austro-Asiatic System of the Thai-Yunnan Periph-
                ery." In Wijeyewardene, G. (ed.), *Ethnic Groups Across
                National Boundaries in Mainland Southeast Asia*. Singapore:
                Institute of Southeast Asian Studies.

Schwimmer, E.
1981   "Le mystère des rizières (a propos de J. Friedman),"
                Anthropologie et sociétés. 5, 2:222–31.

Woodward, M.
1989   "Economy, Polity and Cosmology in the Ao Naga Mithan
                Feast." In Russell S. (ed.), *Ritual, Power, and Economy:
                Upland-Lowland Contrasts in Mainland Southeast Asia*.
                Occasional Paper 14. Chicago: Center for Southeast
                Asian Studies.

Preface

This book was originally presented as a Ph.D. thesis at Columbia University in 1972. It was conceived as a part of a then newly developing marxist inspired anthropology. I have chosen to leave the original manuscript largely intact – apart from several omissions and additional footnotes. I have done so in spite of the fact that I am no longer in agreement with the kind of model represented in that thesis. Since I do not feel that I am in a position to rewrite major portions of the original manuscript, I have taken this opportunity to try and characterise the study in light of a framework that appears more suitable today.

The major thrust of the analysis in this book relates to the mechanisms and dynamics of development of a certain kind of tribal system. That system is defined as a reproductive totality whose properties generate a process of hierarchization leading from a competitive but egalitarian structure to a conical-clan state formation whose properties are discussed in terms of Marx's notion of »asiatic« social formations. The structural tendencies outlined in the model are analysed in two sets of conditions.

The first general environment is that of montane swidden agriculture. It imposes objective limits of intensification on the expansionist social system in such a way that evolving hierarchies tend periodically to break down due to social conflicts induced by the incompatibility between economic growth and the material conditions of reproduction. This model provides for two alternative developments in pure conditions, i.e. in the absence of other social formations, trade routes etc.

> 1) Where former conditions of reproduction can be re-established by dispersal of population leading to decrease in density, i.e. by the long term maintenance of relatively constant population density, there is a tendency for a cyclical pattern of hierarchisation → revolt → equality → hierarchisation to emerge.

2) Where conditions are such that the initial productive potential of nature cannot be re-established, due to permanently increasing population density and ecological degradation, there ensues a series of transformations leading (via increasingly flattened political cycles) toward a politically acephalous and warfare ridden social system based on competitive reciprocity.

The second set of conditions is plains agriculture permitting increasing intensification without significantly declining productivity. Here the tendencies toward hierarchy develop in the direction of »asiatic« state structures.

There are other more complex developments; specialisation in larger trade systems, imperialism – taxing of trade routes and valley populations, that are taken up at some length, but the major focus of the analysis is on the three »pure« developments.

Local versus Global Models
The kind of approach represented in the thesis is one that developed in a context of evolutionism, historical materialism, and structuralism. The two former schools of thought, especially, have tended to be based on the analysis of whole societies in their environments as the only significant theoretical totality. The anthropological object of both of these schools has tended, thus, to coincide with that of the structural-functionalist object of traditional social anthropology – the ethnographically defined society. This correspondence has permitted the use of ethnography as material for evolutionary analysis and has involved anthropology in the evolutionary paradox of not being able to account for the very existence of the ethnographic parallels upon which the evolutionary models are based. A model of progressive evolution cannot account for the fact of non-evolution (Service 1971).

In recent criticisms a number of anthropologists have tried to reconstruct the anthropological object in terms of systems of reproduction rather than societies, which in fact need not be evolutionary units at all (Ekholm 1975, 1976, Friedman 1976). In this perspective, the development of centers of civilisation is accompanied by the simultaneous formation of peripheral subsystems. The most elementary representation of the kind of systems within which the Kachin are found is the general model of the »global system« characterised by center/periphery relations. Within such systems there are centers of accumulation, producing a whole range of manufactured goods, surrounded by peripheries or supply zones – less developed areas that exchange their raw materials and labor power for center-produced goods that are instrumental in defining the power of local elites. A third zone can be added to this representation, one containing »primitive« societies, beyond the center/periphery structure and totally dependent upon local resources, resources which are themselves limited by the expansionist nature of the centers. This general model is discussed in Ekholm (1976) and is part of a more elaborate first attempt to develop a global approach within anthropology.

Now from this kind of perspective, the whole undertaking of the present book can be called into question. First, why can the Kachin be treated as representative of something called a »tribal« system in a general evolutionary framework? What have they been doing for the past thousand years? Second, how is it possible to describe the Kachin in terms of a closed model when they are surrounded by larger state economies and strategic trade routes between China, Burma and India?

In order to answer these questions it is necessary to reconsider my analysis of the Kachin in terms of the place they occupy in a larger economic system that I failed to take into account in my earlier work but which, I think, makes it possible to maintain much of the validity of that analysis.

The larger economic-system abstraction that I would like to suggest here is one that elaborates upon the concentric circle model referred to above (Ekholm 1976). The distribution of structures in this totality is significant. Central economies here are large urban based states, in this case with a large measure of state control and a very large palace sector, developed craft production on a large scale, a merchant class etc. These central states are surrounded by a supply zone for raw materials (often »exotic« goods) and slaves. The structure of these peripheral states or provinces is often described as feudal. They are chiefly hierarchies that in return for raw materials import manufactured items access to which is monopolized by the chiefs and which function as prestige goods circulating as »primitive« money or as wealth symbols of the elite. These societies may be dependent structures insofar as local hierarchy is based on the control over external exchange (Ekholm 1977). These kinds of structures have been reported in conjunction with center/periphery relations in Celtic Gaul (Nash n.d.), Halstatt Central Europe (Frankenstein and Rowlands, in press) and later Roman Iron Age Denmark (Hedeager 1979). In an article reprinted as an appendix here, I discuss some of the structural differences between such prestige good systems and those that function like the Kachin. Structures of the Kachin type exist outside of the periphery and bear a different relation to larger economic processes. They possess an internal reproduction cycle based on the competitive exchange of locally produced products. The formation of hierarchy, of course, implies the extension of exchange networks and the incorporation of increasingly exotic goods into the circulation process. Such goods function as markers of status but do not become sources of control in themselves. While prestige good systems produce for external trade with the centers or with trade routes emanating from the centers, Kachin type systems simply exploit what is available from the centers – by exacting tolls and taking tribute from trade routes and valley states, but without offering anything in return. The goods thus obtained simply circulate within the already constituted exchange relations of the »local« system but tend to be accumulated by the chiefly elite, circulating endogamously with respect to status.

Some interesting correlations can be established for the two kinds of system. Early Thai societies appear to conform to the pattern of a peripheral structure. They have often been described as feudal-tribal formations. Significantly, the local chiefs had monopoly over forest products destined for export as well as over all imported manufactured products (Condominas 1976). Kinship structures tend to be bilineal in many aspects rather than patrilineal, and there is a clear dualism in the hierarchy: The nobility or *tay* seem to have represented outsiders or »conquerors« opposed to the autochtonous servile classes. Expansion among the Thai involved the marriage of incoming nobility with the local upper class, the emergent lineages being defined by the bilineal character of the original relationship (Condominas 1976). Kachin, Chin and others are, unlike the Thai, mainly predators on the larger economy whose products enter into their internal cycles of prestige and status accumulation. These may consist of slaves and staples as well as more exotic goods. The chiefly elite, rather than being represented as a foreign element, are instead the closest relatives of the local ancestor-deities. Those most exploited, on the other hand, are depicted as outsiders.

We might, briefly, sketch the contours of the interrelated functional positions (possibilities) within a hypothetical global system:

A) Center/Periphery structures
   1) centers of accumulation and relatively advanced production where there is a high demand for foreign raw materials and labor power (especially in pre-capitalist industrial economies).
   2) supply zone peripheries – small hierarchically organised »states« that exchange local resources for imported manufactured items and where monopoly over external relations is instrumental in defining the position of the elite.

Between such center/periphery structures there are a number of functional positions, some of which are dependent upon the existence of centers and some of which are not.

B) Dependent structures
   1) specialist producers – groups entirely specialised in specific kinds of manufacture, raw material and specialised agricultural pro-products for a wide region containing several centers. They are linked not to a specific center, but to inter-center trade routes.

2) trade states – groups whose existence depends on their position as middle-men. Trade states are often also specialist producers. The two categories are not mutually exclusive.

B1 and B2 are neither socially nor economically self-sufficient. They often depend upon the import of subsistence requirements and their internal social structures are often entirely supported by a necessary minimum cut of the total wealth flow in the larger system. The Shan states, the Palaung tea producers and Kachin jade producers fall into these positions in Southeast Asia.

C) Independent structures

1) expansionist tribal structures – predatory structures. These are structures containing internal cycles of accumulation and that expand against both A and B, exploiting the flow of wealth in the larger system by extortion. They often expand into small states, sometimes into larger »barbarian« empires – especially in periods of decline of the centers on whom they feed. Examples of such structures are found in northern Southeast Asia, Yunnan, Central Asia etc. Such structures tend to become dependent on their ability to exploit other sectors of the system when they expand into states and empires insofar as they must maintain increasingly elaborate military machines, political alliances and a greatly elaborated court life.

2) »primitive« structures are those that are blocked by their position within the larger system. They are often the prey of centers, peripheries and predatory societies. They tend to lose control over their resource base and labor by violent methods. As a result they may only exist as refugee groups, escaped into the »forests« or as politically acephalous structures that, where not the prey of the system, are nonetheless so blocked in their own expansion (the mechanisms are similar to C1) that they experience breakdown, internal warfare and declining resources.

The notion of »independent structure« is meant to refer here only to the fact that the operant structures in such societies are not connected to the larger reproductive cycles of the system. Such societies are clearly not independent with respect to their material conditions of reproduction.

This very preliminary classification is meant to enable us to place the Kachin and the other groups discussed within a larger context so as to be able to grasp their conditions of existence from a slightly more theoretical standpoint. The »pure« model of the Kachin system is, according to this classification, distributed in a specific way with respect to other types of structures in a larger economic totality.

What now of the evolutionary status of the Kachin model. According to the framework outlined here, evolution is not a local phenomenon. All societies do not simply evolve into increasingly advanced forms or devolve into more involuted forms by means of their own internal mechanisms. There are, rather, various forms of interlocking cycles of expansion, accumulation and decline in systems dominated by the development of powerful centers. The Kachin occupy a zone that has always been more or less in between such centers or centers to be. Such a position implies certain conditions for development. It might even be argued that structures of the Kachin type have maintained a basic set of mechanisms throughout history because of the relative stability of their systemic position following the development of the great valley civilisations. The transformations that such structures may have undergone might then be envisaged as variations and elaborations on a theme rather than a change in the form of accumulation or reproduction itself. In a different position in the larger system such a structure might presumably be totally transformed. The material on the Thai »feudal« states indicates, in fact, the presence of both a Kachin type »asiatic« structure and a more recently superimposed »prestige-good« structure based on incorporation into the economic realm of the Khmer states (Condominas 1976). Thus, chieftainship is theocratically defined and feasts play a crucial role, but the source of economic power seems to depend very much on the monopoly over external exchange and political relations.

The possibility of using the Kachin as a representative of a general tribal model in an evolutionary framework rests on assumptions that are clearly hypothetical. The status of the hypothetical assumptions depends on the way in which they are tested against extant archaeological data to which they would refer (for an attempt see Friedman and Rowlands, M. J. 1977). The structural features of the model help clarify, I think, many problems in the analysis of early state formation, especially in China. The fact that such structures can be treated as more or less independent and closed reproductive systems rather than as dependent structures is, of course, attractive for those who would like to envisage such a model as an original neolithic structure. It might be argued, for example, that this model is an underlying feature of a great number of systems. In Melanesia, for example, it appears that individual societies can easily take on characteristics of either prestige-good or Kachin type systems. Thus the people of Goodenough Island who »fight with food« (Young 1972) are a society that may, in the past, when they were included in the Kula system, have operated more like a prestige-good economy (see appendix). Similarly, some Highland New Guinea societies may have previously had elites that maintained a monopoly over the import of valuables necessary to internal circulation (Vicedom and Tischner 1943–48).

The argument of this thesis depends on the attribution of certain properties of a model derived from the Kachin to a general evolutionary type. Insofar as the properties of the model are capable of generating structures similar to those of the early Shang states, they have obvious theoretical value (Friedman and Rowlands op. cit.). My claim that the general mechanisms of the Kachin model are applicable to the ancient material is clearly open to further testing. As it stands, however, the case for the evolutionary significance of the model might be put in the following way:

The tribal system described in this work has evolutionary significance because it represents, in its »present« historical circumstances, the same general reproductive structure as that which can be attributed to the ancient tribal system. The fact of its survival is due to the fact that its conditions of reproduction, as a »predatory« system situated between larger centers, has prevented its long term transformation where population density has not increased significantly. This does not mean that there has not been elaboration and variation, but only that the basic features of the economic cycle have remained intact. Dynamic systems of the Kachin type can either evolve, devolve or cycle continuously between hierarchy and equality – all depending on conditions that are in the long run external to the dynamic itself.

Replies to Critiques

Since 1972 the original manuscript has been thoroughly discussed and criticized in seminars, letters and, to some extent, in print. In what follows I have divided my attention between criticism that I feel is misdirected and more general issues that are unclear in the original manuscript and have been most under discussion. Most of these remarks are relatively minor, I feel, compared to the general issue taken up above.

I)

The question of the nature of the contradictions of the tribal system has been raised by a number of people. Bridget O'Laughlin, in a critique of the original manuscript (O'Laughlin 1975) has claimed that my model is basically an expression of »technological determinism quite reminiscent of cultural evolutionism« (op. cit. 358). She suggests that the productive forces are an independent variable in that model and that the autonomous growth of population leading to increasing density is the determinant limiting factor of the system. This is clearly a total misreading. First, my discussion of the conditions of production in terms of autonomous material properties in no way implies autonomous functioning of those conditions. It is simply the recognition of the crucial difference between the objective material properties of technology and environment and the way in which they are organized within and dominated by social relations. Throughout this work I unambiguously stress the dominance of the social, that the dynamic of the system is always a social dynamic. This

is quite clear in my discussion of population growth, where, contrary to
O'Laughlin, I state that population growth, far from being an independent
variable, is largely dependent upon a socially determined demand for labor.
I might add here that in my discussion of increasing demographic density the
rate of importation of captives plays a greater role than the local birth rate.

In spite of my use of what I today consider to be a rather inadequate structural marxist vocabulary, I think it is quite clear that my position can in no
way be likened to cultural materialism or even to the »structural causality«
models of some French marxists.

II)

In several places I have made comparisons between the tribal politico-economic cycles and the capitalist business cycle. This is in no way meant to imply
an identity between the two. The comparison is purely formal and destined to
bring to light a feature more general than either system. In one cycle production is increased and converted into prestige and status until certain limits of
internal indebtedness are reached in conditions of declining productivity so
that debt outruns possibilities of repayment. The result is a political crash.
Status incorporated in lineages is lost and the hierarchy collapses. In the other
cycle there is an increase in production up to a certain point determined by the
conditions and limits of capital accumulation – the necessity of converting
increased output into a requisite quantity of money. The result is an economic
recession or even an economic crash, a partial or total devaluation of capital
values. The social mechanisms that generate the cycles are completely different, but there are superficial similarities in the cycles themselves – the rising
ratio of debt to means of payment, the increase in output destined for exchange,
the crisis in economic relations at the top of the cycle and the subsequent
decline in production.

I might easily be accused here of further confusing the notion of exchange
value in capitalism with »exchange value« in the tribal system. This requires
some discussion. First, there is clearly nothing like a capitalist valuation process in the system I describe. Labor time in wage labor capitalism is »incorporated« into the value of the product because it exists as a cost of production for
capital. This is a formal property of a system of wage labor, where even means
of production, also a cost of production, can be reduced to past labor time. It
is also a product of the purely formal abstraction whereby all capital is industrial capital and where there are no other sectors of capital accumulation.
This assumption is clearly contrary to reality. Insofar as the value of capital,
via systematic overvaluation – the non-reckoning of increasing productivity in
terms of devaluation of old capital, speculation, the normal functioning of
money capital, etc., does not correspond to the labor time law of value, the

price of commodities cannot reflect incorporated labor but tends instead to diverge from labor time value. In effect, the capitalist model tends periodically to create an excess of fictitious capital in relation to productive capacity, leading to liquidity crises (Bettelheim 1959, Marcus 1975). In spite of this contradictory aspect of the capitalist process, however, it can be admitted that the existence of labor power as a commodity does create formal conditions for a process of labor-time incorporation, i.e. for the value *form* of commodities. Such a reality does not exist for the tribal system. But this does not imply that labor time has no significance for that system. It only implies that the *formal* relation between labor time and social valuation processes must be of a logically different type if it exists at all. To begin with, in the absence of free labor, there is no social category corresponding to labor time. Thus, the relation between labor and the social process must necessarily be an implicit or covert rather than an immediately socialized phenomenon. Now, in fact, in the tribal system output is converted into status in such a way that, within any one cycle, there is a functional relation between incorporated labor and relative status. In other words, status is a function of accumulated labor (the labor of lineage heads and their dependents). This is what was meant in using the term »exchange value« for *hpaga* value, status position, bride price etc.

In effect, the Kachin exchange system reflects variations in productivity and level of production much more accurately than does a capitalist structure, simply because the means of circulation in that system are not simultaneously capital. There is no M-M' process so that all changes in »value« depend on changes in production. Production is the only way to make prestige among the Kachin. It is clearly *not* the only way to make money in capitalism. As such, it is misleading to write, as I do, of inflation in Kachin society since the level of payments cannot vary independently of production. The way in which indebtedness is created in Kachin is by the unequal accumulation of dependent labor among different lineages and not by the generalized creation of credit at a rate faster than real accumulation as in capitalism. The brideprice inflation to which I refer is an aspect of the process of ranking and cannot be compared to any capitalist process.

This comparison is in no way meant to imply a general similarity between two very different forms of social system. It merely demonstrates that both systems undergo cyclical expansion and crisis, the result in both cases of the accumulative nature of the social system and the limited conditions of accumulation.

III)
A brief remark is required on the subject of forms of control and the place of religion in my argument. It may sometimes appear that »control of the super-

natural« is a real source of economic power in my model, as if such control
were something that could be gotten hold of. Such is not the case. The definition of lineages as ancestral lines, the connection between ancestors and higher
spirits and their socio-economic function, are all constituent elements of the
social space within which hierarchisation occurs. They are, as such, the definition space of the system. The relation between higher deities and particular
local lines is the property of a certain structural position and not a form of
control. A theocratic ruler does not owe his position to his control over the
gods. Rather, his position is defined by his function. Ancestors cannot be monopolized, but a position can be attained which is defined in terms of such a
monopoly. Furthermore, it can only be thoroughly confusing to write that religion functions as economy (Godelier 1973, 1977) in a situation where the
categories we call »religious« are themselves expressed partly in kinship categories and where such categories constitute the space within which *all* production and circulation occur. It is obvious that where kinship categories and
their religious subcategories constitute the totality of social relations they must,
by definition, organize material reproduction as well.[1]

But this, of course, is true only as a tautology. On the other hand, where »religion« does not exist as a discrete cultural realm it cannot be said to organize
anything. It is the above tautology that serves, in effect, as Godelier's version
of structural causality (Godelier 1977) after his hasty rejection of the Althusserian notion that he has so often had recourse to in the past. To say that religion, politics or kinship is dominant if it functions as relations of production is a
contradiction in terms. The very purpose of the Althusserian distinction between determination in the last instance and dominance is to account for the
organization of material production by »non-economic« institutions in terms of
a logically pre-supposed »economy«. However functionalist the Althusserian
formulation might be (Friedman 1974), Godelier reduces it to meaninglessness
by implicitly redefining dominance as determination (Godelier 1977: 15). To
say that religion dominates because it functions as relations of production is
to say that religion dominates because it dominates.

IV)

Finally, in spite of the fact that I use the terms structural marxism several
times in the course of this work, the kind of model which I have constructed

---

[1] It must be stressed here that a definition space does not determine the content of all activities.
The accumulation of dependents, the competition, the intensification of production, indebtedness,
enslavement, etc. are all actions existing with respect to kin categories but not defined by them.
It is the processual relations between categories that constitutes the real logic of the system and
not the »genealogic« itself. The latter is, in fact, very much a product of the former.

is quite unlike the standard structural marxism of French anthropology. The model used by Althusserians and by Godelier is an elaboration on the historical materialist model of determination in the last instance. It expresses itself in attempts to account for social forms in terms of the material relations that they organize. The notion of »structural causality« (Althusser and Balibar 1968, Godelier 1973) is entirely foreign to the approach adopted here, one that would, I suppose, be classified as some dreadful expression of historicism. I consider the basic notion of structural causality – that the economy determines which instance or social structure will dominate its organisation – to be a kind of static functionalism that has no explanatory power. Instead, it is assumed here that the only way to account for the existence of a social form is by laying bare the structural transformation by which it came into being, i.e. by accounting for its genesis. Thus, the starting point of my analysis is a given social form that I do not explain. That could only be done by constructing a further model to account for its emergence, i.e. precisely what is done for all the structures that logically follow from the one posited at the start. It would, of course, be logically inconsistent to explain the basic Kachin structure in terms of its conditions of existence when all the other social forms discussed are derived from the *historical* functioning of that structure.

In this very important respect I find it impossible to accept the major tenet of much structural marxism (Friedman 1974) which appears to converge at many points with American cultural materialism. Determination is systemic and historical and not structural. It is the outcome and expression of the contradictory functioning of systems of social reproduction over time and not of the »logic of the productive forces«.

References to Preface

Althusser, L., Balibar, E. et. al.
    1968   *Lire le Capital*, Paris

Bettelheim, C.
    1959   »Variations du tax de profit et accroissement de la productivité du travail«, Economie appliquée, 1

Condominas, G.
    1976   »Essai sur l'evolution du système politique thai«, Ethnos, 1–4

Ekholm, K.
1977 (1975)   »Varför fungerar inte samhällen«, Marxistisk antropologi
               3, 1
1976   »On the structure and dynamics of global systems«, An-
               tropologiska Studier 20
1977 (1973)   »External exchange and the transformation of Central
               African social systems«, in Friedman, J. and Rowlands, M.
               (eds.) *The Evolution of Social Systems,* London

Frankenstein, S. and *Rowlands, M. J.*
1978   »The evolution of political structures in the European Iron
               Age« (in press)

Friedman, J.
1974   »The place of fetishism and the problem of materialist
               interpretations«, Critique of Anthropology, 1
1975   »Religion as economy and economy as religion«, Ethnos
               1–4 (Festschrift for K. G. Izikowitz)
1976   »Marxist theory and systems of total reproduction«, Cri-
               tique of Anthropology, 7

Friedman, J. and *Rowlands, M. J.*
1977   »Notes toward an epigenetic model of the evolution of
               'civilization'«, in Friedman and Rowlands (eds.) *The Evo-
               lution of Social Systems,* London

Godelier, M.
1973   *Horizon, trajets marxistes en anthropologie,* Paris
1977   »Economy and religion: an evolutionary optical illusion«
               in Friedman and Rowlands (eds.) *The Evolution of Social
               Systems,* London

Hedeager, L.
1979   »A quantitative analysis of Roman imports in Europe
               north of the Limes (0–400 A.D.), and the question of
               Roman-Germanic exchange«, in Kristiansen and Paludan-
               Müller (eds.) *New Directions in Scandinavian Archaeo-
               logy,* Copenhagen
1979   »Processes towards State Formation in Early Iron Age
               Denmark«, in above

Marcus, L.
1975   *Dialectical Economics,* Lexington

Nash, D.
n.d.   »Foreign trade and the development of the state in Pre-
               Roman Gaul« m.s.

Service, E.
1971   »Archaeological theory and ethnological fact« and »Our
               contemporary ancestors: Extant stages and extinct ages«,
               both in *Cultural Evolutionism, Theory and Practice,* New
               York

CHAPTER I

Introduction

Scientific theories, like social systems, have the property of being falsifiable by experience. Social structures necessarily pass out of existence when their internal and external contradictions ultimately force their transformation. Theories, however, have no such direct relationship to material reality and are not subject to the selective forces that eliminate unworkable social forms. Scientific change and growth depend on the creation of a social context in which the confrontation and selection of theoretical constructs can be carried out in the complex dialectic of theory and falsification.[1])

It is especially unfortunate that the conditions for such scientific activity have not been established in the social sciences where a plethora of approaches continue relatively isolated from one another, enjoying the protection of institutionalisation, so that ideas that should have disappeared many years ago still flourish. It should be perfectly obvious by now that without falsification there can be no progress in theory. If this has not seemed evident it is perhaps due to the anti-theoretical attitude that has pervaded most of the social sciences.

The plague of practically all Anglo-American social science, including anthropology, has been its powerfully entrenched empiricist ideology which has largely prevented, if not buried, all attempts at higher level theorizing. At worst, the generalisations that have filled journals and text books have been little more than simple translations of statistical samples. The contributions made by conventional functionalists have been of extremely limited scope; never going beyond the concrete except by straightforward abstraction, ending up with static »models« which are often no more than impoverished replicas of the ethnographic data, and nowhere recognizing that no amount of description, abstraction and comparison can yield an explanation. But it is not only the functionalists, cultural ecologists and statistical sociologists who are embedded in this ideology. Some of those who consider themselves structuralists, like Needham and Maybury-Lewis, have managed to transform Levi-Strauss'

[1]) We follow Lakatos (1970) here, noting that falsification is a complex affair involving the presence of competing explanations and cannot be reduced to the simple yes/no of an experimental situation.

notions of structure into a kind of mentalism where what were formerly categories in the theory become categories in the minds of informants (Maybury-
Lewis/Levi-Strauss 1960). Every explanation is assumed to be present *as such*
in the described reality; if not in actual behavior, then in the conceptual
categories of the society. Even Leach, with his propensity for theoretical generalisations, ends his brilliant analysis of the inner workings of Kachin society
with the anticlimactic low level hypothesis that the oscillation between »egalitarian« (*gumlao*) and hierarchical (*gumsa*) political forms is the result of
»differing forms of compromise between two conflicting systems of ethics«
(Leach 1954:292).

   While paying lip-service to Levi-Strauss' explanation of Kachin development
in terms of the properties of hypothesized models, and criticizing, quite correctly, some of its inadequacies, he retreats into a series of disconnected partial
hypotheses dominated by a notion of ideal polar types (Shan/gumlao),[1] said
to exist in the minds of all Kachin, and which are so localized as to be totally
inapplicable to other »tribal« groups (Chin, Naga) for which he would like to
account. He does this in spite of the fact that he has assembled a tremendous
quantity of ecological, historical, and economic data which, as his analyses
show, could well serve as the basis for a »better« theory.

   The approach adopted here as will be seen shortly, is explicitly theoretical.
The data is practically all from the geographical area covered by Leach's
Political Systems of Highland Burma, that is, Assam, Northern Burma and
Yunnan. It consists of the kind of material that Leach seems to be interested
in: ecological, economic and ritual as well as the normal categories of social
structures. But I have attempted to construct a larger model of social reproduction in which all the above elements are determinate parts of structured system. I consider, at least for the purposes of this thesis, that the model
represents a fundamental underlying structure and that the set of variants
which can be generated from it should be able to account for the actual
distribution of social forms in time and space. The general and specific aspects
of my hypotheses have been made as clear as possible in order to enable them
to be falsified, at least theoretically.

   Before beginning I would like to stress that due to the number of variables
and quantity of data which I shall have to deal with, the exposition will, of
necessity, take the form of successive approximations. Some of the hypotheses
deduced from the properties of the model, especially with regard to its development over time, will only begin to be fully comprehensible after a good deal
of material has been analyzed. An essential part of the following analysis
consists in the reduction of social variation in space to a dynamic time model.
This may appear to be a very questionable, if not far fetched, sort of endeavor.
To this I can only reply that this is a first approximation to a very complex

---

[1] The Shan are stratified valley states in Northern Burma whose princes, according to Leach,
are imitated by Kachin chiefs.

problem and that, precisely because I have, so to speak, taken things to their logical conclusion, the next theory will not be working in the dark. Another serious problem for the whole project has been the inaccessibility or poor quality of certain very important kinds of data, especially domographic, ecological and technological. In most cases I have had to make do with survey reports, gazetteers and ethnographies not dealing primarily with such problems. For this reason, many of my conclusions are not as precise as they might be, and some are questionable on the grounds of insufficient data. In all of these cases, however, the data which could falsify any conclusions are at least available in principle, and it would be falling into the same empiricist trap to avoid any statements not based on actual »hard fact«. Any theoretical construct which is more than simply an abstract description makes assertions about phenomena which have not been observed, or which have only been poorly observed. This is part of the normal process of expanding understanding of the world. Every theory demands further observation. In this sense, »scientific explanation ... is the reduction of the known to the unknown« (Popper 1963).

In any case I would emphasize that if the following work is to have any value it must become part of such a process in which theory and falsification are the prime movers. Knowledge is a social product, and theory cannot be reduced to the status of private property to be defended for its own sake.

»There could be no fairer destiny for any ... theory than that it should point the way to a more comprehensive theory in which it lives on, as a limiting case.« (A. Einstein)

General Theory

The goal of this work is the elaboration of a structural marxist model of a particular kind of »tribal« social formation that will account for the structural variation in time and space which occurs among a large number of groups in Northern Southeast Asia. The only other approach in anthropology which has made any attempt to deal with the relations between levels of a social formation has been »cultural materialism«. In an earlier paper (Friedman 1971–1974) I tried to demonstrate the inadequacy af this approach, and it should become increasingly evident in the course of the present work that a theory of social reproduction is able to explain a great deal which cannot even be approached in the »cultural materialist« framework. In order to be as explicit as possible in delineating the linkages between the categories of the theory and the material to which it is applied it is necessary to briefly discuss some of the principle aspects of this theory.

The Marxist Model

In the past several years there has been a remarkable revival of marxist thinking in the social sciences. Much of this has occurred in Paris where the confrontation between marxism and structuralism has produced substantial theoretical progress. A re-analysis of the methodology of Marx's later works has

revealed some striking resemblences to structuralist thinking. Many of the
concepts of structuralism have been employed to lend precision to notions
which are only vaguely expressed in Marx's writings. The net effect, however,
has been that a number of structuralist concepts have been incorporated into
the marxist framework rather than the contrary. It is Marx's totalistic view of
the social field which makes it possible to formulate hypotheses about social
formations as wholes. In structuralist terms, this would be a framework for
handling the as yet unapproachable problem of »l'ordre des ordres« (Levi-
Strauss 1958:347) or vertical structures which account for societies as entities.
Further, it is the only way one can get at a real theoretical history. The structures of social reproduction are not institutional structures but properties of
dynamic processes which can only be defined with respect to time. It is the
knowledge of such properties, which permits us to predict the way a social
system will behave over time. This is clearly what Marx attempted to do in
Capital.

The principal object of analysis is the social formation,[1]) whose analytical
categories can be represented as follows:

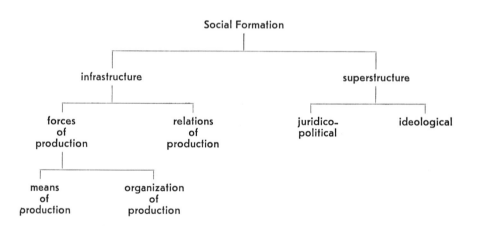

It is necessary here to distinguish between institutional structures and material structures. If we are able to say that kinship structures are also relations
of production, it is because they organize the process of material production
and reproduction, determining who works, how much, and how output is to be
distributed. This is simply a question of taking into account the difference
between the internal properties of social structure and the material effects of
that structure. It is for this reason that we stress that the notions »forces of
production«, »relations of production« and »superstructure« refer only to

---

[1]) The definitions given here differ from those of Althusser in that we assume that »social formation« and »mode of production« are of the same order of abstraction, while for Althusser, the
former term applies only to concrete societies.

functions in the material process of reproduction and not to particular cultural categories. The following quasi-definitions are only meant to distinguish the functions and not to characterize them exhaustively:

1. Forces of production – include the technology and the exploitable ecological niches, the totality of the technical conditions of production and their possibilities of organisation.
2. Social relations of production – are those social (nontechnical) relations that determine the internal rationality of the economy, the distribution of total social labor time and product and the specific way in which the productive forces are organized within the limits defined be the level and previous modes of technological development.
3. Superstructure – refers to ideological and political relations and categories whose contents may or may not be derived from the cultural categories of the relations of production, but whose functions can only be defined *with respect to* already existing productive relations and material conditions of social reproduction. They are thus, functionally, secondary relations which express, elaborate upon, or act upon the relations of production that they presuppose.

Dialectic

The establishment of the preceding categories is only the beginning, for Marx's central contribution was to establish the nature of the relationships between the elements of a social formation, and it is here that structural marxists have concentrated their attention.

The elements of a mode of production (infrastructure) are not linked by simple cause and effect, but, on the contrary, by a complex structure which, if we are content to remain superficial, can only be characterized by reciprocal causality. To assume, however, that this is a sufficient description, as many have done, is to entirely miss the point. Following Godelier's analysis, we will refer instead to intersystemic and intrasystemic contradictions. The latter are contradictions within a structure, for example, between classes, or more generally, between systematically self-contradictory aspects of a social relation; e.g., in asymmetrical connubia, between the accumulation of prestige and the egalitarian political structure implied by the closure of marriage circles. Intersystemic contradictions are those that exist *between* structures. This notion is not found in dialectical sociologies, but it is crucial for understanding the dynamics of any social formation. The fact that, although central to Marx's later works, it has been overlooked is due to the Hegelian tradition which enveloped much of the interpretation of early Marx. Hegelian contradictions are always produced within a unity. As such, the Hegelian metaphor can be extended to cover intrasystemic contradictions with the only result that they appear simpler and neater than they really are. However, the extention of the metaphor to intersystemic contradictions entirely obscures the nature of a relationship which is better expressed in the framework of systems analysis. This relationship is one of mutual constraint. Expressed mathematically, it is analogous to mutually limiting functions in systems of equations which impose inequality side-conditions on one another. Here the functions are autonomous, but the range of values which they can take is limited by the other functions. Structurally, it is a case of constraints on the possible combinations of given elements or on variations in their relations. This is what characterizes the marxist notion of »law of correspondence«.

> »This correspondence which determines the causality of each structure has limits which reveal their objective properties. With the onset of these limits, contradictions appear between structures.« (Godelier 1966:93)

Within this framework, a contradiction is defined as the *limit of functional compatibility* between structures. In Marx's analysis of capitalism, the intrasystemic contradictions (class conflict) are insufficient by themselves to cause a breakdown of the system. Their effectiveness depends on the development of the intersystemic contradiction between forces and relations of production, for it is the latter which sets the limits on the development and stability of the system as a whole.

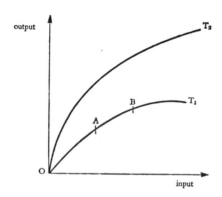

As we can see, intra- and intersystemic contradictions are not of the same order. The former is a property of a structure itself; the latter is the result or effect of the coexistence of several structures in a larger system. In order to give a complete rendering of a social formation we must include the intersystemic relations themselves. This brings us to the notion of structural dominance. The different levels of organization are linked by functional relations which are imposed by the dominant relations of production; hence the characterization of modes of production by the titles »capitalism«, feudalism«, »slavery«, and not by technologies. The existence of intersystemic relations does imply the possibility of making causal or functional statements. In capitalist forms, profit, investment, wages, organic composition, output and consumption are all linked in such a way that a change in one will cause changes in the others. But such relations exist between systems or elements themselves and *not between their structural properties*. Thus, increased investment can raise productivity directly within the bounds of a given production function, e.g., by moving from A to B on the function T1. However, the same kind of relation does not exist between increasing investment and a shift from T1 to T2. Technological change can only be *directly* determined by its own internal possibilities of development (including here the state of technical knowledge and science). New investment can *only* change the conditions in which the technology functions and develops by changing the social selective environment in which it operates.

The key to the whole affair is what has been referred to as the *relative autonomy* of structures, that is, the autonomy of their internal properties.[1]) A contradiction between subsystems occurs as the results of a dominant structure causing intersystemic relations to strain to the limits of functional compatibility, but these limits are determined by the subsystems themselves. It is relative autonomy of structures which entails the necessary existence of two distinct kinds of relationships, those within and those between. And it is the substructures themselves which doubly determine the larger whole; first, by delimiting the kinds of functions which can serve to unite them, and second, by fixing the breakdown limits of those functions.

The principal contribution of structuralism to all this is the notion of »system of transformations« which enables us to reduce superficially distinct structures to a set of variants which can be generated by a single underlying structure. Levi-Strauss' *Structures elementaires de la parenté* is an attempt to show how a great number of kinship systems can be reduced to a few basic exchange structures. For example, taking restricted exchange as a basic principle of organization (in Levi-Strauss' terminology, an invariant), it is possible to generate a number of different social forms by treating as variables such elements as: number of exchanging groups, internal organization of the groups, structural level at which reciprocity is effective (i.e., moiety, clan, maximal lineage, minimal lineage), kind of descent, kind of residence, etc. Dumont's re-analysis of Australian kinship (Dumont 1966) is a brillant example of the way in which such analysis can productively be carried out. His treatment of the Murngin where he shows quite rigorously that a strong tendency toward restricted exchange at all levels (not just between moieties) combined with asymmetrical marriage must result in a complex form of bilineal descent with alternating marriage rules (where what is in fact FZD marriage is represented ideologically as MBD marriage) goes a long way in explaining discrepancies in the empirical data (Barnes 1967; Shapiro 1969) which the simple unilineal model of Leach and Maybury-Lewis (Leach 1951; Maybury-Lewis 1967) is unable to account for.

---

[1]) This definition may differ somewhat from that of the Althusserians whose notion of »relative autonomy« would seem to imply a real functional independence which is denied here in principal.

It must be remembered throughout that Levi-Strauss does more than simply generate structures. Some of his most suggestive chapters are those in which he explores the dynamics of reciprocity over time and the unstable relationship between asymmetrical and symmetrical exchange. His most ignored sections, those dealing with the limits of generalized exchange, have proven to be among the most important for the ideas developed here. Needless to say, they lead us in a direction very different from Needham's overly formalist approach in which it is practically impossible to treat restricted and generalized exchange as anything but opposed static ideal types. On the contrary, they point to the necessity of considering exchange in its larger context. The structuralist can generate variants, but it is only by embedding these in larger models of social reproduction that we can determine the way in which they are distributed in time and space.

The intersystemic relations which govern the process of social reproduction can be represented as follows:

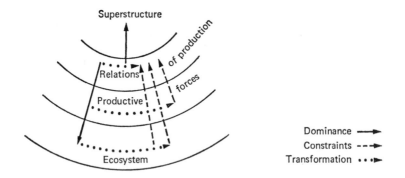

The upward directed arrow designates the hierarchy of constraints which at each succeeding level determines the limiting conditions of internal variation and development. This is equivalent to Marx's notion of determination in the last instance. It implies nothing in the way of direct causality. Rather, it is a selective operation whereby the existence or non-existence of any particular structure is determined by its degree of compatibility with structures at the preceding level. The internal properties of each level remain independent of one another. This is simply to say that the organization of exchange and the organization of machinery are two different kinds of things which cannot be confused without getting us into Hegelian (or cultural materialist) muddles in which different levels of society seem to emerge from one another (Hegel 1956; Harris 1968:4). The downward pointing arrow designates what I have referred to as structural dominance. The different levels of a social formation are linked in a larger system of reproduction whose properties are determined by the dominant relations of production. This implies a specific organization and use of the forces of production within the limits already determined by prior constraints, from which follows, a specific form and intensity of exploitation of the environment. The use made of the environment may in turn result in significant alterations which change the nature of the constraints. These, finally, begin to operate again in the opposite direction. Contradictions arise when specific structures become functionally incompatible with one another. These may be the result of changing constraints resulting from the operation of the system as a whole, or they may be the effect of variation at any one level over time (which is possible to the extent that the constraints are only limiting factors and do not impose necessary forms of organization). Intersystemic contradictions tend to trigger intrasystemic contradictions, and it is not uncommon to find a chain of contradictions systemically linking all levels in such a way that the initial incompatibilities are greatly aggravated. *None of the levels of the social formation are to be considered as specific kinds of organization, but rather as sets of fundamental structural properties from which possible concrete forms can be generated.* The forces of production are not simply meant to represent an existent technology in operation, but rather, the production possibilities afforded by a given level of technological development. Finally, as can be seen on the diagram, relations of production and superstructure are linked in very complex ways. In order to avoid confusion, however, I would again stress that the categories of the social formation are functional, their content being determined by the historical specificity of a particular society. Certain religious phenomena, for example, which appear at first to be superstructural may in fact be an integral part of the infrastructure. It is of crucial importance to distinguish purely ideological phenomena, which are projections (however complex) of infrastructures, from other semantic structures (see conclusion, pp. 273–279) which have a necessary role in the actual operation of the economy.

The general model can be used in two ways. First, it is a way of analyzing the distribution of social forms in space. It may, for example, be used to explain variant forms of kinship structure in different conditions. Second, it can be used to build historical models of particular social forms in time. The two kinds of explanation are complementary. Neither is sufficient by itself. A historical model presupposes a particular combination of environmental, infra- and superstructures. The spatial model examines the variations at each of these levels and the interplay of mutual constraints. A third kind of model which results from the combination of the first two is one in which changing constraints are included in the operation of the historical model, resulting in variations at all levels of organization over time. In order to explain the oscillation of a particular Kachin group between *gumsa* and *gumlao* forms of organization we can make use of a simple historical model. In order to explain differences between Kachin, Chin and Naga forms of organization we might be inclined to use a spatial model, since one might very well expect that these societies were adapted to different sets of environmental conditions (including political). However, after examining the very wide variation which seems to occur in the Kachin Hills alone, it now appears that a model of the third sort might be used to explain a kind of long term evolution of Kachin systems toward Naga systems within the limits of a given technology, in this case, slash-and-burn agriculture. Another long term evolution whose transition is much more difficult to document seems to link Kachin structures with a certain kind of class-state form which may have broad implications for the development of states in Burma, China an Assam. All of the problems implied by these models will be discussed in the body of the thesis.

Transition

To bridge the gap between the general theory and the body of the analysis, it is necessary here to briefly elaborate the general plan of organization. The next chapter will outline the major structural variables and their interrelationships in a larger abstract model. The relations discussed there are designed to be applicable to all later analyses of concrete societies. The model delineates the dominant relations of production and the intersystemic relations linking them to the techno-environment. The properties of the model are analyzed with respect to time in order to determine the internal contradictions of the social formation as well as its possibilities of transformation. Subsequently, I will follow a plan of exposition implied by the general theory outlined above (see diagram, p. 24). That is, I will begin by considering the outermost constraints, those of the ecology, and then work inwards toward the relations of production. At each level, however, I will, of necessity, consider the interaction between the structural dominance of the higher level and the constraints imposed by the lower level. For example, it will be seen that Leach's so-called »ecological zones« are not independent factors, but the result of long-term intensification of a fundamentally extensive slash-and-burn technology in an ecology which was originally quite uniform.

The central part of the analysis is that dealing with the Kachin social system. It focuses on the internal dynamics of the Jinghpaw of the Triangle region of Upper Burma. Since the analysis is to be from an evolutionary standpoint, the choice of the Triangle Kachin is significant, since they are situated at a kind of logical origin of all later developments, i.e., with the least depleted environment, lowest population density, and simplest technological adaptation. Starting from this zero-point, I will apply the model developed in Chapter Two to a detailed analysis of the short and long term developmental properties of the Kachin system. The short term behavior of the system, Leach's *gumlao/gumsa* oscillation, will be shown to be the product of a number of hierarchically related contradictions that emerge with the operation of the economy.

Two major long-term transformations that will be dealt with are devolution and evolution. The first is the outcome of increased population density and environmental degradation (decreasing productivity), both caused by the continued action of an expansionist economy in conditions where further territorial growth is blocked. In other words, the development of the social formation in time has the effect of changing its own conditions of social reproduction, resulting in significant structural transformations. In the chapter on devolution, I will attempt to demonstrate how Chin, Naga and Wa societies can be understood in terms of a single developmental model. In the section on evolution I will examine the way in which the internal properties of Kachin *gumsa* systems might tend to develop in the direction of »asiatic state« formations when the conditions of production are changed in such a way that economic expansion can continue beyond the limits of productivity imposed by hill swiddening. Where technological constraints are lifted, the Kachin economy tends to develop in the direction of social forms which closely resemble the ancient Chinese States.

The unifying theme of the entire analysis is the evolutionary (or devolutionary) transformation of a social formation. »Evolutionary« is not to be understood in its accepted anthropological usage, i.e., where a number of ordered progressive stages are related at most to some single factor such as technology or demography. Rather, our focus will be on a model of social reproduction whose internal dynamic properties generate the variant developmental tendencies that are manifested in the actual distribution of social forms in Southeast Asia. The emergence, in devolution, of proto-feudal property, and the evolution of »asiatic« states on the basis of »tribal« property will both be shown to be related to the functioning of a single social system over time.

CHAPTER II

Specific Theory

The purpose of this chapter is to examine the properties of a specific kind of tribal system. The system cannot be said to be merely an abstract model of the empirical societies to which it shall be applied. If this were the case it would already be apparent in the ethnographic data, and this is plainly not the case. Rather, it is meant to be an explanatory theoretical model which can account for a wide range of societies. This undertaking, however, is not of the same order as recent attempts at generalisation by Meillassoux, Terray and Rey (see bibliography) on the »lineage mode of production« although their discussions merit serious attention. Unlike those authors, we have not attempted to explain the origin or account for the existence of a particular kind of society. According to our general theory this would be out of the question, since a system can only be explained in terms of the system from which it evolved. As there is no direct causation of nor functional necessity for a particular set of relations of production in particular techno-ecological conditions we do not attempt to derive such features as lineage structure, mariage forms, political hierarchy etc. This does not imply, however, that such elements cannot be accounted for, but only that evolutionary models always begin with an arbitrarily chosen »original« structure in order to generate subsequent structures with the consequence that the initial form must remain temporarily unexplained.

All of the above authors, but especially Meillassoux (1967, 1972), consider lineage societies as the outgrowth of agricultural modes of life. This is contradicted by numerous hunting/gathering societies which have lineage structures and by agricultural societies in which lineages are vague local manifestations of larger clans which in no way correspond, as required by the theory, to units of cooperation. The model developed here might apply to the Indians of the Northwest Coast of America as well as to a large number of agricultural societies. It does not depend on the specific form of technology but on the form of *social* appropriation of nature and on the structure of *social* reproduction. The same social form will be found in a wide range of techno-environments, which is possible insofar as the latter are compatible with the social relations that dominate them.

More particularly, I find that the characterization of the »lineage mode of production« is far too specific to certain parts of Africa, to warrant the use of so general a title. The economic conditions on which the model rests seem somewhat more complex than need be assumed to build a model of this sort. The existence of an age division into elders and juniors, which Meillassoux tries to deduce from the technical conditions of agricultural production (1972), is neither necessary nor a particulary widespread phenomenon. The more interesting explanation, that elders often produce or monopolize prestige goods which are necessary for their dependents' marriages, thereby giving them a politico-economic control over social reproduction (Meillassoux 1960), is, I think, the result of a very specific development which might be derived from the model we shall present here. Insofar as these societies might be said to possess both a subsistence and a prestige good production sector, they are more complex than the lineage system we shall describe in which there is no such devision of labor, nor any corresponding division into dominant elders and dependent juniors.

The following analysis makes use of a relatively small number of elements; a local lineage – unit of appropriation, a distributive feast structure, generalized exchange of women, and a representation of the world in which ancestors merge with deities that control nature, wealth and prosperity. There are prestige goods, but they are not produced by society and are integrated into the redistributive and affinal exchange networks in a way different than that indicated for the »lineage mode of production«. They cannot be accumulated independently of the production and distribution of subsistence goods as in the »lineage mode«. The articulation of the above mentioned relations of production in a single system of reproduction determines the forms of functioning and development of this kind of society. I hesitate to talk of a specific mode of production although what is described is certainly a kind of tribal mode. But, until the variation in tribal systems is worked out clearly, and the logico-temporal links between them discovered, is is more reasonable to avoid any definitive sounding nomenclature.

It will undoubtedly strike the reader as strange that no mention has been made of the forces of production which were so summarily dismissed as possible causes of particular kinship relations. In fact, the forces of production are crucial in determining the possible evolutionary paths of the system which we shall discuss.[1]) While it is unnecessary to demonstrate the origin of the social elements of our social formation which, I believe, could have developed in several types of technological conditions, the constraints of a particular technology do determine the specific capacities for evolution. Because of the social systems, I have chosen to restrict myself primarily to swidden agriculture. This should not be taken to mean that there is any necessity for the conjuncture of

[1]) Forces of production refer here to a given set of production possibilities. The latter are more or less constant in a system where productive »investment« implying continuous technological development is not part of the logic of the system. Technological change (intensification) occurs within the bounds of the production possibility function as an effect of the operation of the system, not of its internal logic.

3 Friedman

that form of technology and specific social relations, and a complete analysis would have to consider the evolutionary possibilities of the same relations of production in different initial technological conditions.

Exchange Units and Production Units

We shall assume here that exchange units and production units are indentical although, in later chapters, it will be shown how the extent to which they overlap is one of the major variables in the transformation of the system. As all of this is, in principal, predictable from the model we shall develop here, it would be needlessly repetitive to discuss that kind of variation at this point. The exchange unit is the minor patrilineage, a patrilocal grouping containing several (max. 5–6) households which engage individually in production on a larger communal field. Every household is a single consumption unit although there is a considerable amount of labor pooling and sharing of the product among the members of the lineage. The lineage appears more clearly as a single unit in exchange relations with other lineages, since, to the outside world it clearly represents a single resource and status unit. For most practical purposes, then, it is safe to consider the local lineage as the minimal unit of appropriation, of production and reproduction. We might compare it to Sahlins' »domestic« economic units (1971, 1972), but I would not agree that the apparent self-sufficiency of such units entitles them to the status of a mode of production. As we shall see, their links with other similar groups might be considered both economically and biologically necessary for the long term survival of any one unit, and more important, the alliance relation itself *is* a dominant relation of production whether or not one considers it biologically necessary. It is, of course, this latter criterion which characterizes the mode of production.[1])

Alliance and Exchange

The minor lineages of our model are linked by a system of exchange whose properties have been thoroughly explored by Levi-Strauss (Levi-Strauss 1967). What has been referred to as generalized exchange can be defined in many different ways. For our purposes, Lehman's proscriptive definition (1963) is quite sufficient to determine the conditions in which generalized exchange can take place. The determination is double. One may not give wives to wife-givers, nor may one marry into one's own group. This leaves two possible alternatives. One can marry a real or classificatory MBD or one can marry into unrelated segments. In other words, one can keep up old alliances or establish new ones. This approach greatly clarifies the fundamental properties of generalized exchange and rids us of the prescriptive/preference problem which is a false issue tied to an excessive if not obstinate focus on marriage rules while avoiding the question of the exchange system as a whole (Needham 1961; Maybury-Lewis 1965). For Levi-Strauss, the rules of marriage are the

[1]) See critique on page 45.

results of a particular mode of exchange between groups. Of greater importance than the way the rule is stated is the actual distribution of exchanges over the generations. A so-called prescriptive system might best be conceived as a relatively closed system in which old alliances are constantly renewed as opposed to an open system in which the ratio of new to old alliances is quite high. Lehman has pointed out that the open system corresponds to an expanding population, and we will see later that the two are linked in a single process. In any case, the ratio of new to old alliances in no way changes the underlying properties of asymmetrical marriage itself. The only transactions which can alter the system are patrilateral or bilateral exchanges over extended periods of time. It is best, however, not to treat these three models as static forms, but rather as tendencies or possibilities any one of which may dominate the circulation of women and goods. Among most of the groups dealt with here, patrilateral reversal is quite possible, but the dominance of the asymmetrical mode is demonstrated by the fact that a patrilateral reversal becomes a permanent reversal of wife-giver/wife-taker status, a new unilateral alliance which is enforced by substantial economic sanctions.

Generalized exchange involves some important characteristic relations between minimal segments. Of prime interest is that men and women always marry into different groups. This results in a certain ordering in which any one line has a distinct set of wife-givers and wife-takers. Secondly, the fact that women cannot be exchanged for women, or that like objects cannot be exchanged, implies a certain asymmetry. Women move one way (at least in the patrilineal patrilocal model) in exchange for goods and/or labor. If we add to this the Maussian insight that prestations create debtors, we have already got the basis for an ordered ranking of lineages. In all of the systems we shall discuss, hypogamy rather than hypergamy is the rule. In patrilineal societies this may be true where lineages can only define their rank in the exchange act itself, that is, where rank is entirely relative and equivalent to the degree of »indebtedness«. Where women marry up it is probably a case in which economic class or caste differences are clearly established independently of the exchange. This is not our concern here, however, except insofar as the development of a class society will be accompanied by the replacement of the normal *mayu/dama* relationship by a hypergamous tributary relationship between classes.

The very operation of generalized exchange involves a serious contradiction which has been well described by Levi-Strauss.

> »L'échange généralisé suppose l'égalité, et il est source d'inégalité. Il suppose l'égalité, car la condition théorique d'application de la formule élémentaire est que l'opération c épouse A, qui ferme le cycle soit équivalente à l'opération A epouse b, qui l'a ouvert au debut. Il faut pour que le système fonctionne harmonieusement, qu'une femme a vaille une femme b, une femme b une femme c, et une femme c une femme a autrement dit, que les lignées A, B, C aient même statut et même prestige. Au contraire,

le caractère spéculatif du système; l'élargissement du cycle; et l'établisse-
ment de cycles secondaires entre certaines lignées entreprenantes, et à leur
profit; enfin, la préférence inévitable pour certains alliances, qui aura
pour résultat l'accumulation des femmes à telle ou telle étape du circuit:
autant de facteurs d'inégalité, qui peuvent, à chaque instant, provoquer
une rupture. On arrive donc à la conclusion que l'échange généralisé con-
duit, de façon presque inéluctable, à l'anisogamie, c'est-a-dire au mariage
entre conjoints de statuts différents; que cette consequence doit apparaître
avec d'autant plus de netteté quand les cycles d'échange se multiplient ou
s'élargissent; mais qu'en même temps, elle est en contradiction avec le
système, et doit entraîner sa ruine.« (Levi-Strauss 1967:306)
   The application of the assymmetrical model to a fixed number of lineages
results in a number of circles of varying lengths. This is an unavoidable property of the system if the number of groups is finite. In the simplest case, it
results in the following contradiction:

$$A \to B \to C \to N \to A \qquad > \ = \text{ is superior to}$$
$$A > B > C > N > A$$

The resultant situation would appear to be absolutely untenable if the unity
of the group is to be preserved, but there are several ways to get around the
problem. In most »egalitarian« societies the status difference between wife-
givers and wife-takers is quite minimal and is usually limited to symbolic
behavior. Further, it is usually not transitive. The already minimal status
difference that exists between a man and his MB does not extend to MMB's
lineage. This is extremely important for the possibilities of later ranking. The
»lack of information« about distant alliances affords a great deal of freedom
for any one lineage if the system ever opens up and the exchange networks
begin to expand. The stabilizing influence in egalitarian groups is the non-
differentiation of bride price so that all transactions are in a state of equilibrium. A fixed quantity of wealth or labor circulates from lineage to lineage
in exchange for women, but there is no accumulation. Finally, there is nothing
in the egalitarian system which prevents the formation of a number of small
alliance networks which are quite separate from one another. The formation
of small endogamous circles throughout the population is more an indicator
of an egalitarian than a hierarchical system since the principal means of
establishing rank is through the alliance link itself. However, the existence of
such circles is instrumental in the hoarding of wealth objects and prestige and
is thus crucial in the formation of hierarchy.
   It would appear that while generalized exchange can certainly coexist with
egalitarian political forms, there is a latent or potential contradiction between
the wife-giver/wife-taker relation and the equality implied by the closure of
marriage circles. The phenomenon which must now be explained is the way
in which the hierarchical implications of the asymmetrical alliance structure

can radically transform the originally egalitarian conditions. Levi-Strauss seems to have intuitively grasped the problem by stressing the speculative character of generalized exchange, but as he is concerned primarily with the marriage system itself he is unable to provide the material basis for that speculation which he relegates, quite correctly from his point of view, to external factors.

»Mais c'est du dehors, des caractères concrets, et non de la structure for-melle du groupe, que surviennent les dangers qui le menacent.« (1967: 308)

The external factors for Levi-Strauss are essential internal elements of the marxist model. Levi-Strauss has brilliantly isolated a fundamental contradic-tion within the relations of production, but he has left out some other very important relations of production as well as the all important link between forces and relations of production. We must now attempt to place the minimal production and exchange units into a larger context of social reproduction.

Political Economy of the Minimal Segment

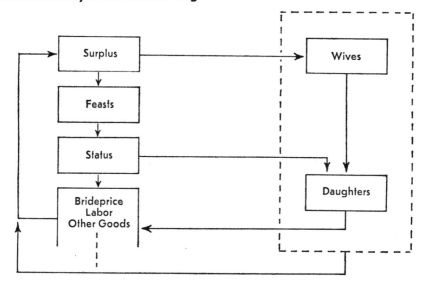

This extremely general model of reproduction applies, with variations, to the great majority of tribal groups in northern Southeast Asia. It might also have broad application to a large number of other societies. The specific character of the model is the way it links feast giving, the distribution of surplus, to the kinship structure. It parallels, in fact, Levi-Strauss' atom of kinship insofar as it presupposes an alliance or exchange relation with another local group, and it might be understood as a kind of elementary structure of reproduction.

There are two significant chains or flows which when merged enable a lineage to raise or maintain its status. The motor of the system is not marriage exchange by itself, but a combination of alliance and distributive feasts. The precondition for the operation of the system is the production of a lineage surplus. This surplus is converted into prestige by means of feasts, that is, by distribution to members of the community. Prestige is passed on to daughters in the form of increased brideprice expressed in wealth items such as cattle which replenish or increase the feastgiver's stock. In the early stages of prestige accumulation, a lineage can maintain its position only through increased agricultural output, i.e., as the result of having a maximal amount of available household labor, and by the intensification of the production process itself — by clearing and sowing larger fields. In the context of expanding demand for surplus, polygyny is a principal means for the provision of additional household labor. This, of course, can lead to problems since the available surplus depends not only on the total labor force but on the ratio of workers to consumers. An excellent discussion of this ratio can be found in Sahlins' recent article (1971). While a large number of wives will increase household surplus, the eventual advent of children is likely to put a damper on this process, since the number of consumers will increase. This effect holds true for any household, of course, and in the long run, the absolute quantity of labor input is the critical factor since, for the purposes of feast giving, total surplus is what matters, and not efficiency.

The ability to give large feasts depends on the absolute size of the surplus produced. Wealth items, such as cattle and prestige goods, are owned by individual lineages, but they can only be accumulated as a result of the production/distribution of agricultural surplus. The existence of such goods does not imply that there is a corresponding productive sector in the total economy. Cattle, in the societies with which we are dealing, have little or no cost of maintenance since they roam freely on non-agricultural land. Their distinctiveness lies in their restricted usage as the representative of value, of the general productive wealth of local lineages, and not in their intrinsic properties. This is the key to their differential accumulation. Prestige goods, even if distributed on ceremonial occasions, can be more than made up for. Cattle lost at a feast are not only replenished by the lineage's own stock. They are accumulated directly through the increase in brideprice paid for lineage daughters. The positive feedback character of this process is the foundation of hierarchization. The control of ritual wealth items by wealthy lines tends to consolidate their position at the expense of poorer groups. As brideprice tends to follow the developing prestige ranks a situation will necessarily develop in which only the wealthy can afford to take wives from the wealthy. In practice, as Leach points out, women do not have fixed values, and the critical determinant of status is the ability of men to pay large prices. But this supposed flexibility in the system simply reinforces the differentiation of status. Any one lineage is faced with several courses of action. To begin with, prestige can be maximized by paying the highest possible brideprice for wives from other wealthy households. Secondly wives can be given to other wealthy lineages in order to replace some of the lost wealth. But they can also be given to lineages of slightly lower status in order to gain »clients«. These latter two strategies will alternate according to political and economic circumstances, but their net effect will be to maintain status differences while increasing the flow of wealth objects from lower to higher groups. Thus, wealth and prestige come to form a self perpetuating vicious circle. The ownership of cattle is redistributed in such a way that wealthy lineages control all titles and consequently find themselves in an increasingly monopolistic position with regard to acquiring prestige.

The combination of accumulation processes, the production of surpluses, their transformation into control of cattle and the consolidation of rank positions by means of the wife-giver/wife-taker relationship produces an ordered series of lineages.

$$
\begin{array}{lll}
\text{Rank} & A > B > C > D & \dots\dots \\[2ex]
\text{Quantity:} \left\{ \begin{array}{l} \text{Cattle} \\ \text{Brideprice} \end{array} \right\} & A > B > C > D & \dots\dots \\[2ex]
\text{Surplus} & A > B > C > D & \dots\dots
\end{array}
$$

It is unlikely if not impossible that the ranking can approach anything like a neat ordering. Rather, there is a tendency for a kind of hierarchy of connected circles to be formed, a spiral in which any one lineage will keep company with a number of equal as well as higher and lower groups. Leach has represented the general structure of such a hierarchy in terms of three levels of lineages, chiefly, aristocratic (elB) and commoner Leach (1961:86). In reality, the number of levels may be greater or smaller depending on how the ranking system comes to be institutionalized, while within any one level there will tend to be something of a finer differential unless the brideprices stabilize and competition between lineages decreases. This would seem to be the likely result of the formation of hereditary rank classes. Once the ranks are established and reinforced by inheritance the alliance alternatives will vary from top to bottom in the following way:

$$
\begin{array}{ccc}
& \downarrow & \downarrow \\
\rightarrow \text{uppers} \rightarrow & \rightarrow \text{middles} \rightarrow & \rightarrow \text{lowers} \rightarrow \\
\downarrow & \downarrow &
\end{array}
$$

$(\rightarrow)$ direction of women

A number of factors enter here to consolidate the hierarchy. Since they will all be discussed later on I will simply outline some of the more important ones.

a) With the increased differentiation of brideprice, a number of households may find it impossible to meet brideprice payments. In such cases, brideprice is commuted to labor service for the father-in-law – a transfer of labor power in favor of the wife-giver which augments his prestige and rank to the extent that increased surplus from his land is converted into bigger and better feasts.

b) The very poorest households who cannot pay any of their debts will attach themselves to very wealthy lineages as bond slaves. This is tantamount to increasing the workforce of the wealthy protector who, while paying the various debts of the lineage in question gains a practically permanent source of surplus labor as well as a political follower.

c) At the highest stage of rank formation, chiefs become entitled to village labor as well as a small percentage of the total harvest. This phenomenon, whose explanation is given further on, depends ultimately upon the structure of the lineage ideology.

d) Expansion of the system may involve the introduction of foreign labor in the form of »slavery« which is not slavery in the normal sense, but rather the addition of a lowest rank. In effect, I will argue later that the demand for labor in these societies is such that the search for outside sources is a basic characteristic of their development.

All of these factors lead to a concentration of manipulable wealth in the hands of the most powerful lineages. The degree to which a single lineage can control all these factors is decisive for the stabilization of the emergent hierarchy. The control by a single lineage over significant amounts of surplus labor and product tightens the network into a rather neat pyramid in which a chief can hold sway over his aristocrats.

Religion, Property and the »Higher Unity«

While native concepts of religion and ritual are discussed at great length by many of the Southeast Asian ethnographers, none have attempted to analyze their functions from the point of view of social control and emergent social hierarchy. Leach provides nearly all the material needed to understand this position in the larger social structure. He shows quite clearly the way in which the »supernatural spirits« or »nats« parallel the segmentary nature of the society and how they are manipulated for political purposes. Leach, like others, has documented the widespread phenomenon whereby the spirit world is an apparent extension of the social world, but he tends to take the position that the spiritual is simply the reflection or restatement of »real« social relations. In a great many lineage societies, the universe is depicted as a segmentary ordering of spirits that descend from a supreme deity to the ancestors of the local lineages. It can be represented as follows:

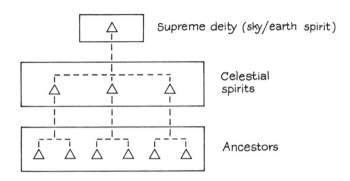

This hierarchy exists for both egalitarian and ranked groups, but with significant differences in internal organization. In egalitarian groups, each local
lineage has its own set of ancestor spirits arranged in comparatively short
genealogies of three or four generations. There is a village spirit representing
the local territory, its »owner«, who is conceived of as a remote ancestor of
all the local lines. It is not clear that this link is necessary – it appears to be
the case among some Kachin groups, but among the Lamet, for example, where
village unity is extremely tentative, the village spirit is more a purely local
being and is not explicitly linked with the ancestors of the lineages.[1]) The
celestial *nats* can be approached by any lineage through the mediation of its
own ancestors. The earth *nat* who controls production (fertility) is usually
approached by the community as a whole through the village priests. The
single most important transformation that occurs in the process of hierarchization is the monopolization of the village spirit by a particular local lineage.
In ranked groups, the chief's ancestors are identical to the village spirits, local
spirits who control all lands belonging to the community. The celestial spirits
are now ranked by age following earthly rules of succession and the chiefly
lineage can now be traced back to the chief celestial deity to whom it is
affinally related. Since the chief is genealogically and thus sociologically
closer to the forces that control the well-being of the group he is entitled to
special privileges. As he is related to the celestial spirits he can also reach the
supreme earth spirit directly, a function which formerly could only be performed by the community as a whole. Thus, the chief, in effect, becomes the
mediator between the community and the forces of nature which provide for
its prosperity. He is able to do this because his lineage has become the territorial or community lineage.

It appears then that this religious structure is more than a simple reflection
of social categories. On the contrary, it has a very clear economic function
and a decisive role in political development. Let me be more precise about this.

---

[1]) It is interesting, however, that the chief-priest, although politically powerless, does claim the
village spirit as his ancestor.

a) Sacrifices of any importance always involve the whole village. The purpose of major sacrifices is specifically to ensure and increase the *material* welfare of the community as a whole, that is, by increasing the total agricultural yield. Its socio-economic function is to establish the prestige of the feast giver. The sacrifice is in itself an act whereby the wealthy man represents the whole community by approaching the spirits on their behalf.

b) The community's relation to the spirits can only be understood as a kind of religion of productivity. The celestial spirits and their earth spirit progenitor represent a superior community whose form is a projection of the earthly social structure and whose function is to control that which the society seems objectively powerless to control beyond certain limits, i.e., prosperity. A good rapport with the spirit world is the only means to a good crop yield and there is a strong incentive to work hard in order to be able to at once propitiate the spirits and gain prestige. A major portion of the local surplus is the input for just this process.

c) The community spirit is the superior unity with which individual lineages can identify. It is the ideological correlate of the village and its territory. Furthermore, it is the only available category by which this entity is conceivable since there is no communal appropriation of the total output, but only distribution through the channels of affinal kinship, channels that link *individual* lineage segments.

d) In the transition to chieftainship, a lineage which before only represented the community at each feast gradually takes on the job permanently. This is possible because of the very structure of the spirit world, which is a supernatural *extension* (not just reflection) of the community's kinship network. Proper manipulation simply identifies the ancestor spirit of the lineage with the spirit of the village who is, after all, only a more remote and powerful ancestor. This is not simply a question of manipulation, however, and there is an internal logic linking increasing rank to gradual identification with the village spirit. *As the ability to feast implies greater surpluses which apparently depend on one's influence with the higher spirits, and since this influence can only be interpreted as closer kinship, one's ancestors must indeed be genalogically closer to the territorial spirit that is the necessary first link in the chain of communication with the supernatural powers* (see p. 269). The result is a very specific set of relationships between the chiefly line, the spiritual world and the community. In a sense, a particular individual can be said to have filled a previously empty category. The territorial spirit is village landlord in the sense that it represents the community's control over a given area. This does not correspond to any specific economic relation between lineages but rather to an ill-defined social and economic space within which take place cooperation and exchanges that are necessary for the reproduction of the social group. The chief by filling this category comes to represent the *community as a whole*, an entirely new social relation. He does not own the land of his village, at least not in the sense of feudal or private rights. It is his land only by reason of his relation to the local deity. By virtue of the fact that he represents the community as a whole, he represents its territory and is able to approach the supernatural on its behalf. In this position the chief is »naturally« entitled to tribute and corvée from the community as a whole, just as his predecessor, the village spirit, was entitled to offerings.

The relation we have just described is a significant social reality which must be distinguished from the normal affinal and consaguineal relations of individual exchange units. The set of independent production-and-exchange units, through internal exchange and cooperation, forms a larger aggregate, embodying in this way a possible second relationship structure which is materialized as the chiefly lineage. This second emergent form is strikingly close to Marx's concept of the »asiatic mode« in which the individual's relation to the land that he works,

>»appears to be mediated by means of the particular community,« (Marx 1965:69)

and where part of the

>»surplus labor belongs to the higher community, which ultimately appears as a person.« (Marx 1965:69)

While Marx does not develop this notion in anything approaching a systematic theory, he uses it to characterize a situation extending from primitive groups through his »oriental despotic« state whose foundation remains »tribal or common property« (Marx 1965:70). For Marx, the individual (or minimal segment) has rights over land, over the forces of production, only insofar as he is a member of the community. It must be emphasized that this is not a simple mechanical materialist statement. The larger community does not correspond to the organization of labor. We are not dealing with a communal work force, since, in fact, labor is organized on a household basis. Marx assumes that individuals have use rights over their own plots of land. Rather, the community represents an aggregate of production units which increases the probability of survival of all its members through the sharing of individually variable outputs as well as serving as a kind of general security against human and natural enemies and a means of ensuring the reproduction of each of the individual families. This is a very general phenomenon which is not meant to suggest anything like a functional ecology of large or small scale distribution of surplus (Vayda 1961; Piddocke 1965) where chiefly feasts serve as a necessary survival mechanism. There is, of course, a relation between the process of production and the notion of »higher unity« in that the local group defines itself socially in terms of the appropriation of a territory to which it must have access in order to survive. Whatever its functional benefits, the definition of the larger group's relation to nature is expressed in the same kinship terms (common ancestry) as the individual lineages' relation to nature. It is thus a question of definition and need not be explained in terms of its effects or survival value.

Godelier has pointed out, in a slightly different context, that the formation of the so-called »asiatic state« involves no basic change in the former property relations.

> ». . . l'apparition de l'Etat et l'exploitation des communautés ne modifient pas la forme des rapports de propriété puisque celle-ci reste propriété communautaire, propriété de la communauté supérieure cette fois, tandis que l'individu reste possesseur du sol en tant que membre de sa communauté particulière.« (Godelier 1969:64)

The very same kind of phenomenon seems to be characteristic of chiefly control of land. By modifying Godelier's diagrammatic representation (in turn borrowed from Tokei 1967 in Godelier 1969:60) we might clarify the transition from egalitarian to hierarchical communities in the following way:

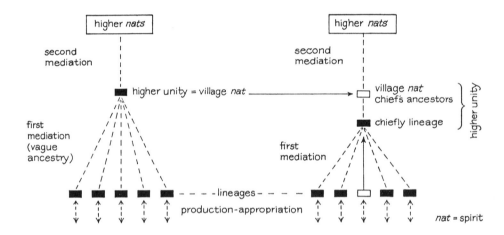

The relationship of lineages to the »supernatural« has an extremely important role in the development of interlineage hierarchy and especially in the stabilization of that hierarchy. A chiefly line that occupies the position we have described has a distinct advantage over its aristocratic competitors. Among the Chin, as we shall see, the ability of chiefs to maintain paramountcy is greatly diminished by weakness or absence of this vertical religious structure.

Relations of Production: Synthesis

The preceding analysis has focused on two principal structures, both of which are related to our model of minimal segment economy. In that model we specified two major cycles related to the utilization of surplus. The first and the most important for establishing rank is the giving of feasts. The second is the affinal exchange. The first corresponds to the religious structure while the second corresponds to the alliance structure. No understanding of the internal development of these societies can be reached without recourse to these two structures and their articulation.

Let me clarify, first, what I mean by »relation of production«. In the earlier discussion I made a distinction between organization of production and relations of production. The former is a part of the (technical) process of production itself whereas the latter determine the control and distribution of the factors of production as well as the output of productive activity. Relations of production are simply the *dominant social structures of the economy*.[1])

The relations of production can be divided into three structures whose internal logic determines the distribution of total social labor and product.

1. A minimal self-reproducing lineage which has appropriation rights over its plots and their output, but where these rights are themselves dependent on the lineage being part of a local group.
2. An alliance network through which are channeled certain rights and duties, significant quantities of wealth (ritual) items and surplus product and labor.
3. A ritual feast-distribution structure which absorbs a good deal of surplus in a double process in which wealth controlling spirits are propitiated and prestige is gained by distribution.

The latter two structures determine the utilization of surplus product and labor. The first, stripped of the larger social and economic context is simply a production-consumption unit. Sahlins has, as we said, characterized the single household economy as the »domestic mode of production« having its own internal structure and economic goals (Sahlins 1971; 1972). He points out that the tendency for the independent reproductive unit is to produce only what is needed; to make minimal use of available labor, and that there is, thus, a contradiction between this self-sufficiency and the demand for surplus by the larger society, i.e., in marxist terms a fundamental contradiction between production for use and production for exchange. We stress again that Sahlins has clearly exaggerated in referring to the domestic economy as a mode of production. While it is doubtful that a domestic unit is capable even of long term biological reproduction without alliances to other groups, there is a more fundamental difficulty in this attempt to associate the »mode of production« with the production unit while relegating relations between such units to »society«.[2]) This implicitly denies the possibility that an alliance relationship can be a dominant relation of production simply on the grounds that it does not occur within the unit of appropriation. It also assumes that the unit of appropriation is somehow technologically determined in the sense that the basic social unit is necessarily the principal unit of immediate production. Contrary to this,

---

[1]) This usage of the notion »relations of production« now appears unsatisfactory to me. See Appendix pp. 314–315.

[2]) For a more complete criticism see the article by Ekholm (1973).

I would assert that appropriation is largely socially determined. With respect to the kinds of tasks which are performed in swidden agriculture, for example, there is nothing that prohibits the formation of larger production and consumption units than the household. There is, of course, a contradiction between the lineage as private appropriator and its links to the larger network of social relations which requires that it produce a surplus. This contradiction is itself embedded in a system which is clearly dominated by our second and third structures (above) which, while part of a process of social reproduction, are also in potential conflict with one another. The dominant relation of production remains the alliance structure, but operating within that structure and providing the very fuel for its development, the ritual feast structure also provides the basis for a new kind of hierarchical relationship which might well become dominant in the long run.

It is significant that Izikowitz discovered the importance of this third structure when working among a group in which ranking is quite minimal.

> »If we examine the expenditures of the Lamet throughout life, we should find that the greatest sums go to the cult of ancestors and to the payments made in connection with the entrance into matrimony.« (Izikowitz 1951: 308).

But he goes further than this simple identification.

> »I should even like to assume that the feast of the ancestors and all connected with it is the driving force in the entire economic and social life of the Lamet.« (Izikowitz 1951: 332).

If we refer to these two major structures which dominate the circulation of wealth respectively as horizontal and vertical, we can represent them in such a way that their potential opposition becomes clear (see opposite page).

With the formation of powerful chiefdoms the conflict between the two structures becomes obvious. A chief may demand both tribute and corvée from the whole village in exchange for his magico-religious services. It is not stretching things too far, I think, to see in this situation a kind of embryonic form of »asiatic state« in which the social function of the ruler is to control fertility by means of his genealogical proximity to the gods.[1] But there is a strain between this emergent hierarchy and the dominant ties of kinship, since rank itself is expressed in the alliance relationship. That is, the dominance implied in the chief/community relation is incompatible with the wife-giver/wife-taker link. Thus, the vertical structure which is the main impetus for the development of affinal hierarchy has within it the germ of a new social relationship which is in contradiction with that hierarchy.

---

[1] We shall see in chapter IV that the segmentary structure of the ancestor world is the basis for the formation of a conical clan, so that alliance rank tends to be represented as a consanguinal relation between lineage ancestors, i.e. wife-giver/wife-taker rank becomes senior/junior rank. In this way, the relative ranking of alliance is redefined in terms of absolute genealogical distance from the territorial spirit, that is, from the chiefly lineage.

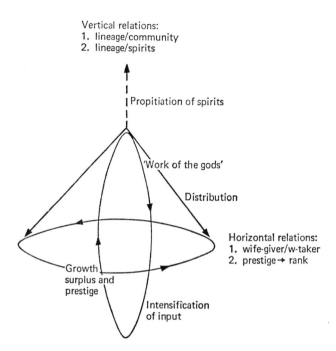

Vertical relations:
1. lineage/community
2. lineage/spirits

Propitiation of spirits

'Work of the gods'

Distribution

Horizontal relations:
1. wife-giver/w-taker
2. prestige → rank

Growth
surplus and
prestige

Intensification
of input

Surplus and the Forces of Production

The simplest marxist notion of surplus is total output minus the necessary costs of reproduction of the work force of society. Necessary costs are the quantities of output needed to reproduce the working population and means of production at the same level of productivity, thus permitting the reproduction of the society at the same economic or subsistence level. Surplus can be represented in either a potential or materialized form. Potential surplus is unused labor time while actualized surplus is the realization of that potential.

We must be clear at this point to distinguish between total social surplus and individual or lineage surplus. Lineage surplus is the operator in the system as we have described it. It is quite possible for a population to underproduce as an aggregate while some of its members produce a surplus. This may be due to variation in the ratio of workers to consumers, to technological and climatic factors, or to intensity of labor input which is our most important social factor.

The possibility of producing a surplus is a fundamental precondition for the operation of the system. Feasts are impossible unless the minimal segment has enough output above and beyond its own needs to undertake such an affair. The alliance structure by itself might not require a significant surplus if it only depended on the transfer of wealth items which had little or no real social cost. However, the fact that it is linked with the prestige ranking of feast giving tends to inflate the costs of affinal relations which involve large feasts and gifts of grain as well as cattle. The way access to cattle is tied into the

accumulation of prestige is itself necessarily linked to the production of surpluses since cattle lost can only be regained if prestige is maintained by continued feast giving. Thus, the increasing accumulation of prestige, brideprice
values, etc. depends on increasing real output. This, of course becomes a
problem when the limits of productivity are reached and surplus can no longer
be increased.

Forces of Production

The limits of output are ultimately determined by the capacity of the technology or techno-environment. In this case the technological base is slash-and-
burn agriculture. In the next chapter we shall discuss the regional variants of
this system. Here, we shall only be concerned with its general properties as they
relate to the social formation as a whole.

I. Organization of Production

The organization of the work process is not nearly as important as is often
assumed in certain oversimplified views. While there are a number of technological and environmental constraints which impose necessary limits on possible arrangements of labor, there is usually great latitude for variation. In
swidden cultivation, the major constraints are the direct outcome of the number
and kind of crops grown. Complex harvesting and planting schedules in which
the quantities of different seeds sown depend on the distribution of soil conditions, stage of fallow, distance between fields, etc. can make large scale
cooperation very difficult. However, these conditions may be partly due to the
social structure itself. A primary relation of production in all of the societies
we deal with is the private household appropriation of the land and its product
which means that a good deal of the decision making regarding specific combinations of crops and location of fields is decentralized, making cooperation a
virtual impossibility, especially where timing becomes an important element.
If the social relations were altered so as to make central planning possible to a
greater degree, large scale cooperation would then seem to be quite feasible.
From this perspective, the way in which a swidden is worked is to a large
extent determined by the social relations. In similar conditions we shall find
that labor, from clearing to harvesting may be organized by households, swidden groups (several households), or larger groups approaching an entire local
clan or even village. The division of labor by age and sex is also quite variable.
At one end we find societies where women do practically all of the agricultural
work, and at the other, groups in which men take on some of the heavier bur-
dens and the division of tasks is a bit more even.

   To clarify this, we need only consider the independent existence of a working population, N, and a given system of cultivation which imposes a set
number of tasks, r, l, m, and p to be executed at a given time. Each task
corresponds to a work group comprising a fixed segment of the population.
Task r, for example, might impose age restrictions; l might impose sex restric-

tions, but this is for the most part highly doubtful as none of the work forms are that specialized. At time t, then, we have:

$$r_n + l_n + m_n + p_n = N \qquad (x_n = \text{work group size})$$

Suppose, now, that only »a« members of the population are eligible for task r. Also suppose, for example, that a > r and that a − r = c. Then, the basic problem of allocation can be summarized in the following table:

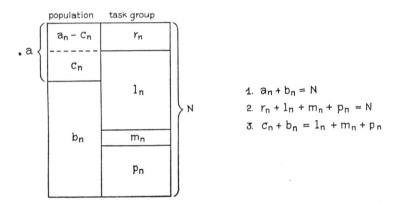

1. $a_n + b_n = N$
2. $r_n + l_n + m_n + p_n = N$
3. $c_n + b_n = l_n + m_n + p_n$

After task r is allocated, the rest of the population, c + b, can be distributed in any combination of age and sex, in small disparate groups or in one large group. Most of the agricultural work in slash and burn technology might be placed in Steiner's category of »uniform labor« (Steiner 1957) or Terray's »coopération simple« (Terray 1969:114) where the division of functions is non-existent or such that no strict allocation of tasks is necessary. This implies an even greater range of freedom. Among the Konyak, women turn the soil and men place the seeds. Among other groups both tasks are the work of a single individual. In very few cases do we find complex forms of cooperative activity where functions are necessarily distributed in terms of a larger organization of work. If the tasks r, l, m, and p are not simultaneous but part of a work cycle. we might be inclined to assume an assignment of people to jobs in such a way that man-hours are more or less equally distributed. This, however, is not necessarily the case especially with regard to women who invariably have a more than equal share of the labor. In any case, it can be said that the activities of the process of production do not strictly determine the division of labor. Therefore, no description of the process of production is comprehensive unless the social context is taken into account.

This applies quite clearly to the composition and size of the group involved in any particular task. While certain anthropologists (Terray 1969) have tried to show that forms of cooperation somehow generate corresponding social forms, I think it more likely that the social relations themselves are instrumen-

tal in the organization of production. To say that the local lineage is a production unit is not, of course, to imply that the fact of cooperation determines
that it will be a lineage. On the contrary, we shall assume that local lineage
appropriation is a socially determined phenomenon. In all of the groups we
shall deal with, the household is the only stable unit of production and consumption. Beyond this, lineage, alliance and common residence relations are
all variously employed to organize production. The way they are used determines the form and composition of the work group and not the contrary.

Generally speaking, the technology of production determines the necessity of
cooperation but not its social form. The specific task does not necessarily imply
anything about the social relations of the individuals engaged in that task. It is
this compatibility which permits the actual variation that does occur. The stability of the household in all of this cannot anymore be accounted for technologically than that of any other social unit. In fact, when we examine the data more
closely there is variation here also. For among some groups the nuclear family
is the principal unit while in others there are large extended families often
including domestic slaves. The size of the unit of immediate production may
depend on the rate of fission characteristic of the minimal lineage, and on
the distribution of authority in units above the nuclear family.

The importance of the organization of labor is not in its direct effects on the
relations of production, for, as we shall see variations in the former do not
correspond to significant variations in the latter. The organization of work is
most meningful in terms of the productivity of the economy as a whole, and it
cannot be separated from the production function of the society. It is the combination of labor-power, technique and environment which determines the
potential for surplus. The organization of work must undoubtedly affect the
efficiency of production as well as the total labor time available for productive
work, i.e. the potential intensity of production.

II. Technology

The determinants of crop yields are extremely numerous and complex, and to
sort them out requires the kind of data which is quite simply unavailable. Questions which would have to be answered in a thorough analysis, those pertaining
to particular plant species, exact slope of hills, local soil conditions, quantity
and variability of sunlight, temperature variability, rainfall surplus, are at this
point impossible to deal with. The best that can be done is to indicate some of
the important variables and delineate the internal properties of the productive
system.

Broadly speaking, we need to consider two principal relations between technology and social reproduction. These are the production of absolute and relative surplus, or, in other terms, the absolute and relative productivity of the
techno-environment over time. We shall discuss the all-important time factor
when we deal with the limits of the system (next section). Here we concentrate
on the statics, i.e., general structure, of the process of production.

There are three measures of relative productivity which are commonly used but rarely related to one another. These are the following:

$$\text{I)} \quad \frac{\text{crop yield}}{\text{crop sown}} = \frac{Y}{C}$$

$$\text{II)} \quad \frac{\text{crop yield}}{\text{area sown}} = \frac{Y}{A}$$

$$\text{III)} \quad \frac{\text{crop yield}}{\text{labor input}} = \frac{Y}{L}$$

I have not come across any materials in which measures (I) and (II) are clearly distinguished. Yield per acre and yield per input of seed are used alternately and it is assumed that they represent equivalent measures. It would seem, however, that they refer to different aspects of a single process, the former representing the productivity of the seed itself and the latter, the productivity of that seed in particular edaphic and climatic conditions. But this distinction is only practicable when the potential productivity of the seed can be determined independently of local conditions. Thus, where only actual local output figures exist, the yield per crop sown represents a combination of environmental factors and properties of the seed itself. Since this kind of mixup cannot be sorted out here I will define a kind of hybrid situation that might permit us to manipulate some relevant variables. I assume that Y/C represents the yield as determined by local average ecological conditions. This leaves Y/A as an indicator of intensification more than anything else. Y/C and Y/A interact in a very specific way. As we have defined things Y/C should be a constant in fixed conditions of soil and climate. This is not the case, however, since increasing plant density per acre, C/A, affects Y/C significantly. Density of sowing may increase the photosynthetic surface per unit of ground area and thus permit the processing of more nutrient materials from the soil. But at the same time, this increased density creates competition for light and nutrients (to a lesser degree) which can eventually reduce total yield (Williams and Joseph 1970: Chap. 4). Thus, Y/C will tend to increase at first and then to decline in conditions of high plant density. Optimal points and the limits of increasing output are determined by the leaf structure of the particular variety of plant. As C/A increases we reach a limit where $dC > dY$, that is, where marginal yield begins to decline as a result of overcrowding. This limit is an index of the level of intensification permitted by the agricultural system. It is also an indirect index of the maximal man/land ratio for any one agricultural cycle. The two technical conditions of production, (I) and (II) determine the labor efficiency of the system along with a number of specific factors: weeding, fencing, cartage and clearing, whose labor costs are to a very large degree a product of those same technical conditions. These latter factors which are necessary labor inputs of the production process vary in cost with the general state of the system as a whole; the degree of ecological maintenance and the man/land balance. The labor efficiency of the system Y/L has an important influence, in turn, on the stability of the social relations of production. The three ratios combine, finally, into a single process of the production which we can represent as follows:

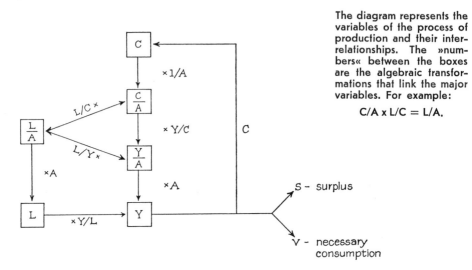

The diagram represents the variables of the process of production and their interrelationships. The »numbers« between the boxes are the algebraic transformations that link the major variables. For example:

$$C/A \times L/C = L/A.$$

The limit condition for the reproduction of the system is $Y > V + C$. There must be enough total output to at least reproduce the working population and the necessary input of seed in order to maintain the same standard of living. If Y/A sinks below a given limit, total acreage must be increased to maintain Y.[1] But this is only possible if there is enough labor available to extend cultivation at this low Y/L level. In very poor conditions, the threshold can be reached at which no population no matter how small or large can support itself in the sense that more acreage per man would be required than available labor input could manage. This is a limit which need not concern us here. In most cases, the productivity of seed Y/C is quite high, rarely sinking below 10/1 and often as high as 70/1. But the degree of intensification is limited in such a way that appreciable increases in output are not really possible without increasing total acreage. Thus, while the Y/C ratio indicates great efficiency, absolute yield obtainable is ultimately the most important factor. If Y/C = 20/1, but if I can only plant one acre where C/A − 40 lbs./acre then my total yield will be 800 lbs. 760 of which are consumable. If individual consumption

---

[1] We assume here that C/A is a constant corresponding to optimal distance between plants. In any case there is little room for variation here unless we assume that cleared fields are only partly sown or sown haphazardly − not a very likely occurrence.

is assumed to be 650 lbs./year, a not particularly high figure, I am left with only 110 lbs. of personal surplus. Any dependents are quite out of luck and the conditions of production (a child) can not even be reproduced. The relatively low cost of seed is only significant if the input per acre is fairly high. Thus, the number of acres cultivated becomes a significant if not all important parameter of the economy. However, in any but the worst conditions, the system operates well above these limits and surpluses are quite easily obtained in a technology where labor input is comparatively low. It is often remarked that the high Y/L ratio of slash and burn cultivation accounts for its popularity more than any other feature. In the best of conditions, the relative surplus of swidden agriculture is higher than many more intensive systems of irrigation, but we must not forget that the limits of intensification imply a relatively low absolute surplus.

III. Surplus and the Contradiction between Forces and Relations of Production

Until now we have considered the properties of the technology of production independently of the time element. Surplus, relative and absolute were treated as simple ratios or quantities of output and potential input. If we now place all of this in a developmental perspective we find ourselves with a production function which describes the variation of input and output as a continuous relationship. It is not necessary to conceive of this as variation in time. We can just as well assume that the function represents a distribution in space of possible input/output combinations. The assumptions of our approach, however, lead us to envisage the variation as a dynamic process implied by the operation of a social economy based on expanding demand for surplus.

Most discussions of surplus in anthropology have not, curiously enough, placed the problem within the context of the process of social reproduction, but, on the contrary, have focused on the mere static existence or non-existence of output above the absolute and »sub-minimal« (Orans 1966:25–6) requirements of *biological* reproduction (Pearson 1957; Harris 1959; Dalton 1960; Orans 1966). Ignacy Sachs, approaching the problem from the point of view of a marxist economist has made matters more comprehensible by his explicit use of the notion of production function. In this way he has avoided the reduction of variables to constants and has been able to get at the dynamic properties of production and reproduction. (Sachs 1965). The following discussion relies largely on his analysis.

The graph next page represents a production function OT and two consumption functions OV and OM. The axes represent output, Y, and labor input, L, which corresponds to seed input as well. Other factors such as total arable land available are held constant thus producing a typical case of diminishing returns after a certain point. The curve can be said to summarize a number of different factors:

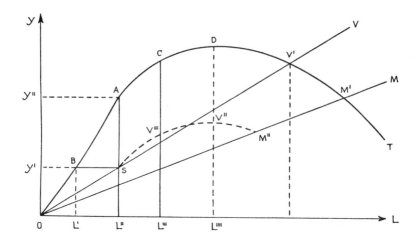

a) Intensification of planting per unit area.
b) Decrease in optimal fallow period due to the extension of land used in any one cycle.
c) Expansion into lands of poorer quality (assuming that the best lands are used first).
d) Labor intensification per unit area in order to maintain maximum yields in worsening conditions.

The function OM is the minimum physiologically defined comsumption necessary to maintain the level of efficiency required by the techniques employed. Beneath this limit, available labor power decreases spontaneously, either through inability to maintain the population size (starvation, underreproduction) or by any number of factors (disease, insufficient energy) which progressively incapacitate the working population. If this limit is ever reached it produces, of its own accord, a spiraling down into famine and disaster: Less food → less labor → less food . . . . . .

The function OV represents the normal level of consumption. It is proportional to the size of the productive population and is equivalent to Marx's notion of variable capital, the cost of reproduction of the work force at a constant level of productivity. It is not strictly physiological but is determined by the socio-historical context. It includes factors which influence economic performance as well as political tolerance. The consumption function represents more than the cost of feeding those actually engaged in the work process. It is the cost of reproduction of the work force. This includes, of course, the support of dependents, entire families, without which the notion of cost becomes meaningless after one generation. Any viable economy must provide for its own reproduction. Consequently, this concept must be the basis of any coherent analysis of a social formation.

A population of producers OL" can produce a yield equal to L"A = OY". Surplus can be represented in two ways here, either by actual product SA or by potential surplus labor SB. In order to support the population OL" only OL' input or OY' output is necessary. As we move along the L axis, total output and consumption change according to the properties of their respective functions resulting in changes in potential surplus product.

Contradictions

If we now analyze our model of political economy in terms of this graph, we can locate the major economic contradictions of the social formation within the process of reproduction itself.

At the lowest level there is what Sahlins has spoken of as the contradiction between domestic production for use and production for exchange. On the graph it is represented by the difference between necessary and potential output of a given labor population. A population OL" need only produce OY' to reproduce itself over time even though it is capable of producing the surplus Y'Y" as well. We can express the contradiction in terms of input or output, i.e., OL'/OL" or 'OY'/OY". This is an *intrasystemic* contradiction. As we have suggested, the decision to produce a surplus is determined by the structure of the relations of production, specifically, the cycle surplus – feasting – prestige, and the asymmetrical exchange between production units which tends to demand increasing surplus as ranking develops in a formerly egalitarian alliance network. This internal contradiction works itself out within the limits of the production function itself; in the range SA, SB.

The *intersystemic* contradiction is manifested by the relation between the requirements of increasing surplus and the cost of producing that surplus. There are several aspects to this relationship which depend on the way we choose to interpret movements along the L axis. In the simplest case, we can think of movement from L' to L" to L"' as increased hours of work by the same population. This, of course, has definite physiological and political limits which may very well go into effect before marginal productivity approaches zero ($\frac{dY}{dL} = 0$), but we can assume that the strains are greatest when the marginal yield per hour of work begins to fall. The more interesting case is the interpretation of increasing L as increasing size of the working population itself. The system as we have described it has a very high demand for labor. As we shall see, this is expressed in the great value placed on large families and the importation of new labor in the form of »slaves« captured from other populations. But there is a fundamental contradiction between this kind of expansion and the output possibilities of the technology. This is clearly visible in the contradiction between the consumption function OV and the production function OT. The former is linear and increases in direct proportion to population growth. The latter only increases up to a certain point, but a decreasing rate, $\dfrac{d^2Y}{dL^2} < 0$, and then, at

that point, $\dfrac{dY}{dL} = 0$, begins to decrease absolutely. Thus, in the interval SV'''

surplus increases rapidly because $\dfrac{d^2Y}{dL^2} > 0$, but from L''' to L'''' begins to fall

off and at L'''' the available surplus is less than quantity SA obtained with a smaller population. From V'' to V' consumption gradually overtakes output until surplus is non-existent. Increased L beyond this point entails decreasing consumption for everyone. There is a functional incompatibility between the consumption necessary for the reproduction of an expanding work force and the ability of the forces of production to provide the material basis of that consumption. The absolute limit of the system is V' but the social relations of production become strained long before that point. The internal dynamics of alliance ranking, feasting, etc., require an increasing surplus which is only possible as long as output increases faster than necessary consumption, i.e., up to L'''. Even if we suppose only a constant surplus, the system soon becomes unworkable. It goes without saying that the growth of the total labor force brings with it increasing work loads, especially when increasing output becomes more difficult to maintain. In a fully formed *gumsa* domain in which a paramount chief takes several baskets of rice tribute from each house, V''' would seem to be an ideal time for a *gumlao* rebellion.

Summary and Conclusion

This chapter has been devoted to the elaboration of a first approximation model of social reproduction. We have indicated the major categories of the social formation and outlined the intersystemic relations that unite them. We have, finally, suggested some of the major contradictions which might emerge in the functioning of the system over time. We have now to see to what extent this model can illuminate the Southeast Asian data. This implies a back and forth process whereby particular societies are analysed in terms of the model, in which hypotheses generated theoretically are used to restructure the data and where the model itself is further elaborated in such a way that its explanatory power is increased. The effect of this process should be that the theory is able to generate structures which more closely approach concrete reality.

The procedure adopted follows the general theory outlined in the preceding chapter. We shall, thus, begin with the outermost constraints, those of the environment, and subsequently work our way in towards the social relations of production.

CHAPTER III

Environment and Technology

In any system of swidden cultivation, the environment plays a crucial role, not simply in determining the conditions of production, but as a part of the technological process itself. Ecological conditions do set limit conditions on the nature and extent of exploitation, but they are subject to change due to the production process itself. In this perspective, I have chosen not to treat the environment simply as a constant. I have deliberately precluded the possibility of dividing the territory into »ecological zones« in the manner of Leach (Leach 1954: Chap. 2). Instead, the following survey will attempt to reconstruct the distribution of techno-environments in terms of whole production systems in which the ecology is both a limiting factor and a variable subject to transformation as a result of human activity.

In the following analysis, I will examine the natural environmental distributions of the Burma-Assam-Yunnan region and attempt to show how Leach's zones are, in fact, historically determined secondary phenomena. The emergent relationships between technology and environment will open the way to an explanation based on a larger evolutionary model.

The territory covered by this analysis includes extensive regions of Northern Burma, Assam, Laos and Southwest Yunnan, where several related forms of slash and burn agriculture are utilized. Let me begin by specifying the range of environmental variation which must be accounted for. All of these areas are what might be referred to as »accidented highlands« (Ho 1960) whose altitudes range from 3,000 to 7,000 feet. Temperatures vary, of course, according to altitude, but they are distributed between a high average of 30 degrees C and a low average of 15 degrees C. Rainfall varies from 75 to 150 inches per year in weather systems of wet summers and dry winters where the dry period is two or three months and occasionally as much as four months. These features fit for the most part into Ho's category of »Humid tropics with short dry season« (Ho 1960:31).

What is the significance of this variation? Is it sufficient for the establishment of a continuum of techno-environmental forms? I think not, but before discussing this it might be profitable to give a clearer presentation of the facts.

The following maps provide a number of partially overlapping distributions of climatic types and give us some idea of the underlying conditions for slash and

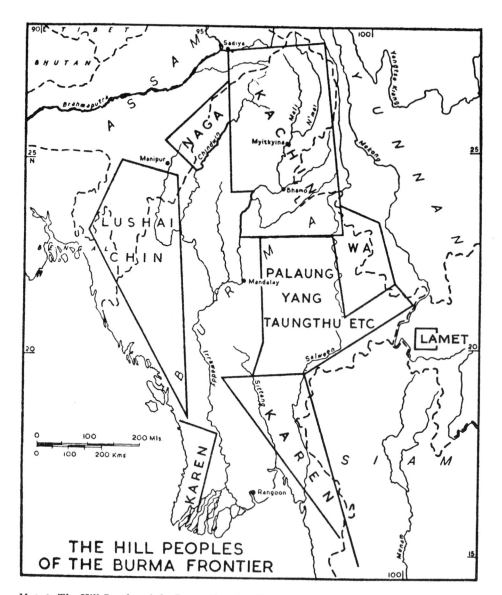

Map 1. The Hill Peoples of the Burma Frontier. From Leach 1954.

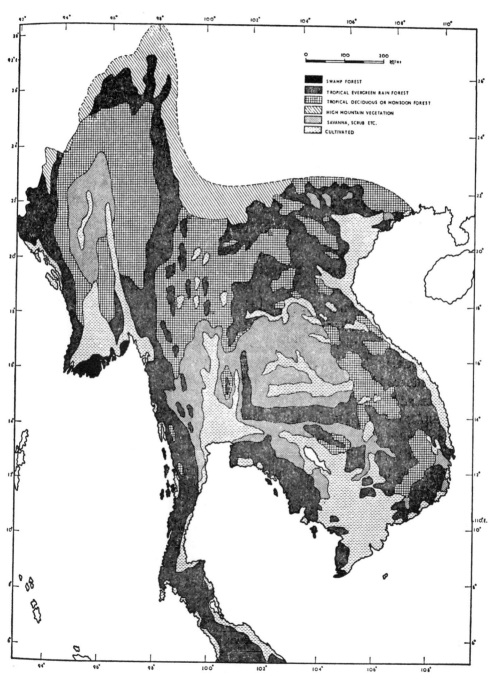

Map 2. Mainland South-east Asia: Vegetation. From Fisher 1964.

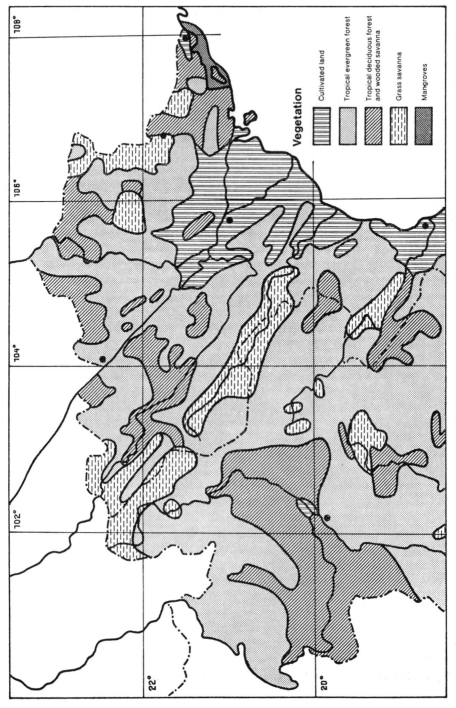

Map 3. Northern Indochina: Vegetation. Based on Hall 1964.

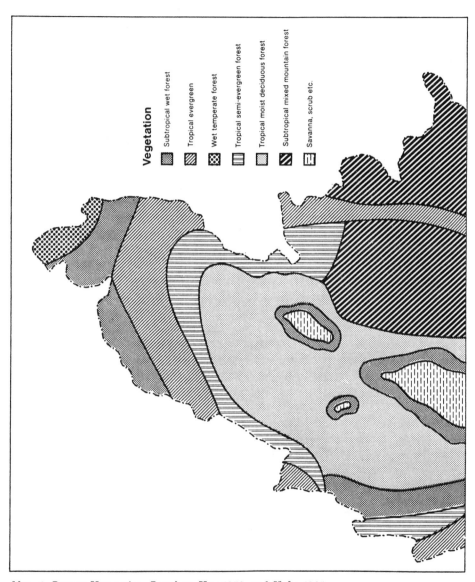

Map 4. Burma: Vegetation. Based on Hoe 1956, and Huke 1965.

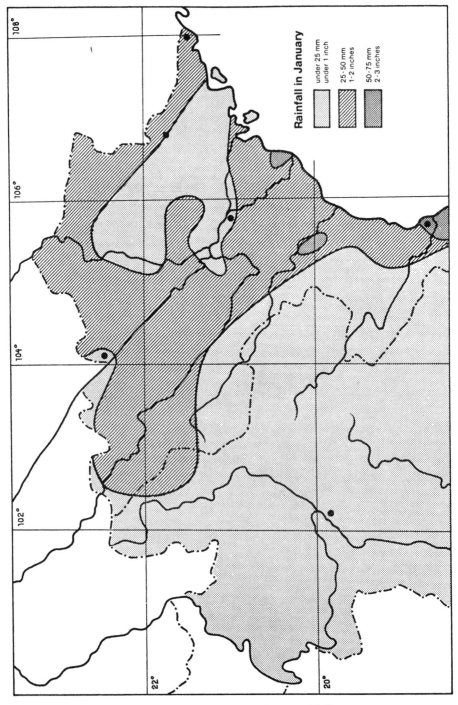

Map 5. Northern Indochina: Rainfall in January. Based on Hall 1964.

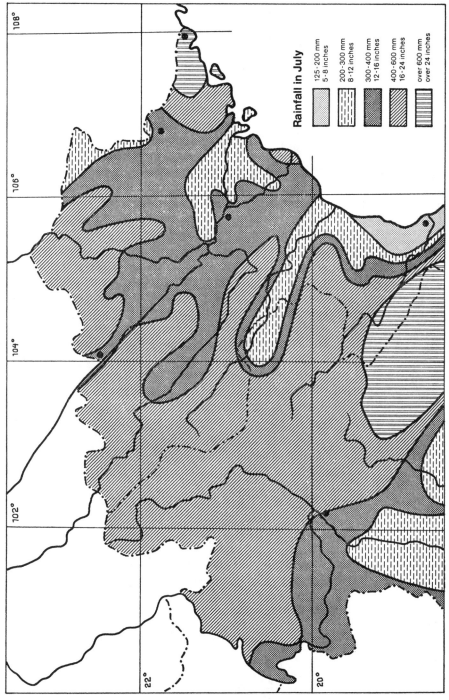

Map 6. Northern Indochina: Rainfall in July. Based on Hall 1964.

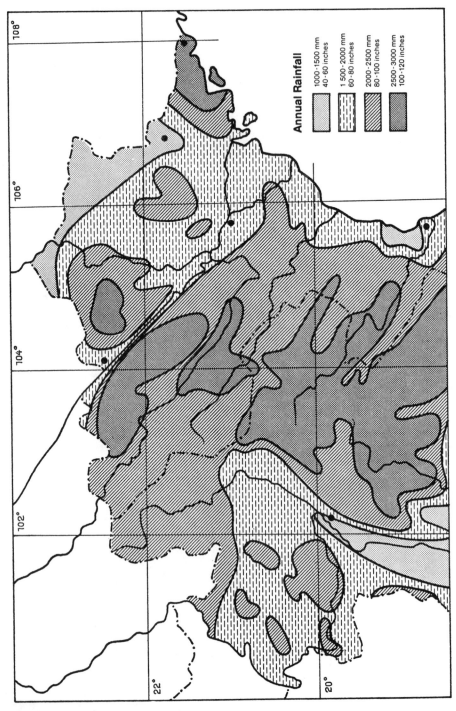

Map 7. Northern Indochina: Annual Rainfall. Based on Hall 1964.

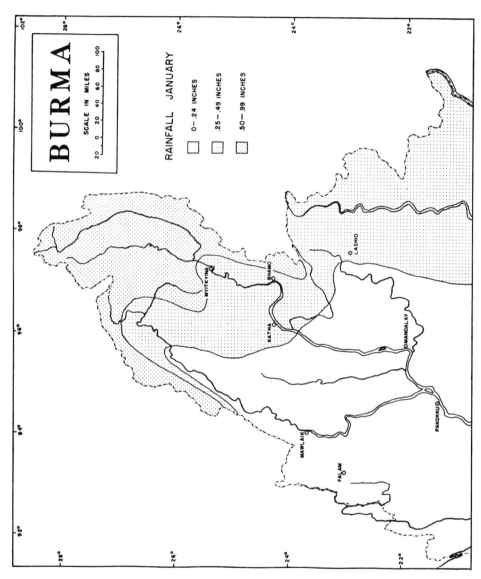

Map 8. Burma: Rainfall in January. From Huke 1965.

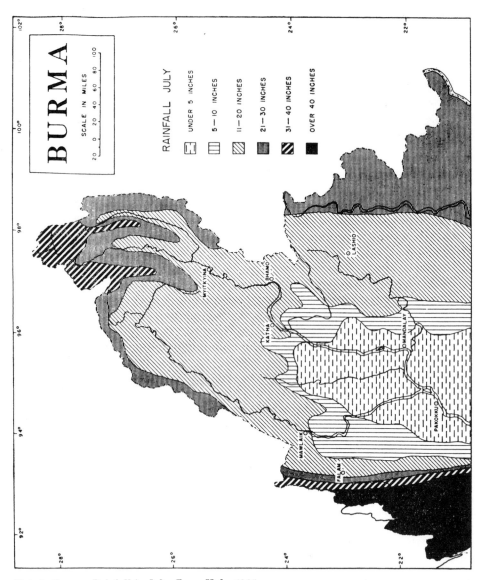

Map 9. Burma: Rainfall in July. From Huke 1965.

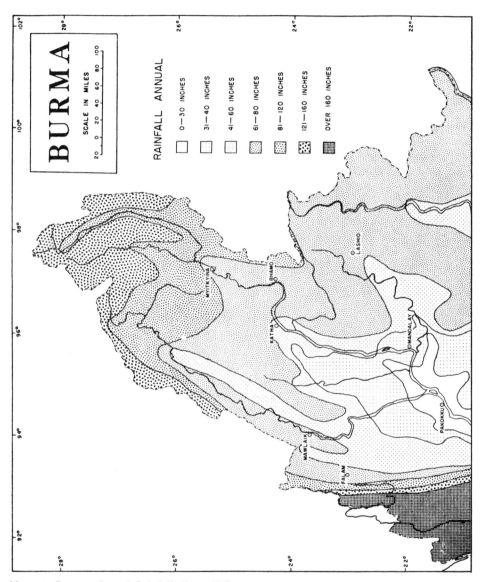

Map 10. Burma: Annual Rainfall. From Huke 1965.

5*

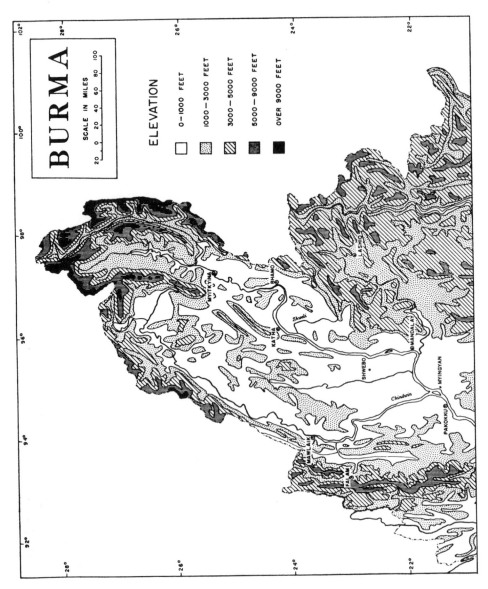

Map 11. Burma: Elevation. From Huke 1965.

burn agriculture. A very important trait which holds for the entire region we are concerned with, is the rainfall average for July which is between 11" and 30". If we take this as a mark of seasonal climatic conditions it is clear that the main growing period for crops is quite similar for all of the upland groups, from the Lamet to the Naga. The more specific area maps incidate that the Lamet fall within the range 16"–24" while the Kachin, Chin and Naga fall in the range 15"–30" – the difference is insignificant. Annual rainfall shows somewhat more variation. On most general maps there are two main rainfall zones. Part of the Naga and Kachin areas fall within the 80–120 inch zone while all the other areas get 40–80 inches. On our more accurate regional maps, the distribution changes. The Lamet now fall into the 60–80 inch range. The Chin, most Naga, the Wa and some Kachin are in the 70–100 inch range, while most Kachin and the northern Naga fall into the 100–200 inch range. This typology increases in complexity as we examine the regions more closely. Different authors have reported different rainfall estimates so that it would not be very wise for us to narrow the range too far. Generally, though, it would seem that precipitation totals concentrate in the vicinity of three separate averages. The lowest average cluster is around 80 inches per year and includes the Lamet, Wa, parts of the Chin and Naga (south) hills and Southwest Yunnan. A higher average centers around the 100 inch mark and can be found in parts of the Chin Hills (Haka and south), Naga Hills (Wokha) and Kachin Hills (Bhamo area). Finally, certain areas of the Kachin Hills (Triangle) and the extreme northern Naga Hills (Konyak) appear to get 120–150 inches quite consistently.[1]

We might well ask whether or not these three variations have any significance for the local economies. Most evidence would seem to indicate that this is not the case. The importance of rainfall is the maintenance of water balance in the soil, and once this is taken care of, more rainfall will not have any long term effect on productivity. Studies of tropical soils (Mohr 1944; Van Brun 1954) suggest that where temperatures lie between 24 and 28 degrees C, 100 mm (3.9 inches) per month is sufficient to maintain water balance in normal conditions of evapo-transpiration. A dry month would be equivalent to less than 60 mm rainfall. Thus, even the driest of our regions easily meets the conditions of water balance. Furthermore, during the agricultural season rainfall is quite ample in all the areas considered, the variations being due to off-season differences. It has been suggested to me by J. Barrau[2] that rainfall (or the lack of it) only begins to become an important factor when it approaches

---

[1] Standard rainfall estimates generally tend to be on the low side because they are based on lowland readings. This may often imply that an entire region is placed in a lower category than is warranted. The rainfall map for Burma made by Huke (1965) is one of the few that appears to take altitude variations into account in an accurate way. Thus in the northeast parts of Burma where valley readings are below the 80"/yr. mark, the mountain readings are well above 100".
[2] Personal communication.

the 60 inch per year level which implies that our variations are not possible determinants of fertility and crop productivity. It does seem likely however, that rainfall may have an effect on the speed of secondary forest regeneraration, but I have no evidence at all on this. If this were true then we would have a good case for a limiting factor, but it still seems unlikely that the interval 80–150 inches is sufficient to establish real economic differentiation. It should also be pointed out, of course, that excessive rainfall in any one period can cause leaching which would certainly counter its positive effects.

Vegetation

As we have nothing approaching adequacy regarding edaphic conditions we must rely on the distribution of vegetation as an indicator of agricultural potential. Even here, we will only be concerned with major types of vegetation. These, however, can be a usefull source of information.

>A study of vegetation is of value to the agriculturalist in two main ways. First, since the nature of the vegetation is, to a considerable extent controlled by climate, soil and topography, which are the principal physical factors determining agricultural potential, it is often a usefull indicator of such potential. Secondly, some types of vegetation possess features of direct agricultural significance. For example, some kinds of forest or woodland are much more difficult to clear than others, and after clearing, it is relatively easy to maintain pastures in some vegetation zones, whereas in others this is difficult because of persistent regeneration of woody species.< (Webster and Wilson 1966:68).

We cannot assume that there is a one to one correspondence here since soil, climate, topography and vegetation form an integrated ecosystem in which all the variables have some influence on each other. When we introduce a fifth factor, man, the possibilities of modification become enormous, especially with regard to soil conditions and vegetation. Aside from human influence, there are some major factors which affect the kind of vegetation climax which are likely to be relevant to agriculturalists.

>The most important way in which climate, soil and topography affect the vegetation is by their influence on the moisture available to plants, taking into consideration, on the one hand, the rainfall and the moisture stored in the soil and, on the other, the losses from surface run-off, subsoil drainage and evaporation.< (Webster and Wilson 1966:69).

The interplay of the above factors enables us to deduce a number of variant conditions affecting natural climax vegetation. Optimum conditions for the development of vegetation (Webster and Wilson 1966:70) occur in low to medium altitude areas with good rainfall and humidity, relatively high temperatures throughout the year, with fairly level, well drained land, deep permeable soils, and in areas sheltered from high winds. Climax formation in these conditions is tropical lowland evergreen rainforest. The most important sub-type of this is a seasonal evergreen formation due to the existence of a dry season. If this season increases in length, the vegetation changes successively from evergreen to mixed evergreen and deciduous and finally to pure deciduous. Drier formations are irrelevant to the areas under consideration here.

The natural climax vegetation forms which concern us are all variations of evergreen tropical, mixed evergreen and deciduous forests. On Fisher's map (Map 2) of Southeast Asian vegetation, Chin, Naga, Kachin, Wa and Lamet areas are all covered by three vegetation types; tropical evergreen, tropical deciduous (monsoon) and high montane. Maps 3 and 4 are broken down into finer categories, and the following correspondences will make their interpretation easier.

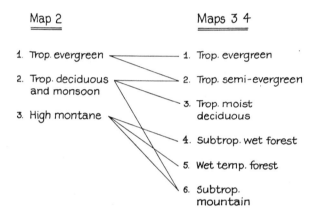

There is some overlap in these categories where the vegetation is mixed. While maps 3 and 4 are quite specific, they are not able to handle the continuous aspect of vegetation changes and can often be misleading. This is especially true in mountainous areas where mixed forest can vary greatly in evergreen content with changing altitude. With reference to the tropical-moist-deciduous zone of maps 3 and 4, ethnographic descriptions indicate that at higher altitudes (4,000–6,000 ft.) these areas contain a good deal of evergreen growth and are closer to the category »tropical semi-evergreen forest« (thus, map 2 is more accurate for the Chin Hills in this way). As such, these two categories will be referred to as tropical mixed forest in order to highlight the internal variability.

The distribution of the »tribal« groups among these categories is roughly as shown in the diagram on page 72.

Does this distribution carry any implications for agriculture? Leaving aside the Wa and marginal Kachin for the time being, all of the other groups fall into the three categories tropical evergreen, tropical mixed and subtropical wet forest. These categories are differentiated along two axes, temperature and rainfall, but the differentiation is very slight. The first and last would appear to get somewhat heavier total rainfall while the last is in a sligtly cooler region where winter temperatures might have an effect on vegetation. The subtropical mixed forest of the Wa may be the result of somewhat lower over-

	wet temp.	trop. wet evergrn.	trop. mixed	subtrop. wet	subtrop. mixed
Kachin	peripheral	main	main	main	peripheral
Naga		main	main	peripheral	
Chin			main		
Lushai			main	main	
Wa		main			main
Lamet			main		

main population

peripheral population

all temperatures combined with lower rainfall. Again, this represents a minor variation since the vegetation is of the same general type. However, there may be an effect on the regenerative capacity of the forest in such conditions when we take a long enough period of time and a sufficient number of slash and burn cycles into account.

When we first discussed vegetation we used, as our model, lowland evergreen rainforest since it was the source of our optimal definition. The three subtypes of lowland rainforest were seasonal, semi-evergreen and deciduous. These follow a continuum toward longer dry seasons. The hill areas we have been discussing are normally classified as lower and higher montane forest, but they do not represent a significant divergence from lowland types for the analysis of productive potential. Webster and Wilson, comparing the lower montane and lowland areas say,

»Agricultural conditions are so similar in the two zones that separate discussion is not merited.« (Webster and Wilson 1966:81).

In Northern Southeast Asia, lower montane vegetation occurs normally as high as 6,000 feet. Thus, our hill zones sort themselves into the lower montane categories of semi-evergreen and deciduous forest. Tropical wet evergreen forest occupied by some Kachin and northern Naga groups are as close as we can get to the optimal vegetation conditions. While there is a dry season in these areas, the total rainfall is extremely high and quite reliable. The tropical mixed forest occupied by the majority of the populations covers a continuum from semi-evergreen to more deciduous formations. The areas with denser evergreen growth have annual rainfalls from 80 to 150 inches. The percentage of deciduous trees increases when rainfall begins to drop below 80 inches. The subtropical mixed forest of the Southern Shan and Wa states has the largest proportion of deciduous trees, although the number of evergreens is probably greater in the high altitude areas. While the nutrient content of the soil is not known it would be unwise to assume that fertility is lower here, since deciduous forest zones are generally higher in this respect than zones with more rainfall. This is due to the fact that there is less leaching during wet seasons. Because of the high altitudes and cooler temperatures in parts of the Wa states, they take on many characteristics of higher montane zones. This is demonstrated by the fact that the Wa often grow their rice as much as 3,000 feet beneath their villages while reserving higher slopes for maize, millet and buckwheat (Scott and Hardiman 1900: Pt. I, Vol. 1:509). In this one case, then, we may have a clear example of environmental constraint. It should not, however, be construed as an important one, since the latter crops are capable of the same kinds of yields as rice.

On the surface, it might appear strange to regard all this micro-ecological variation as basically inconsequential for the agricultural potential of the area. I would argue, however, that this is just the way things turn out in the last analysis. The crucial characteristic, one which applies equally to all the zones, is the relation between vegetation and soil nutrients in all montane environments. The maintenance of fertility in conditions of relatively shallow soils and steep slopes depends on the »balanced, closed cycle of nutrients between vegetation and soil.« (Webster and Wilson 1966:75). Where land is put under cultivation, this cycle is broken, and with traditional methods of swiddening fertility declines rapidly.

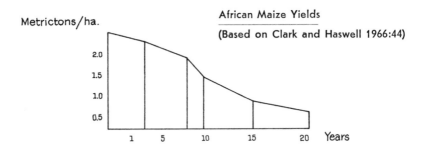

Metrictons/ha.

African Maize Yields

(Based on Clark and Haswell 1966:44)

2.0
1.5
1.0
0.5

1   5   10   15   20   Years

The above pattern from Africa is generally true of all slash and burn systems, but in upland regions (unlike that above), the yield will tend to fall off much more rapidly and it is rare to find cultivation of one cereal crop for more than two years running. The output potential of the different montane zones will, I think, be found to be broadly similar, and emphasis should be placed on the much more important problem of maintenance of fertility which is more a techno-environmental than purely environmental affair. This will be clearly demonstrated when we examine techno-economic zones which, quite contrary to simple mechanical expectation, cross-cut the natural ecological zones in such a way as to render them quite meaningless.

Techno-Economic Zones

These zones are the result of the application of a particular technology and economic organization to the natural vegetation zones we have described above. These zones are also part of a continuum, but one which does not map onto the natural climax vegetation. At one extreme we have a combination of very thick secondary growth with a relatively high percentage of primary forest. At the other extreme is the predominance of coarse grassland with few trees of any kind. Between these extremes lie a number of variants which can best be classified according to the degree of development of thick secondary forest as opposed to lower forms of scrub, bamboo and grass. The Lushai Hills (North) are something of a special case due to the great proliferation of bamboo stands. It is possible that these are a natural formation, but from existing descriptions, it seems more likely that they are the secondary result of cultivation. This, at least, is the opinion of the geographer L. D. Stamp (Stamp 1924). Bamboo stands are cleared by the Lushai but are reported to give lower yields than secondary forest. They might be classified along with poor secondary or scrub growth. We will tentatively make use of the following categories:

A. Heavy secondary forest and primary forest.
B. Heavy secondary forest predominates, little or no primary forest.
C. Secondary forest – high percentage of scrub, bamboo, lighter vegetation.
D. Grasses and scrub predominate.

The »tribal« groups are distributed amongst these categories in a way which appears at first to reflect the natural vegetation zones.

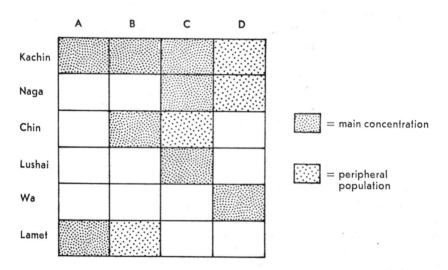

The Kachin span all the techno-economic zones at one extreme, while the Wa, by no means a small population, are confined to a single zone. As with the ecological zones, the majority of the groups cluster in the middle categories.

But this should not lead to the mistaken attempt to find some causal relation between the two kinds of zones. The next table should demonstrate the degree to which the techno-economic categories cut across the natural ones.

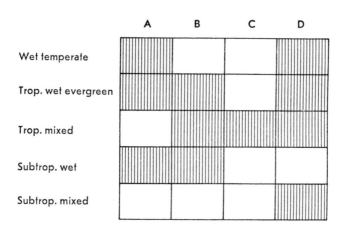

As we can see, the techno-economic zones are quite evenly distributed throughout the different vegetation zones. This is a matter of common sense. A, B, C and D represent the results of increasing intensity of land use over extended periods of time. They represent the long term transformation of natural climax vegetation into grassland irrespective of the original ecological conditions. If, for example, a normally sub-tropical mixed forest is entirely in our zone D, this is not due to some inherent property of that kind of vegetation, but is merely a reflection of the fact that the group occupying that zone is very densely populated and has been there for a long time.

Economics and Ecology: Leach's »Ecological Zones«

Our analysis thus far implies that the dominant factor in the formation of techno-economic zones is the economy itself and not the natural environment. It is, of course, possible that in slightly different micro-climatic conditions the transition from A through D might be accelerated or decelerated, but the stages themselves are pretty well invariant.

Leach's distribution of the Kachin into three »ecological« zones appears, in this light, as both a misnomer and a theoretically misleading approach to the problem (Leach 1954:24). Fortunately, his presentation is so clear that the errors are easily recognizable. He begins by distinguishing three types of hill agriculture; monsoon *taungya* (swidden), grassland *taungya*, and irrigated hill terraces plus a combination of the first two. He then seeks to show that they correspond to three very definite natural ecological zones (see map – next page). His monsoon forest zone corresponds to our techno-economic zone A,

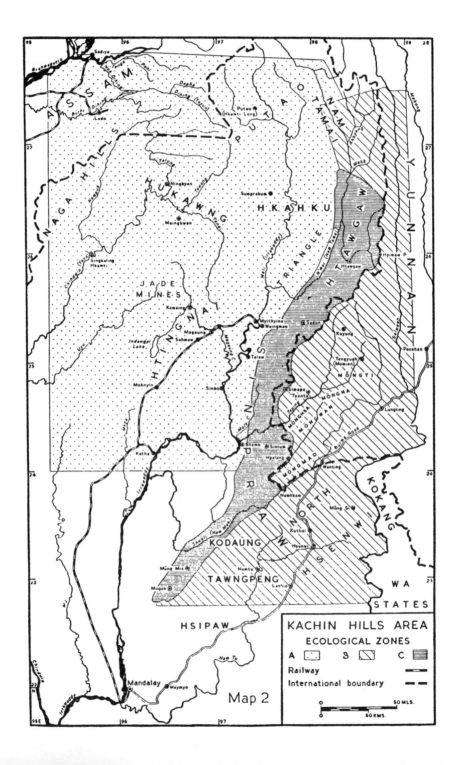

Map 2

KACHIN HILLS AREA
ECOLOGICAL ZONES

A   B   C
Railway
International boundary

but it spans a number of natural vegetation zones. His grassland zone, from his description and according to the Burma gazetteers (Dawson 1912; Hertz 1912; Scott and Hardiman 1900: Pt. I, Vol. I) corresponds to our zones B and C (and some D) in which grassland exists in varying degrees but does not dominate. It spans three vegetation zones and two rainfall zones. Leach claims that »temperature and rainfall here are much lower« (Leach 1954:26) but our information would seem to contradict this statement.

It might be that rainfall is a bit lower in some areas, but certainly not enough to make a difference as great as Leach would expect. The area falls into the 80–120" zone in the south and into the 120–160" zone in the north. These averages appear to be based on very recent readings (Huke 1965). Readings in the Burma Gazetteers are quite variable and tend to be based on valley averages. As the range in any one zone is rather wide, it might be that actual rainfall is in the vicinity of 80–100" rather than 100–120". This, of course, is difficult to ascertain from the maps. Ecologically, however, it makes very little difference. The map indicates that in the northern part of the Kachin Hills, Leach's monsoon forest and grassland zones both fall into the same rainfall area. This would seem to contradict his assumptions. In the southern part of the grassland zone the mountain areas seem to get upwards of 80", and rainfall is lower as one moves west so that Leach's zone C would seem to get less rainfall than his zone B. This again contradicts what he would expect. While there is a general decrease in rainfall as one moves from West to East into Yunnan this is more than compensated for by the North-South mountain ranges that catch large amounts of rain. Real fall-off does not occur until well into China. Leach's third zone is supposedly intermediate between monsoon and grassland and might fall into our zone B. It is significant that this area is affected by rain shadow (i.e. south slopes grass, north slopes forest) so that regeneration of forest on some slopes is impossible. The extensiveness of this condition, though, is not reported, and there is no reason to assume that it is limited to just this one area. In any case, Leach's reasoning runs quite differently since his only determinants are rainfall and temperature which, as we have seen, do not serve to differentiate the zones in any significant way. Kachin of this area practice monsoon and grassland taungya but also terraced irrigation which he claims is the result of political rather than economic decisions.

Leach's zones do not correspond to true ecological zones. His own statements lend ample support to this. Grassland it not a natural climax formation in this region. It is the result of over-intensive cultivation. This is stated quite plainly by Leach. He seems to be saying that certain areas tend to turn to grassland more easily than others and that the three zones simply represent three environmental reactions to swidden agriculture. We have argued contrary to this that environmental differences, if they exist at all are insufficient to account for such radical differences in resultant vegetation. This can be demonstrated with two examples. The Lamet who occupy an »ecological« zone similar in most respects to Leach's monsoon area have a total rainfall of about 70–80 inches which is lower than most of his grassland region. At the other end of the scale, the Garo Hills get the highest rainfall in all of the Burma-Assam upland region, but there are practically no trees there at all, only extensive grass cover. It is evident from these examples that there is no truly ecological basis for Leach's division of the Kachin area. Rather, these divisions correspond to what I have called techno-economic zones whose determinants are not environmental preconditions so much as the socially determined production process itself. The factor which is most clearly related to zonal differentiation is intensity of exploitation over time which itself corresponds roughly to population density.

Population Density (increasing order)	Lamet =	Triangle Kachin <	Nam Tamai Htawgaw Sinlum Kachin <	Garo
Techno-economic Zone	A	A	B-C	D
Rainfall	70"–80"	120"–150"	80"–120"	≽ 150"

It is not my intention to be dogmatic at this point. I do not claim that microclimatic or soil differences are irrelevant here. But I would stress that aside from minor variations, the human factor is decisive. It is a systematic error to treat the environment as an independent variable when it is so important a part of the production process itself. Leach's often equivocal position on the relations between ecology and the social economy is misleading precisely because it is not clearly worked out in theory.

For our purpose, the techno-economic zones are far more important than the original natural vegetation. They form an ordered set which is directly related to intensity of exploitation and indirectly to population pressure. The motive force behind the transition from one zone to the next will ultimately be found in the social structure, but at this level of analysis there is a specific *contradiction between increasing intensification and the basically extensive character of the agricultural system*. The contradiction is most striking in those areas where no modification of the cropping system has occurred to offset the deteriorating conditions. In some cases, however rare, the technology of production has varied in the direction of increased reduction of fallow while still maintaining fairly high yields. Other local adaptations to this contradiction have implied the exploitation of external economic sources such as trade routes or valley dwelling wet rice cultivators, subjects which will be explored in later chapters. In any case, the problem of population growth, technological variation and environmental transition will not be fully understood until we have put together a more complete model of the social formation.

Since the articulation of technology and environment is the central theme of this chapter, the characterization of the techniques of production and their variants is essential to our understanding of the production process as a whole as well as the distribution of techno-economic zones.

Technology: Processes of Production

There are only two major kinds of agriculture to be found in the hill country of Southeast Asia, slash and burn and terraced irrigation. The former is the more important technology and is subject to a high degree of internal variation. But the variations are not simply random. They constitute a well ordered set of sub-types which fit into an equally well ordered set of techno-environmental systems. Terraced irrigation is *not* a distinct technical evolution, but one of the end points of the techno-economic development of swidden systems.

I.   The simplest or classic form of swidden cultivation is practiced by the Kachin of the Triangle area and by the Lamet. There is a single main crop, rice, and a number of subsidiary plants which are intercropped.

Some of these are:

millets	pumpkins
sorghum	yams
jobs tears	beans
maize	taro
sessamum	tomato
melons	spices

These subsidiary crops are common to all of the variants of swidden cultivation and will not be repeated in later discussion. Certain kinds of runner beans cannot be planted with rice due to their rapid growth and tendency to crowd out the young rice plants. Often, early varieties of rice are planted which can be harvested long before the main crop. This also is true of other grains, especially millets, sorghum and jobs tears. Such early harvests maintain a steady inflow of food throughout the summer months in case of a rice shortage from the preceding year.

Fields are planted for only one year, and the fallow cycle for this sub-type is very long, averaging from 12 to 15 years or more. The organization of labor is not the same among the Lamet and Kachin. The former are divided usually into swidden groups of several families each with its own field. The latter usually cut one swidden for the entire village. In both cases, each household has individual use rights over its plots. As with most of the other groups, each household has its own garden in which a number of vegetables, spices and some grain crops are grown.

The distinctive feature of this kind of cultivation is that the work requirements are very low. The soil is rarely worked as burning suffices to aerate, and virtually prepares the soil for sowing. Weeding is not a major issue in these areas where the secondary forest growth is very rich so that weeds do not get a chance to establish themselves. This is reinforced by the fact that fields are used for only one year. The only necessary agricultural implement is the dibble stick. This system is practiced in zone A and in the better parts of zone B.

II.   The Kachin practice a different type of cultivation in zones B and C. Here, rice is again the major crop, although Leach reports that in some areas millet and buckweat are more important (Leach 1954:26). I will concentrate on rice cultures since he gives no information about these other crops which, if grown extensively, might well correspond to increasing grassland conditions as among the Wa. Rice is usually grown for two years running, undoubtedly with a substantial drop in yield for the second year. The agricultural cycle is made more complex by the fact that beans are usually sown the third year (Leach 1946; 1949). This would seem to imply that at any one time three plots were in use:

	PLOTS		
	I	II	III
year	1. rice 2. 3.	1. 2. rice 3.	1. 2. 3. beans

The importance of beans is in the maintenance of fertility. It is not uncommon on grassland to open up a field after the fallow period with a first crop of beans. The fallow cycle is relatively short in this system and the ratio of cultivation to fallow is usually in the vicinity of 2/10, but can fall as low as 2/8 in the Sinlum Hills area which is making a rapid transition to grassland. It is not unreasonable to believe that the ecological conditions in these areas are the result of decreasing fallow leading to increasing intensity of cultivation which finally necessitates the transition from System I to System II. Leach reports that within System I, fallows are often as low as 7 to 10 years which would certainly be enough to trigger this kind of development (Leach 1949). The labor requirements of this system are higher than those of the first. Weeding becomes a much more time consuming and difficult activity and the land must be worked with a hoe. In addition, yields are quite a bit lower so that more land must be worked in any one season. This is evidenced by the fact that three plots are in use at any one time.

    Leach's differentiation between the intermediate *taungya* area and the grassland zone is based entirely on the extent of transition from forest to grassland

and is not a true distinction. Thus, when he says that two kinds of swidden are cultivated in the intermediate zone, he is referring only to the kind of land that is being used and not to some general technological factor. Where millet and buckweat predominate, in some of the worst areas, it is presumably the result of soil degradation. These latter crops are not usually preferred, but they are a good deal less exhaustive of soil nutrients. These crops are grown by the Wa and by certain Naga groups and will be treated as a separate sub-type. The practice of terraced irrigation in the intermediate zone might be one cause of the percentage of forest here since it requires very much less land and is more or less permanent.

III.   The Lushai represent a kind of extreme variant of System II where two consecutive rice crops are sown but where no bean crop is used to restore fertility although peas and beans are intercropped in small quantities (Allen 1906: Shakespear, J. 1912: Chap. II). Other crops such as maize, millet, melons, etc., are grown as in all of the groups. There are two very distinct kinds of vegetation which serve as the basis for two cultivation cycles. Secondary jungle is planted for two years with a fallow of 7 to 10 years. Bamboo jungle is planted for two years with a fallow of only three to four years. Although the bamboo jungle yields are lower than those of secondary jungle it is preferred for a number of reasons. As Shakespear notes, the labor requirements of bamboo are considerably less with regard to felling and there is less weeding (Shakespear 1912:33). Furthermore, given the short fallow period of secondary forest, it turns to coarse grassland quite easily and so would be a rather impractical base for the economy. Thus, in spite of its greater yields, secondary jungle (very secondary) is soon transformed into conditions of very low productivity, much lower than bamboo if nothing remains but grass. In this way, we might regard bamboo jungle as a kind of safety valve for Lushai subsistence as it gives a fair yield with a very short fallow. The two cultivation/fallow cycles for the Lushai are 2/3–2/4 and 2/7–2/10. The long term instability of settlement, to say nothing of warfare is quite probably related to the shortness of their fallow period. These conditions vary in different parts of the hills. From a number of sources it would appear that in the extreme southern portions of the Lushai Hills the crops are generally better, there is more available forest (Allen 1906) and much less bamboo (Lewin 1869). This area, inhabited by some Lushai, but also by Lakher, may be a transitional zone. Another important feature of this system, owing to the presence of bamboo jungle, is the high probability of periodic famine due to the occurrence every 17 og 21 years of a drastic increase in the bamboo rat population.[1] When bamboo flowers and seeds, the rat population increases rapidly. But since the seeding period is short, the rats soon take to the rice fields where they devour everything in sight.

---

[1] Lehman: personal communication.

IV. The system of cultivation practiced by Northern and Central Chin is the most elaborate of all the groups we encounter. It is noteworthy that this system seems to give fairly high yields while keeping the fallow/cultivation ratio relatively low. It is surely the best adaptation to zones B and C. The main crop is maize and not rice which is occasionally sown, but always in separate fields. Other important crops are two kinds of millet (italica and eleusine corocacana), sorghum and jobs tears. Maize and millet are the two most important crops, and millet has a special place as the main ritual crop. Economically, it is important because it can be stored for as long as fifty years and gives a certain amount of security to the system.

Most Chin make use of a large range of altitudes for their crops and there is a distinction between land on the highest slopes above 5,000 feet and fields below that mark which are generally the more important.

The agricultural cycles of the two kinds of field are very different and they are combined in a variety of ways. High land (*zo lo*) is planted only with maize for one year and left fallow from 7 to 9 years. Low land (*lai lo*) is used for all the other crops in a complex cycle which varies from place to place. The land may be used from three to nine years in succession and the fallow is often as long as forty years. The intensity of use depends on a number of factors, population pressure being the most important. In Haka, the ratio of cultivation to fallow is in the range 4/30–5/40. In Falam, the cycles are 6/18–3/12–4/24. *Zo* land is much easier to work, requiring little labor input (due to the nature of maize and the fact that it is only used for one year, i.e., less weeding), and it is sometimes used up entirely before *lai* land is even begun. Where *zo lo* is preferred and abundant, *lai lo* is only used until *zo lo* again becomes available after fallow. Generally, however, *lai lo* is more important because of the number of crops that can be sown and the length of cultivation. In fact, given the short fallow of *zo lo* which is already under some strain, the chances of continual regeneration of secondary growth are slim and it is doubtful that it could serve as a permanent basis for the Chin economy. *Lai lo* agriculture combines a system of field rotation with a system of crop rotation, and it is this latter which makes the long period of continuous cultivation possible.

The system of crop rotation is based on a three or four year cycle in which peas start and end the rotation.

> 1. peas (pigeon pea)
> 2. Ø (in Falam – runner beans)
> 3. sulphur beans (carnavalia ensiformis)
> 4. peas

In each of these years the main crops, maize and millet, are planted along with the leguminous plants. It is not necessary that a field be abandoned after the fourth year and Stevenson has described an elaborate rotation system for Falam, which is very heavily populated, in which there is a cycle of 3, 6 or even

9 years marked by the alternate use of two kinds of sulphur beans. Following is the six year cycle (Stevenson 1968:32):

1. sulphur beans A
2. peas
3. runner beans
4. sulphur beans B
5. peas
6. runner beans

The greater elaboration of this system may reflect the increased pressure on the cultivators. In either case, however, the peas year is the pivotal point in the agricultural cycle which has ritual importance, and in the past had significant political concomitants. The use of peas is perhaps the most common way of maintaining soil fertility over extended periods of time.

»Pigeon pea has been more frequently employed as a restorative crop in experiments of this kind (i.e., fallowing) than any other legume.« (Webster and Wilson 1966:179).

The importance of peas and beans lies in their ability to fix nitrogen in the soil. Peas, especially, with their deeper roots also enrich surface soil by bringing nutrients from lower levels. The emphasis on leguminous crops among the Chin is related in an inverted way to the rarity of rice crops. When rice is sown, it is always as a first crop on a very good field. It is never planted for more than one year.Rice is much more exhaustive, especially of nitrogen, than either maize or millet which are, in consequence, better long run crops for so intensive a system.

The Chin system is surely one of the most intensive of hill swidden economies, and it appears that large portions of the Chin Hills are closer to zone C than to zone B (Lehman 1963:50–51). In more densely populated regions it is not uncommon that newly cleared plots are of »scrub jungle and grass« (Stevenson 1968:38) rather than more developed secondary forest. The labor requirements seem to be quite high especially as regards weeding in the second and third years of cultivation. The hoe is an indispensable item of equipment in these conditions. It also appears that individuals cultivate a relatively large number of acres during any one year (5–6 per household). In spite of all this, however, yields are maintained at a fairly high level and an average family of five might have a surplus of 1,000 to 1,500 lbs. in a good year (Stevenson 1968:114).

V.   The system practiced by the Sema and a number of other Naga populations is similar to both Chin and Kachin (II). It is an obvious compromise between System II and the continuing degradation of the ecology. The main crop is rice which is planted for one year only being replaced by a less demanding millet crop in the second year. Fallow periods vary with availability of land.

»Where there is enough land, seven years is usually reckoned the shortest

time in which the land can become regarded as the normal period for it
to lie fallow . . . . In the Tizu valley, however, and in parts of the Kileki
valley where the population has much outgrown the supply of suitable
jhuming land *jhums* may often be fund cleared after only five years rest.«
(Hutton 1921a:59).
   Millet is not always the second crop. Among the Lhota Naga, rice is grown
for both years with a fallow of 4 to 15 years. As the land shortage is not as
acute in this group, the 15 year fallow is probably more common. Among the
Chang Naga, no rice is grown at all and jobs tears are the staple crop. We find
the same subsidiary crops here as elsewhere and the system appears to resemble
Kachin II except for the absence of a bean crop.

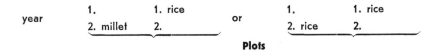

   Hutton stresses that the labor requirements of this system are high due to
the number of fields worked and the necessary weeding activity, especially in
the second year (Hutton 1949). The Naga »tribes« occupy techno-economic
zone C for the most part although some areas are almost entirely turned to
grassland.

VI.   There is very little information on the agriculture of the Wa who occupy
zone D, but it may be similar in many respects to Naga groups like the Chang
or the Maru and Nung north and east of the Kachin Hills. This is Leach's
grassland *taungya* proper. The main crops are millet, buckwheat, perhaps some
maize, with beans and sometimes peas to reinforce soil fertility (Harvey 1933;
Scott and Hardman 1900: Pt. I, Vol. I). Rice is rarely grown and only in small
quantities on lower slopes. Opium, however, for some Wa is a major crop, and
its sale is probably crucial in those areas where staple food crops are insufficient. It is also probable that opium, a winter crop unlike the food staples,
accentuates the already extremely depleted soil of the hills and while it would
appear to be grown on separate fields (Scott and Hardiman 1900: Pt. I. Vol. II:
360) it must be considered a contributing factor to the almost total lack of
trees in the Wa states.
   There is no reliable report on the cultivation/fallow cycle of the Wa, but it
seems to have a very high ratio. The clearings for cultivation are enormous and
one often finds reports of entire hill slopes under cultivation in a single season.
This would imply that fallows are of necessity quite short while cultivation
might continue for at least two years. Scott and Hardiman, in a very brief
discussion of »hai« (agriculture in South Hsenwi whose terrain is »thoroughly

deforested« but not as heavily populated as the Wa region) gives yield per basket of input for rice at 12/1–20/1 which is quite low. This might be somewhat higher for millet and buckwheat since they do better in poor soils. In any case, with a yield below 20/1 the area which must be put under cultivation is much larger than in regions like the Triangle where the yield is anywhere from 30/1 to 70/1. This explains Scott's remark that the Wa as opposed to the Kachin »are diligent cultivators with immense clearings.« (Scott 1893 in Harvey 1933:13–14). Grassland fields are often burned more than once, both the vegetation and soil being scorched to get maximum friability. This too may contribute to long run depletion and increase the quantity of nutrients that can be leached during the rains. But it appears, unfortunately, to be a necessary condition of a good yield in any one season.

It is not clear that these conditions hold for other parts of what Leach refers to as grassland *taungya* where there is still a good deal of secondary growth. Certain areas of the Naga Hills may have similar conditions and the region northeast of the Irrawaddy populated by large Maru and Lashi settlements would also seem to fall into this sub-type. However, I tend to think of the Wa as a very extreme case in which the agricultural base has been degraded beyond all repair. It does not appear that other groups are this far along. In Tawngpeng State (Palaung), which gets lower yearly rainfalls, the yields of swidden rice average between 16/1 and 39/1 for each basket sown (Scott and Hardiman 1900: Pt. II, Vol. III:261).

VII.   Terraced irrigation is the most intensive land use pattern found in the hills. It occurs in zones B, C and D, but more particularly in zone C and D with heavy population densities though not necesserily in the densest region. It is found in its most elaborate form among the Angami Naga, but also exists among Kachin Lashi and Atsi groups in Leach's intermediate zone, especially along trade routes. Some Sema Naga groups near Angami country have also recently switched to this form of agriculture.

This system, which is devoted exclusively to rice, entails a very heavy demand on labor, especially since in most cases no traction animals are used, the work being done entirely by hand. While there is no burning or clearing each year, the construction and maintenance of terraces represent a major investment of labor. The cultivation cycle involves hoeing, planting and transplanting, the latter being the peak work season of the year. Dikes must often be repaired in a climate with heavy rainfall, and in spite of the fact stressed by Hutton (1949) that weeding is greatly reduced, it is quite clear that this method of cultivation is a very laborious one. Not only is the system labor intensive, but the yields per acre are not increased that much. Leach reports an average of 25 to 40 bushels per acre (1,210–1,742 lbs./acre) which is not bad at all. Good swiddens among the Kachin will yield 1,800 lbs./acre or more and with much less labor input, while poor swiddens may require a great deal of work for a return of 1,000 lbs./acre or less in some areas. Two points are of paramount importance here. On the one hand, terraces provide a fairly stable yield over time out of the same piece of land. In a fifteen year period they are fifteen times more intensive than the best Kachin swiddens and are capable of being maintained indefinitely. But, by their very nature, they represent a blockage to expansion. Swidden cultivators can easily increase the amount of acreage sown in order to increase absolute yield or to make up for decreasing relative yield per acre. The terrace agriculturalist can not maneuver in this way. Expansion requires a new large scale investment which can never be effected at the last minute. In addition, the work requirements are such that expansion of terraced fields might run into serious limitations with respect to available labor power. Thus, there is a ceiling on the possible output due to the fixity of total cultivated area, a limitation which does not exist for swidden agriculture.

The enforced stability of terracing may be one of its major drawbacks in the kind of economy described earlier which puts a premium on expansion over time. It is certainly not a preferred form of agriculture.

»All the Angamis, however, do not practice this wet cultivation, as the Chakroma Angamis living nearer to the plains have so much *jhum* land that they are able to live on this alone, and good *jhum* land, cleared once in twelve or fifteen years, say is said to produce a better crop than 'panikhets' or terraced fields.« (Hutton 1921:72).

Leach, in an article which demonstrates the superiority of swiddening from the point of view of the laboring population concludes,

»I believe that hand cultivation of wet rice in terraces gives a poorer return for labor than any other form and is only found where shortage of land overrides all other considerations.« (Leach 1949:27).

This last system is an adaptation to severe land shortage and not an evolution of a new more productive form of technology. Where it does occur it represents a means of overcoming the kind of situation that might develop in the Wa region. Irrigation is not practiced everywhere and it might develop out of various combinations of circumstances. Leach suggests the following order of causality:

Military need → large agglomerations → terracing

I would suggest that the military need which appears as the first cause is itself caused by increasing population density, a phenomenon closely linked to the functioning of the social system over time. However, the triggering effect of warfare which leads to rapidly increasing agglomerations separated by greater distances may occur before all available land is exhausted. We are dealing here with a social system in expansion and not simply the properties of land usage and total man/land ratios. The terraced communities in the eastern hills of the Kachin region are in an area of heavy trade between Burma and China, where control over routes makes permanent settlement an advantage, especially where population is already dense and competition for control is quite strong. In an area where trade revenue is needed but also restricted, population density must be measured in terms of the circumscribed revenue area and not total available land.

In sum, terracing is an adaptation to an increasing need for large aggregates which is itself the result of land deterioration and increasing population pressure. It is successful to the extent that it represents a relatively stable source of subsistence, but it is not well adapted to a socio-economic system with expansionist tendencies. Kachin terrace communities are all associated with external revenue. Angami terraces are usually supplemented by swidden cultivation and in both cases warfare is common although it is much more serious among the Angami who have no »imperialist« safety valve.

We have now described seven systems of cultivation, six of which are broadly similar. Most of the technologies fall into zones B and C and only one is able to maintain itself in zone A for any length of time. Following is the approximate distribution of the cultivation systems in the techno-economic zones:

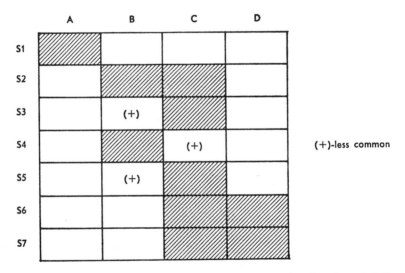

The generally diagonal clustering is the long term result of reduced fallow and increased cultivation period. But the chart by itself tells us little except that S2, S3, S4 and S5 seem to be variant adaptations to the B and C zones. Excepting S4 (Chin) for the moment, it is clear that S2, S3 and S5 are very similar kinds of techniques. All have a two year succession of cultivation with a relatively short fallow of usually less than 10 years, and at the most, among certain Lhota Naga, 15 years. But even this is still a ratio of only 1/7 or so. All of these systems tend in the long run to degrade their environmental base. S6 is the extreme form of this development. If we were to represent the development of these systems in terms of transition probabilities we would get something like the following:

p = transition
probability

S1: $\;A \xrightarrow{\;\;p2\;} B$ $\;\;\;\curvearrowright p1$

$p1 > p2$, unless $\dfrac{\text{cultivation}}{\text{fallow}} \lessgtr \dfrac{1}{12}$

S2: $\;B \xrightarrow{\;\;p4\;} C \xrightarrow{\;p4\;} D$ $\;\curvearrowright p3$

$p4 > p3,\; p4 > p2$

S3: $\;B \xrightarrow{\;\;p6\;} C \xrightarrow{\;p6\;} D$ $\;\curvearrowright p5$

$p6 > p5,\; p6 > p4 > p2$

S4: $\;B \xrightarrow{\;\;p8\;} C$ $\;\curvearrowright p7 \quad \curvearrowright p7$

$p7 > p8,\; p8 < p4 < p6$

S5: $\;B \xrightarrow{\;p10\;} C \xrightarrow{\;p11\;} D$ $\;\curvearrowright p9$

$p10 > p9$, decreasing: $p11 > p10 \geqslant p6 > p4 > p8$
fallow

S6: $\;C \xrightarrow{\;p13\;} D$ $\;\curvearrowright p12$

$p13 > p12,\; p13 > p11 \qquad p10 \geqslant p6 > p4 > p8$

S7: $\;C \xrightarrow{\;p15\;} D$ $\;\curvearrowright p14 \quad \curvearrowright p14$

$p14 > p15,\; p15 < p2$

While there are no exact figures here, we can rank the systems according to an ordinal scale of transition probabilities (above) which measures the rate of environmental degradation. These probabilities yield the following order:

Rate of degradation: S7 < S1 < S4 < S2 < S3 ≤ S5 < S6

When we compare this ordering of the systems to their places in the techno-economic zones we can get some idea of their developmental possibilities. But the way in which they are distributed cannot be fully understood outside the context of the social system. As such we leave it to a later chapter to fully integrate this data. One thing, however, is clear right now. The technologies and techno-economic zones cannot be dissociated from one another. They are part of a single scheme in which the pivotal variable is increasing intensification of land use without adjustment of the soil nutrient balance which results in long term transformation of dense forest into grassland.

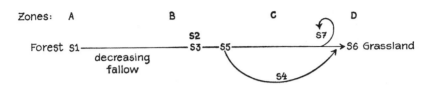

The above trajectories represent the three ways or rates at which this transformation may be accomplished.

Contrary to simple expectation, the transition from dibble stick to dibble stick plus hoe, the transition to more complex fallow systems and finally the transition to irrigated terraces, do not represent technological advances, at least not in terms of overall efficiency. On the contrary, they are ways of adapting to increasingly poor conditions of production which are the very result of the application of those technologies. While S1 is capable of maintaining itself in a given environment, S2, S3, S5 and S6 are by their very nature, self destructive. S4 is also relatively stable, but along with S1 it tends to come under increasing pressure for shortened fallow. In all cases the increased pressure is due to factors which are not inherent in the technology itself. Swidden agriculture is neutral with respect to environmental degradation, and if used efficiently it can maintain the ecological balance virtually intact. In order to understand the disequilibrium we will have to wait for a more complete model of the social formation.

The exterior factor to which the technology must adapt if the economy is to be maintained is increasing land shortage. If fallow is reduced and cultivation increased the economy destroys itself over time. The Chin are our only case where the cultivation/fallow cycle is manipulated to hold productivity per acre fairly high while raising the cycle ratio to as high as 1/3. This is accomplished by keeping a long absolute fallow period of at least 12 years and as much as 40 years while preserving fertility during extended cropping periods by rotation and heavy use of legumes as nitrogen fixers. In this way, Chin agriculture can support fairly high population densities with much higher yields than the Lushai or Naga.

J. M. Blaut, in a general discussion, has described a situation for Malaya that could very well serve as an outline for the major themes of this chapter.

»Total yields for villages overall territory will continue to increase at successively shorter fallows – as evidence the demonstrable increase in population – up to a limit set by the low level of biomass accumulation per fallow period. (Available farm labor is increasing at, if anything, a greater rate than acreage under cultivation at any one time, so labor shortage is unlikely to be a factor limiting yields.) Long before the limit is reached, however, the constantly rising level of demand for food will have outstripped the more slowly rising territorial yield. Thus as fallow-

length declines toward and into the *belukar* stage (brush and low wood-
land) the point will be reached where, regardless of any further intensification of labor input and assuming no change in technique, food shortage will appear . . . .

». . . . Some of the differences in structure between the degraded forms of
shifting agriculture and the one described earlier seem to be the following:
greatly reduced fallow and increased intensity of labor input, with greater
proportional effort devoted to tillage and weeding, much lower yields per
acre for fields under cultivation, a change in the array of crops favouring
those which yield reasonably well on poorer soils (cassava, sweet potato,
coarse grains, etc.) over those which do not, and in some situations, favouring cash crops which enjoy comparative advantage in trade for food
produced elsewhere.« (Blaut 1960:192).

In this chapter I have analyzed what I consider to be the important features
of environment and technology and their combination in the process of production. I have given little space to the actual organization of work, since it is
similar for all the cultivation systems. Although, often, the size of groups
involved in any one task may differ, it does not appear that this is significant.
The variations which do occur are invariably the product of the larger socio-
economic context and not the technology itself. The division of labor does take
on importance only where it puts significant constraints on the productive process as a whole, as when important tasks such as weeding are left entirely to
women while the men do nothing, thus greatly reducing the labor force at a
time of peak need. Weeding is a crucial factor in raising yields to the maximum, especially in less than optimum environmental conditions. In a table
fallowing this chapter, I summarize the general features of the work cycles. I
have also summarized in tabular form some of the available data relating to
several Southeast Asian highland economies. In all of the cases where nume-
rical information exists there appear to be very high yields per acre, and the
availability of household surplus is a certainty in all of these cases. The figures
also imply that the population densities which are often as low as 5 per square
mile and not higher than 30 per square mile (Chin) are below carrying capacity.
If we take the Kachin data at face value and assume that an acre will support
a little less than two people (5/3), then the potential poupulation per mi^2 is
about 71. For the Chin it might be almost twice that. These potentials are
greatly exaggerated due to the fact that they assume that all land is flat and
arable. Aside from this, however, it suggests that the question of the relations
between population density and economic structure are more complex than
might be expected were we only to consider simple technological relations.

Group	Village Altitude	Annual Rainfall	Main Crop	Cultivated / Fallow	Yield / Input	Yield / Acre	Acre/Year Household
Kachin (Leach)	4000' –	Zone B & C ≈ 100"	Rice	2/10–3/10	≈ 25/1	> 900	2.5–3
	6000'	Zone A ≈ 150"	Rice	1/12–1/15	30/1–70/1	⩾ 1742	2.5–3
Lamet (Izikowitz)	3280'	≈ 78"	Rice	1/12–1/15	35/1–60/1	> 1200	4.32
S. Chin (Matupi)	3000' – 3500'	≈ 110"	Rice	1/6–1/10	30/1	1600	5–6
(Lehman)							(?)
North Central Chin Stevenson & Lehman	4000' – 7000'	≈ 100"	Maize Millet <Italica Eleusine Corocacana Sorghum <Red White	Haka: 4/30–5/40		1000–1333	3–6
Lautu (Bareigts)	4000' – 6000'	≈ 100"	Jobs Tears Beans – carnaualia ensiformis Peas – »bush peas« (every 2 or 3 yrs.)	Hnaring ≈ 4/20		1112	≈ 1.9 (?)
Hanunoo	984' –	100"	Rice	2/12–4/12	48/1	1959	1.7–2.47

Mo.	Kachin Zone A	Kachin Zone B & C	Kachin Irrigation	Sema Naga	Angami Naga Irrigation	Northern & Central Chin
J						End of pea & bean harvest – sulphur bean & great millet harvest
F	Felling Fencing			Felling		
M	Burning	Clearing		Burning	Rice seeding sown in dry nurseries	Burning
A	Burning	Burning Hoeing	Hoeing	New fields sown (rice) Old fields (millet) worked	Terraces dry out – maintenance of channels	Burning (hoeing)
M	Sowing	Hoeing	Sowing rice in nurseries Hoeing	Heavy Weeding	Transplanting	Sowing
J		Sowing	Repair dykes Hoeing	On second year fields	Weeding	Weeding
J	♀ Weeding ♀	♀ Weeding	Transplant rice to main field	Millet Harvest		Millet Harvest (panicum miliare)
A S			Weeding	Rice		Millet & Maize Harvest
O	Early rice harvest			Harvest	Harvest	
N	Main rice harvest			Clean old fields for 2nd crop (♀) Clear new forest (♂)	Harvest	Rice Harvest Start pea & bean
D		Harvest	Harvest			Felling in new Swiddens

CHAPTER IV

The Kachin

This chapter is an application and an elaboration of the model described in chapter two. I will try not to restate that model verbatim but to re-present it in the guise of what Leach might call Kachin categories. A number of different levels are linked in the abstract model of social reproduction. These include: local organization, lineage structure and inheritance, affinal relations, and »religion«. I propose to outline these categories and to put them together step by step.

After analyzing the articulation of the different structural levels, I will discuss the nature of the economic flow that is channeled through these structures. It will be seen that the properties of the social system determine the way it will develop over time – the transition from *gumlao* to *gumsa,* the expansion of the system, the formation of domains, the accumulation of prestige and control over the labor of the community; these are all linked in terms of a single set of structural properties.

Local Organization

There are three main levels of local organization, villages, village clusters and domains which form an inclusive hierarchy.

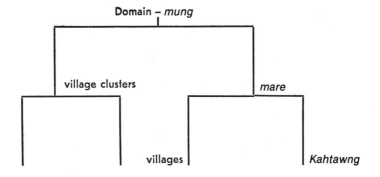

The village is the only stable political unit in this structure. Clusters and domains are larger scale political forms which emerge in *gumsa* development. The village is a self-contained economic unit and also the largest political unit in what Leach refers to as *gumlao* organization (we will discuss the terminology later). Villages are very small settlements of often no more than ten houses and rarely more than thirty houses. The combination cluster – village represents a dispersed settlement pattern found in most Kachin areas and among the Lamet to an even greater degree. Settlement density is a variable in our model, however, and even among the Kachin the village cluster may become a single large village in conditions of higher population pressure.

Lineage Structure, Property Forms, »Religion«

Ideologically, the Kachin segmentary system is a neat hierarchy containing minimal, minor, major, maximal and clan levels of affiliation. In practice, however, most of these levels are not operational. The only true exogamous level is the local lineage which is made up of one or more households that share the same hearth spirits (*nats*). The local lineage is a corporate group by all appearances. Expenses for important occasions are shared, there are common religious functions, and the rule of exogamy is quite strict. It also seems to be the unit of political decision-making at the village level. In *gumlao* systems where all lineages are »commoners« so to speak, lineage genealogies are short, rarely more than four generations. The local lineage is the extension of the minimal or household lineage over time, but as genealogical memory is weak, an automatic fissioning process takes place so that a minimal line, which in the space of sixteen generations gives birth to twenty households may in fact be divided into four or five local lineages. This is an extremely important property of the system which is often overlooked. It permits a great deal of maneuverability by allowing the relatively easy transformation of kin into affines which is a fundamental means of creating lineage hierarchy at the local level. Aside from this, there is a formal ritual whereby local lineages can split, in which a new segment adds a *nat* (spirit) to the previous hierarchy of household spirits. The result of these internal mechanisms is that the local lineage is usually a small group, rarely containing more than five or six households.

All higher levels of lineage segmentation become increasingly open to political manipulation. Related lineages in different localities are not unified in any necessary larger unit and certainly do not form a corporate entity. Endogamy above the village level is increasingly easy, again creating the means to hierarchization within higher levels of lineage segmentation. The clan, or highest level of inclusiveness, is not quite so manipulable as are intervening levels. This is due primarily to the existence of a relatively small number of mythically sanctioned clan names. Rather than invent clans, the Kachin usually manipulate their lineage ancestries to fit into one or another of the maximal categories. However, the distinctions between levels are not always clear. Ruling lineages that control large domains keep elaborate genealogies linking them to a major clan, but sometimes a lineage name will be added to the list of traditional titles. This variability is evident in origin myths where the number of clans is five, seven, eight, or even nine, but where only three clans are always present; Marip, Lahtaw and Laphai. In the Triangle area, the traditional home of the Kachin, clans are often associated with large territories, even where, as in the Duleng region, the ruling lineages have lost their power. But the degree of association between fixed territories and particular clans is not clear and may be the result of the continued existence of *gumsa* domains for extended periods of time. In any case, it is not important politically since any emergent chief can always »trace« his genealogy to the clan of his choice. Outside of the traditional homeland, ruling houses often claim descent from these same clans. But I suspect that in the past, the expansion of Kachin domains brought with it an increase in clan names. This seems to have been the case for the large state-like forms that established themselves west of the Triangle in the Hukawng and Assam (i.e., Tsasen clan).

It is impossible to fully grasp the inner workings of the lineage structure without analyzing the entire ideological matrix of which it is a part. »Ideological« is the wrong word here, for, as we shall see, the religious or mythical universe of which the lineages are a part have instrumental political and economic functions.

The cultural categories that divide groups into their constituent elements, provide the map for genealogical reckoning, the skeletal structure of the mythology etc. are all equally fictitious, but they can and do function as one of the dominant structures of Kachin society, organizing such things as land tenure and political hierarchy. In fact, I would argue that to divide Kachin society simply into economic base and superstructure is not theoretically useful if it is based on the intrinsic semantic content, kinship or religious, of cultural categories and not on their function within the material structure of social reproduction. In this particular case it would be more accurate to say that the lineage structure has ideological as well as material aspects but that both are part of a single entity.

The Kachin mythical universe is not a mere reflection of something more real, and we shall see how it plays a critical role in *establishing* dominance. That this is possible should only appear strange to someone who is mystified into the belief that landed property and money are somehow real objects and not social fictions, just as fictitious as gods and spirits, but which in capitalist society dominate social relations of production and the entire economic process. In the marxist framework, the content of categories is functionally irrelevant. Only their place in the social system is of importance. In this framework, an element is considered ideological because of the structural position it occupies in the social formation and not because it is not part of the material object world.

The Kachin mytho-social universe is organized on a lineage basis of inclusive hierarchy, but one which is neater than any on the ground relationships.

It includes all the most important spirits and links the celestial with the earthly world by means of descent.

The genealogy of the universe (see next page) establishes the kinship connections between three levels of ancestors. It is unfortunate that the only collected data of this sort is from *gumsa* groups in which the fundamental relationships have been elaborated in rather complex ways. I have outlined (dotted line) the main genealogical levels in order to simplify matters. The most distant ancestor is the earth spirit, sometimes represented as man and wife, sometimes as a single individual of indeterminate sex. Leach refers to the couple as »a sort of personification of earth and sky« (Leach 1954:269) Only the male half, *Shadip*, is usually worshipped. The children of this union are the celestial *nats* and a number of other spirits. Also at this level is Ning-gawn-wa, ancestor of the human race, whose nature and origin are somewhat obscure. He might be considered a son of the *ga nat*, but in one version he is constructed out of a pumpkin and various contributions from other celestial *nats*, (Scott and Hardiman 1900: Pt. I, Vol. I:417) and in a third becomes the *Shadip (ga) nat* after his death. In any case, he is regarded as half human, half divine and the obscurity with regard to his celestial kinship may express the contradictory implications of being descended directly from the natural (in the sense of nature) deities, a conflict which seems to be a correlate of the ambiguity of blood versus affinal relationships. The Kachin always express major rank differences in terms of alliance. If Ning-gawn-wa is half divine, his children are quite human as the result of his marriage to an alligator. This animal is used to mark major differences in rank at all levels, gods/men and aristocrats/commoners. This emphasis is most certainly a property of *gumsa* versions and would seem to be incompatible with *gumlao* variants. To continue, however, the ancestor of the Jinghpaw, Shapawng Yawng, is one of the sons of this divinity/animal union (youngest son in *gumsa* versions). His descendents are the ancestors of all the Kachin clans. In *gumsa* versions, this is restricted to chiefly clans while commoners are the result of another alligator intervention which has two variants. They are either descended from the daughter of Ning-gawn-wa by an alligator's son or an orphan, or from the daughter of another *nat*, Musheng, married to the same husband. In either case the general form descent is from celestial male + animal female to daughter of celestial male + human male to the male ancestor of clans and then lineages. The major divisions of *nats*, which are themselves organized into lineages, correspond to human lineage ancestors, celestial *nats*, and the earth *nat*, all linked in a single genealogy, but where the clarity of the links varies with the degree of *gumsa* development. Even in *gumlao* systems, however, the universe is still structured in such a way that a ritual hierarchy can be easily established by working out the logical relations implied in the already given mythical universe. Thus, both *gumsa* and *gumlao* systems work out of the same genealogical matrix.

The only difference between this generalized schema and the *gumsa* mythical variants is that two kinds of hierarchy are mixed in the latter forms,

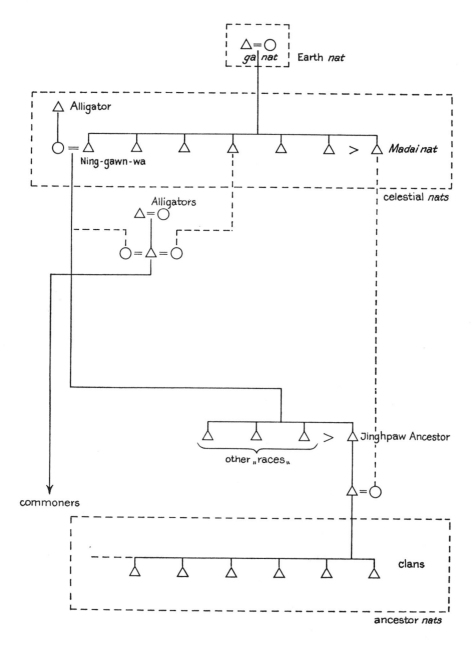

sibling rank and affinal rank (not present above). The former distinguishes chiefs from aristocrats and the latter distinguishes aristocrats from commoners. The use of affinal and sibling rank in a single hierarchy has important effects on the development of *gumsa* systems.

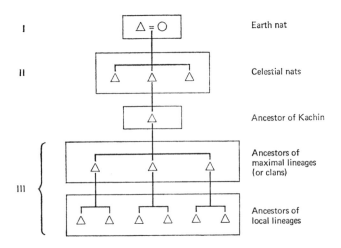

A most interesting aspect of this encompassing structure is that it defines a necessary endogamy at all but the lowest levels of organization. In this way, affinal ranking within larger lineage units gives rise to a ranked clan whose features are similar to the Tikopian *kainanga*, a kind of patrilineal conical clan (Firth 1963:316–320). This is a point I would like to stress since it has important implications for Kachin evolution. While much attention has been concentrated on the local level exogamy of Kachin lineages, this may be the expression of a bias in the anthropological literature which insists on the dichotomy between unilineal exogamous and conical clans. Not enough emphasis has been placed on the articulation of degrees of exogamy and endogamy within the larger segmentary system. While the conical aspects of Kachin structure are merely latent in the »ideological« extension of kinship into the supernatural world, they serve as a spring board to a kind of hierarchy which is not that different from Polynesian political systems. For the time being, I suggest that we use the principles of lineage structure in their widest application, for it is in this way that we will be able to get at a certain unity of organization which is overlooked by applying rigid distinctions between levels which are assumed to exist a priori.

The organization and control of land on local and supralocal levels takes on a very different meaning when seen as part of the larger lineage structure. In contrast to Chin and Naga systems, land does not appear to be owned in the sense of a negotiable title. Use rights are vested in each lineage and it is probable that they have prior rights in land that they have cleared. A local lineage (or household. Leach does not clearly distinguish between the two) can be said to »own« use rights to all of the plots which make up its production cycle, cultivated plus fallow fields. Leach refers to this as permanent tenancy. The only evidence of a stronger property relation is the fact that lineages can apparently let out unused land for a token rent or simply lend it out at no cost to the borrower. Leach only mentions it in passing, and its absence in other ethnographic works indicates that it is an insignificant aspect of land tenure (Leach 1954:155).

The one form of property in land that is well developed is based on chiefly rights in village or domain land, well developed in the sense that it is deeply rooted in the social structure itself. As a form of control over land it is extremely weak. Kachin chiefly property is the direct outgrowth of, and might even be deduced from, the combination of the lineage structure and the local settlement and land use pattern. In the hierarchy of *nats* there is an intermediate level which is not explicit in the previous exposition. While every local lineage has ancestor *nats*, there is also a village *nat* or local territorial *nat* which provides the bridge between local and lineage organization. In the earlier discussion (pp. 40–44), I mentioned that among the Lamet there was no clear genealogical connection between the village spirit and the ancestor spirits. The former represents the community as a whole and controls the local territory. It is the communal condition of individual usufruct. The ancestor spirits on the other hand, represent more particular interests which might, theoretically at least, be at odds with the larger community. Among the Kachin where lineage ideology is more developed, the village spirit is incorporated into the larger spirit hierarchy by making it an ancestor of all the local lines (*gumlao*). In *gumlao* communities the village spirit functions as a sacred ancestor of the local group. In *gumsa* communities, however, the village *nat* is the *mung* or domain *nat* who is also the *uma nat*, the ancestor *nat* of the ruling lineage. In this case, the chief represents a lineage whose ancestors are the sacred founders of the village. He has, so to speak, moved one step up the fictitious hierarchy towards the celestial *nats* and his control over the village territory is a function of his position in this segmentary structure. This is what was referred to earlier in pointing out the similarity to Marx's concept of the asiatic mode. It is important not to confuse this with other forms of landed property, i.e., Chin, which may correspond to analogous political forms but which are more truly feudal in nature, i.e., where landed property is negotiable and the tribute relation is more correctly described as rent. One has only to read the early colonial administrators on Chin and Kachin organization to see the importance of a distinction which is obscured by an uncritical use of the word »feudal« on the part of the more sophisticated.[1]) Whereas Chin chiefs are compared to »feudal barons« who collect »yearly tithes from their tenants,« (Carey and Tuck 1896: Vol. I: 201) the situation among the Kachin is that »the land is regarded as belonging to the whole community as represented by its *duwa*.« (Scott and Hardiman 1900: Pt. I, Vol. I:416).

The question of property relations is a very delicate one. Kachin land tenure exists side by side with well developed concepts of moveable lineage property.

---

[1]) Leach appears to use the word »feudal« quite indiscriminately throughout his writings for any form of aristocracy.

Even certain kinds of land, such as house gardens are privately owned. Leach divides moveable items into three main classes:
a) Perishable foodstuffs
b) Livestock
    1) water buffalo
    2) pigs, chickens, humped cattle
c) Non-perishable valuables:

necklaces	swords	gongs
pipes (silver)	spears	silver
iron pots	cloth	(slaves)

The above items may serve in two kinds of exchange, ritual and trade, categories which are not necessarily closed since some items can have both trade and ritual value. Perishable foodstuffs are used in trade and are part of tribute payments. Of the livestock, only water buffalo is technically a ritual wealth item and a man's status is measured by the number of these animals in his possession. Buffalo are destined for the most important sacrifices. While other livestock may be substituted, they are usually used in less important rituals. Non-perishable values are used for a number of different transactions most of which are ritual. Most of the items have little or no economic cost for Kachins, and, as they are not consumable, or directly convertible into land or labor, their role in ordinary circumstances is of a symbolic nature. That is, they delineate the network of legal obligations or »hka« that exist between individuals and lineages. When inflation sets in, however, they play an important role in the process of wealth concentration. One item that does not fit into this analysis is »slaves« who seem to be part of the brideprice of aristocratic marriages. The social status of slaves is treated elsewhere, but it should be pointed out that while slaves are transferable in this way, in most other respects they are like ordinary commoners. In fact, this is one of their distinguishing characteristics as a category. Slaves are a border line case. They are property, i.e., true slaves only in a marginal sense and usually for only short periods of time, and while they represent an economic element of unparalleled importance for the Kachin system, it would be misleading to treat them as property any more than women who are transferable in a much more generalized way.

The two kinds of property I have described emerge from the two major aspects of Kachin segmentary-local structure. The organization of land reflects the aspects of Kachin segmentary-local structure. Land organization reflects the unity of the community and in *gumsa* society, the *single* hierarchical formation of a number of lineage segments. Local organization is based on the unity of the various levels of segmentation. Moveable property, on the other hand, belongs to individual lineages or even households and is an expression of lineage independence and fission. The two forms of property are contradictory and their opposition is one of the motive forces in Kachin evolution and devolution. The former is linked with a redistributive system while the latter implies balanced (or unbalanced, i.e., asymmetrical) exchange between local lines.

Articulation of Alliance and Descent: Kinship Space
The basic properties of Kachin marriage exchange have already been covered, and we need not repeat them here. In our earlier discussion, however, we assumed that the exchange units and production units were one and the same and that no larger categories were involved. In some ways the Kachin are very close to this simple model, but there are some important modifications involved in considering the complications of an emergent segmentary structure.

The simplest way to envisage these modifications is to start with the simpler model and see what happens when it is run over several generations. The first result is the formation of local lineages, that is, groups of several households with common descent. If we now add the other characteristics of the expanding Kachin model there will be a number of problems which have to be dealt with; ranking of lineages, segmentation, increasing population, etc. The manner in which these problems are met is not part of a conscious decision-making process, but emerges from the articulation of a variable, lineage structure, and a constant, asymmetrical alliance.

Generalized exchange divides kinship space into three broad categories, wife-takers, wife-givers, and ego's group or parallel kin. In an expanding population (or any group with a large number of lines) a fourth category, unrelated lineages, is added. In Kachin terminology, the last category combines both distant parallel relations and unrelated lines.

1. *Kahpu-kanau ni* (*hpu-nauni*) – local lineage plus any lines which might be added as part of the exogamous group.
2. *Mayu ni* – recent wife-givers.
3. *Dama ni* – recent wife-takers.
4. *Lawu-lahta ni* (*hpu-nau lawu lahta*) – lines distantly related to ego.

The above categories form an open system, open in two ways. At any one point in time, categories (1), (2) and (3) can be considered closed while (4) serves as a pool for new *mayu/dama* relations. Category (4) is not a closed category, but serves as a bridge between distant relatives and totally unrelated lines. Thus, not only is there a continual possibility of establishing new affinal links, but the pool from which these groups are chosen is itself open. The categories, taken together, form an operator in a dynamic system and should not be confused with static three-category systems like those of the Old Kuki tribes described by Lehman as a »small remnant people living in alien territory with, perhaps, a reduced population and range of lineages,« (Lehman 1963:99) in which new lines are not being produced over time and where as a result, wife-givers and wife-takers form a fixed group for any one lineage. These systems tend to turn in on themselves in such a way that all the lineages eventually become affinally related (see next page).

If we begin with an egalitarian system and study it diachronically, a number of distinct processes emerge. First, as we have said, the number of segments in any local lineage will tend to increase so that every lineage contains several minimal lineages or production-exchange units. This, in turn, implies that an

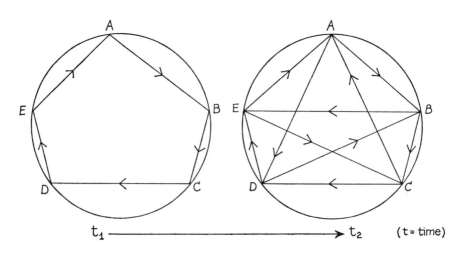

Generalized exchange in a closed system (Old Kuki).

increasing number of alliances can be made over time. The direction of affinal exchanges is controlled by the local lineage itself so that individual alliance patterns will not tend to conflict with one another in normal circumstances, that is, local lines will not allow reciprocal exchange of the following sort:

$$\left(\begin{array}{l} a1 \longrightarrow b1 \\ a2 \longleftarrow b2 \end{array}\right)$$

Each local lineage containing four or five households, then, coordinates its own affinal politics, not necessarily as a conscious policy, but simply as a direct structural effect of the categorical distinction between kin space and alliance space coupled to a generalized rule of marriage whose reference is the local, rather than the minimal lineage. Thus, a household will not take wives from lines which have given wives to other members of its local lineage. Beyond this, there are no specific regulations, but rather a general tendency to keep up affinal relations over the generations. It is not necessary that the flow of women be constant for this to occur, since the act of giving or taking establishes a categorical relationship which need only be renewed periodically to be kept in good working order.

The shallowness of genealogical memory operates to maintain the size of the local lineage below a limit of six or seven households so that, as population increases it is expressed not in terms of segmentation but as fission, ie., the formation of new local lines. The effect of this is to continually shift relatives from category (1) to category (4) and from categories (2) and (3) to category (4) this time in its extended meaning, i.e., non-related lines.

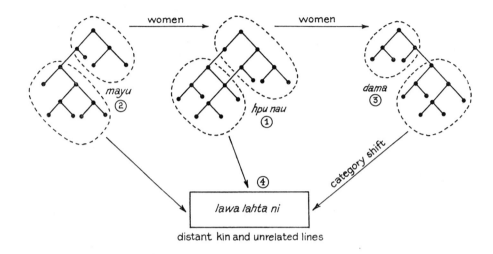

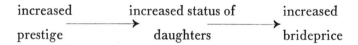

distant kin and unrelated lines

This process is an important mechanism in a system of expanding population and increased ranking and we will refer to it often in the course of this analysis. It is a measure of the *ability of the system to turn kin into affines.*

Until now we have not assumed the existence of ranking, and none of the categories outlined above can be said to be more *gumsa* than *gumlao*. If we now take the model of lineage political economy outlined in Chapter Two we can try to explain the structural transition from egalitarian to ranked forms in the context of Kachin lineage and local organization.

The differentiation of status among minimal lineages begins with the cycle;

surplus product → feast-distribution → prestige

and is continued into the cycle;

| increased prestige | → | increased status of daughters | → | increased brideprice |

As this process takes place, alliances will tend to reflect the emergent situation in which wealthy lines intermarry continuously. This is simply because only they will be able to afford the increasing brideprices. This differentiation operates first at the minimal lineage level where surplus is produced and distributed at feasts, but is reinforced by mapping onto the existing affinal network. Where households have accumulated a great deal of prestige, *mayu/dama* relations begin to express real rank differences. In cases where a *dama* group manages to gain prestige, it can succeed in reversing a previous relationship, or at least in breaking it. This realignment of alliance patterns will gradually come to look like a series of ranked marriage circles.

How does this process combine with the local organization? The local lineage is solidary in terms of prestige accumulation, and it appears that changes in status are transferred to all its members. Lineage unity is further evidenced by such economic functions as mutual aid in the payment of bride-price and debts and by the existence of the levirate (Leach 1954:169). At the same time, however, the lineage is growing and fissioning, thereby producing new potential affines whose local distribution is instrumental in the ranking process. The Kachin have a dispersed settlement pattern in which small villages of ten to thirty houses are most common. This may be due to a number of factors. One might be that, under conditions of optimal fallowing where the cycle is upwards of 1/14, a small settlement will imply less traveling to and from fields (i.e., less work) than a larger settlement whose acreage increases by a factor of *14* for each member of the working population. In egalitarian systems with by and large equal inheritance, a larger family means that new fields will have to be cleared. Thus, where plenty of virgin land is available, there will be a tendency to expand rather than to increase population density in any one locality. Numerous explanations for ultimogeniture have stressed the fact that it is linked to an extensive system of cultivation which must constantly be increasing its total land area if its population is growing. I would prefer not to treat population growth as an absolute since I believe that it is closely linked with the nature of the political economy of the group. This explanation does have a certain inner logic to it as a long term phenomenon. Where population is stable, however, ultimogeniture loses much of its importance since in such cases an equilibrium will be reached between cultivated area and family size. It seems reasonable that the development of *gumsa* systems, with their high demand for surplus and thus for labor, could explain the relation between the two forms of inheritance and population growth. That is, since the *gumlao* system is relatively stable, politically (at first), there is no growing demand for labor and no increase in population size – thus no need for ultimogeniture. When the system begins to expand, however, the situation is reversed and ultimogeniture takes on its full significance as a means of dispersion.

When ranking is in process, however, ultimogeniture takes on even greater importance as a political shrinking valve. By excluding most siblings from the source of wealth it creates new lineages which, if they remain in the village, are ranked as junior lines, or, if they move away (more common), become possible future allies. Thus, the expulsion of brothers increases the tendency to local segmentation or fissioning in a very definitive way.

For the sake of this argument, no assumptions need to be made about population growth. We might simply have begun with the assumption of dispersed settlement, in which case the category of »distant kin« should be almost entirely replaced by real non-relatives. What is important is that where expansion does occur, the dispersed settlement pattern will have very significant consequences for the ranking system. The most important of these is that the great majority of the population will always be in the categories of affine or potential affine. As a result, the possibility of extensive ranking by exchange is decisive. In the *mayu/dama* structure, related lines are clearly ranked, but brothers are more difficult. Within the lineage and among sibling lines (exogamous), domination can only be in terms of the senior/junior distinction which cannot be reinforced by an alliance relationship. The larger the number of segments in the local lineage, the more difficulty there will be in establishing a hierarchy of seniority. Thus, the ability to keep the lineage small is necessary to make the whole process workable. Not only are there then fewer sibling branches to worry about, but those that have been sloughed off can eventually become *dama*, i.e., of distinctly lower rank. As such, dispersion further enables a supralocal structure to emerge in a neat segmentary (and affinal) hierarchy. While within the village there are very few potential competing sibling lines, outside the village where endogamy is possible, there is a virtually open field with regard to alliance possibilities.

Within the territorial lineage organization and the kinship space generated by its articulation with the exchange structure, we can see that a minimal line in the process of elevating its status position has a great deal of maneuverability. This is due to the mechanisms outlined above which result in the mapping of the social functions of production, exchange and exogamy onto a single corporate unit. Later, among the Chin, we will see how the extent to which these functions do not overlap can seriously hamper the process of hierarchization.

Gumsa Structure
The formation of *gumsa* structures is not simply a matter of long term competition between big-men for social status coupled with the consolidation of rank by the asymmetrical exchange of women. It involves the entire social formation. We have tried to show to what extent the kinship structure was a generalized phenomenon, organizing, among other things, relations between and within lineages, control of property, and religion. It would be a great error to try to separate these spheres functionally; for even if we succeed in putting them back together again, the relations uniting them which are material (in the marxist sense of relations of production) might, as in Leach's treatment of religion, end up as mere metaphors for presumed »on the ground« structures whose internal dynamics must then be relegated to circumstances beyond the scope of the analysis.

This model of relations of production is an attempt to distinguish and articulate the two main circulation systems of Kachin society. The horizontal system is dominated by the alliance relations between local lines. The vertical system represents the distributive-redistributive exchange and its linkage with the *nat* hierarchy and the production cycle. The model of lineage political economy purports to show how the two exchange systems form a larger unity, to whose properties we now turn.

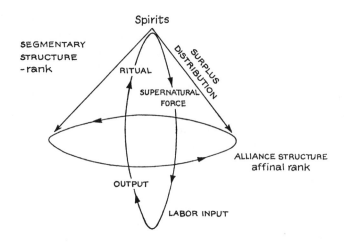

As might be guessed from the earlier discussion, the two kinds of exchange in the above model correspond to two aspects of the kinship structure. The transition from »rich-man« to big-man to chief is linked to the way one can use the affinal system to insert oneself into the genealogical structure of the larger community. But the only existing larger non-local structure is the segmentary lineage organization which, as *gumsa* hierarchy develops, becomes clearly established. While the entire transformation from *gumlao* to *gumsa* is based on material accumulation and conversion into prestige, the new structure can only take shape in terms of the emergent segmentary political form that is already embedded in the spirit hierarchy. For it is here that the latent segmentary possibilities of kinship organization (latent in the sense of currently inoperative: clan, maximal, major lineage) are expressed.

Claims to status are based on genealogical reckoning; the accumulation of ancestor *nats*, and the ability to trace them back to original clan or tribal founders. In *gumsa* polity, chiefs and aristocrats keep elaborate records of their ancestors, and it is a major function of a particular religious officer, the *jaiwa*, to trace aristocratic families back to the beginning of time. Commoners, on the other hand, like *gumlao* Kachin, have little or no lineage memory. This point is of some significance since it allows the commoner to attach himself to the chiefly clan of his choosing. Lack of information implies freedom of choice. It also represents a loophole in the system, for any up-and-coming lineage can create a genealogy to suit its particular political needs. A well established aristocratic lineage, however, is stuck with its past to the extent that it becomes public information, and its position may become more or less fixed. The fixing of lineage ancestry has a way of filling in the maximal lineage or clan structure in such a way that many of the former competitive possibilities may be lost for those closest to the top. The relatively long term durability of some of the semi-state like formations of the Triangle area may be due to a kind of genealogical stability that set in.

Manau feasts are very closely tied in with the development of long gene-alogies since both are functions of the same kinship space. There is no infor-mation regarding the nature of *gumlao* feasting, but among the Lamet (Iziko-witz 1951: Chap. 15) who are structurally similar to *gumlao*, feasts given to ancestors involve distributions to the entire village. A great many purposes are served by such feasts which are, in the Maussian sense, total social phenomena. Ancestor *nats* have a good deal of control over village lands as they are part of that larger hierarchy which controls fertility. Thus, propitiating the *nats* is a community service of the highest order. It should be added, however, that the ancestor is more particularly interested in the well being of the feast-giver's lineage and will surely increase his next year's crop. At the same time, the feast-giver immediately enhances his own status by distributing his surplus output to the rest of the village. The simultaneous transactions, literal and figurative, that are involved in a feast have crucial implications. The prestige of the feast-giver is raised as is that of his local line, and his ancestor *nats* become more important to the village as a whole. For if a lineage can conti-nually feast the community its ancestor spirit must be very powerful indeed. And as this power can only be expressed in kinship terms it means that the lineage in question must be genealogically closer to the village *nat*. I would suggest that the monopolization of the village spirits by a powerful lineage is *intimately* related to these social distributions of surplus, and that the increase in social prestige is transformed into social authority because it is attached to the supernatural power of the lineage *nat*. When a man's lineage ancestor be-comes the village *nat* he is no longer a big-man, but a chief. The advent of hereditary authority is bound to, is even an expression of, the permanent po-sition of the chief's lineage in the ancestral hierarchy of the community. What is important here is that the transition to hereditary *gumsa* chieftainship is effective *within a single pre-existent structure*. One of the failings of Leach's analysis, I think, is that he does not attempt to show the functional role of the supernatural in political transitions but is content with it as a simple reflection of more »concrete« social relations. Thus, while he might be able to explain how a *gumlao* big-man could become a *gumrawng* chief, i.e. a wealthy, »boast-ful« headman whose prestige is not widely accepted, he can only account for the transition to true *gumsa* (hereditary) as a kind of usurpation of power or an imitation of Shan princes. The present argument, on the other hand, is that this development is an internally determined evolution, the outgrowth of the ope-ration of the political economy within a pre-structured kinship system. Thus, the transformation to ranked hierarchy can be explained without any external references. Nothing new has been added, but certain relations have emerged as dominant on the social level which were previously only latent in the super-natural realm. A headman becomes a chief by taking on some of the properties formerly possessed only by the deities.

As we have said, the chiefly lineage's control over land is based on the place of its ancestor in the spirit hierarchy of the community. The monopolization of

the supernatural by a chiefly line is clearly expressed in the organization of
gumsa ritual. In all Kachin communities there are three community *nats* or
classes of *nats* which are a central part of the life of the village. These are: the
village *nat* (in *gumsa* – *mung nat*), representing the »higher-unity« of the
local community; a representative of the celestial *nats* (in *gumsa* – the *madai
nat*), giver of general prosperity; and the earth *nat* (*ga nat*) or fertility spirit.
Every community has a local shrine or *numshang* which in *gumlao* society
houses these three guardian spirits and is the place of community sacrifices.
But the distribution of the *nat* altars is slightly different for *gumsa* society.

	gumlao	gumsa
ga nat	numshang	numshang
celestial (madai) nat	numshang	chief's house
local nat	numshang	chief's house

In *gumsa* society, two out of three of the village *nats* are the personal posses-
sions of the chief. The territorial (local) *nat* is identical with his own ancestor
so it is natural that it's shrine should be in his house. Further, *madai*, chief of
the celestial *nats*, is *mayu* to his ancestor which implies that the chief has an
immediate line of communication to the supernatural forces. The *ga nat* that
remains in the *numshang* is, as parent of the *madai*, also under the direct
influence of the chief. Thus only he has ritual access to this most powerful of
spirits. Only he can represent the entire community before the powers that
govern the fortunes and prosperity of all.

It is worth comparing this to the *gumlao* ritual. The only extant material is
from the Duleng-clan area which had been *gumsa* in the recent past and was
probably returning to that state when studied (Carrapiett 1929). In this particular *gumlao* system no clear distinction was made between different celestial
nats. Offerings to the *ga nat* were an affair of the village as a whole, although
actual sacrifices (as in *gumsa*) could be made only by the priests (who had little
or no other political power). As for the village spirit, any community member
could make offerings. In *gumsa* communities, commoners sacrifice to their
ancestors and to the *musheng nat* (a lesser spirit) who is *mayu* to their ancestors. Chiefs sacrifice to their close ancestors who represent the community,
and through them to *madai* and shadip (*ga nat*) who control prosperity and
fertility. In a system where identity is a lineage matter, it cannot be stressed
strongly enough that the chief's identity is entirely merged with that of the
larger community.

The political structure that evolves is more than the affinal ranking of lineages that would result from the horizontal exchange system alone. It is pyramidal and segmentary in form and can serve as the basis for a different configuration, in which one's rank is determined by genealogical distance from the village or domain or clan ancestor, and is thus equivalent to the conical clan. The typical conical clan is almost always an idealized hierarchy which never quite fits actual lineage relations (see chart). Among the *gumsa* Kachin it is an emergent tendency more than an established structure. The very mechanics of its development are such as to breed inconsistencies. If we take the diagram below to represent a local domain structure, Ao is the *uma* (yoS) lineage which traces its ancestry back to the YoS of the founder of the clan or maximal lineage. All other lines are more or less junior offshoots of this main

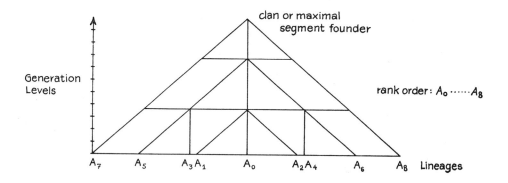

lineage. In the traditional domains of the Triangle region, the situation often approximated this state of affairs. A domain was the territory of a single clan headed by a paramount chief under whom there were a number of secondary chiefs of junior rank of the same clan. Thus, for the uppermost levels of the hierarchy, at least, there is evidence of a conical clan system in good working order. The whole thing is made more complicated, however, by the affinal ranking which exists alongside this sibling lineage stratification and is the basis for it. The clan, even at the highest levels is not normally exogamous. On the contrary, it is not unusual to find several domain chiefs of the same clan linked in a circular marriage system. Ideologically, conical rank is the product of sibling ranking in the process of succession and inheritance. I say »ideological« because it depends on the ability to keep »disinherited« lineages from making claims to higher status. The *mayu/dama* relation is more definitive in this respect since it establishes relative position for an entire local lineage in the exchange process itself. A lineage that wishes to maintain paramountcy is in an excellent position if its junior lines are also *dama* to it. The affinal exchange network is the dominant structure here, certainly in the evolutionary sense. The possibility of eventually forming a conical clan rests on the affinal ranking of lineages in the local political economy. The conicization, so to speak, of the clan is in large part due to the differentiation of local lineages within a clan structure which only comes into play as a result of the former affinal process.

If we ignore global hierarchies for a moment and concentrate on the relations themselves, we can delineate two kinds of status determination which in *gumsa* society operate at all levels. Two lines can be related by exchange or by siblingship. The former establishes a higher/lower dichotomy in terms of the wife-giver/wife-taker relation while the latter arrives at this distinction in terms of being nearer/farther to (from) a senior lineage or founding ancestor. The two relations can exist simultaneously. We have already stated that *mayu/dama* relations may exist within domanial clans, thus combining senior/junior and wife-giver/wife-taker differentiation. But even among lineages that are entirely unrelated with respect to clan origin, there is still a point of reference which is used to reinforce the affinal structure, i.e., to ratify it in terms of the segmentary ancestral structure of the group. Where such lineages are ranked affinally and simultaneously trace their histories back to clan or maximal lineage ancestors, these founders who are themselves brothers are then ranked in terms of segmentary seniority. Thus, where there is no sibling lineage relationship at lower levels the ranking process is simply relegated to higher levels of inclusiveness, or even to the mythical past. In this way, the segmentary system might be referred to in Dumont's terminology as »englobant« (Dumont 1966) with respect to the more dominant affinal structure. The formation generated by the two together is represented in the following chart (next page). The entire tribe, or any kin unit which is considered most inclusive is always descended from a common ancestor. At each level, affinal rank is doubled by sibling rank at a higher segmentary level. This implies a hierarchy of inclusive categories where the degree of endogamy varies inversely with rank. While there are a number of reasons why the global structure is never fully materialized, the mechanisms which in a vacuum would give rise to such a system, are present and dominant in the social relations of the local lineages. Many of the groups, especially in the South Triangle may have approximated this global design rather closely.

Where we find extensive domains (*mung*) some of which contain two or three smaller domains, the conical structure can be realized to a very high degree in the local hierarchy. A domain is clearly organized into political levels; village, village cluster, domain and superdomain, all of which have headmen or chiefs in a definite order of rank. Here, where each position is attached to a specified portion of territory or number of villages, the hierarchy can be well anchored. This is not to say that the conical clan structure is somehow floating in mythical space waiting for a domain on which to land. On the contrary, the formation of *mung* polities is the base on which such conical structures can be elaborated. The domain of the Laphai clan in the South

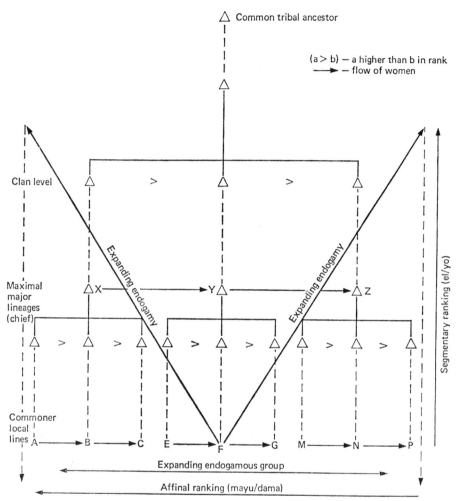

In this chart, two kinds of rank are represented simultaneously. Affinal rank, shown horizontally, is transformed into segmentary rank for lineage ancestors. But ancestors are not simply a time-depth phenomenon. They can be taken to represent 'older', and therefore, senior branches. Structurally, age-ranking and affinal ranking are equivalent since they are generated in the same genealogical space. While, for example, X, Y, or Z appears as the parent to three sibling lineages, it is in fact a senior branch to them. It is not merely an ancestor, but a living local lineage having affinal relations with other lineages of the same 'age-rank' (corresponds to Leach's rank-class). The transforming of affinal rank into segmentary rank implies that local lineage exogamy will always define a larger endogamous group at a higher genealogical level, which is by definition a higher level of social rank. In this way, the formation of a domain entails the formation of conical clan structure.

Triangle is a good example of what appears to have been such a conical clan of the purest variety. The domain of the Laphai chiefs consisted of several smaller *mung* each ruled by a lineage of the clan (Leach 1946:168–9). The paramount chief was Shadan Tu, leader of the senior branch.

But is it necessary for the clan to have preceded the domain for this kind of unity to exist? Given the nature of Kachin genealogical space it would certainly have been relatively easy for rising chiefs to trace their ancestry to the senior lines of the Laphai clan. Leach argues quite cogently that political uniformity tends to cause »cultural« conformity. Let us say, in this case, that lineal or clan conformity is used in the act of political unification.

The mechanisms we have been discussing need not be restricted to a single hierarchization process, and the expansion of the Kachin out of the Triangle area has led to cases where chiefly lineages in distantly separated regions attach themselves to the paramount of the »homeland« even though nothing in the way of political control is established as a result. In the following genealogy, Gauri and Atsi lineages attached themselves to the Shadan Laphai maximal lineage (senior of the Laphai clan) (Leach 1946:565);

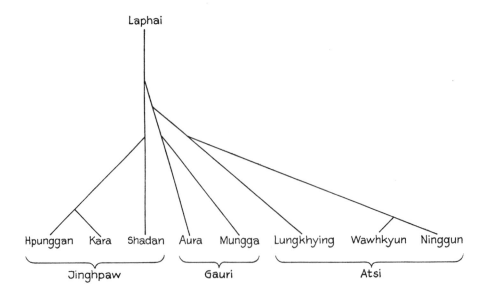

The Gauri and Atsi lineages controlled two strategic areas of the China-Burma trade routes east of Bhamo. That they linked themselves to the dominant western clan indicates the political significance of the segmentary structure. Jinghpaw, Gauri and Atsi are three different dialect groups all which are part of a single conical clan. The question of political control here is another problem. The Shadan Tu lineage had no say at all in Gauri or Atsi internal affairs, and the ranking cannot be said to have had any implications other than ideological. But at the local level, the fact that individual Gauri or Atsi who controlled a given area got together to form a single major lineage, points to a process of political hierarchization. If, for example, by a combination of politico-economic success and affinal exchange, one of these lines became senior with respect to the others, we would again have a hierarchy resembling a conical (territorial) clan with a paramount chief, junior chiefs, headmen and commoner lineages.

As we have said, it is not necessary that the ranking of lineages take place within a larger clan structure since there are other points of reference by which one can convert affinal into sibling rank. Leach gives the following example of the network uniting the major chiefly lines of the Triangle (Leach 1954:233):

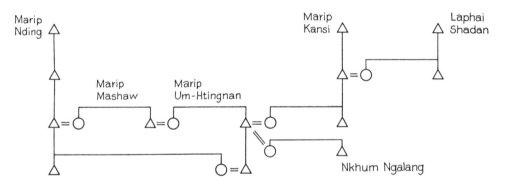

By rearranging this we can show clearly the status relations involved (see next page).

The first diagram expresses affinal rank irrespective of lineage segmentation. The second combines the two. The first diagram might be considered more realistic politically since the hierarchy is in fact established by marriage exchange. However, the second structure is available if the polity ever becomes more rigid. In this case the conical tribe would be superimposed on the conical clan. I only note this as a possibility here since it is quite improbable that it can develop in the existing economic conditions. Shadan Tu's lineage is paramount and undoubtedly can manipulate the mythical past to conform with an overall tribal hierarchy, but in terms of real authority, there is nothing more than a loose confederation. My point here is that the clan is not essential to conical formation. The process of segmentation is more general than that, and as we have seen, it organizes the whole of social space. This must be stressed since there is a tendency among anthropologists to treat such thing as if they were objects, hard-and-fast structures, immutable organizations. The segmentary principle discussed here is a generative mechanism that *tends* to order social relations in hierarchies of lineages, clans and gods. It is *not* an established

Two stages of Ranking

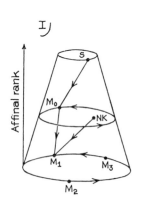

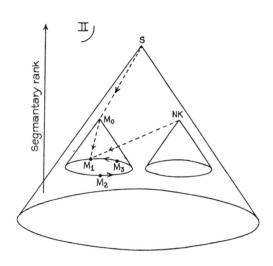

S : Laphai Shadan M_2 : Marip Mashaw
M_0: Marip Kansi M_3 : Marip Nding
M_1: Marip Um-Htingnan   NK : Nkhum

social form. Just as, at the highest levels of the chiefly lineages, there is no necessary connection between ranking and clan membership, at the lowest levels of organization the chief of a village cluster and his village headmen are very often of different clans and their relations are of a strictly affinal nature. The tendency to clan hierarchy is only one of a number of tendencies. It must be remembered that we began with only a set of local lineages whose ancestral interrelations were ill-defined (*gumlao*). From this point of origin and throughout the evolution toward *gumsa* forms, the affinal exchange is the effective basis for ranking. If the local groups that partake in this network are of different clans, the ranking will quite simply cut across the clan boundary. While segmentation is generative, the extension of clan affiliation is more limited and appears to be consciously manipulated by powerful lineages to suit their political ends. Lineage ranking across clan boundaries will not produce ranked clans in any meaningful sense except where the lineages involved are senior lineages of already conicized larger segments. This is important since it implies that clan ranking, if it exists at all, will only take place at the level of domain chiefs. At lower levels the clan is less important, genealogical memory is shallow, and the local lineage dominates political ideology. Three kinds of formation are generated by the combination of alliance ranking and conicization.

    a) At the earliest, or least evolved stages of the process, lineage rank is present with little or no reference to a larger segmentary organization. At a slightly later stage increased genealogical reckoning will rephrase some of the existing hierarchy with reference to the lineage or clan ancestors.

b) Ranking across clan lines exists on a domain level.
   1) Between the heads of already formed clan hierarchies, it represents a very weak tendency toward supra-clan tribal hierarchy.
   2) Between different local domanial levels, chief-headman, paramount chief-junior chief, it continues to be simple lineage ranking. In many cases, a *mung* chief will be a member of an important clan and his domain may be said to belong to that clan. But, if subordinate chiefs are members of different clans, the ranking will not be any more than a supralocal affinal structure.
   c) In the fully developed conical clan, affinal rank is turned into segmentary rank and all lineages are absorbed into the dominant clan. This process seems to have been very thoroughly carried out in some areas of the Triangle region where chiefs, aristocrats and even commoners all belong to the same domanial clan.

Note on the Clan
There is practically no information on the existence of the clan in egalitarian forms. Leach says that »all *gumlao* within any one local area are likely to maintain a fiction of common clanship.« (Leach 1954:205–6). This is apparently based on data from the Duleng area which was fairly recently a *gumsa* domain, and the clan unity of the area is not, I think, understandable except in terms of the history of the area. The word »clan« as I use it here has no *a priori* meaning, but is merely a way of designating the primary level of segmentation, i.e., the highest level of lineage inclusion after that of the »tribe.« Thus, it is present as a formal device which can be used in many ways. Common descent from a single ancestor may well date from the existence of a former exogamous clan. If we assume, then, that as a result of the political economy we have described, local lineages took on a dominant political function, and the clan was dispersed, losing its exogamous unity, the formal ideology of common descent might still reappear in the later endogamous hierarchical clan. Thus, the clan remains a kind of field in which the development of *gumsa* forms takes place. Its function merely changes from a regulator of exogamy to a passive genealogical space in which local lines compete for dominance.

The tendency which I have called »conicization« has never been discussed with reference to the Kachin for several reasons. To begin the conical clan has always been assumed to be a finished product. Among the most evolutionary of anthropologists, it is closely related to the development of stratification (Kirchoff 1955; Fried 1957;1967) and Fried is quite explicit in stating that »some form of the equalitarian exogamous clan preceded all forms of the conical clan.« (Fried 1957:6). But it has usually been assumed that since the conical clan was associated with class formation defined quite mechanically as differential access to strategic resources, it has also been assumed that its evolution was the result of some exterior development of resource control rather than the evolution of the structure itself. By adopting the second approach I think we might well see the Kachin as an intermediate level where actual formation of conical structures is in process. Leach provides all the data necessary for this argument, but his own exclusive emphasis on the local lineage has forced a fragmentation of the social field in such a way that higher levels of segmentation, religion, and property are all put into separate analytical boxes, even though, by using his own discussion one can, in fact, reconstruct a very different picture of the way things work.

It would seem natural that in the politically strongest domains, the tendency toward clan homogeneity would also be the strongest. This is due quite simply to the nature of territorial organization in such conditions. If the villages of a domain are all the »property« of a chiefly line of clan A, the village spirits should also be descended from the same ancestors. This is no more than a question of logical inclusion. Thus a legitimate headman of a different clan, i.e., whose lineage is descended from the village *nat*, is theoretically in an ambiguous position with regard to the ruling clan of the domain. If the village *nat* is of a different clan than the ruler this would imply that the village territory is somehow *dama* to the chief's lineage. This is a clear example of the contradiction between affinal and segmentary modes of organization. We must keep in mind that a domain may include large tracts which are directly under the *nat* of the chief but are allied to it by the *mayu/dama* system. This heterogeneity can always be remedied by reference to a higher level of segmentation, but there is good reason to believe that in the strongest domains where control of territory is strongly enforced, where subordination is maximum, the land will all be under the same maximal lineage or clan spirits. In the areas of highest political development within the swidden economy, the South Triangle, clan homogeneity was extensively maintained, while east and south of that area where domains were generally quite small and weak there was more of a mixture of affinal and segmentary hierarchies. We might summarize here by noting that in a relation of superordination/subordination there are three possible combinations which in order of potential authority are:

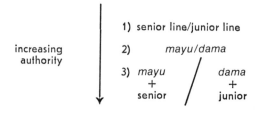

Rank Classes

As we have said, the process of ranking is dominated by the affinal political economy of the local lineage. In Chapter Two we desribed the process of status differentiation, in which local surplus is converted into prestige and then into relative rank in such a way that a hierarchy of lineages emerges over time. In terms of alliance alone, it seems that groups will tend to divide themselves into two categories. Among the Lamet, for example, there are commoners and rich men. The difference is based entirely on the distinction »able to give feasts/not able to give feasts«. The two categories have very little political significance and Lamet villages are both politically isolated and »egalitarian«. It seems likely that this is the earliest stage of development away from the strictly egalitarian (hypothetical) form in which no differences in status exist. While there may be a continuum of economic wealth or rather potential wealth, the categories available to divide the population are the crucial variables here. *Mayu/dama* categories serve to distinguish any two exchanging groups, but they too, if generalized, only provide a dichotomous system. Where, among the Kachin, *gumsa* relations are evolved to the point where a headman has established himself as a chief, it is always with reference to the segmentary hierarchy of the lineage ancestors. It is here, as we shall see, that we again find the basis for structural evolution.

The primary binary division into big-men and commoners is translated by the distinction *daru magam/darat daroi* or »authorities« and commoners (Maran 1967b m.s.). The meaning of *daru magam* implies nothing in the way of hereditary position which is why it would seem to correspond to the Lamet category of big-man or rich-man which has wide application in Southeast Asia and Melanesia. The development of hereditary aristocratic lineages is based on the monopolization of the village *nat* as we have shown. In this way, *daru magam* becomes *du magam*. Within this class there are two subdivisions: chiefly lines, *du baw amyu*, and aristocratic lines *magam amyu*. This distinction reflects the difference between wealthy-prestigious lines and youngest-son lines who are the closest direct descendants of the territorial spirits. The chiefly lineage is *uma*, youngest-son branch, while the aristocratic lines are called »eldest-son lineages«. Thus the distinction between chiefs and aristocrats is made on the basis of segmentation even though it may have originally been a matter of affinal rank. Even where affinal rank remains the only distinguishing feature, the fact that aristocratic status is expressed in terms of junior line of a larger lineage is evidence of the strain in the conical direction. Generally, chiefs are at the heads of domains which include a number of villages or village clusters. Leach describes the class-rank relations in terms of superimposed marriage circles.

»There are thus always some women of a chief's local descent group who marry away from the domain into other chiefly lineages; others however will marry with men of the aristocrat lineages of the chief's own domain. Typically the local descent group of a village headman is of the aristocrat class and will be *dama* (wife taking) in respect to the chief's local descent group.

Similar alternatives operate at the aristocratic level. The typical aristocratic lineage is the lineage of a village headman. Some aristocratic males will marry women of other aristocratic local descent groups in the vicinity – especially those of other village headmen in the domain. Some aristocratic females marry aristocratic males, others marry commoners of their own village.« (Leach 1961:85).

Leach represents the above system diagrammatically as a vertical spiral of lineages. By modifying this to fit the local organization we can get a fairly clear picture of the hierarchy of affinal exchange relations in any *gumsa* domain.

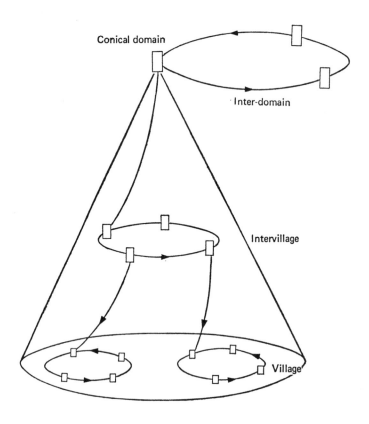

It should now be clear that the rank classes are defined structurally in terms of the segmentary system. Chiefs belong to *uma* lineage of the domain. Those who can demonstrate direct descent from this lineage may be considered of chiefly rank, but their number is naturally quite limited by the principles of inheritance and by the structure of genealogical space which tends to cut off sibling lineages from the source of power.

»When a lineage has acquired a 'depth' of four or five generations it tends to split, but of the two residual lineages only one retains the class status of the parent lineage; the other tends to 'go down hill' (*gumyu yu ai*).« (Leach 1961:84).

The local lineage organization is an almost perfect analogy of the segmentary hierarchy. Each village has only one village spirit, therefore only one village »*uma*« lineage. A domain has only one territorial spirit, therefore only one chiefly lineage. The political economy of domain formation is one of successive levels of status competition. At the village level, the combination of affinal ranking and monopolization of the village spirit produces village headmen. Economic-affinal competition between headmen then produces a supralocal domain chief who monopolizes the *nat* representing the territory of all the villages. The marriage circles at each level imply status equality, but they also imply a certain instability since at any moment a partner can claim superiority on the basis of its record of wealth accumulation and distribution. The circle is up-ended and new circles are formed in an increasingly rarefied political atmosphere. Every time a local or territorial *nat* is monopolized, however, it introduces a new stability at lower levels by eliminating the goal of the competition.

The aristocratic class is the product of a number of overlapping mechanisms.

a) In terms of territorial organization there is a clear distinction between village headmen and domain chief. The *mung* chief and his headmen (*salang*) constitute the main decision making body of the domain, defining, in this way, a functional ruling group.

b) The internal process of wealth accumulation and distribution which gives rise to the local lineage hierarchy is also a function of affinal ranking, so that the relations between chiefs and aristocrats, aristocrats and commoners is always a *mayu/dama* relation. In an already existing *gumsa* structure, a wealthy lineage can convert itself into an aristocratic line by a dual process involving:

1. Claiming genealogical ties
   (a) to the local *uma* lineage (conical tendency)
   (b) to a chiefly lineage in some other locality
2. Becoming *dama* to the domain chief, i.e., able to pay the high brideprice.

c) The process of shedding at all levels in which all but one lineage »go down hill« gives rise to literal eldest-son lines.

1. In expanding situations these lines may establish new villages in the

same territory, becoming aristocratic headmen under the chiefly lineage. This is the process of conicization.

2. They may go to other domains where they become aristocratic *dama* lineages to other chiefs – the process of affinal hierarchization.

3. They may stay at home in which case they either become potentially disruptive or go »down hill« to a secondary aristocratic or even commoner rank.

The mechanisms a, b, and c are all aspects of the same social process of »aristocrat formation« and cannot be separated from one another without sacrificing the properties of the larger whole. Local and lineage ranking, (a) and (b), are part of the same segmentary process. Ranked lineage segments are formed on the basis of local segmentation of villages into village clusters. But the process of local segmentation is itself an expression of the process of lineage shedding.

In a fully formed domain, many of the properties described earlier for the conical clan are reiterated. One very important one is expansion of affinal links as rank increases. In a conical clan, the lowest level is the most endogamous and the degree of endogamy decreases with increasing rank. This distribution of alliances is the result of the ranking process itself and is common to both lineal and affinal hierarchies. A commoner can take women from any other commoner in the village. A headman must take women from someone of at least headman rank. He therefore takes a bride from another village. Finally, a *mung duwa* can only take principal wives from lineages of equal status, i.e., from other domains. Thus, what is represented in a conical clan by increasing lineage exogamy is translated here by increasing local exogamy. Even if the system it not a conical clan, it has the structural properties that would enable it to represent itself as such. The only difference between a patrilineal conical clan and the affinal hierarchy we have described is the nature of political-ideological incorporation. I again use »ideology« in an ambiguous way.[1]) It is more than that. The segmentary structure is ideological to the extent that it reflects the actual process of ranked lineage segmentation over time. But to the extent that this genealogical mechanism operates to unify and reinforce control over territory, it is infrastructural since it determines rights over land, surplus and the services of other lineages. As the domain becomes more rigid, more pyramidal, the segmentary hierarchy will tend to dominate the affinal one. For the latter cannot, by itself, lead to the centralization of authority among a large number of lineages. It is interesting, however, to consider the effect of being able to claim rank in exactly the same way through affinal or patrilineal genealogies. The result would be the elimination of the difference between the two modes of rank recognition and the estab-

---

[1]) The ambiguity in the use of the word »ideology« is due to the effect of the structural transformation that occurs in the evolution of conical chiefdoms. It is because the segmentary ancestral hierarchy which is functionally ideological in the *gumlao* stage becomes an instrumental part of the infrastructure in the formation of the chiefdom.

lishment of a *de facto* ambilateral conical clan. In a purely speculative way, the Kachin system might be capable of two possible evolutions or transformations given the proper economic conditions.

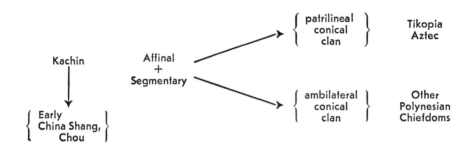

I do not insist that these developments are necessary. I only would like to call attention to the structural possibilities and point out that the two derived forms are not unrelated. In fact, rank recognition is a very complex affair, and the ability to trace status through female lines is not in conflict with a basic patrilineal structure. Descriptions of pre-Han China seem to indicate the existence of a strong patrilineal lineage system in which rank could be established in either male or affinal lines (Hsu 1965:3–7). The main structural difference between the ambilateral and patrilineal systems is that for the latter, all female lines are also affinal lines. This means that, theoretically, one should only be able to trace rank through one generation, to WF or MF, whereas in a true ambilateral system affinal lines are completely transitive. But since it is genealogical distance that counts, the two systems are in fact quite similar. While in the patrilineal case, ego cannot trace his status back through his MMM line, the transitivity of affinal ties implies the same result. His position is simply defined in a different code (MMM = FWFWFW). In an evolutionary perspective it is of the utmost importance to go beyond the superficial classifications and consider the common structural basis which would permit us to generate those classifications.

Slaves

This is an extremely difficult category to deal with. Slaves in the classical sense do not exist among the Kachin. Leach describes the status of slavery as equivalent to a poor *dama* relation. Furthermore, as a social category, slavery is generated by secondary features of the socio-economic structure. It is not a simple derivative of the kinship system, but the result of internal contradictions of economy. The category *mayam* applies to three different social groupings,

  a) subordinate villages or households
  b) debt slaves

c) captured slaves

Debt slavery is produced by the working of the economic system itself. The Kachin economy is highly inflationary and poor individuals or households will often find themselves unable to pay brideprice and other important debts. In such cases they may or must borrow the requisite sums at high interest rates and in the long run fall into greater debt than before. Persons totally unable to meet the wealth requirements of the expanding system can sell themselves or their children into debt bondage to a wealthier household. In such situations, the individuals involved become a kind of added labor force for the wealthy family. They have no property themselves and as members of the new household are only a cost insofar that their brideprice must be paid and that they consume a portion of the agricultural output to which they contribute. But their *entire* surplus belongs to their master who also receives the brideprice of their daughters. Debt slaves do not necessarily remain so *in perpetuo,* they can be freed by relatives or friends (i.e., by proper payment), or even granted membership in the lineage of their master.

Captured slaves appear to fall into a situation similar to that described above. In the past this sub-category made up the large majority of slaves among the Kachin of the Triangle and the Hukawng valley. In both cases, slaves were almost always the exclusive »property« of chiefs or village headmen. They represent a much more significant category economically than socially, although the long term effect of this swelling or chiefly surplus might have critical social consequences. Economically, slaves are equivalent to an immediate and relatively cost-free growth of the household labor force, i.e., a great increase in *absolute* surplus available for distribution at feasts. When it occurs within the community as debt bondage it is analogous to the phenomenon of capital concentration. Here the labor power of poor lineages is shifted to that of the chief, giving the latter an economic advantage over possible competitors by raising his potential output.

Subordinate villages, *ngong mayam*, are created either by conquest or by willful submission to Kachin rule in exchange for land and/or political security. The subordinate group retains sovereignty over its land and is in most respects a simple addition to the larger Kachin community. However, these villages are required to give their masters,

> »amongst other things, every alternate calf born, the first bunch of plantains of each tree, half the marriage price of a bride and so much labor, etc., etc.« (Leach 1954:299).

There is some evidence that *mayam* villages may become integrated into the regular rank class system by means of the same kind of mobility that applies to every Kachin of commoner status (Leach 1946:452–453). An interesting variant of this territorial slavery is indicative of a kind of »creeping feudalism« which is inherent in the Kachin system. Poor families or groups of immigrants can receive land in *exchange* for *mayam* status. Members of such groups are »in many respects similar to the serf« (Leach 1954:299) since their access to the land appears to be the result of a transaction between landlord and land-less laborers. However, to the extent that such groups are integrated into the domain they lose this serf status and simply become the bottom rung of the rank-class system.

The *mayam* communities and households represent a significant innovation. They are much closer to a real economic class than the normal ranked categories of kin. While there seems to be a tendency for them to be incorporated into the larger kinship structure, their presence, which is maintained by continued slave raids and inflation, represents a source of chiefly revenue unlike others since it is based on the extraction of a considerable portion of their surplus. The extent to which this surplus is redistributed in some form is not clear, but one could surmise that there is a germ of class exploitation in these relations. I would add that the only areas where *mayam* villages are wide-spread is the Hukawng Valley and Assam, both areas where the technology is not slash and burn but wet rice. If slave villages did exist in the Triangle, they were probably quickly incorporated into the larger ranking system. The predominant form of slavery in the hills was household slavery which if similar to the Chin *tefa* system, as suggested by Leach, would have the following form. Slaves lived in the house of the chief (one reason for the very large size of these buildings, often more than one hundred feet in length). If they were married they sometimes set up their own households although their status continued as *mayam* (*ngong mayam*). After a number of generations it seems probable that they would become ordinary commoner local lineages, often of the same clan as their former master. In this way there was a kind of circulation of labor into chiefs' houses as internal (*tinung*) *mayam*, then out of the houses as external (*ngong*) *mayam* and finally integration into the village community as commoners.

The status of female slaves is different than that of males, as they often form part of a chief's concubine, bought from other masters for something resembling a reduced brideprice. In a system where labor is in high demand, concubinage appears to be a way in which chiefs can increase their own labor force at minimal expense. In fact, concubinage need not be restricted to slave women but might include any female of the »lower classes.« (Leach 1961:85). It is noteworthy that this represents a secondary form of hypergamy in a system dominated by hypogamous relations, a point to which we shall return later.

A very important economic property of slaves is their easy transferability, and it is this which makes them a kind of property. Their negotiability seems to serve as a means of redistributing labor power among wealthy aristocrats.

The category »slave« is clearly unlike other rank-classes we have discussed and it is preferable to treat it separately. When we discuss the economics of Kachin expansion it should become clear that the size and nature of the slave class is a variable dependent on a number of infrastructural contradictions. *Mayam* are generated by the hierarchical strains in the system. They do not form a primary category but are rather a secondary product of the operation of the system over time. *Mayam* tend to become commoners in the long run and the class can only be maintained on a large scale by importing outsiders. On the other hand, slavery, as a product of the Kachin economy, is extremely important in the expansion process and may develop into class exploitation in areas where the technological base is transformed.

Summary

Ordinary language, being linear, is a serious obstacle to the clear presentation of structural relationships which are thoroughly paradigmatic. I can try to overcome this problem by emphasizing the essential coherence of the system I have been describing. We began with a model in which two relations of production, one vertical, the other horizontal, were articulated in a single structure. Our analysis consisted in demonstrating certain correspondences between segmentary kinship and the vertical »exchange,« and affinal kinship and the horizontal exchange. By showing the way the two articulate in a larger whole, it appeared that the major social categories (surface structure) could be generated and that the transition from *gumlao* to *gumsa* could be explained in terms of a single complex process. Briefly, the structural forms corresponding to the two exchange systems are:

Vertical	*Horizontal*
1. *manau* feast-distribution	1. affinal exchange
2. segmentary principal	2. *mayu/dama* relation
3. lineage-clan structure	3. affinal ranking
4. spirit hierarchy (segmentary)	4. spirit ranking (affinal)
5. conical ranking	5. local lineage (transferable)
6. »asiatic« property	property

These structures are in turn articulated with a process of local segmentation into villages, village clusters and larger domains in which the hierarchy that emerges can best be described as an unsettled combination of patrilineal and affinal relations, a limited ambilateral rank system with strong patrilineal tendencies. While the vertical and horizontal structures are in conflict in very important ways, they are also part of a single process of emergent *gumsa* polity and cannot be treated as separate systems. The system of rank formation is equally the result of the two exchange processes.

$$\text{vertical:} \quad \text{feasting} \rightarrow \text{prestige}$$
$$\text{horizontal:} \quad \text{prestige} \rightarrow \text{affinal rank}$$
$$\text{vertical:} \quad \text{affinal rank} \rightarrow \text{segmentary rank}$$

This can be described as a dialectic where two exchange mechanisms which are necessary parts of a single larger structure are in contradiction with one another. The contradiction is indeed integral to the functioning of the larger system, but it is in no sense hegelian. It is not the vertical and horizontal structures as entities which are contradictory, but rather, the implications which each of these structures has for other levels of organization. If land were to become a negotiable (affinal) item, it would destroy the basis of chiefly authority founded on the monopolization of certain segmentary lineage positions which keeps land off the »market« as opposed to moveable property. In the very process of ranking, the necessity of turning kin into affines is a contradiction between the two structures. Junior lines can only be definitively subordinated by making them *dama* relatives. The entire instability of *gumsa* domains revolves around tendencies toward conical clan structure on one hand and loose affinal ranking on the other. All of these inconsistencies and conflicts are implications of the vertical-lineal and horizontal-affinal aspects of the ranking process which are themselves quite inseparable.

Thus far we have concentrated on the main structural categories of Kachin social existence and the way they combine with one another. In the next section we move on to consider the same model in terms of economic flows. We shall then be in a position to put things together into a more comprehensible system of social reproduction with its own internal »rationality«.

Economic Flows in Gumsa Hierarchies

The main economic flows in Kachin society are by-and-large covered by the Chapter Two model. There are two major categories of exchanges, one vertical and the other horizontal. In *gumlao* society, at the start of the process of hierarchization, these two exchanges consist in brideprice and *manau* feasts which are linked in a single cycle, already described, of prestige accumulation and rank formation. None of this need be repeated again. Instead, we shall look at some of the particulars of *gumsa* economics.

For the sake of comparison it should be kept in mind that non-*gumsa* society is equivalent to a big-man economy in which the wealthy must continually validate their social status by feast-giving. At the earliest stages it is *distribution* rather than re-distribution. An individual or local line is entirely dependent on the resources it can muster to gain prestige. This amounts to working harder to get larger total yields. With the onset of ranked local lineages the flows begin to go both ways. The prime mover here is the value of women. Inflation of brideprice increases the flow of cattle and other goods and services from lower to higher ranks. In the right conditions this can mean that the expenses of feasting are reimbursed. If the increment to cattle stock by reproduction and inflow of bridewealth is greater than the outflow of brideprice, then *manau* feasts can be given with no trouble. Of course, the ability to give feasts rests more on the output of rice, i.e., the quantity of disposable surplus, than on the possession of cattle, but the two are linked by the conversion of prestige into increased brideprice. However, if inflation goes too far, it can create strains in the system by absorbing available cattle in the marriage transactions leaving nothing for feast giving. This kind of tendency would seem, in fact, to be realized, leading to the concentration of cattle in the hands of one or two lineages so that other lineages wanting to give feasts have to borrow or buy cattle from the monopolists. The same tendency applies to all *hpaga* ritual exchange items, which are the measure of a man's status. *Hpaga* goods have little or no social cost of production relative to agricultural goods, and they function as a kind of money which, as a prestige good, can be transformed into status rank or converted into other forms of wealth.

The accumulation of *hpaga* is intimately linked with the development of ranking and is crucial for any understanding of that process. In Leach's treatment, *hpaga* are closely linked to *hka*, debts, in which form all social obligations are expressed. Following is a list of some instances of such debts:

»a. If A borrows money from B: B owns (*madu*) the debt; A drinks (*has*) (*lu*) the debt.
b. If A steals anything from B: B owns a debt against A.
c. If A gets B with child: B's lineage owns a debt against A's lineage.
d. If A kills B either intentionally or unintentionally: B's lineage owns a debt against A's lineage.
e. If A has an accident, fatal or otherwise, while employed by B: A's lineage owns a debt against B's lineage.
f. If A fails to complete the stipulated terms of a contract (such as a brideprice agreement) with B: B's lineage owns a debt against A's lineage.
g. If A, not being a fellow clansman of the chief, fails to pay to his 'thigh-eating chief' B tribute of the hind leg (*magyi*) of an animal he has slaughtered, B owns a debt against A.
h. If lineage A and lineage B are *mayu-dama* and a boy of lineage B marries a girl of lineage C without first informing A and paying token compensation, then lineage A owns a debt against lineage B.
i. If a man of lineage A dies leaving a widow of lineage B, and no other male of lineage A 'picks her up' as a levirate wife; lineage B owns a debt against lineage A.«

(Leach 1954:152–3).

All debts are paid in negotiable quantities of *hpaga* goods.

Hpaga payments are always ranked according to the social status of the parties involved. The most important transactions usually occur in connection with brideprice. Leach indicates that some debts are always left outstanding between *mayu* and *dama* lines as a matter of principle (Leach 1954:153), and that this is a mark of the continuity of the relation. In point of fact, the inflation of brideprice will often make immediate payment impossible so that *dama* relatives are necessarily maintained in an asymmetrical relationship over several generations.

How do *hpaga* wealth items fit into the productive process? Quite simply, in order to obtain *hpaga* one must have the non-ritual wealth which would enable one to give a feast. The circulation of ritual wealth does not take place in a vacuum, for if it did, it would be possible for anyone to acquire status since there would be no way of gaining permanent control over available wealth. *Hpaga*, fit into our model of lineage political economy at two critical points of conversion of one type of wealth or status into another.

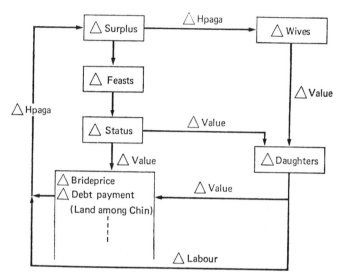

Value refers to an implicit transfer of status as opposed to real transactions (hpaga, labour)

Ritual wealth expresses the social value of the lineage. The social value of the lineage, however, is rooted in its ability to produce a distributable surplus. Thus, control over production is crucial, in that the ability to accumulate ritual wealth depends on the ability to distribute lineage surplus to the village. For any one lineage there seems to be a long term balance in certain kinds of *hpaga*, especially cattle, which, as they move up the hierarchy as brideprice are also slaughtered in feasts and thus redistributed to lower ranking lines in the form of food. In general, however, the leveling off into rank classes would seem to have the effect of maintaining important differences in *hpaga* ownership by means of stratified brideprice and debt payments. Any lineage in the process of raising its status will have to at some point pay a very high brideprice to an already established aristocratic lineage. Leach makes the following remark about such payments:

> »If the brideprice in such cases were fixed according to the status of the bride, the system would break down, for the men of junior status would seldom be able to raise the necessary quantity of cattle and *hpaga*.« (Leach 1954:151).

Leach seems to be implying here that somehow the payment can be avoided without any particular consequences, since it is only a question of raising the husband's lineage status by paying as high a price as possible. This does not appear to be the case. For one thing, the debt system is perfectly capable of transforming the inability to pay a high price into an increased rank differential. On the other hand, this inflation tends to sort out the wealthy lineages from those not so well off by grouping together affinally all those who can afford a similar range of payments. It is quite probable that rather than there being some adjustment to the solvency of the lineages involved, there will be a long run accumulation of debt at all levels of the social structure. This is the logical outcome of any inflationary process and is one of the major strains in the system.

Inflationary tendencies are the result of the accumulation of *hpaga* by wealthy lines and the increase in all payments in such a way that it becomes more and more difficult for lineages to meet the prices demanded.[1]) The increase in debt has a number of immediate effects. If a man is unable to pay brideprice he may be forced to do bride service for a number of years. This is the equivalent of free labor over and above consumption needs and contributes to the surplus of the *mayu* lineage in such a way as to reinforce the pre-existent situation. Families that have accumulated enormous debts over the years may be forced into debt bondage which again increases the labor force and the potential absolute surplus of the headman or chief in such a way as to give him a decided advantage over other lineages. A third result might also be a feud between *mayu* and *dama* lines.

»In principle any outstanding debt, no matter what its origin, is potentially a source of feud.« (Leach 1954:153).

As debts accumulate throughout all levels of the system, the potential for feuds also increases. This might be more important at higher levels where followers can be gathered for such occasions. Poorer lineages of low status must be content with debt slavery. If debts become feuds, it is because they strain the normal *mayu/dama* relationships. The problem of inflation is that *hpaga* values (payments) increase faster than real output, and the inability to pay is transformed into increasing debt ratios until a breaking point is reached, perhaps a *gumlao* rebellion, in which all values are drastically reduced. If the process looks like a business cycle, this does not mean that the Kachin have a capitalist economy, but merely that the measure of value increases faster than real output. It is a contradiction in any economy where there is a difference between value determined by exchange and by production. The debt-feud relationship is the expression of the major contradiction in the Kachin social system. It will be reanalyzed in terms of the intersystemic relation between forces and relations of production.

---

[1]) Green (1934:71) remarks on the facility with which debts can be contracted and on the rapacity of creditors.

Expansion

The economy we have been discussing is an expanding economy in which in order to maintain one's position, it is necessary to produce an increasing surplus. There are definite limits to the internal availability of labor for any one family of a given size and there are several means by which lineages attempt to accumulate more working members. First, there is no doubt that children are highly valued. Infanticide is non-existent and it is the goal of every family head to have as many children as possible (Gilhodes 1911:174–5). Those who have produced large surpluses and have been able to raise their status may often accumulate enough *hpaga* to have more than one wife.[1]) Only one wife is the primary wife, i.e., of equal or higher status. Secondary wives are either from lower ranking lines or are slave concubines. In either case the brideprice is much lower but the return on that price is well worth it. Since the family can be expanded, more land can be cleared, a larger surplus yield can be reaped and converted into higher or better consolidated rank position. There is evidence that polygyny is used quite consciously as a means of economic advance.

>Les polygames ne sont pourtant pas très nombreux et ont rarement plus de deux ou trois épouses. La première est appelée *latung* ou *natung*, la seconde *lashy* ou *nashy* et la troisième *labai* ou *nabai*. La première est la principale; *mais la plus considerée est celle qui a des enfants et travaille le mieux.*« (Gilhodes 1913:374) (my underline).

Gilhodes adds that polygamy is common in the following circumstances:
>1. quand la première femme est sterile ou n'a que des filles;
2. quand une seule femme ne peut suffire à tout le travail de la maison;
3. quand à la mort d'un frère, il n'y a personne de libre pour épouser la veuve dont on a charge, etc.« (Gilhodes 1913:374).

Aside from the absolute necessity to beget a male heir, the most important considerations are purely economic. Labor power can also be concentrated in the hands of the wealthy lineages by:
a) debt bondage
b) importing of slaves

The first is a transfer from poor households to aristocrats, usually headmen and chiefs. In exactly the same way captured slaves add to the *family* labor force of the chief. In sum, polygamy, debt bondage, slavery and bride service are all means of labor accumulation by lineages of high rank. Let me clarify what I mean by »means of accumulation.« In the ordinary *mayu/dama* relation, or even in cases where a tribute of rice is exacted by thigh-eating chiefs, we are dealing with independent households in which only a small portion of the surplus is being raked off. In a large »family« or household which results from the above mentioned processes, *all the surplus*, i.e., all output over and

---

[1]) The age of marriage in the Triangle is 18 for boys and 15 for girls (Green 1934), and premarital sex is frequent between *mayu* women and *dama* men.

above consumption is in the hands of the master of the house or lineage. Thus, while there is increased household consumption, there is also increased total yield and available surplus, and to a much greater extent than would be the case if total labor power remained distributed among independent households.

Vertical Flows and Stabilization

We have now discussed the economic flows associated with an expanding *gumsa* hierarchy. While feasting, a distributive, vertical exchange, is a central part of the process, the dominant relation of production is the affinal, horizontal, exchange which establishes rank differences. In a fully formed *gumsa* domain, however, a combination of monopolization and increasing authority has a tendency to transform the horizontal flows into vertical flows.

A *gumsa* chief may be »thigh-eating« or not. The former is the true chief of a domain, while the latter represents a chief going either »up hill« or »down hill«. The traditional domain, however, is always headed by a *gumchying gumsa du*.[1]) The domain chief finds himself at the focal point of two exchange systems. First, he is the greatest accumulator of *hpaga* and cattle. Second, he is entitled to several important forms of tribute and corvée. It is these latter, the specifically vertical aspects, which appear to become more developed as centralized authority increases. The three services due to a chief are:

1) Labor on the chief's land at clearing, sowing, weeding and harvest.
2) At least three baskets of paddy per season.
3) The hind quarter of any animal sacrificed or hunted in the domain.

While it might be argued that four times a year isn't much in the way of corvée labor, it is practically all that matters in shifting cultivation. Clearing, sowing, weeding and harvest are the times of most intensive labor during the year. The fact that that labor is owed to the chief at these times, means that his fields can be larger than the others, and that his own work load is minimal. The chief's plot is a kind of community farm in terms of labor input. The laborers are fed during their time of service from the chief's stores which were, of course, filled by previous years communal labor. Every house is required to pay three baskets of rice each year. It is not clear whether members of the chief's clan are also required to make this payment, but it would appear that exemptions only apply to very close kin who could not become wife-takers. Unfortunately, there is no information on the volume of the »baskets«, but such harvest baskets among the Chin (Stevenson 1968:114) hold approximately eighty lbs. which means that a tribute of three baskets might be equal to a bit more than 13% of an acre yield, i.e., a fairly small percentage of the total output. It is, of course, quite possible that such tribute was higher during the history of any one domain and there is no reason to assume that it is a constant. The contribution of a thigh of any animal killed is more of a token gesture

---

[1]) *Gumchying* chiefs are the traditional »thigh eating« chiefs of the Triangle region. For a full discussion see p. 229.

than a real economic tribute. However, as with the rice, in a large domain, such tribute could amount to considerable quantities for any one person to control. For example, rice tribute from only 100 households (a relatively small domain) would amount to 16,000 lbs of rice (assuming a tribute of only two instead of three baskets), a harvest more than five times greater than that produced by an average family of five, i.e., certainly enough to give quite a large number of feasts. The Chief's house is with good reason referred to as the »paddy store« (*htingsang*).

In return for tribute and corvée, the chief gives great feasts and is officially in charge of entertaining visitors. The chief's *manau* feast, *nut manau* or wealth feast, is a very large scale redistribution. There are a number of other redistributive occasions. Scott and Hardiman mention two important feasts. One is when,

> »The *Duwa* acts as representative of the community in offering sacrifices, as for example in the yearly festival 'of the *nat* of the earth' (*ga nat*), and every villager is obliged to assist him and contribute offerings.« (Scott and Hardiman 1900: Pt. I, Vol. I: 414–15).

Then in good harvest years,

> »The *duwa* as head of the community holds high festival for three of four days on end (*manau ka law*), to which *all neighboring communities are invited.*« (Scott and Hardiman 1900: Pt. I, Vol. I: 415) (my underline).

The redistributive system is based on the place of the chief in the segmentary hierarchy we have described. His lineage is that of the territorial spirit. His *uma nat* is the *mung nat*. Only the chief can make offerings to his own ancestral *nat*, spirit and protector of the entire domain. And it is only through this channel that he can approach his distant *mayu* relative, the *madai nat*, giver of general prosperity and the *ga nat*, who controls fertility. Thus, in this religio-economic structure, the chief occupies the nodal point as representative of the entire community to the higher spirits who control the life processes of the group. According to Leach,

> »The chief's political authority is based, ideologically on his ability to preserve the prosperity of his domain by making sacrifices to the sky spirit *Madai*, and to the earth spirit *Shadip*.« (Leach 1954:129).

I would suggest that this is more than simply ideology – it is not a mere reflection of a pre-existent authority structure, but the social form of control itself. We have shown how through greater productivity and political manipulation, a given lineage could have monopolized the community *nat* and become the sole means of communication between the human community and the higher community of gods which is responsible for the economic prosperity of all. But, the fact that the anthropologist knows all this to be fantasy should not prevent him from treating it as social fact. It is the materialist Engels who tells us that even in communities where there were no social classes, »there were from the beginning, certain common interests the safeguarding of which had to be handed over to individuals« some of which were, »when conditions were

still absolutely primitive, *religious functions.*« (Engels 1969:214) (my underline). Aside from his implicit functionalism, Engels, who had very little data
to go on was not far off, I think. In any case, religious activities can be of crucial
importance. We have seen that among the Kachin (and Lamet) they are at the
center of economic activity. Thus, the chief's function at the focal point of the
redistributive network is both superstructural and infrastructural. The situation
has enormous evolutionary potential as Engels and Marx were quick to see.

>»Here we are only concerned with establishing the fact that the exercise
of a social function was everywhere the basis of political supremacy.«
(Engels 1969:315).

The Kachin vertical structure is not some very peculiar phenomenon, but
seems to be very widespread as a form of development. To cite only one
example, in Tikopia,

>»It was through his special relation with powerful gods that he was
believed to exercise his superior role in the social and economic as well
as in the religious spheres.« (Firth 1961:53).

And Fried in a general work on political evolution suggests of chiefs that,

>»It seems more accurate to believe that such small power as they control
is likely to stem from their ritual status, although even here there is minimum possibility of transfer from one situation to another.« (Fried 1967:
141).

Earlier I attempted to show how the economic and the »ritual« were intimately connected in the evolution of ranking and here it is clear that the
process may be quite a general one. It also appears, contrary to Fried (above),
that the power of a Kachin »thigh-eating« chief is not so minimal, and further,
that it tends to increase with time – at least until the emergence of serious
contradictions. It cannot be determined whether or not the Kachin domain is
ever capable of verging on class structure, but there is, in any case, a very thin
line between redistribution and exploitation, and there is no better substitute
for a real return than a ritual return in the form of »increased fertility.« The
redistributive system can be represented as in the model on next page.

I again stress here that such payments as corvée are not to be confused with
feudal corvée which is a kind of contract agreement whereby labor is exchanged for a portion of land. On the contrary, as Leach says in spite of his use of
the word »feudal«,

>»The chief's hut is built and his field sown as a communal duty.« (Leach
1954:135).

This community labor is included with other duties which are controlled by
the chief:

>»Such purposes include the clearing of paths and the clearing and fencing
of the annual village rice field.« (Leach 1954:135).

The *duwa* is not a feudal lord. Rather, he is the precursor of Marx's Oriental
Despot, in that his position is squarely within the »ideological« structure of the
community. As he represents the »higher unity« of the group, it is perfectly

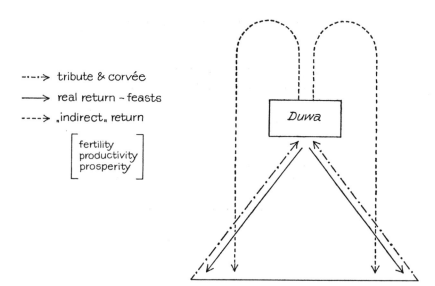

logical that tribute and labor service belong to him as communal activities and not as the result of contractual exchange.

A certain amount of stabilization is introduced in the final stages of domain formation. The *duwa*, through his monopoly of the spirit hierarchy puts something of a damper on the affinal competition which was previously so rampant. A decisive component of his monopoly is the *nut manao*, wealth *manao*, the most important feast which can only be given to the *madai nat*. Leach mentions only four kinds of *manao* feast:

a) *nut manao* – This is a lavishly expensive feast. Leach suggests that it is similar to the Chin Feast of Merit, but we shall see that it is slightly different in form and function. *Nut manao* can usually be given only by a chief. If given by someone else, the chief must be present to invoke the *madai nat*.

b) *iu manao* – roasting feast – is similar to the wealth *manao*, but given by a whole village. Again, since the *madai nat* is invoked, a chief must be present.

c) *padang manao* – victory feast – ends a feud or war. It is particularly important if the purpose of the feud was the annexation of land, since it is the confirmation or legalization of a new land title. The defeated party is heavily feasted, but also contributes to the affair.

d) *gumran manao* – is a feast given when a chiefly lineage splits. It is a symbolic splitting of the *uma nat* between junior (elS) and senior (yoS) branches after which each can claim status as a thigh-eating chief. The Yo Son line, however retains theoretical supremacy. This appears to be a private ceremony in which an el B buys title to thigh-eating status from his yo B.

The first feast appears to be the only where a wealthy individual can transform his accumulated wealth into prestige by feasting the entire community.

As we can see it is probably very difficult for an individual to be completely independent in such a feast. The entire situation is controlled by the chief. Only he can make the feast truly meaningful since he controls the spiritual half of the activity. As for the second *manao*, it is not clear how such feasts are organized, but it is again a matter of chiefly control over the ritual half of the activity. In neither case is there a functional resemblance to the feast of merit common among the Chin and Naga. Among these latter groups, feasts of merit are primarily competitive *affinal* feasts. While a large part of the village community may serve as witness, affinal relatives are marked for special portions of the sacrificial animals. Furthermore, the feast is not made to anything that could be called a higher village spirit or *madai nat*, i.e., no vertical segmentary structure is present.

Aside from the monopolization of the celestial, prosperity giving, spirits, there are a number of purely economic closures which would appear to make competition very difficult between any but those occupying nodal points in the segmentary structure: lineage heads, village headmen, and domain chiefs.

a) Slaves, either from debt bondage or by capture, are usually the property of chiefs and sometimes headmen. These lineages, thus, have substantially increased labor forces. Further, as most imported slaves are adults, they are ready for heavy field labor immediately, i.e., without the added cost of childhood. Slave owning lineages are in superior economic position with regard to all exchange since they always have a lot more going out and therefore a lot more coming in. *The wealth of a lineage, it will be remembered, it not measured by what it has accumulated, but by what it can afford to give away. The greater the quantity of goods put into circulation, the higher the lineage status.*

b) As the chief of a domain is the ultimate »owner« of everything in it, all property, landed or otherwise, reverts to his possession in cases of extreme poverty, lineage extinction, etc. The fact that land is not negotiable means that this kind of control is restricted to chiefs only.

c) The vertical flow tends to divert both surplus labor and product from the individual lineage political economy (horizontal) to the increasing demands of the already existing hierarchy. This is a critical phenomenon since it is a clear case of conflict between the vertical and horizontal exchange structures.

d) The rank-class structure, which is just as much affinal as segmentary, is organized so that those who are already in important aristocratic or chiefly positions are on top of the debt structure. The value of their daughters brideprice is established as highest and they have a decided adventage in the maintenance of their rank since there is an assured inflow of:
   1. debt payments
   2. brideprice
   3. debtors and slaves – i.e., labor

Summary
The two kinds of economic flow discussed so far are linked to two different aspects of Kachin political economy. There is a fairly clear differentiation between the political economy of the independent lineage and that of the larger hierarchical domain. The two exchange systems are more or less contradictory since they both make claims on the same production process. Thus the political question becomes one of the allocation of local lineage surplus.

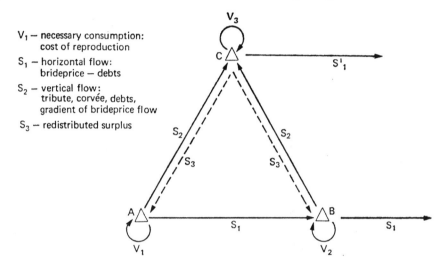

V_1 — necessary consumption:
    cost of reproduction

S_1 — horizontal flow:
    brideprice — debts

S_2 — vertical flow:
    tribute, corvée, debts,
    gradient of brideprice flow

S_3 — redistributed surplus

The above diagram recapitulates the main flows in a *gumsa* domain. S1 here represents the local lineage political economy. To simplify matters, I have assumed that it includes the feast-prestige accumulation cycle as well as the affinal exchange cycle. Since C is of higher rank than A there will necessarily be a difference in its distribution of surplus. S'_1 will probably be of larger magnitude than S1. There are several determinant relations implied in the diagram. The ratio S2/S1 measures the relative strength of two exchange systems. The ratio S2/S3 is a measure of the degree of reciprocity in the redistributive sector. S/V is the marxist »rate of surplus value« which here represents the productivity of the technology.

In the course of *gumsa* evolution I suspect that the following developments occur. S2/S1 tends to increase as does S2/S3, i.e., increasing hierarchization of the economy and decreasing reciprocity in the redistributive sphere. As a result of these changes and the increasing monopoly over labor, the chiefly surplus will tend to grow at the expense of lower level accumulation. At the same time, the inflationary tendencies will place growing demand on all lineage surplus in such a way that S1 + S2 increases, creating a number of strains in the system. Some of these are manifested in the form of debt slavery and in a growing demand for imported labor (captured slaves) for an expanding economy. If we now let S_t stand for total surplus and S_c for that part controlled by chiefly lineages, the following tendency would seem to be implied by what we have said.

$$\left.\begin{array}{l} \dfrac{d^2S_2}{d\,S_1{}^2} > 0 \\[1.2em] \dfrac{d^2S_2}{dS_3{}^2} > 0 \\[1.2em] \dfrac{dS_t}{dt} > 0 \end{array}\right\} \implies \dfrac{dS_c}{dS_t} > 0$$

t: time $\implies$: implies

This is merely a more precise way of saying that the chiefly lineage controls an increasing portion of the increasing total surplus of the community. There are, of course, very stiff limits on the possibilities of continuing this kind of accumulation. These are not only of an economic nature (diminishing returns), but include a massing of contradictions at all levels.

Note on the »Gradient of Brideprice«

While affinal exchange is assumed to be part of the horizontal system, in an already formed *gumsa* domain there is a necessary tendency for it to be verticalized. The gradient expresses the extent to which affinal wealth is channeled toward nodal points in the segmentary structure and is thus accumulated in the same way as tribute. Its value depends on the actual brideprice differentials and on the percentage of hypogamous marriages.

The system of economic flows is the dynamic aspect of Kachin social structure. It should be clear from our analysis of this flow that vertical and horizontal exchanges are part of a single system of reproduction. If we were to isolate the dominant relation of production, however, it would be the affinal-horizontal structure since it is at the heart of the process of ranking and remains instrumental in the maintenance of the hierarchy. But the vertical structure tends to move into a dominant position in the fully formed domain, first through the translation of affinal rank into conical rank, then by the sanctification of the whole process in terms of the spirit hierarchy, and finally by the imposition of vertical redistributive exchange structures on the former alliance network.

Conclusion

I have, thus far, attempted to characterize the basic properties of Kachin relations of production and the several subsystems which determine the nature of *gumsa* development. By analysing not only the static properties of the social relations but also the dynamic properties of the material flow that they generate, I have tried to go beyond the usual ethnographic type of analysis which lacks any time dimension beyond that of the life cycle. The fact that kinship relations may appear to be static does not exclude the possibility that they might have dynamic consequences that, in turn, may transform those relations. The existence of cumulative processes and contradictions, even the formation of chiefdoms, have all been derived from the bits and pieces of standard ethnographic data that normally lie in state, awaiting the procession of functionalist anthropologists whose comparative generalizations sanctify the fossil-like appearance of the »primitive« society.

CHAPTER V

Expansion and Contradiction

I. Structure

In this chapter we shall discuss both the intra- and intersystemic contradictions of *gumsa* social forms and attempt to show how they articulate with one another. We shall analyze the structural strains that develop with territorial and demographic expansion of the domain and how these are related to variations in the degree of ranking. The main arguments will center around the contradiction between forces and relations of production in the context of expanded reproduction. We shall see how the properties of the economic flow cause an inevitable breakdown in *gumsa* social relations; how the divergence between exchange value and real output causes increasing debt, loss of status, »slavery«, and increasing horizontal and vertical conflict. Determination in the last instance by the level of development of the forces of production[1]) will be demonstrated by the way in which *gumlao* tendencies emerge in the expanding system and their ultimate explosion at a given point in *gumsa* evolution.

The Kachin system is a growing economy with very strong inflationary tendencies. It involves a high demand for surplus output and therefore a high demand for increasing input. This expansion is not in any sense caused by the techno-environment. It is a product of the relations of production of Kachin society. Growth is thus generated at the level of productive forces[2]) in terms of increasing population, increasing intensity of labor input, extension of cultivated land, etc., but the process eventually encounters serious limitations. Here we shall be concerned with the expansion process at the level of relations of production and the contradictions that build up within the social structure.

The Kachin tend to maintain small villages and, as a result, local fission would appear to be a rather frequent occurence. I have suggested that this fission is closely tied to ranking and the need to shed siblings and sibling lineages in an effort to consolidate one's position. Ranking is an affinal process and it tends to dominate any tendency toward the expansion of the exogamous

---

[1]) Not to be understood in the »orthodox« or structural-marxist sense, but as discussed on p. 28.
[2]) Not *by* the productive forces which have no internal dynamic. Population growth, intensifications, etc. are an effect, not a cause.

lineage with which, moreover, it is entirely incompatible. The practice of ranked inheritance is the main mechanism for getting rid of blood kin (Leach 1954:165).

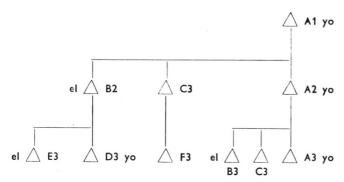

rank order in generation 3: A3⟩B3⟩C3⟩D3⟩E3⟩F3

The above chart exhibits a maximal degree of ranking in succession to office or inheritance. Youngest sons are the sole inheritors of property and are highest in rank after which follow eldest sons and then the rest in descending age order. After several generations, the sibling order becomes the rank order of the lineages with respect to the youngest son line. Where there is polygyny, children of the principal wife are superior to those of the second, third, etc. This is also true of the levirate. Where affinal ranking is being maximized, collateral memory will be quite short. Rather than form a difficult to maintain exogamous ranked maximal lineage, there will be a strong tendency for lineage ties to be forgotten all together, especially if the junior and senior lines do not remain in the same locality. In this way kin are quickly turned into potential affines, either by complete fission or by at least assimilating close sibling lines to more distant clan relatives who are marriageable. The only clearly exogamous group remains the local lineage which never contains more than five or six families. Beyond the village, the possibility of endogamy increases markedly. The Kachin are much more strict about reversing an alliance (FZD marriage) which calls for a heavy fine, than about clan or lineage endogamy which appears to be quite common at all levels of segmentation except the village.

In this situation, an elder son has a number of choices. If he remains at home he must of necessity accept a thoroughly subordinate position to his younger brother. Rather than be resigned to this fate, a noninheriting son of chiefly status will often take some members of the parental village and establish a new village either in the same domain or in that of another chief. This choice will probably depend on the chances for increasing status and will vary with political circumstances. An elder son may buy rights to thigh-eating status from his younger brother, in which case he becomes a junior chiefly segment of the domanial maximal lineage. The expansion of local settlements within the parental domain tends to develop a relatively homogeneous conical structure of the kind described earlier, that is, if hierarchical relations can be maintained. Otherwise the cone will be truncated and a number of chiefs of equal status, all claiming paramount rank, may end up marrying in a circle or becoming involved in a feud. By buying title to territory belonging to another chief, a heterogeneous domain structure develops in which affinal links predominate. In most cases, domains will contain some mixture of the two kinds of structure, but even where there is a high degree of homogeneity senior/junior sibling rank will have to be reinforced by *mayu/dama* relations.

Local fissioning and lineage fissioning are part of the same process whereby large tracts of land are increasingly populated by small local segments tied to one another by lineal and affinal relations. Whether the domain becomes a series of smaller domains, a loose confederation of chiefs, or a tighter conical system depends on the ability to keep junior and *dama* lines in their subordinate positions. While a *mung* may be fairly stable for an extended period of time it is unlikely that a large system containing three or four smaller tracts can be maintained, and it is more likely that these structures will devolve into a number of allied domains of smaller size.

The major contradiction of any kinship hierarchy is kinship itself, especially, in this case, the accumulation of brothers, i.e., possible pretenders to paramount status. By turning kin into affines, i.e., *dama*, an *uma* (yoS) line can better preserve its rank, since the exchange relation cannot be so easily manipulated as a genealogy that becomes increasingly fictitious with the passage of time. The Kachin system, whether based on ultimo- or primo-geniture is still predicated on the ousting of brothers. Leach's reasoning on this point is not altogether clear.

»a) *gumsa* theory presupposes a *taungya* system of agriculture and the necessity for constant segmentation of the local group.
   b) *gumsa* theory supposes that authority over land is derived from birth status only.
   c) These two postulates together provide the basis for succession by ultimogeniture.« (Leach 1954:262).

Unless Leach assumes here that birth status is already by ultimogeniture, I see no reason to suppose that the eldest son should be the one to leave rather than the youngest. In any case, what counts is the maintenance of a thin population and the expulsion of brothers. The predominance of ultimogeniture appears to be of purely political significance. That is, it might well be argued that the sending off of elder brothers (still under the sway of their fathers) to new territory is an instrumental part of the expansion of local control at least as long as distant offshoot lines can be kept within the realm in the following generations.

Given the nature of Kachin kinship, the net effect of this process is that a primary contradiction is avoided, i.e., rival siblings are turned into potential affinal lines. But the contradiction returns as a threat to the control of the larger domain since former lineage brothers who establish themselves in new territory may have the economic wherewithal to gain prestige equivalent to that of the paramount.

In the *gumsa* domain, as we have described it, there is a strong tendency toward a centralization of wealth in a single redistributive network. But this is a kinship network, one which implies a minimum of social distance. Now while the advent of the hierarchy is rooted in the manipulation of those kinship relations, its ultimate stability is severely limited by a central component of kinship, reciprocity. The contradiction between kinship and emergent central authority has been admirably analyzed by Leach.

»*Gumlao* revolt emerges at precisely that point in the political cycle at which the *gumsa* chiefs themselves have been led to infringe on the formal rules of the system.« (Leach 1954:263).

The other side of the coin is,

». . . that the *gumlao* revolutionary leader is in no sense an aberration from the Kachin norm. As a character he is just the same kind of person as the chief against whom he revolts, an ambitious seeker after power who treats economic facts with greater respect than ritual origins.« (Leach 1954:263).

What Leach refers to as »formal« and »ritual« are the constraints of the kinship structure. Both of the above contradictions are inherent in the process of expanding and consolidating the domain purely on the basis of kinship. But conflict can break the system at any number of levels and it is not necessary that there be a *gumlao* revolt. At the highest domanial levels, it can result in fission, the creation of smaller domains which might be no larger than village clusters. All of this can take place within the same *mayu/dama* network while still keeping hereditary powers of leadership in each resultant segment.

In the above cases, each local lineage chief can retain his hereditary claims to office. The only breakdown is at the higher level of hereditary segmentation. This, of course, is only saying that the process of increasing domanial inclusiveness is reversible with respect to time. In the village cluster studied by Leach, Hpalang, there is no clear hierarchical structure above the village headman level. Leach claims that the system was in transition from *gumsa* to *gumlao*, but, structurally, this is impossible to decide.[1]) What is clear, however, is that while higher leadership positions are not established, the headmen of the villages are still hereditary. But since hereditary rights are only based on claims of descent from local *nats*, it is quite conceivable that intra-village competition between lineages could make the system entirely *gumlao*. It is clear that the distinction between hierarchy and equality, based on the existence or non-existence of hereditary titles in an emergent or disappearing segmentary

---

[1]) As we shall see, however, there are ample economic grounds for supporting Leach's assertion.

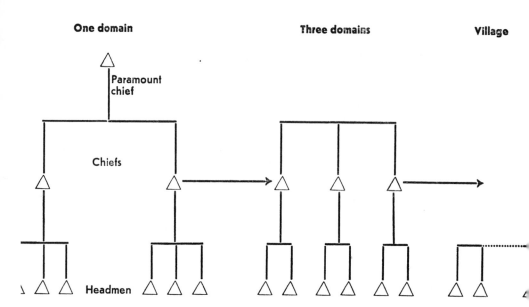

organization is not a matter of clear cut opposition. When we examine this in the larger context of the actual process of rank formation and its ties to the production process, the categories *gumsa* and *gumlao* prove to be more of a hindrance than an aid to understanding. Rather, what seems to be the case, is that the degree of hierarchy is nothing more than the degree of transformation of prestige into rank and then into ritual control of territorial *nats*, all of which depends on the existence of an *expanding surplus*. In this respect, it is most significant that the Hpalang community had:

1) Lost control of the Shan valley population and trade routes which was a major source of revenue, and
2) thus, had to depend on its own agricultural resources which, as a village in our techno-economic zone C, were probably not capable of providing a sufficient surplus to maintain the pre-existent *gumsa* domain.

The differences between various degrees of *gumsa* hierarchy are necessarily of a different order than the dintinction between *gumsa* and *gumlao*. Three domain chiefs who marry in a circle are in many ways the structural equivalent of a *gumlao* system. The difference between hereditary chiefs and non-hereditary big-men is a claim on segmentary status, a claim based on a fictitious link between a lineage and the ancestor spirits of a given territory. This claim can be exercised over a village, village cluster or set of village clusters. Most *gumlao* systems might be characterized quite simply by the absence of supra-local polity and the absence of hereditary headmen, i.e., the absence of segmentary political structure.

The most extreme *gumlao* principle, however, implies more than this absence of hereditary authority. While all of the above variation is centered about the segmentary hierarchy and claims to ritually defined status, the true *gumlao* revolt would, in its most extreme form, consist in the repudiation of the principle of *affinal* ranking altogether. Thus, it would be a much more radical activity, going right to the fundamental contradiction of Kachin society, that which enabled rank to develop in the first place. A true *gumlao* revolt is not quite the same as the more-or-less-*gumsa* variation we described above. It cannot be determined to what extent this repudiation of ranking applies to the alliance system, since early reports of *gumlao* revolts do not make reference to that level of organization, but where the final situation was one in which all local lines were of equal rank this would have had to have been the case. In true *gumlao* villages,

>»Rank differences between *mayu* and *dama* are avoided a) by keeping brideprice low, b) by developing local patterns in which three or more lineages marry in a circle on an exclusive basis ... each lineage having equal rights.« (Leach 1954:205).

True *gumlao* revolts take place in well developed *gumsa* domains. A most recent example is reported for the North Triangle area:

>»The story goes that the daughter of Ning Bawa, *Duwa* of Sumpawng Pum, was sought in marriage by two men: Khawle, who is described as a Maran *Akyi* (headman), and Lapushaung. Ning Bawa, however, chose neither, but gave her to Naw Pwe, chief of Ngumla, a village beyond the confluence, two days north of Wantu. Upon this Khawle and Lapushaung joined forces. Khawle killed the Ngumla Chief and Lapushaung disposed of Sumpawng Pum and each seized his victim's villages. This raised an appetite for more and they proceeded to kill or drive away all *Duwas* who would not yield and efface themselves. Major Fenton remarks that 'Simwa, *Sawbwa* of Sakipum, and numbers of minor *Duwas* saved their lives by consenting to give up their emoluments, and were made *akyis*, apparently a purely honorary title.' The movement was not confined exclusively to the Lepai tribe as he says, but was found also among the Lahtawngs and Marans. It is extraordinarily widespread, considering its recent origin, for there are villages in the upper defile, just north of Bhamo, where within a few years of the annexation the *Duwas* were driven out and *akyis* established.« (Scott and Hardiman 1900: Pt. I, Vol. I:414).

The proximate cause of the *gumlao* revolt was the failure of the chief to fulfill certain affinal obligations to his inferiors. This, at least, would be the reason given by the headmen involved. In fact, the behavior of the chief does not seem so strange and he would appear to be well within his rights. What is more evident is that,

1. There is a structural conflict between the chief's reciprocal obligations to his *dama* relations and his ability to act independently of the will of his inferiors.

2. Conditions exist where this conflict was able to create a break in the
   system of ranking and even to bring it down completely.

Carrapiett, referring to the same area remarks,

>»Certain tribesmen who found the yoke of the *Duwa* irksome and were
impatient of control, declared themselves *Kumlaos* or rebels, threw off
their hereditary connection with the *Duwa*, and settled themselves in
solitary villages of their own.« (Carrapiett 1929:81–2).

To all appearances, the *gumlao* revolt is an indication of the limits of development of the system. It represents a kind of breaking point, a revolt against
authority which has become oppressive. It seems clear that if the headmen who
began the North Triangle rebellion were only decapitating the top of the
pyramid, they would have been able to establish their own smaller domains.
But this did not occur, and the system collapsed entirely. A social contradiction only becomes a point of rupture when the strain is sufficient to make it so.
In order to explain why the contradictions remain latent in some domains but
lead to collapse elsewhere, we must take into account those factors that make
the *gumsa* system oppressive. This is where the economic flow is crucial, that
is, where the strains on subordinates are so great that the semblance of reciprocity can no longer be maintained.

The *gumlao* rebellion and the more/less *gumsa* variation are the same kind
of phenomena structurally except that the extreme *gumlao* form repudiates
alliance rank, i.e., the basis of all conical rank, whereas the former is limited
to a particular segmentary level. In both cases, howewer, we are faced with the
contradictions inherent in an expanding kinship system, expanding in two
ways, in space and in rank. But contradictions are not disruptive in themselves,
they only point to the limit conditions of a structure. The degree to which the
contradiction will materialize as conflict or remain latent depends entirely on
the way it is linked to the process of social reproduction, to the circulation of
labor, debts, and material wealth in the society.

II. Social Reproduction

In the growth cycle, a number of elements are linked in a single social structure
of reproduction. In a very rudimentary way, the growth of surplus which is at
the root of the entire process as well as its ultimate limitation might be envisaged as tied to two kinds of expansion (next page).

I am assuming, here, a rather unorthodox position with regard to population
growth, but one that I think is perfectly logical. The theory handed down by
many population theorists is that population increase is essentially an independent variable that tends to follow a »j-shaped« or sigmoidal curve depending on the distribution of environmental constraints. This modified mal-
thusianism is based primarily on the observation of animal populations in
which survival is based on very high if not maximal net rates of reproduction.
In human populations, however, most of this theory does not hold since in the
majority of cases, fertility is substantially below (potential) fecundity, and

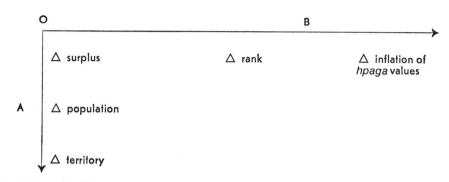

Two kinds of Kachin expansion.

total population increase tends to slow down long before any economic or ecological limits are reached. This is especially true of those social systems with the greatest potential for population growth, i.e., advanced industrial capitalist economies. Without going deeply into the question, I will simply make what I consider to be some common sense assumptions about population growth as applies to the Kachin economy.

a) I will take as pretty well constant, a potential mortality rate which is probably quite high among the Kachin, Chin and many other populations of this area. Most victims appear to be young children or infants. – This may be controlled to some extent through special care and quality nutrition.

b) The birth rate is essentially a socially controlled variable which depends primarily on economic demands, i.e., demand for labor.

This implies that control of population growth rate above equilibrium replacement will be almost entirely conditioned by social factors. As we have already seen, the Kachin place an extremely high value on children and they link this directly to their own prosperity. But in ideal conditions, the techno-economic conditions of swiddening, especially in zone A, a large number of laborers is *not* required. Thus, I would conclude that the high value of children is quite directly related to the expansive nature of the economy; the demand for surplus in order to maintain or raise rank implies a heavy demand for labor.

But the Kachin system it not content with a merely internal growth rate. It goes so far as to pump outside labor into the economy in the form of captured slaves, not slaves that serve as a new form of exploitation, but rather slaves that eventually become commoners. Thus, there are no basic structural changes in the system.[1] It is merely enlarged.

In any case, there is a great deal of hearsay evidence that something like a population explosion occurred in the Kachin Hills in the recent past (Peebles

---

[1] We shall see that slavery can indeed become structurally significant as part of the general transformation involved in state formation (see chapter VII).

1892; Scott and Hardiman 1900: Pt. I, Vol. I) just as there was an older one in the more heavily populated Chin Hills (Lehman 1963:25). In both cases we are dealing with similar expansive systems in which population growth implies territorial growth. What appears historically as an explosion is more probably the effect of this continual expansion encountering some sort of political block-age, most likely in the form of other expanding populations.

In a system of swidden agriculture, the demand for labor, if realized is immediately converted into a demand for territory. In order to maintain pro-ductivity at a maximum the Kachin technology requires a cultivation/fallow cycle of 1/12 to 1/15. This means that the available arable land must expand at 12 to 15 times the rate of increase in the labor force. If we take 1/14 as a starting point, simple calculation tells us that a household of five can be sup-ported by three acres (Leach 1949). Then the maximum population density assuming flat totally arable land is about 71/mi², e.g., using Carneiro's formula:

$$P = \frac{\dfrac{T}{R+Y} \times Y}{A}$$

T: total arable land = 640 acres = 1 mi²
R: fallow period = 14
Y: cultivation period = 1
A: area of cultivated land per individual (acres) = 3/5
P: population

$$\text{we get } P = \frac{\dfrac{640}{14+1} \times 1}{3/5}$$

$$P = \frac{43}{3/5} \cong 71$$

The conditions implied by such a calculation are quite simply not the case for the Kachin where a large portion of the land surface is unavailable for cultivation. Without more specific information it is quite difficult to make anything like a good estimate of the possible population density, so we will have to use other indicators for the most part. If we believe reports about the Wa country and about the Angami and Sema Naga, the limit would seem to lie somewhere below 50/mi², and this in a system of much shorter fallows. These numbers have no clear significance, however, and speculation would have to depend on somewhat better data. Leach, in an unpublished work (1946) claims that the maximum density under optimal fallow conditions is 14/mi². It is not clear how he arrives at this figure, but it implies that the average plot is more than three acres per person per year which would seem to be well above requirements. This problem cannot be solved at present, but a number of things can be made clear. In the Triangle area of optimal fallow conditions, which is *the starting point of our theoretical discussion*, population density is extremely low, not higher than five or six persons per square mile. As such, we can begin with the assumption that there is plenty of room to exercise a policy of maximal expansion and colonization of primary forest areas.

Leach's figure of 14/mi² is interesting when compared to our derived 71/mi². It indicates how in a system of very long fallow, a small increase in acreage cultivated per year can drastically reduce the limits of maximum density. If we make the simple assumption that the Kachin political structure must include allowances for such very likely increases in labor input, then the territorial rate of expansion must be far greater than our postulated 12 to 15 times the rate of increase in the working population. We must, then, take account of this very important political factor when analyzing the territorial growth of the system.

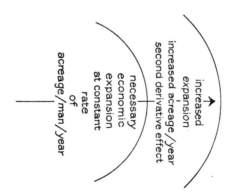

This diagram may be taken to approximate what I would distinguish as two kinds of demographic and territorial expansion. The inner circle represents the rate of necessary expansion, the rate being equal to 15 times the increase in working population where a given acreage per man is cultivated every year. The outer circle represents the increase in territory implied by keeping the rate of population growth constant but adding to the number of acres per worker, i.e., by increasing surplus with the same labor force. We might also add here a kind of »second derivative« effect, whereby enough territory must be available to account for future expansion, i.e., the acceleration of the system.

If the labor force increases at a rate, r, then total available land must increase at the following rate:

$$\frac{dA}{dt} = 15r \qquad\qquad \begin{aligned} &A - \text{arable land} \\ &t\ - \text{time} \end{aligned}$$

And if, on top of this, the average per man per year is increased at a rate p, then the total available land must grow at a faster rate:

$$\frac{dA}{dt} = 15rp$$

Neither of these assumptions appears to be far-fetched. Both are implied by the internal logic of the system itself.

Kachin economic expansion maintains a high level of productivity and output by keeping its population density low. This, however, implies a long term contradiction. Since land is in fact somewhat limited, overall population density will eventually increase, and it is certain that conflicts will arise when expanding domains meet each other head on.

Warfare is said to have existed among the Kachin although it does not appear to have been a major phenomenon. There is, however, a special *manau* feast to celebrate a victory in which new lands have been annexed. There is no information on whether or not secondary forest would be sought in place of primary forest, especially if it were to run the risk of a feud, but there is, in any case, no reason to assume that warfare is a mechanism for attaining optimal population distribution, as suggested by Vayda (Vayda 1968; 1971). On the contrary, warfare, where it did occur was the simple *result* of expanding economic units in collision. From the standpoint of maintaining optimal man/land ratios, the best practice would certainly be to clear virgin forest, or not to expand at all.

We have outlined a very important tendency in the Kachin system whose effects can be critical for the maintenance of *gumsa* hierarchy. If density is increased enough, there will almost certainly be a need to decrease fallows. This, in turn will have severe effects both on the cost of labor input, and on the obtainable yield, and a great deal of strain will be put on any system which requires constant if not increasing surplus. We shall return to this problem in due course.

The very wide distribution of Kachin populations throughout Northern Burma, Yunnan, and Assam is ample evidence of past migration. It seems reasonable to postulate that on various occasions in the past, large numbers of Kachin left their homeland, *hkaku ga*, to seek their fortunes elsewhere. Such emigration to the West, East, and South was probably the result of internal political pressure. The powerful domains of the Triangle area have been able to keep their power by holding down population density. This necessarily implies a periodic expulsion of some portion of the accumulated population.[1]) The present distribution of population densities seems to bear this out. The Kachin who inhabit the area East and Northeast of Bhamo, i.e., those Kachin in Leach's zones B and C, are a good deal more densely populated than the Triangle area, reaching fifteen to twenty to the square mile. This represents a threefold increase in density and has severe consequences. Zones B and C are characterized by a high degree of deforestation and a much less productive technology.

Interestingly enough, this appears to be exactly the opposite of a phenomenon found among the Yanomamö of Venezuela called »social circumscription« in which density increases in the center of an area because outlying districts are already occupied by former emigrants or by other populations (Chagnon 1968:Vol. III, 249). Carneiro goes so far as to use this for a population density theory of social evolution in which overall density stays low but increases rapidly in centrally enclosed areas, leading to increased warfare and, of course, the state (Carneiro 1970).

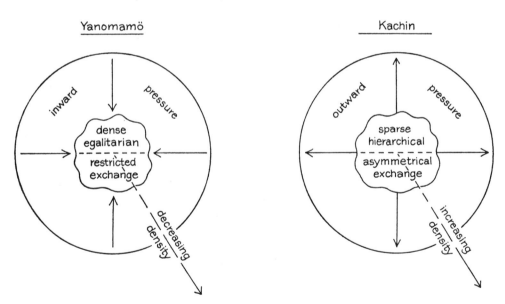

While both the Kachin and Yanomamö have expanding populations, the egalitarian group has no way of expanding territorially while the Kachin are able to do just that. The resulting distributions are, as we can see, exactly

[1]) This is not meant to imply anything in the way of teleology. The mechanisms by which population is distributed do not depend on any such functional assumption. Expansion can be completely accounted for in terms of the internal politics of the Kachin system.

opposite to one another. Peripheral density increases among the Kachin while decreasing among the Yanomamö. Thus, while there is no problem of »social circumscription« for the Kachin, they must continually shed their extra population if the political structure is to be maintained.

While we have discussed at some length the process of transformation of increasing surplus into rank and the inflation of *hpaga* goods, we have still to consider the long term accumulations implied in this process. In a developing *gumsa* hierarchy the combination of increasing rank and inflation of *hpaga* goods will tend to have the following effect:

$$
\left.
\begin{aligned}
1)\ & \frac{d^2 S_2}{dS_1{}^2} > 0 \\[2ex]
2)\ & \frac{dS_1}{dY} > 0
\end{aligned}
\right\}
\longrightarrow \frac{dD}{dt} > 0
$$

S1 – individual lineage economy
S2 – tribute, corvée, brideprice gradient
D – debt

Y – total output

Increasing rank and inflation make increasing demands on the total surplus output of the group. If these demands are greater than the rate of increase in output there will be a rapid accumulation of debts. It is, of course, people at the lower levels of the social hierarchy who are most jeopardized by such a situation. Consequently, a number of lineages and households may find themselves on the border of debt slavery. This, in turn may increase the differentiation at higher levels of the social structure, by adding labor power and surplus to the ruling lineages of the community. The result is further inflation. This plus the accumulation of captured slaves can have important effects on the rank-class structure. According to Leach,

> »The weakness of the *gumsa* system it that the successful chief is tempted to repudiate links of kinship with his followers and to treat them as if they were slaves.« (Leach 1954:203).

In terms of the process we have just outlined, however, bond slaves do not simply result from chiefly whim. Rather, it is likely that the system tends to produce a very large number of households that are completely unable to meet their »obligations« and thus become bond slaves. Among some Chin groups, where this process is extreme, the proportion of slaves reached 85% of the population in some villages (Stevenson 1968:179). It is no wonder then that,

> »From the *gumsa* point of view, the *gumlao* had formerly been their 'slaves'.« (Leach 1954:257).

I suggest here that in the normal course of functioning of *gumsa* society an increasing number of individuals go into debt bondage. This does not necessarily mean that they will be exploited in the strict sense since the larger portion of their surplus which is controlled by the headman or chief is still to be returned in redistributive feasts, or at least this would be a sure way of avoiding a *gumlao* revolt. It must also be remembered that there is a continuum of debt service and that not all such individuals need become actual slaves, i.e., live in their master's house, forfeiting permanent tenure rights on their fields. More important for now is that since increased debt means increased obligations, a very large part of the population will be manipulable by the powerful few.

If left to his own devices, a *gumsa* chief will accumulate slaves, *hpaga*, debt slaves and territory, all as a result of the internal mechanisms of circulation of wealth, women, titles and authority. However, the *gumsa* chief is not left to his own devices.

III. Reproduction of Contradictions and the Contradictions of Reproduction

In this section we will attempt to get at the main contradictions of the *gumsa* system and show how they articulate with one another over time.

Territorial Expansion – Kinship – Political Authority

The contradiction between the territorial growth of a domain and the possibilities of holding it together are fairly obvious.

»Local group segmentation is unfavourable for the development of any large scale stable political state.« (Leach 1954:262).

The problem of size, of course, is similar for any polity with pretentions to some sort of unity. The prime means of centralizing authority in the domain is by the ties of kinship. Either *mayu/dama* or senior/junior or both may be used to cement the rank sytem. But if a distant headman succeeds in accumulating a great number of slaves, wealth, etc., he can break free from the parental domain and form a new one. Fission at the domain level is undoubtedly quite common in the process of expansion. Population growth and village segmentation are local processes within the larger domain, and they have the following implications:

a) Newly founded local segments will be attached to the domain but only by virtue of having budded off from a local parent settlement. Thus, their allegiances will tend to be primarily to the latter.

b) Alliance ties will be stronger between new settlements and their parent villages than with other settlements in the larger domain.

c) If there is a particularly rapid accumulation of population and therefore surplus (potential) in a given local area of a domain, there is a strong possibility for a local headman or junior chief of accumulating a large following.

The next diagram shows the possibilities of domain fission which result from increasing spheres of influence developing at lower levels of the segmentary structure. A chief can hold his domain together only by somehow enforcing the allegiance of his subordinates, a very difficult task in a system based on kinship ties. As a result, the maintenance of a hierarchy must in large measure depend on the ability to preserve economic superiority, that is, the ability to monopolize most of the *hpaga* of the entire domain. This can be effected to some extent by keeping chiefly brideprice very high, by ensuring a steady

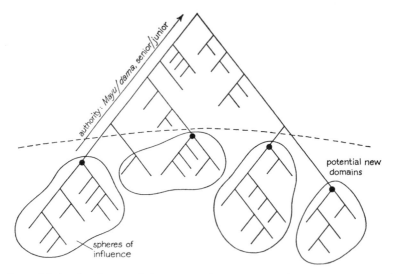

inflow of wealth in the form of slaves, cattle, debts, an finally, by stressing the ritual aspects of his position. In spite of all this, however, the domain probably has an upper size limit after which the predominant form of organization is a rather loosely knit confederacy of domain chiefs. This is the usual case in areas of highest political development.

The process of territorial expansion thus leads to the segmentation of domains, the formation of new political units exactly like the old ones, which work on the same principles and have the same internal contradictions. These are all the direct effect on the *gumsa* structure of demographic growth, where kinship based domains are stretched to certain spatial limits after which fission occurs and the process begins again.

Forces of Production/Relations of Production

We now come to the fundamental intersystemic contradictions of the Kachin system. These are all based on the demand for surplus and the long run possibility of producing it. If we return now to the two processes of expansion outlined in the last section, it can be said that the main incompatibilities are those which take place within and between expansion A and expansion B.

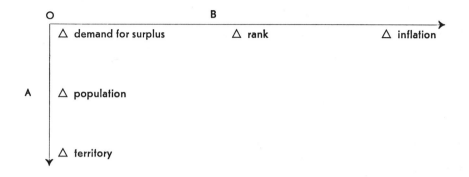

The full elaboration of expansion A yields the following:

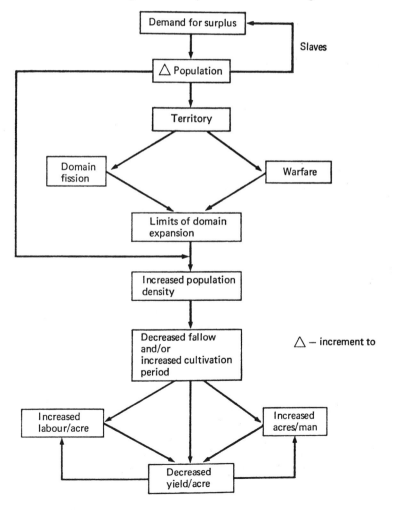

When a domain reaches its capacity, it divides into two or more smaller domains, but the process of surplus accumulation does not simply start all over again from scratch. The kind of fission we discussed several pages ago is related to the ability to maintain ties of rank over large areas. Segmentation at the highest levels of the *gumsa* hierarchy does not bring with it a concomitant devaluation of *hpaga* values. Thus each new domain continues to accumulate in the same manner. A tendency which I think is quite reasonable to expect, then, is that population will increase faster than territory after a certain threshold of »political density« has been reached, i.e., when it becomes more difficult for segments to go out and find unclaimed land. Thus begins the final part of the expansion process.

1) $\dfrac{dS_0}{dt} \geqslant 0 \implies$ 2) $\dfrac{dP}{dt} > 0$

P – population
A – land
S_0 – demand for surplus

but   3) $\dfrac{d^2A}{dP^2} < 0$

4) $\left\{ \begin{array}{l} \dfrac{dP}{dt} > 0 \\[2mm] \dfrac{dA}{dt} < 0 \end{array} \right\} \implies \left\{ \dfrac{dF}{dt} < 0 \right\} \implies \left\{ \begin{array}{l} \dfrac{d^2Y}{dA^2} < 0 \\[2mm] \dfrac{d^2Y}{dL^2} < 0 \end{array} \right\}$

F – fallow
L – labor
A_c – land in cultivation per person per year

5) $\left\{ \begin{array}{l} \dfrac{d^2Y}{dA^2} < 0 \\[2mm] \dfrac{d^2Y}{dL^2} < 0 \\[2mm] \dfrac{dS_0}{dt} \geqslant 0 \end{array} \right\} \implies \left\{ \begin{array}{l} \dfrac{dA_c}{dt} > 0 \\[2mm] \dfrac{d^2L}{dA^2} > 0 \end{array} \right\} \implies \left\{ \dfrac{dL}{dt} > \dfrac{dY}{dt} > 0 \right\}$

A larger population on the same territory means that more land per year must be cleared or that fallows must be shortened. This brings on eventual diminishing yields per acre as well as diminishing yields per unit of labor time. Thus it must lead to a further increase in acres cleared/man/year to make up for the loss in total output/acre. There is, finally, an increase in the total labor input on the land caused by increasing acreage per year and lower yields per unit of labor. In the long run, then, there is a contradiction between the surplus demanded of the system and the ability to produce such a surplus. In order to meet even an unchanging demand, more labor will be required. Even if the demand for surplus can be met, the condition

$$\frac{dS_0}{dt} > \frac{dL}{dt}$$

implies that an increasing portion of the total increasing yield will be absorbed by such demands, or in other words, that a greater percentage of the time worked will be surplus labor time. The above inequations do not necessarily imply that the absolute limits of the system have been reached. The agricultural system might still be very productive in the sense that yield can still be rising faster than consumption. That is, where V = necessary consumption (see graph below) we have,

$$\frac{dY}{dt} > \frac{dV}{dt}$$

which is simply to say that while people are working harder, the yield is quite sufficient to meet the increasing needs as well as surplus demands. This all depends on the productivity of the technology and the degree of environmental degredation that has set in.

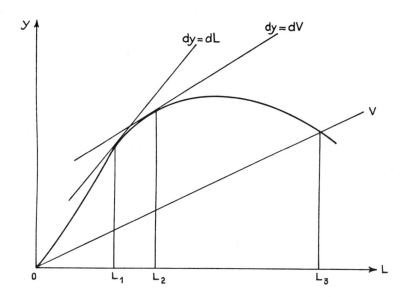

To make this perfectly clear we again have recourse to the production function. We are confronted here with not one but two limits. When labor input
increases to L1 we are at the first limit described above, that is $dY = dL$ or
$dY/dL = 1$. After this point increased input gives decreasing yield per unit.
But it is not until we get to L2 that consumption begins to rise faster than
output. Further it is not until we get to L3 that the system reaches its physical
breaking point. This is extremely important. It implies that the contradiction is
not determined by an environmental crisis, at least not at the stage of environmental evolution to which we are referring. The entire region between L1 and
L2 is an area of political conflict. There is no doubt that the system experiences
real political crises long before L3 is reached. In fact, it is likely that, given the
very strong tendency to dispersed settlement, *gumlao* rebellion occurs very early
in the cycle, probably between L1 and L2.

In order to determine the reasons for this early cut-off of the cycle, we must
now consider the other expansion process (B) and the build up of internal
contradictions at the level of relations of production.

The B expansion taken to its logical conclusion results in the following:

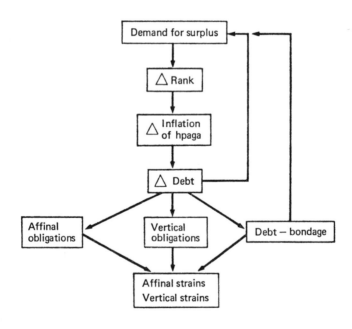

This is a self reinforcing system whereby prestige is converted into rank and
then into obligations, on those of lower rank, at an increasing rate. Increasing
debt has the effect of transforming, however slowly, the lower rank classes
into *mayam* (slave) or semi-*mayam*, families who are hopelessly indebted to
their superiors. This in turn has the immediate effect of an increased accumula-

tion of the community surplus by aristocrats and chiefs. We can divide the effects of increasing debt into three categories. First, with increased rank differentiation, *dama* relatives will owe more of their surplus to their *mayu*. Since most of these obligations turn out in one way or another to be related to food and drink (rice beer) this is a direct strain in the economy of production. Secondly, headmen and chiefs are theoretically entitled to the highest payments with regard not only to marriage, funerals, etc., but also for various infractions of the »law.« Finally in extreme cases, inability to pay accumulated debts will cause families to go into debt bondage. What does all this imply? Most of the changes are only expressed in terms of ritual status. Thus, for example, a chief will pay for the brideprice of his slaves, and he receives any payments that would normally go to them. *Mayam* are worse off only in one major respect. They lose their economic independence which amounts here to the ability to participate in the prestige-rank process. This, in varying degrees, is true of all lineages that begin to become caught in the web of inflation.

A Note of Clarification on »Debt«

With the growing inability to meet inflated prices, lineages do not go into debt in the normal monetary sense. The situation is at once more complicated and more structurally significant. It may have appeared in our discussion as if all the payments to which we refer are set prices which must be paid. In fact, as implied in our model of lineage political economy, all of these exchanges are »gift exchanges« or prestations in the Maussian sense of the word. But an »obligation« to give is a kind of paradox which only makes sense in the context of relative ranking. Thus, as Leach says,

> »In theory, gift obligations are scaled according to class .... In practice the payment depends on the economic standing of the defaulter, not on his class status by birth.« (Leach 1954:148–9).

Debt is not incurred in a straightforward manner. On the contrary it is translated into loss of status.

> »If a man fails to pay what is proper, he loses face and risks a general loss of class status.« (Leach 1954:149).

As such, value is not to be considered an inherent property of the items being transferred in an exchange. This is clear in affinal relations where the,

> »scale of the payment tends to be determined by the class status of the man rather than that of the woman.« (Leach 1954:149).

The implications of this are as follows. While no one can be made to pay a requisite sum, his own rank is always implied in the amount he is willing and able to give. Just as in any system of gift exchange, one's status varies directly with the size of the prestation.

But a *gumsa* system is more than an open competition for status. Rank classes already exist and values tend to become fixed or stratified in such a way that failure to meet payments has a negative effect instead of a non-positive effect. That is, one does not simply miss a chance to gain status, one loses status. This is the particular importance of the notion of debt which is very highly operational in *gumsa* society where careful tabulations are made to keep track of debits and credits.

Debt and the Meaning of Rank Distinctions

»When a Kachin talks about the 'debts' which he owes and which are due to himself, he talks about what an anthropologist means by 'social structure'.« (Leach 1954:141).

This has special importance for the question of ranking among the Kachin. It has long been accepted that exchange and debt are two sides of the same coin. Levi-Strauss' *Structures élémentaires* is founded on this notion developed by Mauss. As we have seen, in a asymmetrical marriage system where women are the valued »object« the debt relationship is one between *mayu* and *dama*. He who receives valued objects has certain obligations toward the giver. The asymmetrical nature of *mayu/dama* is the structural basis for the Kachin notion of debt, and it permeates all aspects and levels of the Kachin social order.

If, as we have indicated, status varies directly with the ability to pay one's debts, then the relation between rank-class and indebtedness is clear.

a) a member of a chiefly line who is unable to pay his debts will become an aristocrat in time.

b) an aristocrat who is unable to pay his debts will become a commoner.

c) a commoner who is unable to pay his debts will become a debt slave.

The loss of rank status and the accumulation of debt are one and the same. The definition of an aristocrat in affinal terms is one who is *dama* or indebted to a chief. A commoner is likewise *dama* to an aristocrat. But where a commoner gets into so much debt, i.e., has more obligations to his affines, whether aristocrat or not, than he is able to meet, he is, so to speak, *hors de combat*, insolvent. The category *mayam* is not a rank-class like the other kin categories. That is, it is not clearly generated by the principles of affinal and segmentary kinship. Although, in terms of debt, the slave is simply one step below the commoners, his economic position is not equivalent to any other rank-class member. Chiefs, aristocrats, and commoners are all similar in one very important respect. No matter how great their indebtedness, they are still able to pay brideprice, tribute, etc., they are economically independent. The *mayam*, however, is characterized by the opposite condition. He cannot acquire wives, pay tribute nor make any other payments on his own. This situation can be dealt with in two ways:

a) If the debt is taken seriously, the *mayam* is liable to lose his independence. He may move into the chief's house, till his fields and become a member of his household.

b) If the condition of debt is very wide-spread it seems reasonable that *mayam* would cause a leveling of certain values like brideprice. They would not move into the chief's house, nor would their debts be taken seriously. Instead, their indebtedness would be translated into a kind of *generalized mayam status.* Their obligations to the chief, in terms of tribute and corvée would be augmented, but they would remain in their own houses and retain their usufruct rights.

In the first alternative, the chief pays the brideprice of the slave's son and receives that of his daughter. He takes care of them in the same way that he would a member of his own »family«. In fact, it is usual for a house *mayam* to join the clan of his master. It is interesting in this respect that marriage between a man and his female slave is considered incestuous. The first alternative, thus, results in an expansion of the household, or chiefly familial work force. The second alternative is more serious. Instead of the chiefly lines taking on their *mayam* as family, they devalue their debts, but at the price of a general loss in rank for all of them. In this way, a kind of *mayam* class is created, a class of »permanent debtors« (Leach 1954:160) who are under much stronger obligations to their superiors. This kind of »slavery« was very common among the Chin and in all probability the Kachin groups of Assam and the Triangle in the nineteenth century. It is significant that a high-born informant of Leach left the commoner category out of his description of rank-class structure.

»All men are either *du baw* (chiefs), *magam amyu* (aristocrats) or *mayam* (slaves).« (Leach 1946:177).

To return now to expansion B, it might, I think be granted that there is a very strong tendency for differential access to rank to develop after a time. Chiefs and some aristocrats accumulate other people's debt payments, in the form of brideprice, indemnities, tribute, corvée and bond slaves. If we add to this the captured slaves from expansion A, it is quite clear that a few chiefly lineages or even just one lineage will become increasingly powerful over time, and that this will be effected for the most part at the expense of other lineages' rank, labor and output.

To get an idea of the contradictions inherent in this process, we return to some of our previous equations.

a) If we start with increasing *hpaga* value we have:

H — *Hpaga* value

S_o — demand for surplus

S_t — total surplus

I — inflation

D — debt

$$\text{1) } \frac{dH}{dt} > 0 \implies \frac{dS_o}{dt} > 0$$

$$\text{2) } \frac{d^2 S_o}{dS_t^2} > 0 \implies \frac{dI}{dt} > 0 \text{ or } \frac{dD}{dt} > 0$$

Thus, if the demand for surplus is greater than the actual increase in surplus forthcoming, there is inflation and increasing debt. Increasing debt means, in a general way, increasing tension between affines and between segmentary senior/junior lines, i.e., increasing possibility of feud. But it is only a contradictory tendency that need not be materialized. That is, it depends on the state of the system as a whole.

b) Within the general inflation, there is a more important conflict between local subordinate and superordinate lines for control of available surplus. As we have pointed out, chiefly lines accumulate labor in the form of corvée and slaves, and product in the form of tribute. To this is added what I called the gradient of affinal exchange which is the rate of flow of bridewealth to the top of the hierarchy. This wealth is accumulated at the expense of the entire community.

$$
\left.
\begin{array}{l}
\text{S1 - horizontal} \\
\text{S2 - vertical} \\
\text{Sc - chiefly accumulation of S} \\
\text{St - total S}
\end{array}
\quad
\begin{array}{l}
\dfrac{d^2 D}{dSt^2} > 0 \\[2em]
\dfrac{d^2 S2}{dS1^2} > 0
\end{array}
\right\}
\Longrightarrow
\dfrac{d^2 Sc}{dSt^2} > 0
$$

Aristocratic competitors lose relative rank and commoners may eventually lose their independence. It seems that such differential accumulation should cause tension among lines competing for wealth and prestige. But it is not a critical situation as we have defined it, or rather as we have not defined it. For we have not indicated whether or not there is a strain on subordinate lineages, in the sense that they cannot meet their vertical and horizontal costs, or that one is met at the expense of the other. Now, in fact, this depends on another very important factor, the productive process itself.

c) The above situation is non-critical when total increasing surplus can be produced without any strain on the workforce. First we must make clear the conditions of appropriation by adding the following to the above set of equations.

$$
\frac{dSt}{dt} > 0
$$

This, when coupled with the other two equations implies that the chief appropriates an *increasing portion of an increasing surplus*. If we specify the relation between surplus and total output we might add that in initial conditions,

$$\frac{d^2 S_t}{dY^2} > 0$$

that is, total surplus increases faster than total output. This establishes the following possibilities of surplus appropriation:

$$\left\{ \begin{array}{c} \dfrac{dY}{dt} > 0 \\[2em] \dfrac{d^2 S}{dY^2} > 0 \end{array} \right\} \left\{ \begin{array}{c} \dfrac{dS_1}{dt} > 0 \\[2em] \dfrac{dS_2}{dt} > 0 \end{array} \right\} \left\{ \begin{array}{c} \dfrac{d^2 S_1}{dL^2} > 0 \\[2em] \dfrac{d^2 S_2}{dL^2} > 0 \end{array} \right\} \left\{ \begin{array}{c} \dfrac{d^2 S_1}{dY^2} > 0 \\[2em] \dfrac{d^2 S_2}{dY^2} > 0 \end{array} \right\}$$

Thus, with expanding real yields, expanding at a rate fast enough to both cover increasing consumption and provide increased surplus, there is still a great deal of maneuverability within the system. The yield on labor is still increasing which means that the surplus output per unit of added labor will be expanding. Surplus is not only a substantial but also a growing part of the total yield. The conditions in which this surplus can cover rising inflation are determined by the following:

$$\boxed{\dfrac{dS}{dt} \geqslant \dfrac{dH}{dt}} \qquad \text{H} - hpaga \text{ values}$$

This condition is not necessarily met, as we said in section (a) – i.e., $dS_0 / dS_t > 0$ – and for a very definite reason. Since surplus is converted into *hpaga* and is differentially allocated from the start, it will tend to increase fastest in higher ranking groups. We then have a situation like the following:

$$\text{Rank:} \begin{bmatrix} A > & B > & C > & D \\ dS > & dS' > & dS'' > & dS''' \\ dH > & dH' > & dH'' > & dH''' \end{bmatrix}$$

Wealthy groups continually make higher demands on lower groups in the form of increased brideprice, etc. In this way lower groups are faced with a continually rising demand for surplus. This is not, as we pointed out, a simple scheme of rising prices, since it is the giver of prestations who determines the price. It is, rather, a *rising demand on the ability to validate or increase one's own status*, and since groups at the top are always able to raise their status faster than lower groups, the overall effect is that *hpaga values will increase faster than surplus.*

There is some question again as to whether this is any more than a super-ficial strain. It all depends not on whether *hpaga* value outdistances real output, but on whether surplus to cover the implied debts can be produ-ced. Thus, for example, a man working to make a good marriage might not have the necessary brideprice to cover the ceremony, but if he has the economic potential of coming up with it eventually, he can easily borrow the necessary wealth items for the occasion and pay them back later. Or, as is often the case, he can pay brideprice over a number of years. It is quite normal that *mayu/dama* transactions continue over several gene-rations, and if there is a constant supply of wives from one to the other, the *dama* line will constantly be in debt, but in debt that it can manage to control. It is, in fact, the common state of affairs that »some debts are always left outstanding« (Leach 1954:153) in order to ensure the »conti-nuity of the relationship« (ibid.).

In the above case, although there is strain in the system it is not critical because inflation serves as an impetus for increased output which can be reali-zed. There are serious problems only when inflation is faster than potential surplus. Thus the limit might be more accurately expressed as:

$$\boxed{\frac{dSp}{dt} > \frac{dH}{dt}} \qquad \begin{array}{l} Sp - \text{potential} \\ \quad\quad \text{surplus} \end{array}$$

Potential surplus indicates the degree to which a production unit is capable of turning out a surplus as opposed to what it may actually produce at any one time. The effects of this limit are most acutely felt in lineages with a labor shortage or in poorer lineages generally. It is the immediate cause of debt bondage.

The question of potential surplus takes us back to the notion of the produc-tion function. Thus far we have revealed the relative indeterminacy of the system (except for the poorest lineages). As long as dS/dt and dS/dY are both increasing, there is ample freedom of manoeuvre for any one lineage since S1 and S2 can both be growing. The problem now is to determine the nature and limits of this growth (see graph next page).

The indeterminacy expressed by our earlier equations can be seen quite clearly on the graph. The condition $dY/dt > 0$ holds for everything up to L3. After that, total yield begins to fall. The more interesting condition $dS/dY > 0$

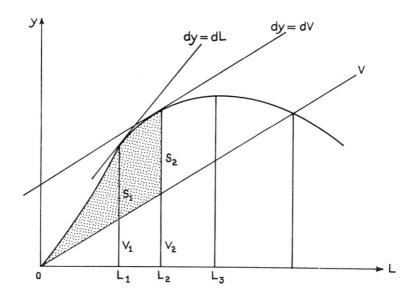

holds true from 0 to L2 which is the point at which dY = dV, after which consumption grows faster than yield and, consequently, surplus diminishes. In terms of these two criteria, the entire shaded area is indeterminate with respect to potential conflict, since up to L2, S1 and S2 can both be increasing and there would seem to be enough to cover all costs.

Things get more interesting, however, if we narrow our conditions in such a way as to focus on the more specific properties of the production function. The single most important property here is expressed by the second derivative of the function and it determines a new inflection point at L1. At this point $d^2Y/dL^2 = 0$, dY = dL, and the space above 0L2 is divided into two significant regions:

$$\text{0L1:} \quad \text{where} \quad \frac{d^2Y}{dL^2} > 0$$

$$\text{L1L2:} \quad \text{where} \quad \frac{d^2Y}{dL^2} < 0$$

In the first region, yield and therefore surplus increase faster than labor input. This is the most productive part of the curve. In the second region, however, things begin to slow down. Output grows more slowly than before and, in a manner of speaking, the cost of producing a surplus is increased since it takes more input to get the same yield.

Thus, within the region in which surplus is still an expanding portion of the total yield, there are two divisions, one in which it increases at an increasing rate, and one in which this rate is decreasing.

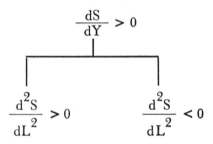

This is implied by the previous conditions with regard to yield, i.e., that what is true of d^2Y/dL^2 is also true of d^2S/dL^2 since the only difference between them is the consumption function $f(V)$ which is a linear function.[1] If we take this one step further we have:

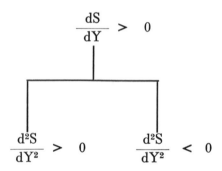

This adds some significant information. It indicates that the rate of increase of surplus with respect to total yield is increasing in the first region and decreasing in the second, which implies that up to point L1, a lineage has a very rapidly growing surplus available for its exchanges, vertical or horizontal. This is the period of maximal expansion of the system and permits the greatest amount of politico-economic freedom at the local lineage level, i.e., at the level of the basic production-exchange unit. Following this, however, the expansion of surplus slows down and is obtained only with increased effort on the part of the producers. This, by itself, does not imply that a crisis is imminent, but if we place these conditions in their socio-economic context we can, I think, point to a severe strain which begins at point L1.

If we begin in the first region in which there is maximal expansion of the system, we can characterize the economic situation by the following:

[1] Any change in Y can be expressed by an equivalent change in S since $S = Y - V$ where V is a constant multiple of L.

$$\left. \begin{array}{l} \dfrac{dY}{dt} > 0 \\[2em] \dfrac{d^2S}{dL^2} > 0 \\[2em] \dfrac{d^2S}{dY^2} > 0 \end{array} \right\} \Longrightarrow \dfrac{d^2H}{dt^2} > 0$$

The reasoning here is simply this. An increasingly available surplus is being transformed into prestige, *hpaga*, rank, etc., at an accelerated rate. This implies a very high rate of inflation, but it is not a strain on the economy as a whole since productivity is rising. Thus, demand for surplus can be met with relative ease, i.e., surplus is at its greatest potential for growth.

What happens now when we begin to move into the second region after total labor is increased to point L1? If the system were entirely controlable we would undoubtedly get the following:

$$\left. \begin{array}{l} \dfrac{dY}{dt} > 0 \\[2em] \dfrac{d^2S}{dL^2} < 0 \\[2em] \dfrac{d^2S}{dY^2} < 0 \end{array} \right\} \Longrightarrow \dfrac{d^2H}{dt^2} < 0$$

But here we have a serious contradiction. Why should the value of *hpaga* goods be adaptable to changing rates of surplus output? For this to be true, it would be necessary that all groups begin to feel the increasing pressure on the productive process. This, however, is not the way things turn out.

a) In the accumulation process, we have seen that those at the very top of the pyramid increase their wealth at a faster rate than those lower down and that they do so by and large to the detriment of the others. That is, while the system is in maximal expansion, the chief is accumulating faster than anyone else. By the time point L1 is reached he is in a very powerful position. He has a large labor force, is owed more debts, has higher prestige and is in a position to give more and bigger feasts than anyone else.

$$\boxed{\dfrac{d^2S_c}{dY^2} > \dfrac{d^2S}{dY^2}}$$

b) If we now examine the cycle, surplus – prestige – rank – inflation . . . . one
thing is unmistakably clear. At any given time, the thing that counts is
absolute surplus, not productivity nor any other measure that might tell us
about long term properties of the system. Thus, a chief who has accumulated large amounts of absolute quantities of tribute, corvée, slaves, etc.,
is in a position to do more than make up for the declining rates, d^2S/dY^2
and d^2S/dL^2, by simply increasing the cultivated acreage to cover the loss
in productivity. Thus, if d^2A/dt^2 is increased to offset a declining d^2S/dt^2 in such a way that,

$$\left.\begin{array}{l} \dfrac{d^2S}{dL^2} < 0 \\[2em] \dfrac{d^2A}{dt^2} > 0 \end{array}\right\} \implies \dfrac{d^2S}{dt^2} \geq 0$$

then the inflationary spiral begun in better conditions has every good
reason to continue in the same way.

c) Another point is that once exchange values have been established at high
levels, it is hard to devalue without some equivalent of a depression.
Hpaga values are the result of a political economy which is dominated by
individual independent lineages. For them to get together to revalue the
cost of women would be structurally difficult if not impossible.

Since the accumulation of *hpaga* is fastest at the top, the obligations placed on
those below will be determined by the chief's own feasting activity. As we said
earlier, all of the lineages in a domain are linked asymmetrically so that the
accumulation of debt at any level is more or less determined by the rate of
accumulation of surplus at the top. Where »A« is a chiefly lineage and »D« a
lower ranking group we have,

$$dD_D = f(dS_A). \quad (\text{D}=\text{debt})$$

In such a situation, the ability of a chief to accumulate labor may offset declining trends in productivity. It is the divergence between local chiefly accumulation and the average productivity per unit of labor input that is the basis of
the contradiction. In other words, the increasing control over the labor of the
community is in direct contradiction to the real rate of potential production so
that the chief appears to maintain a higher rate of surplus production than
would seem possible in the given technical conditions. Hence, accelerating
chiefly accumulation implies accelerating debts for all members of the alliance
network. We can represent this as follows:

$$\left\{ \frac{d^2Sc}{dt^2} > 0 \right\} \Longrightarrow \left\{ \frac{d^2H}{dt^2} > 0 \right\}$$

I take this to be the basic tendency in the situation described above. It is in contradiction with the requirements implied by a decreasing acceleration of surplus production. Thus, instead of the sensible situation where inflation is controlled by potential productivity, we get:

$$\left\{ \begin{array}{l} \dfrac{dY}{dt} > 0 \\[2mm] \dfrac{d^2S}{dL^2} < 0 \\[2mm] \dfrac{d^2S}{dY^2} < 0 \end{array} \right\} \longleftrightarrow \left\{ \frac{d^2H}{dt^2} > 0 \right\}$$

Here we have what I would call a critical strain in the system. Any lineage of non-chiefly status is faced with a rapidly increasing demand for surplus, increasing more rapidly, in fact, than its own ability to produce that surplus. This means that $dSp/dt < dH/dt$, which is in conflict with the continued amicable maintenance of *mayu/dama* and senior/junior ties. It increases the social distance between chiefs and all other ranks, as well as the probability that debts will turn into feuds. It is not by chance that the word for »feud«, *hka*, is the same as the word for »debt«.

»The groups that make feud are, in the long run, the same groups that are *mayu-dama*«. (Leach 1954:151).

It might seem strange to a functionalist that a contradiction like that described above could ever occur. It might seem even stranger that such a contradiction is the *systematic result of the inner workings of a social system*. However, there is nothing particularly astonishing about this result. In a marxist framework it is a normal outcome of any expanding system of this type. The basis for the contradiction is that »exchange value« (*hpaga*) is produced within and in terms of the properties of the social relations of production without regard for the possibilities or limits of its realization.[1] Thus, there are two structures involved in the contradiction, each with its own internally determined laws of

---

[1]) The question of exchange value is rather complicated in these societies. The accumulation of wealth goods of the *hpaga* type can be said to be a measure of exchange value in the sense of embodied labor – insofar as their quantity does indeed reflect a corresponding amount of past labor input necessary to gain the prestige enabling one to accumulate such goods. In other words, the accumulation (in the sense of control) of *hpaga* goods varies directly with the ability to produce a real surplus of given magnitude. Our use here of the words exchange value is in no way equivalent to the capitalist category, since the process of »embodiment« of labor time is structured by a different social form.

functioning. The crucial relation of production is the affinal exchange system. It is asymmetrical and is conducive to maximum political mobility and wealth-prestige differentials, unlike restricted exchange. Thus, there is a possibility, even a tendency, to increase value at a differential rate in such a way as to produce stratified »exchange values«, debts-obligations, lineages, etc. But this process cannot take place without being linked to the process of production (i.e., of »use values«), for otherwise, differential prestige, the starting point of the accumulation could never be attained. That is, without the conversion of surplus into prestige, none of the other developments are possible. Now in fact, the process of production (forces of production) has properties of its own which set limits on population density, maximum yield, etc. But these properties are not taken account of by the social relations of production, or to avoid metaphors, the two structures are such that in the course of the reproduction of the system over time, certain functional incompatibilities appear. The social relations make demands on the technology which cannot be met – leading to social strains at all levels.

There is a contradiction between forces and relations of production beginning at point L1 on the graph. But it can only be manifested at the level of the social relation themselves, simply because this is the only »lived« level. The contradiction is the unconscious result of the incompatibility of two subsystems of the social formation.[1]) However, members of the society do not experience the contradiction directly, only its resultant effect on everyday life. The intersystemic contradiction is transformed into the increased aggravation of intrasystemic contradictions. Thus, the major strains occur, as is well documented by Leach, between affines, and between sibling lineages in the senior/junior relation.

The Hierarchy of Contradictions

We have so far discussed only the first major contradiction of the system. As L increases the production function flattens out and the ability to maintain the political structure is weakened considerably. By the time we get to L2 on the graph, increasing output has slowed to the point where $dY = dV$. After this point the production of surplus (as opposed to its acceleration which is now negative) slows down considerably. This region of the graph is characterized by the following functions:

---

[1]) »Unconscious« is used here in the sense of »non-conscious«, i.e. unintended, so that the properties of behavior are hidden from the actors by the very categories that organize that behavior.

$$\left\{ \begin{array}{l} \dfrac{dY}{dt} > 0 \\[2ex] \dfrac{dS}{dY} < 0 \\[2ex] \left(\dfrac{d^2S}{dY^2} < 0 \right) \end{array} \right\} \implies \dfrac{dS}{dt} < 0$$

While total yield is still increasing, albeit at a negative rate of acceleration, consumption now begins to overtake this growth, $dY/dt < dV/dt$. Thus, not only is the labor cost of output increasing, but *absolute* available surplus is decreasing. If the chiefly line, however, has managed to accumulate a large enough portion of the total labor force, it may not be affected by this trend. In other words, while the majority of the community experiences absolute diminishing surplus, the chief may still maintain an increasing surplus. These are conditions which, as we have seen, have a very high probability of occurrence. While the rate of increase for chiefly lines might be slowing down, what is important is that it not be slowing down as fast as the general rate.

$$\frac{dSc}{dt} > \frac{dS}{dt}$$

That is, chiefly surplus is growing faster than total surplus, or is decreasing at a slower rate. If we add to this a second condition, that chiefly surplus is growing faster than the general rate of consumption, we have

$$\frac{dSc}{dt} > \frac{dV}{dt}$$

This is perfectly reasonable since, as we have said, the chief can be making up for lost productivity with increased acreage worked by an increasing number of slaves. This second inequation implies,

$$\frac{dSc}{dt} > \frac{dY}{dt}$$

But this implies further that,

$$\frac{dSc}{dt} > 0$$

That is, the chief's surplus is not merely maintaining itself at a higher rate than that of the community. It is still increasing. If we put this all together the picture becomes quite clear.

$$\frac{dSc}{dt} > \frac{dY}{dt} > \frac{dV}{dt} > 0 > \frac{dS}{dt}$$

This is an unbearable political situation. While before, the chief was accumulating an *increasing portion of an increasing surplus, he is now accumulating an increasing portion of a decreasing surplus.* We are speaking now of absolute surplus, absolute wealth which is translated into prestige, rank, etc.

In this region of the graph, lineages will be faced with the growing impossibility of meeting their debt payments. The conflict between affines and between different lines in the segmentary hierarchy is now of a much more serious nature. It is no longer a struggle for appropriation of an increasing surplus, but struggle over a diminishing surplus. There is now an absolute contradiction plainly manifested, between rising (*hpaga*) value and a real decreasing ability to cover it with real output.[1]) Since debt varies inversely with rank, and since debts are increasing faster than ability to pay them off, large numbers of lines are either going to lose relative rank or go into debt bondage which is the same thing expressed at different levels of the hierarchy.

The next major inflection point occurs at L3, where $dY/dL = 0$, i.e., where the marginal yield shrinks to zero. After this point, absolute yield decreases at an increasing rate. The surplus portion of this yield is decreasing even faster than it did before. This is because, while consumption is increasing at the same constant rate, total yield is decreasing which has the effect that surplus, $Y - V$, decreases faster than the total yield. We have then:

$$\left\{ \begin{array}{l} \dfrac{dY}{dt} < 0 \\[2ex] \dfrac{d^2S}{dY^2} < 0 \\[2ex] \dfrac{dS}{dY} < 0 \end{array} \right\}$$

The entire economy is in decline and a new conflict begins to emerge between the local lineage as a reproductive (i.e., consumption) unit and the demands of the larger social structure. This is Sahlins' household level of produc-

[1]) See footnote on page 189.

tion (DMP) at which the whole basis of the exchange process is threatened. In its extreme form, it can dissolve the entire social structure, leaving nothing but the minimal lineage unit.

Finally, when we get to L4, we reach the physical breaking point of the system after which exchange becomes a virtual impossibility insofar as it depends on the existence of surplus. Either it devolves into a tokenism or the entire society collapses, which is more likely, given the intersystemic relation between the exchange structure and the production process. At point L4 we have the following conditions:

$$\left\{ \begin{array}{l} \dfrac{dY}{dt} < 0 \\[2ex] \dfrac{d^2S}{dY^2} < 0 \\[2ex] Y - V = S = 0 \end{array} \right\}$$

This implies that any further increase in the labor force will provoke a rupture in the material sense of not having enough goods to go around. That is, in the region beyond L4 we have $dY/dV < 0$, or in other words, $V > Y$, which is equivalent to starvation on an increasing scale.

The Hierarchy of Constraints

What we have just described is, in effect, an ordered system of barriers or limits. Every time a limit is passed, the contradictions at the social level are more aggravated. Thus, we can represent the contradictions between forces and relations of production in terms of a hierarchy of constraints in which, with each limit a new constraint is added to the older ones. As we move from 0 to L4 on the production function we do not simply progress from one conflict to another. On the contrary, the effect is one of accumulating contradictions which render the maintenance of the social system increasingly difficult in an increasing number of ways.

The graph and hierarchy on the following page summarize the development of contradictions between forces and relations of production. It is highly doubtful that the system could ever approach zones III and IV, and I have tried to show that in fact, the contradictions that begin in region II and continue into III are quite sufficient for a *gumlao* rebellion. Following is a brief description of the kinds of strains and breakdowns that might be characteristic of each region of the graph.

Region I: This is the sector of maximal expansion where surplus is forthcoming at an increasing rate. This implies both the possibility of maintaining a strong hierarchy for the most part as well as the possibility of individual

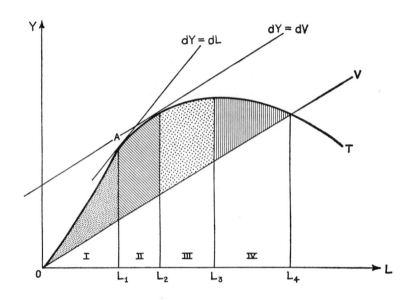

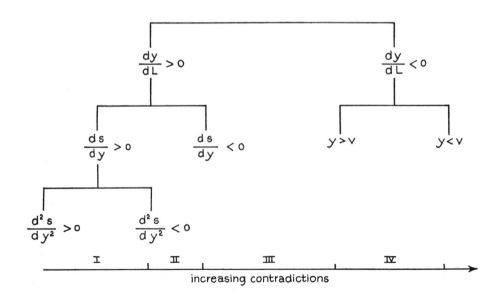

accumulation of wealth. The kinds of strains that emerge here are thus related to the expansion process itself and not to inter-systemic contradictions.

a) As the domain increases in size, outlying groups may tend to become new centers of accumulation and power. Thus, segments that are not well integrated by ties of tribute, debt and ritual will tend to break off and form new domains.

b) Within any existent domain, accumulation of wealth and prestige at some lower level in the hierarchy can always lead to rupture where a new potential chief is in a position to challenge the paramount.

In both of these cases, the conflicts occur as part of the expansion of population, surplus, rank, etc. Fission occurs at the highest levels of ranked segmentation. This is not the same as a *gumlao* breakdown, but takes place with reference to the same affinal and segmentary structure. Fission becomes more difficult however, as time wears on and accumulation becomes increasingly centralized.

Region II: Here there is a major change. The cost of surplus begins to increase. Output begins to decelerate while inflation continues to be rampant. Debt increases, and, at lower levels, begins to convert commoners into *mayam*. The high demand for surplus turns into a conflict over increasing available output. Strains build up at two levels. Among aristocrats and chiefs there is a struggle for the maintenance of prestige by the former in face of the increasing dominance of the latter. At lower levels there is a strain on producers to meet the rising costs of bride wealth, debts, etc. The potential for *gumlao* revolt is high in this region and increases as we move toward L3. Due to the hierarchy of *mayu/dama* relations, revolts are most likely to be led by members of the aristocracy who have been excluded from the accumulation process of their senior lineage kin. But the system is indeterminate at this stage because there is enough potential surplus to meet the growing costs (vertical and horizontal).

$$\frac{dS}{dY} > 0 \implies \left\{ \frac{dS1}{dY} > 0 \quad \text{and} \quad \frac{dS2}{dY} > 0 \right\}$$

Region III: Now the strains become much more severe. Since absolute surplus is now decreasing and demand is still rising, subordinate lineages find themselves in a position where an increasing portion of their now decreasing surplus yield is going to their superiors. Not only has production become a more costly activity in terms of labor input, but less and less of that output is available for individual use. We are beyond the indeterminacy described for region II where S1 and S2 can both be expanding simultaneously. Our situation is now more of a real conflict.

$$\frac{dSt}{dY} < 0 \implies \left\{ \begin{array}{l} \dfrac{dS1}{dY} > 0 \\[2mm] \dfrac{dS2}{dY} < 0 \end{array} \right\} \quad or \quad \left\{ \begin{array}{l} \dfrac{dS1}{dY} < 0 \\[2mm] \dfrac{dS2}{dY} > 0 \end{array} \right\} \quad or \quad \left\{ \begin{array}{l} \dfrac{dS1}{dY} < 0 \\[2mm] \dfrac{dS2}{dY} < 0 \end{array} \right\}$$

Here, for the first time, there is a real competition between vertical and horizontal exchange systems for a dwindling quantity of surplus. For the local lineages the process has become one of relative exploitation since more and more of their labor time is being used to produce an output which is appropriated by others. Structurally, this is not necessarily a question of class exploitation since most of the surplus is redistributed, but there is no doubt that classes are in the process of being formed, especially at the extremities, chiefs and *mayam*. I would venture to say that the occurrence of full scale *gumlao* rebellions is almost inevitable within this region of the graph. Certainly their probability is extremely high and it is not absolutely necessary that it be an aristocrat that is behind it all. The rebellion may indeed start with a discontented headman, but once started, it becomes generalized to all levels of the system.

Region IV: In this region we are in many ways, »over the hill«. The system is in decline with respect to both surplus and total yield. Increasing demands cannot be met at all, in any of the exchange networks. In fact, in order for the system to work at all, there has to be a constant devaluation of *hpaga* goods following decreasing yield. Further, by this time, it has certainly become obvious that the environment is in a state of rapid depletion. It seems unlikely that a *gumsa* system could be maintained at all in these circumstances, since the whole accumulation process is predicated on the existence of an expanding total output. As we can see, however, it is more than likely that the system will collapse before it gets to this point.

Gumlao Revolts

The *gumlao* revolt as we have described it can best be seen as an extreme form of fission or breakdown in the segmentary and affinal system of ranking. Depending on internal strains, rupture can occur at any of the hierarchical levels, but a true *gumlao* revolt is one which leaves no ranking in its path.

According to the preceding section, *gumlao* revolts do not, in all probability, occur when the economy is on the decline, but rather when the contradiction between expanding »exchange value« and real output places increasing strains on the affinal and lineal network that holds the system together. This is an interesting parallel with a typical business cycle in capitalist society; rapid periods of credit expansion followed by crises and then devaluation. This kind of cycle will apply to any social system where:

1) The exchange structure is a dominant relation of production (i.e., asymmetrical exchange for the Kachin).
2) Where the exchange system has inflationary tendencies.[1])
3) Where the relative autonomy of the exchange system from the productive process on which it rests makes it possible for exchange value to increase faster than use value (i.e., real output).

The preceding properties are similar for both capitalist and Kachin societies as well as for many other systems with dominant exchange sectors. In the Kachin system, however, the entire political-economic structure collapses with each cycle, unlike capitalism. This is quite simply because rank and position are entirely determined by the exchange process itself whereas in class systems, social position is determined by exterior means, i.e., property, previously accumulated capital. The typical capitalist recession is a relatively superficial phenomenon in that it leaves a large part of the accumulated exchange values untouched as well as the basic property relations which are at the foundation of the system. The Kachin economy is such that rank is determined by »generosity«, by accumulation *and* negative accumulation. Thus it stands to reason that an economic cycle will also be a social cycle. In class societies, however, position is determined *only by accumulation*, so that accumulated and controlled property is in the last analysis outside the cycle.[2])

This comparison should not be taken as a rapprochement in any way. There is a world of difference between a system in which the goal of accumulation is prestige and one in which it is the appropriation (permanent) of real wealth.

A true *gumlao* revolt, one that flattens out the society, is basically an act which abolishes all hereditary status. We have seen that *gumlao* revolts occur as the result of accumulated affinal and segmentary strains in the ranking system. These develop at all levels of the society, but there is a tendency for revolts to be led by headmen or petty aristocrats. This is primarily because, as long as the hierarchy still exists, embittered headmen will be the logical focal point for discontented lineages to gather around. The *gumlao* revolt of the 1850's was led by a very minor lineage head Maran Khawle, and a commoner, Labu Shawn.

The Dumsa and the Mythology of Revolt

It is most interesting that in Kachin mythology, *gumlao* revolts are always linked to the *N'Dup-Dumsa*, »blacksmith-priest« lineage, and are led by a priest. The status of blacksmiths is not clear historically, but they are today found

---

[1]) Inflation among the Kachin occurs as increased demands in the form of debts. Unlike the situation in capitalism, this is not the result of the accumulation of money capital, i.e. fictitious value that must be converted into real production, but the result of the asymmetrical distribution of labor in the hierarchy. *Hpaga* are, in the Ricardian sense, merely a means of circulation whose value is no more than the prestige (resulting from real production) which they symbolize.
[2]) For a full discussion of the question of value see introduction.

among virtually all the tribes and they never seem to have any special social rank. Priests, however, and especially the *dumsa*, are a different story. The position of priest is non-hereditary though it can be filled by an aristocrat. In spite of its non-hereditary nature, however, it is a potentially powerful position, and priests often have a great deal of personal authority. This is based on their special powers of communication with the higher *nats*. While the chief is descended from very important spirits, only the *dumsa* can communicate with them, and if the chief is an intermediary between the community and the celestial powers, he cannot be effective without a second intermediary, the *dumsa*. Thus, ritually at least, the priest is more important than the chief. He is necessary to communicate with *nats*, but at the same time he is excluded from the lineage to whom they »belong.« According to Leach, the importance of the *dumsa* as a mythological leader of the revolt is related to the fact that the position is most often filled by an individual »whom the rule of ultimogeniture somewhat defrauds.« (Leach 1954:263). This may be true, but is not indicated in the available data. In any case it is not absolutely necessary that the *dumsa* be an aristocrat. Another possible explanation lies in the very structural nature of the position. The *dumsa* has considerable power, potentially equal to if not greater than that of the chief, but this power is maintained *only* by means of his ritual function. Secondly, his position is not hereditary. Thus, structurally he represents the inverse of the chief; his authority is the direct result of his control over the supernatural. For the chief, on the other hand, control of the supernatural is the expression of authority achieved in the politico-economic sphere. As such, the priest represents a structural threat (and in this way mythological – since it need never be materialized) to the very foundations of power. The *dumsa* is outside of the *gumsa* hierarchy and in a sense alongside of it. He represents a different kind of authority, not based on the »rules of the game.«

In this respect, it is important to note that the myth of the priest-led rebellion is associated with the Kachin community of the Hukawng valley, a community which, in fact, was based on irrigated rice and approached a Shan state very closely. If this be the case, then we must also point out that priest (or monk) led rebellions were a very common phenomenon in the Shan states of the past. (Scott and Hardiman 1900: Pt. I, Vol. II: Chap. 10). The Shan *pongyi*'s place was structurally analogous to that of the Kachin *dumsa*. As the main ritual authority, he served to ratify, by his services, the ritual connections of the chief, yet at the same time, he represented a major threat to chiefly or princely authority.

»Thus, the *pongyi* was a power in the government of the country, a power constituted and fostered so as to place a salutary check on the tyranny and oppression of officials on the one hand, and to reconcile the people to the existing form of government on the other.« (Scott and Hardiman 1900: Pt. I, Vol. II:2).

The place of the priest in the social order explains his place in mythology,

but the fact that this particular myth is from an area where priests were probably much stronger (in Shan states, the priesthood is a highly developed institution with its own internal order and hierarchy of officials), in an area where
a Kachin *gumsa* organization, through technological transformation, was able
to evolve in the direction of a petty state, indicates a particular set of conditions
which may not apply to the same degree for hill Kachin.

Be all this as it may, however, it makes absolutely no difference who leads a
gumlao rebellion as long as it has the same consequences. In none of the known
cases of *gumlao* uprisings were priests the leaders.

I have added the previous discussion of the priests in order to dispel what
appears to me to be an erroneous interpretation on the part of Leach. His
argument supposes that a *gumlao* priest-leader is merely an enterprising aristocrat who has been somehow excluded from the inheritance of his chiefly
brother.

> »In brief, the mythical archetype of the *gumlao* leader is that of a minor
> aristocrat of ambition and ability who might himself have been a chief if
> the accident of birth order had not dictated otherwise.« (Leach 1954:263).

While I have stated my agreement that aristocrats or minor headmen are
often *gumlao* leaders, a priest is not necessarily an aristocrat, and, as we have
shown, there are genuinely structural reasons for his place in the mythology
which do not depend on his being an over-ambitious elder brother. Secondly,
and this is a more serious objection, Leach appears to imply that *gumlao*
revolts are the work of ambitious aristocrats. But to lead such a revolt would
indeed be a foolish undertaking for any power-hungry individual. After all,
how does one compete for positions of authority which no longer exist? The
explanation offered here places emphasis on the intersystemic contradictions
between forces and relations of production and the consequent aggravation of
internal contradictions in the latter (kinship/rank) in such a way as to bring
down the entire political structure. I do not deny that ambition plays a role in
the system but only that it is an independent variable. If there are economic
strains in the society, they are bound to be strongest where the kinship ties are
closest. We have seen that the greatest accumulation takes place at the top of
the pyramid and that it goes on in spite of everyone else's increasing debt.
There is no doubt that this imposes an especially great burden on lower ranking lineages, but they are more distant in the kinship structure than are aristocrats. The potential for rupture is greatest, i.e., requires the least economic
pressure, between aristocrats who are losing rank and their chiefly relatives.
Aristocrats feel the contradiction rank/kinship most acutely because they have
everything to lose if rank succeeds in replacing kin ties. Thus, they are more
than qualified to lead a *gumlao* revolt, or at least to start the ball rolling. But
it is doubtful that they would be willing to have things go as egalitarian as
they might where the revolt is successful.

Summary

This chapter presents the central argument of this book. We have examined the internally determined development of the major structural levels of Kachin *gumsa* systems and attempted to show how they articulate with one another over time. It has been shown that the social relations of production generate an economic flow whose properties are in contradiction with the output potential of the techno-environment. We have shown how this contradiction, expressed in the growing divergence between accelerating »exchange value« and decelerating real output causes unbearable strains in the very relations of production which originally gave rise to the growth and development of the system. We will see, shortly, how both evolution and devolution take on precise meanings in terms of this discussion.

Appendix: Some New Material On Kachin Expansion.

Since completing this book, Maran La Raw (personal communication) has graciously offered me some new material on the nature of Kachin political expansion that tends to confirm, I think, some of the hypotheses suggested in this chapter.

Chief's sons who do not succeed to their father's office must, if they are to become chiefs in their own right, move out of the local domain and secure new land. In other words, status maintenance depends upon territorial expansion. Apart from this, however, there are a number of things which must be done in order to become a *gumchying* chief associated to a paramount. This applies to sons who move out as well as to those aspirants from adjacent areas who wish to become domain chiefs.

1. The contender must be able to distinguish himself in his local group.
2. He must »step down«, *gum yu,* renounce his chiefly status, temporarily becoming a commoner.
3. He must be sponsored by an already established *gumchying* chief. This usually depends on his paying an enormous brideprice, greater than any paid in »living memory«. This, of course, is an extremely inflationary sort of activity.
4. He thus becomes a *gum yu du,* a sponsored future chief with no ritual position.
5. This sponsorship should last about seven years during which time the aspirant must give many feasts and build up his prestige.
6. At the end of this period the candidate gives a great *manao* feast to which the sponsor is invited. At this time he is granted his full status as a *gumchying* chief.

This process implies both territorial expansion and a high rate of inflation, both of which are indicated in the model we have proposed. It also partially reveals the areas of contradiction in the expansion process itself. A *gumyu* pretender to chiefship can only maintain himself in such a position so long as he has the resource base to continue feasting throughout the period of his candidature. If domains expand into areas where such resources are not as easily obtainable, there are bound to be conflicts. In such cases a situation where there is high ratio of *gumyu* to *gumchying* chiefs can easily become a *gumlao* situation. There is reason to believe that this may have been the case in the Duleng area of the northern Kachin Hills.

The situation in the Eastern Hills (Sinlum, Sadon) may have been somewhat different. Here, access to trade routes as an important direct source of wealth may in itself have disturbed the traditional patterns insofar as it need not have been based on large domains and the control over agricultural labor. I would argue, however, that the same kind of phenomenon might have occurred here as that described above. There were probably a great number of *gumyu* chiefs in the area (due to the availability of trade) who with the major dislocations of trade flows in the nineteenth century would have lost the resource basis of their claims to high status. The result would have been *gumlao* rebellion, or, at least, a *gumrawng* situation in which chiefly positions could not be definitively established. It is noteworthy that chiefs in this area associated themselves with the great chiefly lineages of the Triangle.

CHAPTER VI

The Short Cycle and the Long Cycle

In the preceding chapter we analyzed the functioning of the *gumsa* system in optimal conditions of production. We now turn to a longer term discussion in which the properties of the production function are allowed to vary over time. The crucial distinction to be considered is whether or not the Kachin economy reproduces itself in exactly the same way in the course of its *gumlao/gumsa* cycles. In effect, we will see how social reproduction, in conditions of increasing population density and environmental degradation, leads to transformations at all levels as well as to new »adaptations« to exterior resources where available. The combination of diminishing internal production possibilities and external exploitable resources gives rise to a set of variants which corresponds to the actual distribution of Kachin systems throughout the hills region.

Since we are dealing with a great many variables which may be difficult to keep in order, I will begin here with a brief summary of some of the main intra- and inter-systemic contradictions of the Kachin system.

Gumlao: The main intrasystemic contradiction in Kachin relations of production is the wife-giver/wife-taker relationship, which, as pointed out by Levi-Strauss, is based on equality but permits and even fosters the development of inequality.

When this is linked to the political economy of the local lineage and the production-distribution-feast system the contradiction of the exchange structure is materialized in the transformation (or rather modification) of the affinal relation into a ranked *mayu/dama* relation. The fact that women are not exchanged against women means that differential values can be established. If, in the other cycle of exchange by feasting, wealth is transformed into prestige and prestige into rank by means of differential brideprice, the egalitarian *gumlao* system is up-ended and becomes *gumsa*.

The »determination in the last instance« remains the conditions of production, i.e., the possibility of procuring a surplus without which the above transformation cannot occur. The best conditions for this are determined by region I of the production function (Leach 1954:28).

Gumsa: Here the intrasystemic contradiction is between the affinal (and later, segmentary) kinship relations and the rank differences that have become established. More generally, there is a contradiction between what I have called the vertical and horizontal aspects of the kinship network. To be as concise as possible I will divide the contradiction vertical/horizontal into two parts, both of which are manifested on the exchange level as a conflict over lineage surplus.

a) vertical/horizontal → affinal gradient of exchange.
The affinal gradient of exchange measures the rate at which horizontal exchanges become verticalized, i.e., the rate of flow of brideprice and affinal goods in the direction of the chief. In terms of competition for surplus, that which appears to be in category S1 is really in category S2. It tells us how much surplus can be gotten hold of by the chiefly lineage in the affinal exchange system.

b) vertical/horizontal → conical/affinal – tribute/alliance.
This distinction is a more clear cut opposition between two qualitatively different kinds of exchange systems. The vertical here stands for the conical-segmentary structure and its implications for the flow of surplus. It is linked to an explicit redistributive system in which control is exercised by means of monopolization of the spirit world in a religion based on production and prosperity. The chief, at the summit of this pyramid amasses tribute and corvée (which is transformed into surplus product) which is in turn used to propitiate the gods, as the source of large scale redistribution. It also appears to be used for entertaining guests – in a very big way – possibly a form of inter-domain rank competition. This is certainly the case at marriages when the *local community often contributes to its chief's brideprice* (Scott and Hardiman 1900: Pt. I, Vol. I:415). The question here is how much of the collected surplus (S2) is returned and how much is used for other purposes. There is good reason to believe that the redistributive relation is *not* entirely reciprocal.

1. This latter should be singled out as a contradiction within the redistributive system proper and not one between the two exchange structures. On our earlier graph (p. 135), the potential contradiction of the redistributive relation was represented in the ratio S3/S2, the degree of reciprocity in the inflow-outflow of goods. I have suggested that S3 < S2 although this is not necessarily a severe inequality. On closer examination of the material, however, there is a clear exploitation by the chief, at least of a temporary nature, with respect to corvée. It appears that the chief has his large field worked by the whole community. Thus, even if the entire output over and above chiefly consumption is returned to the community, it is still the case that the chief is by and large supported by the work of others (i.e., that he does little or no work on the land required to support his own family). Secondly, in terms of the accumulation of *hpaga* values, the chief gets the *entire* benefit of the labor of others.

Beyond this contradiction, S3/S2, there is one between the vertical exchange process as a whole and the affinal process, i.e., between S2 and S1. This is manifested as a conflict over the allocation of surplus, between the demands of tribute and corvée and the demands of the local lineage alliance network (which, due to the gradient of exchange, may itself be more vertical than appears to the lineage).

There are two social structural contradictions which correspond to the contradictions in the economy outlined above. The first is between the ties of kinship and alliance with their implied reciprocity and the growth of segmentary conical ranking. The second is between the tendency for the development of a class structure in which all surplus is absorbed in tribute and corvée and the egalitarian tendency implied by the continued independence of the local lineage as a production and exchange unit.

These internal contradictions are linked to the process of production in the form of an intersystemic relation between the increase in *hpaga* values and the increase in real surplus needed to keep up the circulation of exchange values. The limits of the system are clearly determined by the production function. Likewise, the intensity with which the contradictions within the relations of production manifest themselves depends on one's position on the production curve. The system works best when surplus is increasing rapidly, but as we move into regions II and III of our graph, the conditions of reproduction of the same political structure are severely jeopardized. A *gumlao* rebellion brings the process around full circle, reproducing an egalitarian form with all the same internal contradictions that tend, again, to cause an evolution in the *gumsa* direction.

Secondary Contradiction: Slaves (mayam)

Gumsa society does not begin with the institution of *mayam*, nor is it based on the exploitation of slaves. On the contrary, the category *mayam* is generated by the working of the *gumsa* system itself. This is what is meant by the term »secondary.« Slaves are gotten in two ways:

1) The high demand for surplus and thus for labor puts a very high value on captured individuals who can be put to work for men in authority.
2) The problem of accumulating debts and the inability to produce the surplus necessary to meet them, drags many commoner lines into a state of permanent indebtedness in which they are so heavily obligated to their headman or chief that they lose their free status.

Mayam can either be interns (*tinung mayam*) or externs (*ngong mayam*).

1) *Tinung mayam* are household slaves. They have no rights to land. They are, in most ways, members of their master's lineage except that their status remains very low. That they are included in the local lineage is evidenced by the fact that they are able to sacrifice to the lesser *nats* of their master.
2) *Ngong mayam* are slaves who have their own separate houses, cultivate their own fields and »when living in a *mayam* village share in the ownership of communal land.« (Leach 1954:299). They are heavily bound to

their master by payments of dues such as »every alternate calf born, the first bunch of plantains of each tree half the marriage price and so much labor, etc.« (Leach 1954:299). Briefly *ngong mayam are that part of the community which has come under the domination of the vertical relations of production.* That is, most of their surplus would seem to be absorbed in the tribute-corvée system.

In many ways, *mayam* can be conceived to be the property of their masters although the degree to which this holds for *ngong mayam* is not clear. They are transferrable and appear to be a common item in the brideprice of chiefs. In other respects, however, they are similar to lower ranking commoners.

Slavery represents a very ambiguous social category for the Kachin, and it is implicated in two contradictory processes or tendencies. On the one hand, the slave is non-kin, he »belongs« to his owner, and to the extent that the system is verticalized, he represents the germinal form of a truly exploited class, i.e., where one group is charged with reproducing both itself and another group. If a large portion of the *mayam* are debt slaves, this represents a serious contra-diction since former kin are being turned into non-relatives and exploited as if they were outside the community. The tendency for an exploited *mayam* class to be formed seems to have materialized in some areas, notably where the shift was made to irrigated agriculture. It may also have developed on a minor scale in the North Triangle. Another equally powerful tendency is to transform slaves into kin. It is common for house slaves to become adopted into their master's clan and it appears that in the space of several generations they be-come commoners. This is certainly true of captured slaves and in this sense they are merely an added labor input for the community that temporarily satisfies the demand for increased surplus.

These two opposed tendencies do not operate at the same point in the evo-lution of the system. Slaves become kin in the period of rapid expansion, since there is a high probability of being able to procure the surplus necessary to pay for their freedom. As the production function becomes more inflected, how-ever, the opposite tendency, kin to slaves, is the stronger and develops at an increasing rate. But this latter tendency is never fulfilled, not, at least, in an economy based on swidden cultivation, because *gumlao* rebellion will have usually occurred before that time.

The Short Cycle: Gumsa/Gumlao

There are two possible interpretations of the production function we have been using. One is based on the local time/space conditions of expansion and the other is a long term accounting of the relation between yield and labor input on an indefinitely large tract of land into which the population slowly expands.

In any one *gumlao/gumsa* cycle, the production function must take into account certain constraints which do not exist for the long term interpretation. Diminishing returns and eventual decline in output are not simply the effect of a necessary shortening of the fallow period, but a complex of interrelated factors. The outside limit of domain expansion, as will be recalled, is set by political considerations and not by economic contradictions at the level of the production process. Thus the *gumsa* domain is a relatively enclosed political territory and consequently, an artificial limitation on the expansion process. Further, the centralization of authority in the chiefdom brings with it the accumulation of a large number of slaves and dependents in the community. The growth and continued maintenance of his prestige depend on his *control over a large local population, i.e., a denser population.* Thirdly, as the system expands a greater strain is being put on each individual in the form of increasing demand for surplus. People begin to work harder. Now, in an extensive system of agriculture, when one begins to cultivate an increasing number of acres, the work process must of necessity become less efficient.

All three of the above constraints imposed on any *gumsa* community tend to cause what I have called a short cycle. That is, where the inflection of the production function is due not to an inherent property of the techno-environment, but to local-historical constraints. The long cycle simply represents the technological production function without taking any of these short term effects into account.

We can represent the determinants of the short cycle in the following way:

A_t – total land
A – total land available, i.e., domain land
P – population
L – labor input
S_o – demand for surplus
L_o – demand for labor
L_i – labor input per person

1) $A_t > A \cong$ constant, i.e., $\dfrac{dA}{dt} \longrightarrow 0$

2) $\dfrac{dP}{dt} > 0 \implies \dfrac{dP}{dA} > 1 \implies \dfrac{dL}{dA} > 1$

3) $\left.\begin{array}{l} \dfrac{dS_o}{dL} > 0 \\[2mm] \dfrac{dL_o}{dP} > 0 \end{array}\right\} \implies \dfrac{dL_i}{dA} > 0$

Thus we have:
1) A tendency for territorial expansion of the domain to slow down.
2) A rising demand for surplus and thus for labor in an area that has ceased to grow.
3) A demand, especially by chiefs, for a large concentration of labor under direct control (e.g., slaves) leading to a local increase in population density.
4) A demand for surplus rising faster than the growth of population leading to increased input of labor per person in an extensive cultivation system resulting in declining efficiency and increase in the labor cost of surplus.
The above are basically non-technological conditions which greatly effect

the shape of the production function, especially with regard to the major in-flection points. Diminishing returns will set in earlier and the system will be unworkable in the economic sense long before it is unworkable in the tech-nological sence.

Gumsa/Gumlao: Reproduction of the Short Cycle

As we have seen, even within the short cycle production function, the *gumlao* rebellion does not wait for real diminishing returns to set in. There are other social contradictions which fire the political cycle while the absolute yield of the economy is still on the upswing. In other words the *gumsa* system will not normally reach the point of maximum output. Its internal contradictions bring it down before this is attained.

A question which has not been discusssed but which is of utmost importance is whether or not the *gumsa/gumlao* cycle reproduces itself in unchanging conditions. That is, after a *gumlao* revolt, do the newly formed egalitarian communities find themselves in the same »environment« as the previous *gumlao* society? The answer to this question depends on two factors:

1) state of the techno-environment
2) population density

The state of the techno-environment is determined, for the most part, by the previous intensity of land use, the length of cultivation and the length of fal-low, factors which are themselves directly linked to population density. The latter, then, is the crucial determinant of the state of the environment after any one cycle. If population has increased, the new *gumsa* development begins in slightly different circumstances. If there have been a number of *gumsa/gumlao* cycles with increasing intensity and population, the shape of the production function will be modified accordingly. If there has been a temporary increase in intensity leading to temporary loss of forest cover, it is possible for the envi-ronment to be regenerated if a longer fallow is re-established, i.e., if popu-lation density is reduced.

It appears that the Kachin of the Triangle area have been able to maintain their population density quite low by extensive out-migration.

This may take place in the framework of *gumsa* organization, but it is probably more difficult since there is a heavy claim on labor and a tendency for population density to increase within the domain. We have seen how, among the egalitarian Yanomamö, the effect of increased population density is caused by the existence of already occupied peripheral land, a process referred to by Chagnon as »social circumscription.« Among the hierarchical Kachin there is an equivalent effect produced by an opposite cause which could be called »political circumscription,« which is the attempt to hold and increase population within a fixed area by a central authority. This is a wide-spread phenomenon among state societies referred to by Lattimore as »centri-petalism,« (Lattimore 1962a: Chap. 15; 1962b) but which is structurally simi-lar in any centralized political form. It has been suggested, for example, that the great wall of China was not simply a device to keep out the »barbarians« but to »hold frontier populations within the Chinese orbit.« (Lattimore 1962: 480). It would, however, be something of an overstatement to stress this centripetal tendency in *gumsa* society, at least with regard to the highest levels of the rank system. I am referring here to the mutual repulsion of elder and younger siblings. It is probable that some long-distance migrations of aristocrats and their following have been caused by segmentary and affinal conflicts. In fact, there might be major migrations during the *gumsa* periods due to a kind of balance between internal and external pressures. That is, while there is a tendency for density to increase at the center of a domain, marginal areas (having no great wall), are probably subject to a centrifugal tendency.[1]) Groups in these areas will try to get as far as possible from the domination of powerful chiefs. It is this double action which may account for the large scale emigration from the Hkakhu region into Assam, east into China, and south into the Shan states of North and South Hsenwi. At the same time, however, it is undoubtedly true that central populations tend to increase in density. The mythical representation of *gumsa* local organization is one where there are »numbers of houses very close together.« (Kawlu Ma Nawng in Leach 1954: 200). On the other hand, while *gumlao* settlements tend to disperse, there is no reason to believe that they undertake distant migrations unless there is pressure to do so, and they might present a problem except for the fact that in the Triangle area there seems to have been an easy outlet toward the west. There might have been a steady migration in both *gumlao* and *gumsa* periods.

Because the Kachin of the Triangle area have been able to maintain a low population, they have been able to reproduce the *gumsa/gumlao* cycle more or less intact each time. This is a real oscillation where each time one returns to the *gumlao* state, the conditions of population and environment are either the same, or, if the environment has been utilized too intensively because of the *gumsa* economy, fallows can again be increased, population dispersed, and the productivity of the land can be returned to its original state. Each cycle is thus faced with the same production function and has, consequently, the same possibilities of expansion and collapse. Furthermore, as we have said, the *gumsa* system breaks down before it gets to maximum output. This means that the population in any one *gumsa/gumlao* cycle does not grow as rapidly as it might if the system were more successful in its expansionist tendencies.

---

[1]) As noted earlier (p. 139) the normal expansion process of a *gumsa* domain implies that non-inheriting sons leave and establish new domains outside the former territory if they do not want to lose their chiefly status. In this way, new territory is constantly being added, a phenomenon which could conceivably accommodate the internal build-up of population. As this applies primarily to chiefs, however, and since the demand for labor still tends to increase, it is likely that density, especially at the center, will grow. This is simply reinforced when the domain can no longer expand, or only at a slower rate.

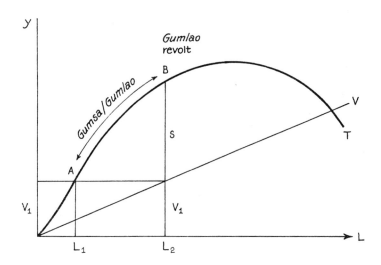

We can represent the *gumsa/gumlao* cycle in an exaggerated way in the movement between A and B on the above production function. If L1 represents the working portion of a population P capable of a maximum input of L2, we can say that the *gumsa/gumlao* extrema correspond to two input/output ratios. The necessary cost of reproduction of the population P is, in terms of output, equal to V1. This is the yield that will by definition cover the reproduction costs of the whole population, i.e., laborers and their dependents. I include here, for the sake of simplicity, technical costs of reproduction, i.e., tools, grain for sowing, hunting equipment, as well as some excess grain that might be taken as a kind of security (note, however, that famines are not a common phenomenon in this particular area). V1 is, thus, a measure of the cost of reproduction at a given level of existence (*gumlao*), defined in part by social structural needs. This is not to be confused with a biological minimum. The output V1 suffices for the maintenance and reproduction of a *gumlao* structure. It might be asked here why no surplus is necessary to pay brideprice. The answer is that in the *gumlao* system all brideprices are equal so that there is no need for there to be a surplus production. Outgoing brideprice is more or less covered by incoming brideprice and in any case the quantity is small enough so as not to make much difference. In a formal sense, the payment of brideprice might, however, be considered as a minimal surplus since it is not necessary for the reproduction of the society. But I think it could well be argued that in a system of asymmetrical exchange, some form of bridewealth is a *structural necessity*. The return of women and bridewealth is theoretically assured by the »long cycle« (in Levi-Strauss' terminology 1967 : Chap. 27).

This is a matter of a number of generations, depending on how many groups are involved in the marriage circle, if it is in fact a closed circle (implied by

Leach, for *gumlao* especially). Thus, there is no surplus, I think, in the sense of social reproduction because brideprice is required by the exchange structure itself. Furthermore, to the extent that the price is merely a token payment and not a potlatch (as defined by Rosman and Rubel 1971) it can be considered part of the category V1.

Now, if a *gumlao* system, at the start, produces only what is necessary for its own reproduction, the labor input will only be L1 which is all that is needed to get a yield V1. In the course of *gumsa* development, labor input is increased to L2, total yield increases to B and the surplus product goes to S. Thus, in the simplest kind of cycle, where population stays constant, the transition from *gumlao* to *gumsa*, A to B, consists in the transformation of surplus labor L1L2 into surplus product S. When the system breaks down, everything is returned to its original state. *Gumsa/gumlao* oscillation is a back and forth movement between A and B on the production function which, theoretically, can continue indefinitely. A more accurate representation of the situation we have been discussing would permit a temporary increase in population. In this case, labor input would increase beyond L2 and B, but the *gumlao* revolt would still return the system to points L1 and A.

The oscillation which would appear to occur in the Triangle area depends on the maintenance of a constant techno-economic balance. Where this is not the case, i.e., where population increases, where fallow is shortened in the long run, then the conditions of social reproduction are permanently altered and the new *gumlao/gumsa* cycle is faced with a changed production function.

The Long Cycle

The long term production function is not limited by the constraints of the short term cycle. It is a simple technological input/output function. Its shape is determined by other techno-environmental constraints; increasing population density as a permanent phenomenon and environmental degradation or loss of productivity over time due to overintensification of a basically extensive system.

The long and short cycles are related in a very definite way. If, instead of holding the original population density more or less constant, we let it increase continuously, we shall get, with each significant techno-environmental shift, a new set of conditions which will be expressed in a new production function. The long term function is nothing more than what is called the envelope of the short cycles. The meaning of the word »envelope« should be clear from the graph next page.

Here, the short cycles distribute themselves along the inner surface of the long cycle, each being tangent to the long term function.

Thus, the long cycle expresses the potential yield for each successive combination of population size and resultant techno-economic conditions. The short cycles are naturally below this curve since they have the added political and economic constraints which we have already analyzed. If the Kachin system

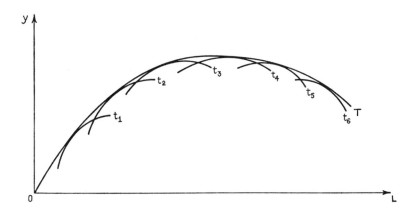

were to develop in the direction of increasing population density, it would not continually be faced with the same production function T1; rather, it would move from T1 to T2 to T3 and so on. We should recognize that the lowest population density does *not* represent either maximum productivity or maximum total yield. Productivity and yield can be maximized by having the greatest population density permitted by the optimal cultivation/fallow cycle. Thus, for example, to get maximum output in the Triangle one would try to increase population density as far as possible, up to the point where fallow would have to be shortened. As we have seen, however, the short cycle never gets that far.

In comparing different domains, we may find that they are at different points along the envelope and thus in different positions with regard to maximal yield and productivity. In fact, if we were to divide the long term curve into regions analogous to those of the short cycle we would find that there are four different classes of *gumsa/gumlao* oscillations corresponding to our regions I, II, III and IV. The most important change that occurs as we move toward the top of the curve is that the short cycle flattens out. There is less of a rapid growth period. This would seem to imply that such systems have more difficulty expanding. At the same time, however, they might be more stable internally, since on the one hand, the accumulation of debts has been much slower, and since the curve is flatter, there is less of a jolt when moving from region I to region II. Finally, in regions III and IV, the possibilities are greatly reduced and if pursued lead to rapidly diminishing returns.

The question of long and short term functions brings up an issue that is entirely overlooked by Leach is his discussion of *gumsa/gumlao* variation. He all too tacitly assumes that the system constantly reproduces itself over time without any qualitative change in the nature of the cycle. While it is certainly to his credit to have discovered that democratic and autocratic variants in North Burma and Assam are not separate societies but linked in a temporal model, he has, by concentrating only on the social structure and not trying to grasp the larger system, been led to make the false assumption that *gumsa/gumlao* variation is always of the same order. He never, for example, suggests that there might be variation in the nature of the cycle in different parts of the Kachin Hills, and he goes so far as to assimilate the democratic/autocratic variants of the Chin and Naga Hills to the same pattern. This is to some extent the result of his own emphasis on the opposition between two ideal types and his consequent failure to compare other structural features which are quite different but not unrelated in an evolutionary sense. In the second introduction to his 1954 *Political Systems of Highland Burma*, he seems acutely aware of this problem.

»Considered as category structures, the *gumsa* political order and the *gumlao* political order are ideal types which necessarily, at all times and all places, correspond rather badly with the empirical facts on the ground. If this be so, it seems reasonable to enquire whether there is any analysable social process which can be attributed to the persistent discrepancy between the facts on the ground and the two polarized structures of ideal categories. The thesis of chapters VII and VIII is that the outcome *for any one part of the Kachin region*, is a long phase political oscillation, though, since the facts at the end of the cycle are quite different from the facts at the beginning of the cycle, the 'system on the ground' is not in equilibrium in the same way as the 'system of ideas!'« (Leach 1954 (1964 ed.): xiii).

While it is not quite clear what Leach means when speaking of the »facts at the end of the cycle« and the difference between the »on the ground« and ideal states of affairs, it does appear that he might be referring to some of the problems we have raised. But in his most recent harshly worded critique of Levi-Strauss he has gone back to a strict equilibrium model where *gumsa* and *gumlao* variants »are in oscillatory movement about a central position.« (Leach 1969:283).

The problem seems to be that Leach refused to expand his view of things to systematically account for other levels of the social formation. His only structures are »verbal categories« and »systems of ideas.« The on the ground facts are believed to have no structure at all. This is a serious mistake which is deadly as an a priori assumption since it precludes the possibility of larger explanatory models. This is, perhaps, the greatest failure of *Political Systems*. There is a *gumsa/gumlao* oscillation and there are a number of contradictions in both forms which could make them equally transitory, but the dynamics is left to the unintelligible, random morass of external political and economic factors. In effect, the oscillation is not explained theoretically at all, because Leach has not put the bits and pieces of his structures together. We will return to this presently. Suffice it to say here that by taking account of the production function of the society both as a long and short term phenomenon, we can, I believe, explain much of what Leach leaves to the caprice of external circumstances, external, that is, to his own theoretical framwork.

Short Cycles, Long Cycles and the Distribution of Kachin Political Systems
There are two possibilities for the Kachin *gumsa/gumlao* cycle when viewed diachronically. The system can either repeat itself in exactly the same economic conditions, or it can, by the process of accumulating population, transform its conditions as it moves the length of the long cycle. The second alternative is ultimately the only one since the first depends on their being somewhere for migrating populations to go. It is probable that the Triangle societies have been able, by and large, to get rid of their excess population, but other hill areas which at one time or another may have received the »original« emigrants have not been able to do the same, at least not to the same extent. In this section we address ourselves to the relations between the distribution of population densities, techno-economic zones, political systems and exterior economies.

We must first examine the theoretical implications of movement along the long term production function. This is, fundamentally, an increase in population density, a cumulative process which continues from one short cycle to the next.

$$\frac{P}{A} = \frac{\text{population}}{\text{area}}$$

$$P2 > P1 > P0 \quad \left[\begin{array}{cccc} \text{Gumlao} \longrightarrow & \text{Gumsa} \longrightarrow & \text{Gumlao} \longrightarrow & \text{Gumsa} \\ \dfrac{P0}{A} \longrightarrow & \dfrac{P1}{A} \longrightarrow & \dfrac{P1}{A} \longrightarrow & \dfrac{P2}{A} \end{array} \right]$$

The increase in density changes the properties of the short cycle in the following ways:

a) In discussing the nature of Kachin expansion, we noted that there were two components, one purely technological and the other, a kind of political elbow room to provide for increased intensity of production and further territorial expansion at some later date. In order to keep the fallow cycle optimal, to preserve maximum productivity, territory must increase about fifteen times faster than the size of the working population. On top of this, there must be a great deal more room to provide for future generations as well as a possible increase in cultivated area per year. Thus, the typical *gumsa* system must expand at a very rapid rate if it is to maintain its economic efficiency for any length of time.

The most obvious effect of increasing density is that it makes such expansion more difficult. There is less available land at any one time, and since several domains are likely to be expanding simultaneously, there is bound to be an increasing amount of friction, feuding and warfare.

b) Labor intensification of a relatively fixed area, the domain, is the result of the impossibility of expansion as well as the tendency of domains to be somewhat centripetal (i.e., accumulation of a labor force in the chiefly settlement – general attempt to hold subordinate population within bounds where they can be controlled). We have stressed that the expansionist tendencies of the domain entail, for these reasons, an increase in density within a particular area. Demand for labor is constantly increasing even after the area of the controlled territory has ceased to grow. The long term results of this process are a decrease in fallow and/or an increase in cultivation period. This brings with it a degeneration of the environment, decrease in the amount of primary and secondary forest and eventually transition to scrub and grassland.

c) If this process is allowed to continue, a *gumsa* system will become more difficult to maintain. Interlineage competition will become more intense, debt will be taken more seriously. Increased warfare between the fragments of larger domains may lead to the formation of larger aggregates for the purpose of military security. Villages will be independent fortified units and the *gumsa/gumlao* cycle will find itself, if at all, on a new social structural as well as economic base. What is meant here is that certain segmentary processes which were crucial for the hierarchization of the group now become impossible. What does one do with elder brothers that cannot be gotten rid of? Is genealogical memory increased by proximity of kin over the generations? How does the local lineage maintain its independence of the larger lineage that has not been able to disperse? If rank is less easy to maintain between affines, how does this effect the exchange network and the tension between *mayu* and *dama* relatives?

d) Are there any alternatives to the kind of evolution suggested above? The two most obvious possibilities that come to mind are:
1. Change the technology to adapt to increasing population as well as expansionist tendencies, i.e., become a valley system.
   Here, of course, we may be faced with a completely new set of variables and constraints.
2. Find an exterior source of wealth to meet the demands for surplus. This can involve a number of options.
   (a) Imperialism – »protection« of valley Shan populations in exchange for needed economic goods.
   (b) Imperialism – »protection« of trade routes in exchange for tolls.
   (c) Specialization in a particular widely demanded trade item – integration into the larger exchange network of the valley states.
   (d) Political integration into valley state systems, as part of larger Shan states.

We can summarize these »multilinear« possibilities in the following way:

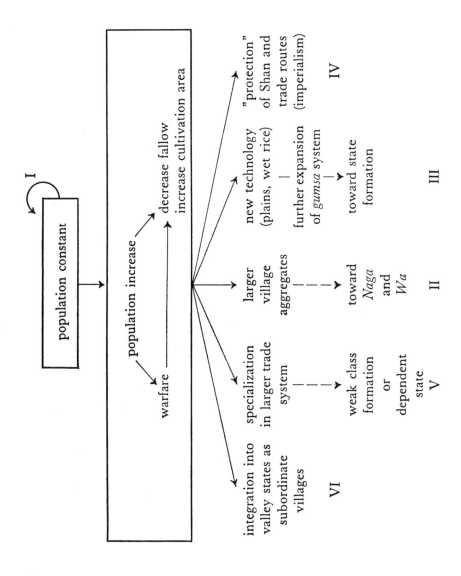

Not all of these possibilities are natural deductions from the preceding theoretical framework. In fact, there are only four kinds of development which can be derived from the earlier discussion.

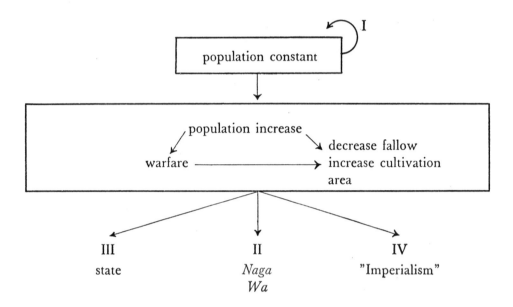

In this chart, only minimal assumptions are made about the outside non-Kachin world. System I is the normal state of affairs as long as population density can be maintained. (II) is, in most respects the result of the fact that the tribal areas are more or less surrounded by state societies that represent a political as well as demographic barrier. (III) is another natural development out of (I) which can take place in a vacuum. In fact, it doesn't, which is why there are no states in Northern Burma that have not been affected by a high degree of diffusion. (IV) makes the assumption that there are sources of exploitable wealth outside the swidden technology which could reinforce *gumsa* polity and possibly serve as the basis for further development. (V) and (VI) on the previous chart make a more specific assumption, which is that Kachin can become integrated in one way or another into the already existent Shan societies of the valleys. These are rather special cases which depend in large measure on the particular structure of the larger inter-group economy.

For the time being, we shall be concerned exclusively with the evolution of the hill systems. We use Leach's map of the Kachin »ecological« zones as a starting point. It will be remembered that for that author, the zones are not in any way connected with the Kachin social formation itself but are independent constants which have no particularly clear influence on the distribution of *gumsa* and *gumlao* type societies. This kind of non-correspondence is good medicine for the mechanical materialist, hoping perhaps to find that all *gumlao* are in one zone while *gumsa* are in another. In our own framework, however, the environment, is, as principal object of the process of production, completely integrated into the evolution of the *gumsa/gumlao* cycle considered as a whole.

Leach's zones A, B and C (see map next page) correspond more or less to our own techno-economic zones with some modifications. His B and C zones are probably not as distinct as they appear to be. His zone B, for instance, should by his definition be equivalent to our zone D, grassland. But while there is grassland in this area, there is also some secondary forest and scrub growth. As such, it is more like a transitional state between our C and D zones. We have already discussed the classification of so-called »ecological« zones and it was shown that these are more properly techno-economic zones whose natural features are the result of varying intensity of land use.

If the Kachin groups of the Hkahku area were somehow able to rid themselves of »excess« population, we cannot assume that this is true in all the areas into which migration took place. The most important factor here would be the barriers imposed by exterior demographic and political conditions. Now, in fact, the area west of the Triangle was relatively unpopulated at the time of the various Kachin expansions so that migration in this direction would have been fairly easy. However, to the east and south, there were both demographic and political problems since in these directions lay the Shan states of North and South Hsenwi and Tengyueh as well as Lolo and Lisu populations in the northern-most areas of the China-Burma border region. Thus, in the east and south there was evidently enough pressure to slow the Kachin expansion enough to permit population density to increase greatly. These are the areas in which, in fact, population is most dense, and which correspond to Leach's »ecological zones« B and C.

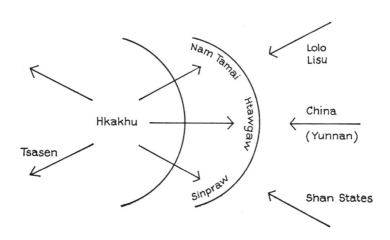

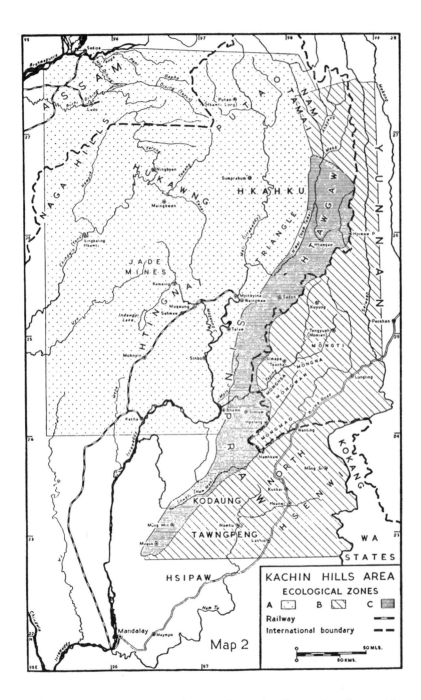

A: monsoon forest. B: grassland. C: mixed (transitional) secondary forest with terraces.

A Note on Linguistic Diversity and Theoretical Analysis

In the Nam Tamai and Htawgaw regions there are dialect and even substantial language differences especially among the Nung and Maru populations who make up the majority of the inhabitants. Both these languages are closely related to Kachin, and it would not, I think, make much sense to treat them as totally different populations. The Maru, at least those living in the Triangle area, are practically indistinguishable from other Kachin with regard to social structure and local organization. In any case, it is not necessary that other groups in these areas all be of the same origin. We are concerned with the structural properties of social systems, and if the Maru immigrated from the east (which is quite possible) they will also be assumed to have been part of an expanding system of the same type. The following »tribal« tree from Maran La Raw (next page), certainly the most knowledgeable of Kachin linguists, should indicate the degree to which we may speak of the area as a kind of unity. He states with reference to this chart:

»It would surprise quite a few readers that the common name of reference 'Jinghpaw' is not listed among the members of the set Vt in tree II at all. This is because 'Jinghpaw' refers to all the members of the universal set Wungpawng and does not narrow itself to refer to any single group.« (Maran 1967b:11).

This kind of argument might appear superfluous in a study of this sort, but it is very common for anthropologists in the area to criticize certain analyses on the basis that they »mix up« groups of different origins that speak different languages. Leach, who was one of the first to argue the primacy of underlying structures criticizes Levi-Strauss' confusing of Chin and Kachin on purely cultural grounds (Leach 1961:78) even though the latter made use of the material on purely structural grounds. It is not necessary to drag this out, but I would stress that in a theoretical analysis which purports to explain the distribution in time and space of a number of social forms, the onus is on the critic to disprove the hypothesis by showing that it does not explain that distribution. To claim from the start, however, that the analysis cannot be made on linguistic or cultural grounds is to beg the question out of existence.

Although it is a pretty well accepted fact that census figures are notoriously unreliable, it is possible to use them to establish quantitative trends of a very general order, especially when there are enough of them over a long enough period of time. One very definite trend does emerge from the census figures. While in Leach's zone A the population densities average about 5 per mi^2, the figures for zones C and B are upwards of 15 per mi^2.

	Kachin Tract	Population	Density
Zone A	Myitkyina	6,411	5/mi^2
	Mogaung and Kamaing	17,534	6.5/mi^2

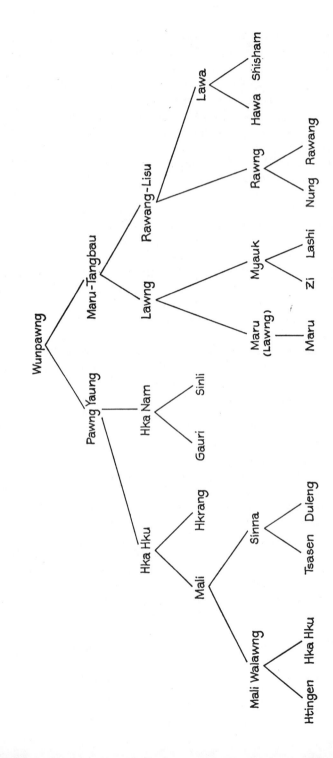

Wunpawng Amyu Ni : Kinds of Kachin

From Maran La Raw, 1967 b.

	Sima	10,416	16/mi²
	Sadon	12,355	17/mi²
Zone C	Htawgaw (incomplete)	17,305	11/mi² (?)
	Sinlum	44,035	28/mi²

The above figures (Burma Gazetteer, Bhamo and Myitkyina Districts, Census Tables 1921) give a very rough idea of the distribution of population in some of the areas we have been discussing. The figure for Htawgaw is most certainly on the low side. That area was only recently incorporated under British rule at the time of the census and the figures which only cover part of the area in question are especially inaccurate. Leach puts the density of all of zone C between 15 and 30 per square mile (Leach 1954:236). Sinlum is, as we can see, very high relative to the other zone C areas. There are no density figures for Nam Tamai (zone B), but judging by the absolute population estimates (Leyden in Leach 1946) it would seem to fall into the same category as zone C, perhaps a little higher. The other areas of zone B include the Northern Burmese and Chinese Shan states. There are no density figures for the hill areas of the Shan states, but the population densities of these areas are a good deal higher than any of the Kachin regions, including valleys and towns (Harvey 1933).

Tengyueh	44/mi²	
Lungling		zone B
North Hsenwi	37/mi²	

These, of course, are not really high figures for valley dwelling populations, but a very large portion of the inhabitants of these areas are hill peoples. In North Hsenwi, for example, we find roughly the following breakdown (Scott and Hardiman 1900: Pt. II, Vol. I):

	Population
Shan	43,140
Kachin	36,270
Palaung	16,680
Chinese	14,950
Miaotzu	2,500
La and Wa	2,000
Lihsaw (Lisu)	250
	118,290

It might well be assumed that at one time or another, about half of the population practiced hill swidden cultivation. It is possible, furthermore, that due to this state's unusually turbulent past, there has been a fair amount of emigration, so that in the past the area might certainly have been more heavily populated. It must also be recognized that these states, besides being more heavily populated, would, with their organized hierarchical class structures, make any independent Kachin domain a very difficult proposition. In these areas we do not find anything like the Kachin *mung* of the Triangle. There are either *gumsa* Kachin who have become Shan (e.g. Möng Si), or smaller communities that are incorporated into Shan administrative districts.

It seems plausible, to say the least, that Leach's zones are not constant ecological facts, but the result of a definite evolution of the *gumlao/gumsa* cycle under conditions of »expanded reproduction,« i.e., where population is increasing markedly enough to cause environmental change. We saw earlier that, in terms of climate and vegetation zones, there was no cause for Leach's distinctions, but we can admit that certain secondary factors might speed up the transition from techno-economic zone A through B, C and D. The most important of these is the nature of the terrain itself. In many parts of Sinpraw and especially Htawgaw, slopes are somewhat steeper. This could make erosion proceed at a faster rate and would certainly reduce the available land per square mile.

Leach is not unaware of the determinant aspect of population density, and in some places makes an argument similar to the one put forward here (Leach 1954:290) but he never ties it all together and is left, finally, with a population-free definition of »ecological zone.«

Htawgaw, Nam Tamai and Sinpraw have broken away from the simple reproduction of the Triangle area and have started on what we have referred to as development II (p. 194). The distribution of these areas in terms of our techno-economic zones is the following:

	A	B	C	D	Technology
Myitkyina & Jademines	////				S_1
Sinlum		////	////		S_1 S_2 S_7
Sadon, Sima, Htawgaw		////	////		S_1 S_2 S_7
Nam Tamai			////	////	S_7

We now have a number of correspondences which can help us to account for a certain amount of the Kachin variation. Myitkyina and the Triangle area generally have, by keeping population to a minimum, been able to maintain a technological system at high productivity per acre and per man hour. Increased population has affected all the other areas of the hill country. In the eastern and southern areas, shorter fallows and increased cultivation periods (2/7– 2/10) with some rotation of a bean crop, have been coupled to irrigated terraces as an adaptation to environmental degradation. In the northern area, Nam Tamai, there appears to be no terracing and therefore more grassland. In terms of technological succession we have:

$$S1 \underset{S7}{\overset{S2}{\diagdown}} \qquad (pp.\ 87-89)$$

It is possible that in areas where terracing has been used, it prevented the transition to grassland. In spite of these variations, however, it is clear that long fallowing preceded the other two forms wherever possible and that the technologies are not simply local adaptations to pre-existent ecologies. In areas where density is still a bit lower, there are attempts to preserve the older fallow system. Evidence for this kind of suggestion is difficult to find, but we do have this much. In the Myikyina gazetteer (Hertz 1912) which covers the Sadon and Sima tracts as well, the cultivation period is reported to be only one year, and there is no mention of the loss of forest land, which is an important point since the British blocked off a good deal of forest in the form of reserves. The gazetteer remarks that virgin forest is often cleared, but it also says that fallow is sometimes as low as eight to ten years. If this applies, in fact, to the Sadon and Sima tracts it is clearly a transitional state. In the Sinlum area as reported in the Bhamo gazetteer (Dawson 1912) forest land is a very big problem. There are complaints that the Kachin have denuded much of the area. The reason suggested for this is precisely the one we have put forward, i.e., that population pressure had reduced the fallow period. Needless to say, there were conflicts over the British claims on primary forest since this could only further destroy the basis of the Kachin economy, but the increased population pressure of this area was a major factor (Leach 1954:116). The use of grassland *taungya* technique is probably more widespread here, for both real grassland and scrub growth, as opposed to Sima and Sadon where the population density is only about 15/mi^2.

We are still faced with some discrepancies which we shall attempt to sort out now that we have established a reasonable explanation for the so-called »ecological« distribution. We would expect that Htawgaw, Sima and Sadon, having had similar techno-economic evolutions might, in fact, have similar social forms. We might further expect that Sinlum would be slightly different given the increased intensity of exploitation. After all, from the material we have

analyzed, it appears that all of these areas have gone through the same development and that Sinlum is simply further along the way. If this were the case
we would expect to find:

   1) Similar local organization due to the growth of warfare and concomitant
      growth of village size.
   2) Similar political cycles of *gumsa* and *gumlao*, except for increased diffi-
      culties of maintaining *gumsa* in the southern area (Sinlum).

Neither of these expectations is entirely born out for the simple reason that
not all of the groups follow development II. We can use the distribution of
village sizes as a first indicator of what is occurring in the different areas.

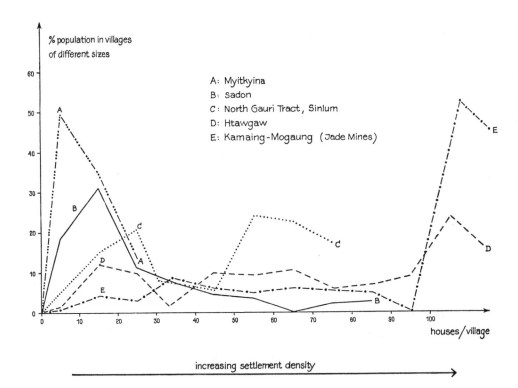

The above graph is practically identical with the one in Leach (1946).
Myitkyina and Sadon are treated separately here in order to accentuate the
transition toward increased settlement density.

We shall not be concerned, for the time being, with the Kamaing-Mogaung tracts (jade mines). As for the others, however, they show an interesting distribution. In terms of averages, we have the following progression:

	Average village size
Myitkyina	9 houses/village
Sadon	13 houses/village
Gauri Sinlum	24 houses/village
Htawgaw	43 houses/village

We must, of course, be wary of such averages since they are difficult to interpret. For example, the high average for Htawgaw is not a result of a large number of villages with between forty and fifty houses. It is due to a more even distribution coupled with the existence of a large number of villages of one hundred or more houses. Likewise, in the Sinlum area, less than twenty percent of the villages come near to the overall average of twenty four. As such, the actual distributions of the graph are more important indicators. In both Myitkyina and Sadon tracts, the large majority of the villages are quite small. In Sinlum, there are two cluster points, one at 25 and the other at 55–60. In Htawgaw, there is a fairly even distribution except for the fact that 25% of the population is in villages of over 100 houses.

Does this correspond with that we would expect from development II? Not exactly. If we compare density rank with village size we get:

density: Myitkyina < Sadon = Htawgaw < Sinlum

village size: Myitkyina < Sadon < Sinlum   < Htawgaw

We may be tempted to think that the data are incorrect. Leach implies in his thesis that the Htawgaw tract is more densely populated than any other area (Leach 1946). This is possible and would certainly corroborate the hypothetical development II. However, since there is little other information to go on than the census, we shall have to stick by it for the time being.

The above discrepancy is no longer a problem if we take one more factor into account; external resources. Sadon, Sima and Sinlum are all on the main trade routes from Burma to China. In the past, the routes served to bolster the Kachin economies of these regions. In Htawgaw, there is mention of the Hpimaw pass, but it is all that is mentioned, and it does not seem to have been anything like the revenue source afforded by the southern routes. Another point is that in the Sinpraw area, the Gauri and Atsi, for example, are known to have dominated valley Shan populations from whom they took tribute in rice. Thus, especially here, it seems that given the proper exploitation of exterior resources, a relatively high population density can be supported without any of the effects which accompany development II.

If we make the simple assumption that village size varies directly with density and inversely with availability of resources, the difference between the tracts begins to make some sense. A dispersed settlement pattern can be maintained in fairly high density situations if competition for swidden land can be avoided. Now, if an outside resource can be transformed into a means of getting rice, either directly as with the Shans, or indirectly, by taxing traders and buying food, then the evolution toward increased warfare and larger aggregates can be put off indefinitely. Where such resources are not available, development II will simply continue. The Htawgaw tract is inhabited by Maru and Lashi groups. There is no mention of dominance over Shan valley settlements. The large Lashi terraced villages on the Hpimaw pass are all *gumlao* while those near Sadon are *gumsa*. It is not clear that the Hpimaw settlements are doing a great trade. They can certainly support themselves with irrigated cultivation, but I would tend to think that a *gumsa* organization would be very difficult to maintain. Htawgaw settlements appear to be similar in most respects to those further north in Nam Tamai. Unfortunately there is little information on this northern area, but the main difference between them seems to be that Htawgaw has terraces instead of grassland.

A distinguishing feature of both Htawgaw and Sinpraw is the existence of terracing. Leach has suggested that the primary reason for this is military, in that relatively large and dense populations could be supported for the purpose of dominating trade routes as well as maintaining the favored positions against the possible encroachments of other Kachin competitors (Leach 1954:28). This appears to be a bit too specific as an explanation. If we go back to the economic properties of terracing we are, I think, on better footing. This form of irrigation has the specific property that it can support a large population on a small amount of land. As such it could serve a great many purposes, but I would suggest that where it does occur it is not simply a positive economic or political choice. In areas where there is already a good deal of population pressure and a few prospects for continuing the old expansionist political economy, the exploitation of trade routes or other populations is the only alternative means for preserving the system. The competition for trade route land in areas of high density may well be a cause for the military need of such large settlements. Leach in various places has argued as if the trade routes themselves were the cause of the population density since they attracted large numbers of Kachin (Leach 1949, 1954:28). It is just as plausible that things go the other way around. That is, population pressure leads to the military need for large agglomerations and that this may in turn lead to the construction of terraces. This may happen earlier or later. If, in fact, there is a possibility of getting something out of trade routes, then the land along them will be the target of competition. If agricultural land becomes scarce, terracing may be a kind of last resort. Leach points out that the Angami are on the route from Imphal to Dimapur and that this can explain the existence of their terraced villages (Leach 1954:28). This is rather hard to believe, though, since there are a number of other Naga groups who theoretically could get first crack at the trade. I have found no mention that the Angami did engage in this kind of domination. Furthermore, it might be noted that the Angami probably do not have enough land to indulge in swiddening even if they wanted to (Allen 1905). If, in fact, Leach's hypothesis about the relation between trade and terracing were correct, we would expect to find the largest agglomerations in the Sinpraw area, especially the south. However, there seems to be an inverse relation between availability of trade and the existence of terraces. That is, the further north we go, the more terraces we find. In Htawgaw where trade can only have been of very minor significance, we find by far the largest terraced villages. Contrary to Leach, it appears as though the large villages in Htawgaw are the result of competition for a small volume of trade, and it is the very scarcity of this trade which accounts for the number of very large villages. Generally, the lack of outside resources means increased dependence on interior resources. This in turn implies internal competition for land. It is not, I suspect, necessary that land be absolutely scarce, but only that it be scarce in terms of the expanding nature of the economy which demands a territory far greater than its actual needs of the moment. I would suggest that, particularly in Htawgaw, the existence of terracing may have little to do with trade and more to do with a combination of internal economic pressure and the existence of steep slopes. It is not uncommon, for example, that dry terracing is practiced on slopes where erosion and soil loss is a problem. But it is only a short way from here to irrigated terracing and this kind of development may have occurred in Htawgaw as well as in the Angami Hills in exactly the same way.

The problem of terracing still remains largely unsolved on the basis of existing data. It appears to be an economic »choice« which may or may not occur in conditions of extreme population pressure on available resources. We suggested earlier that the construction of terraces imposes a great number of constraints on a formerly expanding system, and it may be that the existence of this form of irrigation is determined by local microhistorical political and economic factors. In the above discussion, however, we have suggested two related underlying causes. In a declining swidden economy there comes a point at which available outside resources must be appropriated to prop up a collapsing *gumsa* system. Large settlements will then be necessary to secure positions along trade routes, not necessarily because the trade is so profitable, but because the combination of tolls and irrigated rice is a better economic choice than the continuation of swiddening alone in degraded conditions. Note, however, that in all of these settlements, swidden cultivation is often still the major form of agriculture. At a more advanced stage of deterioration, irrigation may become an absolute necessity simply because there is not enough land for swiddening. Where there isn't any outside economic resource to draw upon

and warfare takes on some importance, larger settlements may be forced by
their size alone to take up irrigation.

The similarity of population aggregates in Sinlum and Htawgaw is due to
equivalent economic effects of different combinations of factors. In terms of
abstract economic wealth, the increase in population density is offset in Sinlum
by a massive increase in external exploitation. Although population density
in Htawgaw is lower, it is sufficient, given the threshold effect which triggers
warfare, to significantly alter the settlement pattern in conditions where external resources are not available in great quantities. In either case, terracing
may occur where there is a narrowly circumscribed area of revenue, either in
the form of exploitable outsiders or as agricultural land. Sinlum with a density of $28/mi^2$ and outside resources experienced a general increase in village
size. Htawgaw, with a density of perhaps $15/mi^2$ and no outside resources,
still has a majority of small villages but a very significant minority of very
large villages.

Political Systems

It remains for us now to examine the distribution of political forms in the
various regions we have discussed. For this discussion we will make partial use
of the recent analyses of Maran La Raw (Maran 1967a, 1967b) who has
substantially sharpened some of Leach's vocabulary by systematic usage of
Jinghpaw terms to reveal finer distinctions than *gumsa* and *gumlao*. I say
partial, because there are a number of problems with his definitions.

Maran defines three kinds of chiefly office, two of which are non-hereditary:

a) *Gymchying gumsa du* – »The old traditional chief in office.« (Maran
1967b:16).

b) *Gumrawng Gumsa magam* – »The proud and free system which ack-
nowledges no hereditary paramount chief, and to whom a claim to chieftainship must be justified ritually as well as in terms of capable of
leadership.« (Maran 1967b:16).

c) *Gumlao magam* – »Another not strictly hereditary chiefdom whose
dependence on opium cultivation as a cash crop has brought vast changes
in the general social structure ... while every *gumlao magam* or republican chief must be sponsored by a *gumsa* chief to become a *'gumlao magam'*
he could be disposed of by the republicans at will. That is, ritually and
symbolically, a republican chief not only models himself after the hereditary chiefs but also must be approved by the latter to justify his claim
to being *magam*. However, since lineal succession is not the determining
criterion, he could never be referred to as *'Duwa!'*« (Maran 1967b:16).

This last definition seems to be extremely narrow and based on a particularly recent state of affairs. Opium cultivation is not a prerequisite for
gumlao political forms. Maran himself uses the word in its traditional anthropological sense and indicates that *gumlao* chiefs can become *gumsa du* (Maran

1967b:16). Further, it would be a contradiction in terms for a recent *gumlao* revolutionary to claim authority on the basis of backing by a *gumsa* chief, but this might be a much later development. Until this issue is cleared up I would prefer to keep the definition employed by Leach. We do, after all, have some descriptive information on *gumlao* areas which indicate that *gumlao* »chiefs« are what would normally be called »big-men« in egalitarian polities.

The other two definitions, however, bring a needed distinction between two different kinds of *gumsa* organization. One is the traditional hereditary domain chief (*gumchying*) of the Triangle area. The other is a not strictly hereditary domain chief who must make his claims through ritual. Maran is not clear on the nature of this ritual, but the *gumrawng* chief seems to correspond to a weaker form of *gumchying* structure. In this sense, *gumrawng* ritual claims would be attempts to link the local territorial *nats* to the chief's ancestry. As we have shown on purely structural grounds, the possibility of being an official hereditary chief depends entirely on identifying one's lineage with that of the local spirits. Thus, a *gumrawng* chief would simply be one who had not achieved this position, or where it was still open to competition.

Without getting into a discussion of Maran's critique of Leach which would involve questions which are not relevant to a structural analysis, it is important to stress one point. The distinction *gumsa/gumlao* as we have been using it it not one between autocratic/democratic, at least not necessarily. Rather, it is one between hereditary/non-hereditary. This again is in accord with our structural analysis, since the only hereditary positions are those that exist by means of claims on the *nat* hierarchy. Thus, what I referred to as »true *gumlao*« is simply the removal of hereditary functions at all levels including the village. Differential brideprice will also be removed, but real equality cannot be established without abolishing the relation between exchange and kinship, i.e., by neutralizing the political-economic aspect of marriage which is the basis of the social structure. If this were done, then *gumlao* could never again become *gumsa*. Thus, while a *gumlao* rebellion is by implication egalitarian, it is perfectly possible for ranking to exist in a later stage of *gumlao* development.

Extremely interesting for our analysis is the distribution of different kinds of *gumsa* societies. We might well assume that the *gumrawng* type can occur anywhere as a transition to or away from the hereditary *gumchying* model, but Maran adds that the *gumchying* chiefs occur only in the Triangle region.

> »The first is the *gumchying gumsa*, the original traditional ideal Kachin model, whose adherents are upland farmers, confined to the Triangle region of extreme northern Burma. Second is the *gumrawng gumsa*, an intermediate type whose chiefs generally become powerless figureheads. Most lowland settlers seem to derive from this type of society. *It is associated with the practice of terraced cultivation on mountainsides.*« (Maran 1967a:139). (My underline).

This corresponds quite well with what we would expect. The areas of terraced cultivation, Leach's zone C, is the area of higher population density where *gumsa* hierarchies depend for their maintenance on outside resources. It is not clear that there were never any *gumchying* type communities in this area. It appears that the main trade route from Bhamo to Loilung was organized as a large domain under the paramountcy of the Gauri chief Mahtang. One report lists thirty-six village chiefs who appear to have been his subordinates (Sladen 1868). In fact, this particular domain was something closer to a Shan *möng* than the typical Kachin *gumchying* domain, and in Maran's terms the two are polar opposites, since one represents an incorporation of Shan culture while the other is the highest development achieved within the purely Kachin framework. In terms of an a-cultural argument, however, we might be more inclined to treat the Mahtang domain of Möng Hka as a special case, a kind of petty trade state. This in itself makes it different from a *gumchying* type economy and it is a point which must be absolutely clear. In both a Shan domain and a *gumchying gumsa mung*, the chiefs draw their revenue from the internal surplus produced by their own subjects. The wealth of the Mahtang or any of the chiefs of Leach's zone C is based primarily on the control of external resources. It is, of course, true that Guari chiefs extracted tribute and corvée from their villagers. But the degree to which this could develop, the number of villages that could be controlled was entirely at the mercy of the flow of trade and the ability to exploit valley Shans. In other words, the hierarchical system in this area is supported by very special circumstances and is liable to break down when the circumstances change.

The entire Sinpraw area has probably always been in a kind of flux for precisely this reason, but the British permanently changed circumstances by cutting off Kachin access to Shans and traders. The area was bound, after this, to become more or less like Leach's Sinlum community of Hpalang, where feuds were prevalent and no domain hierarchy could be maintained. An interesting myth collected soon after the advent of the British indicates the potential lines of fission in Guari *gumsa* communities in which chiefly control was shrinking. In this myth about the origin of chiefs, *du ni,* and commoners, *tarat ni,* we are told that the latter who originally had moved south due to overcrowding (significant in itself) were at first egalitarian. But there were so many disputes that, if they didn't have the good fortune to find som *du ni* to regulate their feuds, there might have been a disaster, a total breakdown in social relations. As myths so often do, this one seems to have neatly reversed the situation while making the social contradictions even more obvious. The following is a description of the Mahtang domain in 1921.

> »The Laphai *Duwas,* who once ruled the Gauris have now fallen into complete insignificance. They have less standing than even the village *salangs* (headmen) or elders. While visiting the tombs of this once illustrious family, I met the present *du,* Sau Dwe, cutting wood in the jungle while his wife carried home the logs.« (Enriques 1923:126).

The situation in this area quickly degenerated after the outside sources of surplus were cut off. A chief who formerly received a large revenue from tolls and Shans and could subsequently afford to give large feasts could no longer do this. Thus the distributive economic base of the wider domain network began to disintegrate and the authority that accompanied it was bound to fade.

Generally, however, domains in the Sinpraw area are small, rarely containing more than one or two village tracts, perhaps 500 people at the most. Even in times of greatest prosperity, political units of the largest scale did not grow to be anything like the great domains of the Triangle area, where, for example, the paramount chief Shadan Tu headed a domain of perhaps 16,000 people (Leach 1946). Early colonial administrators often remarked on the extreme political disintegration of the area east of the Irrawaddy, and intervillage feuding appears to have been quite common and widespread. The following quotes give some idea of both colonial mentality and the state of affairs in these economic systems which had been permanently broken by the British.

> »In approaching these tribes we had to deal, not with nationalism, but with groups of small independent savage communities with no inter tribal coherence.« (Scott and Hardiman 1900: Pt. I, Vol. I:353).

> »Our opponents here were the *Kumlao* (*gumlao*) Kachin, whose principal characteristic is that they do not own the authority of any chief, even in single villages.« (Scott and Hardiman 1900: Pt. I, Vol. I:363).

> »Since their defeat, the disturbances have been purely local and insignificant. They have chiefly arisen from the Kachin's peculiar and stubborn ideas on the subject of debts and from the many land disputes. In many parts the country is too thickly inhabited, and the people have difficulty in supporting themselves with their present rude agricultural methods and their scanty crops. The question of boundaries is therefore fought out with great bitterness.« (Scott and Hardiman 1900: Pt. I, Vol. I:367).

The last quote is the key to the first two. It speaks of feuds related to debts and feuds related to land. This is precisely what the model predicts. Increasing population and decreasing productivity imply two kinds of contradictions. First, demand for surplus is greater than the actual rate of increase in productivity; we have

$$dS_0/dS > 1 \implies dD/dt > 0$$

that is, increase in debts and decreasing ability to pay them. Consequently we have debt feuding. Secondly, as the agricultural system is already somewhat depleted as well as overpopulated, the expansionist nature of the economy will lead quite naturally to land disputes. Such a system is clearly on the point of breakdown unless some other economic source can be found. When the British removed this source, disintegration was bound to occur. Some areas seem to have had *gumlao* rebellions.

> »There are villages in the upper defile, just north of Bhamo, where within a few years of our annexation the *Duwas* were driven out.« (Scott and Hardiman 1900 Pt. I, Vol. I:414).

In other areas there was a slower disintegration. These breakdowns may

have been very unlike the typical *gumlao* movements of the Triangle. These
latter, it should be remembered, usually occur as the result of the *internal
expansion of the gumchying system*. In Sinpraw, however, this kind of expansion did not take place to the same degree. Domains were much smaller and
when extended, they were not based on the internal economy of the local hill
communities.

With external economies removed, the pre-existent inflation of exchange
values is faced with an internal economy which is totally incapable of paying
for itself. In consequence, there is a depression, expressed here in the deflation
of status. Where claims are made, they are difficult to validate since the
economic base of validation has disappeared.

>Hpalang in 1940, in my view, was probably in process of changing from
a *gumsa* to a *gumlao* type of organization.« (Leach 1954:87).

Instead of a *gumlao* rebellion, a rejection of hereditary rank which returns
the system to »go«, we have a slow distintegration of a supralocal hierarchy in
which claims on former hereditary positions are made until the end.[1]

While, as Leach has said, *gumlao* and *gumsa* occur in both his zones A and
C, there are some crucial differences that are overlooked by this simple dichotomy. It is only in zone A that the *gumchying* system is a long term possibility.
In zone C, the degree of hierarchical development is generally much lower and
in a much less stable state. Most of the systems in this area are *gumrawng
gumsa*, where competition is still open and the size of domains is rather small.
All of this is in accordance with Leach's data, but he has never incorporated
it into his explanatory framework. If he had worked from the political economy down to the »ecology« he might have seen things very differently. At
the end of *Political Systems in Highland Burma*, he makes use of another set
of classifications which cut across his earlier »ecological zones«.

>A *gumlao* type organization seems to have persisted throughout most
of the northern part of zones B and C (Map 2, Htawgaw and Nam Tamai
areas). Here, dialects (Maru and Nung) change every few miles, almost
from village to village.« (Leach 1954:289).

». . . in most of zone B and in the southern part of zone C (Map 2, Sinpraw
area), because of relative dryness and relative high population density,
the economy of the hill communities is essentially unbalanced. Temporary
stability can only be achieved by political and military expedients. In
these zones, both in *gumsa* and *gumlao* areas, *the only continuing unit of
political structure is the village*.« (Leach 1954:289) (my underline).

This more sensible classification contradicts his earlier discussion. First, he

---

[1] »The chiefs have not the influence that they have in the north, and, owing to the pressure of
population and to there being little opportunity for the sons of chiefs to migrate and form their
own communities, there are often several *Du* households in every village. The chiefs, having lost
influence and power, have degenerated. In one big village, the chief lives in the smallest tumble-
down shack in the village. The people are now in most cases governed entirely by their elders.«
(Green 1934:307).

seems to have assimilated conditions in the southern part of zone C to those in B. But these conditions should also hold for the northerly areas. Why then does he find political differences between them? Quite simply, the northern parts of B and C are not balanced by an inflow of goods. Thus, the *gumsa* supralocal organization that is maintained in the south is not possible in Htawgaw and Nam Tamai.

We have already seen that the areas north and east of the Triangle are characterized by larger local aggregates than are found elsewhere. There is, unfortunately, virtually no ethnographic data on the Maru and Nung populations, although it is probable that they do have a system of generalized exchange (Barnard 1934; Benedict 1941). While Leach claims that they are mostly *gumlao*, this may be his reading of the fact that they have no supralocal organization. This, however, does not necessarily preclude the existence of hereditary village chiefs. It appears that the Maru and Nung may have begun on a development similar to that of the Naga, Wa and Lushai in which large villages are the basis of either hereditary or non-hereditary chiefship, but in conditions of increasing environmental degradation and population pressure. It may seem out of place here, but it is true that the fact that the Maru, Wa and Naga all consume dog meat puts them on the lowest rung in the Kachin scale of values since dog is considered the most unpalatable of foods. It would be nonsense to accept this at face value, but there could very well be a correspondence between the consumption of dog meat and the degeneration of a Kachin type system.[1] In any case, the little we do know about the Maru would seem to indicate that they are headed in a Naga-Wa direction.

> »Among the Marus every village is a separate community and has its own chief, and thus there are no sub-tribes, unless indeed every village can be called a separate clan.« (Scott and Hardiman 1900: Pt. I, Vol. I:383).

The *gumsa/gumlao* distinction might apply here in the strict sense of hereditary/non-hereditary, but the entire organization must now be based on a single large independent village community. There is certainly a great difference between a domain chief and an hereditary headman. Why doesn't this kind of development occur in the Sinpraw area? It appears to have begun when the British removed Kachin access to external resources, but it was halted by the colonial administration itself. Leach, in reference to the decomposition of Hpalang *gumsa* organization says:

> »It was restrained from completing the change over only by the arbitrary dictates of the paramount power whose officers objected to the *gumlao* system as a matter of principle.« (Leach 1954:289).

What is important here is not the anti-*gumlao* attitude in itself, but that the existence of a »paramount power« carried with it the same functions as those of a domain chief, i.e., authority over local affairs and especially the regulation

---

[1] It is not unreasonable to assume that where forest is destroyed, the *mithan* will become scarce, there being less available land on which they can survive.

of disputes. The feuding which existed at the start was stopped by the superior authority of the British, thus preventing, not only the disintegration of larger political units into smaller ones, but also the reorganization of the small dispersed settlements into large villages. It is significant in this respect that with the high population densities of Leach's zone B Shan states, the village communities remain small and somewhat dispersed. This, I maintain, is due to the same kind of political authority as that exercised by the British. Kachins that moved out of the Sinpraw area and into the Shan states eventually became Shans or subject Kachins in some level of the larger state. If *gumsa* organization seems prevalent in this zone, it is due to the fact that Shan domains are structured according to hierarchical principles which do not admit of independent village communities any more than do *gumchying* domains.

In the Shan states, Kachin communities were integrated into the larger economic system. Where they were able to exert some kind of dominance over valley Shans this was institutionalized by the state. Where there were single Kachin communities they were grouped into Shan administrative divisions with appointed representatives. When Leach says that all of Zone B is *gumsa*, however, he conveniently forgets the Nam Tamai area which is most certainly not. But this region is also independent of any larger state apparatus.

If we go back now to summarize the distribution of political types, we find that they do not vary at random, but are part of a larger socio-economic evolution which can only be properly understood as a developmental whole.

At the beginning of the development we have the Triangle area where population density is kept low and there is a *gumchying gumsa/gumlao* cycle which can repeat itself indefinitely. The shift away from this system takes place in the whole border area east of Leach's zone A. This includes his zones B and C, but in terms of the real techno-economic situation, it is only one environmental zone in transition to grassland. Here the population is higher, the yields lower. Three possibilities emerge:

a) Make use of outside resources:
    1. exploitation of trade routes   Sinpraw
    2. exploitation of valley populations
b) Where outside resources are not available:
    1. Increased feudings due to the inability
       to match rising demands for surplus with   Htawgaw
       rising yields.   and
    2. Feuding or warfare resulting from   Nam Tamai[1])
       competition for land.
    3. Formation of large independent villages.

[1]) Villages in the northern reaches of the Nam Tamai river tend to be rather small. They do not fit into the pattern we have outlined. This is probably due to the fact that the area was constantly under attack by Kachin slave raiders. Thus, in spite of the density and extreme environmental degradation, villages remained small, hidden from main roads and often on the move. In the southern part of the area, there was a good deal of warfare and larger villages.

c) Integration into Shan states:
   1. Communities remaining in the hills will be grouped into the Shan administrative hierarchy.
   2. Communities can move into the valley – possibility of becoming a Shan sub-domain.
   3. Hill Kachin can dominate valley populations – will be institutionalized by the state. If not, it means a great deal of instability – this last possibility is exactly like (a) above.

We can, then, explain the distribution of the different Kachin systems in terms of a single development model in which there are relatively few variables. The following chart should help bring together some of the main variables and

	P/A	exterior resources	local organization	political organization	technology	techno-economic zone	developmental path
Triangle	—	—	dispersed	gumchying ↕ gumlao	S_1	A	I
Sinpraw	+	+	dispersed	gumrawng ↕ gumlao	S_1 S_2 S_7	B-C	IV
Shan states (hills)	+	+	dispersed	gumrawng (Shan)	S_2	C-D	
Htawpaw	+	—	concentrated	independent villages	S_1 S_2 S_7	B-C	II
Nam tamai[1]	+	—	concentrated	independent villages	S_2	C-D	

P/A - population density: + ≥ 15/mi²
                          — < 10/mi²

[1] See footnote p. 234.

their interrelationships. Some of the subclasses of variants are left out, but the major trends should be clear enough.

The three preceding developmental paths are distributed throughout Leach's ecological zones in the following way. Development I is found in zone A. Development II occurs in the northern part of his zones C and B, and development IV occurs in the southern part of those zones. The interpretation of the distribution is a fairly simple matter now. In development I the short cycle continually reproduces itself in the same form. In development IV, movement along the long cycle with increasing population density and deteriorating conditions of reproduction causes a number of social contradictions which are kept in check by the exploitation of the outside world. In development II, this outside world is not available and the contradictions manifest themselves: increased feuding, lower standard of living, a breakdown in supralocal organization and consequent emergence of large independent villages with chiefs of their own. If the gumsa/gumlao cycle operates, which is a clear possibility, it is now only within the village.

The one variation for the hills that we have not discussed is the jade mines (Kamaing – Mogaung) district. The reason for this is that it is not simply a case of the utilization of an outside resource to solve internal contradictions. On the contrary, the mining of jade was done entirely by the Kachins themselves, and the economy of the dominant Kansi chief's domain represents a significant shift in technological base, but one which was dependent on international and not local demand. The jade trade developed in the eighteenth and nineteenth centuries and the rise of the Kansi lineage is closely linked with this very lucrative business as the first and largest mines were located in its domain. There is not a great deal of information about the internal organization of the Kansi domain, but it is clear that the chief's revenue was nothing short of enormous. The mines were worked exclusively by Kachin. As an activity, it did not interfere with agriculture since it was during the winter months that rain slackened and the pits were dry enough to be worked. But it is not clear whether Kachin miners did any cultivating at all since there is mention of a regular rice import in the mine areas (Hertz 1912). In any case, the jade trade brought a tremendous amount of wealth into an area which was already in very good economic condition and not in need of outside resources for the maintenance of a gumsa hierarchy. The Kansi chief can best be considered as a very wealthy Kachin prince, wealthier than some of his Shan neighbors in Hkamti Long. He received a tax on all jade brought up as well as a percentage of the take in the numerous gambling halls that grew up in the area, most of which were frequented by Burmese and Chinese traders. It also appears that the largest mines, those at Tawmaw, were worked exclusively by members of the Kansi's lineage which would certainly have increased the wealth of that lineage. There is, unfortunately, very little information on the internal economy of the Kachin community since most of the official documents are concerned with international aspects of the trade. There is some data on the chiefly family, however, and from this we can ascertain that the Kansi chief was similar to a Shan domain prince who was married into Shan as well as other Kachin lineages.

Very little more can be said about the jade mines tract. It is clear, though, that the *gumlao* half of the normal Kachin cycle could be avoided since the increased surplus was not dependent on swidden agriculture. Just as with the shift to lowland irrigation, the increase in total labor input continued to give such high yields that the *gumsa* system was not only not strained, but it could develop in the direction of a small state.[1] The increase in village size so evident in the graph is the result of the totally altered economy and the concentration of wealth in a very small region. This may have brought serious problems with it in the past. The gazetteer mentions that the power of the Kansi chief is quite recent and due to external political support. In the past, Kansi was only able to maintain his position by buying off other chiefs in the area.

For the purposes of the present analysis, the jade mines tract is a special developmental case. The political and economic structure of the area is inseparable from the larger Burmese and international economy. From the very beginning, the administration of the jade mines was in the hands of both the Kansi chief and numerous Burmese officials. In spite of the fact that we know very little of the internal Kachin organization, it is safe to say that the local evolution cannot be explained as a properly Kachin development. Structurally, however, the exploitation of the mines may well have led to the expansion of a *gumchying gumsa* domain into some form of small, very specialized state. It is, of course, possible that the Kansi was no more than an extremely rich *duwa* whose position depended more on the Burmese than on his internally exercised authority. To answer this question we would have to know who worked the mines and who didn't, and how wealth was distributed, or redistributed.

We leave this problem for now. As there are several examples of the evolution toward class structure which are somewhat clearer, we need not try to draw conclusions from so little data.

Summary
We have attempted to account for Kachin variation in terms of a single model of social reproduction set in the context of a particular set of external circumstances. In the next chapter we will concentrate on the two most interesting multilinear possibilities: evolution and devolution, both of which might be said to be internally determined, i.e., with no reference to exterior conditions. In all cases, however, we are dealing with the same models, those elaborated in chapter V. The successive transformations of the basic Kachin structure are the result of the changing, if socially induced, properties of the production function. In this way, we are able to generate the distribution of social forms in terms of an historical model, i.e., one whose variables function with respect to time.

[1] Of course, if the jade mines were depleted, the same kind of diminishing returns would undoubtedly cause the system to crack.

CHAPTER VII

Evolution and Devolution

The major theme of this analysis has been the evolutionary transformation of social forms. We have discussed a number of variants of Kachin structure, not all of which are relevant to the following section. The particular ways in which Kachin groups have adapted to or rather exploited exterior resources are a special kind of dead-end evolution. Once a Kachin group becomes part of another economic system it is no longer possible to consider it in isolation, as a single reproducing society, any more than it is possible to understand one class of a stratified society independently of the larger structure. The Kachin – Shan, Kachin – trade-route relations represent a kind of imperialism on a small scale. Outside resources are extorted from another laboring population in order to maintain a system that might otherwise succumb under its own internal contradictions. The development that would normally lead from Kachin dispersed settlement *gumchying/gumlao* systems to the large independent villages of the Htawgaw and Nam Tamai area is blocked by the control over exterior populations.

In the following section we will be concerned with developments II and III, each which is an internal evolution where there is a specific correspondence between forces and relations of production within a single social formation. Thus, we will be focusing on the developmental possibilities of a *single* »mode of production«. Development II is what I have chosen to call devolution, increasing population density without major changes in the technological base, i.e., without increased potential productivity. It corresponds to the emerging dominance of the horizontal exchange structure and the gradual disappearance of the vertical system which characterized the *gumchying gumsa* model. It is a kind proto-feudal development in which landed property, incorporated into the horizontal exchange system, becomes the basis for hierarchy. Development III is the evolution of *gumsa* society to its logical conclusion in conditions of increasing absolute surplus, i.e., where the technological base is changed significantly to permit *gumsa* tendencies to work themselves out without the intersystemic contradictions implied by diminishing returns. This corresponds to the emergent dominance of the vertical exchange structure and the disappearance or at least total subordination of the horizontal. It represents the simultaneous development of a state and class society within the framework of »asiatic property«.

Feudal vs. Asiatic Modes

The vertical and horizontal structures which characterize Kachin *gumsa* formations are two ways of establishing relations between men and between men and things. The two structures, as we have seen, are not compatible in the long run, and one tends to become dominant. Before taking up the question of devolution, we must clarify the property relations implied by these two modes of organization.

Among the Kachin, there is theoretically only one kind of claim to land that can be called »property« as opposed to usufruct. This is the claim which is exercised by the youngest son lineage of a domain, and it exists by virtue of descent from the village or territorial ancestor spirit. This is only meaningful in a system where lineages form a widely ramifying segmentary system which can be traced back through the ancestors to the celestial spirits. This entire supernatural vertical structure is part of a ritual system of sacrifice and redistribution in which the chief represents the entire community to the spirit world in an attempt to increase productivity and prosperity. Thus, control over land is expressed in terms of a segmentary hierarchy of ancestor spirits for each village. As each increasingly inclusive local area can only have one *nat*, it can only have one *uma* lineage. The hierarchy of local inclusion is expressed in a hierarchy of local lineages, and community title to land is transferred to this hierarchy. In this system, land title is a product of the development of *gumsa* ranking and not vice versa. Land still belongs to the community as a single entity, but since this community represents itself by a founding ancestor spirit, the chief, by merging his own line with that of the ancestor comes to represent what Marx called the »higher unity«.

The economic process which leads to the formation of this hierarchy is dominated by an affinal exchange system. The conversion of surplus into prestige by community wide feasting is the economic base of the system which is the root of the »asiatic-mode« property described above, but it is only through the alliance system that a hierarchy of lineages can be developed. The horizontal structure, which dominates all other forms of property, has a tendency to invade the categories of land tenure and consequently, to play a secondary role in the transfer of title. I say secondary here because the transfers all take place *within* an already established *gumsa* domain where the dominant form of landed property is asiatic.

a) A non inheriting son of a chief can go with followers to another domain and *purchase* rights of tenancy from his new chief. His rank in the new domain will depend on the price he pays.

> »Indeed the transaction itself closely resembles a marriage ... it would be normal in such circumstances if the subordinate tenant chief became in fact son-in-law (*dama*) to the superior chief.« (Leach 1954:157–8).

b) In cases of conflict between patrilineal kin, or in cases of extreme poverty, a man can settle in the village of his wife-giver, thus becoming a dependent *dama* lineage whose,

> »Inferiority rests on dual grounds, firstly that the *mayu* 'were there first' and therefore have superior land title, and secondly that the founder of the *dama* lineage by adapting matrilocal residence admitted his inferior status.« (Leach 1954:69–70).

In both of these cases we have a kind of encroachment of an affinal property relation on the pre-existent segmentary structure. While both can be interpreted as being the result of shifts in residence within already established domains, there is nothing to prevent a more general interpretation which suggests that in any system where rank is determined affinally there are two simultaneous property relations. The first is title by virtue of being the *uma* (yoS) lineage. The second implies first settler status with regard to subordinate wife-takers who have bought tenancy rights. This is a rather complex situation which takes us back to the contradictions between affinal and kin relationships.

In the diagram below there are two kinds of property relation just as there are two kinds of kinship relation. If we assume that the concentric circles represent the land controlled at each level of the hierarchy, the incompatibility between the two forms becomes clear. The dominant property structure can only be represented by one circle, that of the domain. The chiefly lineage at the top is the only youngest son line and therefore is sole title holder of the entire territory. His subordinates only have access to their local position by being lineal relatives of the chief. Transfer of title is out of the question here since there is only one title, one domain, and the only means of access to any segment of the domain is through the chief himself.

The alliance relationship cuts right across this segmentary hierarchy. It is an exchange relationship between an original land holder and a tenant in which rights are partially transferred from a *mayu* to a *dama* relative. This might

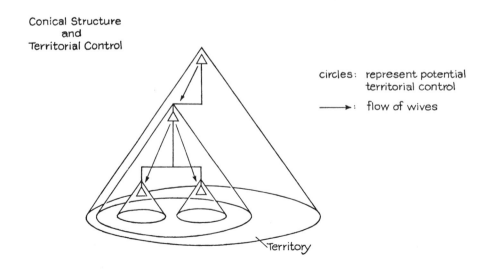

Conical Structure
and
Territorial Control

circles: represent potential territorial control

———▶: flow of wives

Territory

properly be called a proto-feudal relationship since title to land is part of the exchange process. This is not a matter of outright ownership. Except in extreme cases (some Chin groups) tenancy rights are quite inalienable. If we interpret the above diagram in terms of *mayu/dama* relations we no longer have a hierarchy of lineages where control over territory is determined by genealogical distance from the single domain title holder. Instead, we have a hierarchy of land titles or better, a partial transference of tenancy rights. The chief is the first settler and has ultimate sovereignty, but at each succeeding level below him there is a partial transfer of land rights to lineages that have bought into the domain and become *dama*.

It is not necessary to assume here that lineages are actually moving from domain to domain or that *mayu/dama* ranking depends on matrilocal residence. This would be accepting the ideology at face value.[1])

On the contrary, as we have seen, the proces of ranking is based on the *mayu/dama* system and thus, the proper interpretation here is quite simply that wherever rank is expressed affinally, this proto-feudal relationship will be implied. I have no intention of getting into terminological problems related to the use of the word »feudal«. I employ it here primarily in opposition to the notion of »asiatic« property. In its most general sense, »feudal« refers here to a hierarchical transference of rights over land in which there is a theoretically sliding scale of tenure.

These two property forms do not really come into conflict in Kachin society. The asiatic structure is everywhere dominant and such transfers as we have mentioned are quickly assimilated into the segmentary mode. It will be remembered that this hierarchy can be expressed either as a patrilineal or ambilateral structure. That is, *mayu/dama* relations can easily co-exist with the segmentary rank system so that position can be traced both affinally and consanguineously.

The contradictions would become apparent only if the transfer of land titles came into conflict with *uma* rights, i.e., if a lineage could collect land titles at will through its affinal transactions. This would be equivalent to making land a freely transferable item like other movable goods. It would also mean the destruction of the basis for the vertical segmentary system since ritual position would no longer necessarily correspond to real control over land. It is this evolution away from the asiatic property form which characterizes the devolution of Kachin structures toward Chin and Naga structures. This is, in turn, part of a larger transformation in which vertical relations breakdown and the horizontal system absorbs the entire exchange process.

---

[1]) Both Fried (1967) and de Heusch (1971) appear to be guilty of this error. For further discussion, see the concluding sections of this book.

I. Devolution

The principal determinants of the transformation of Kachin type society into
Chin and Naga types are, on the surface, purely techno-economic; increasing
population pressure, decreasing productivity, concentration into large villages.
But these factors are not independent variables in the historical perspective
we have chosen. They are the result of the perfectly normal expansion of a
gumsa/gumlao system which encounters one very important limiting factor,
space.

In the chapter on technology and environment we discussed a linear progression of technologies adapted to a more or less linear progression of environmental conditions. The only problem area there is the Lushai since the condition of the environment is not entirely clear. It must also be added that the
Lushai hills were until the mid-nineteenth century much more densely populated than they now are and that the present condition is due to a war in which
most of the groups which then occupied the northern hills were ousted or
decimated by the southern Lushai. I am referring here to the expulsion of the
Kuki tribes into Manipur and surrounding areas. It is likely that at the time of
the major ethnographies, the area had not yet adjusted to the depopulation. It is
wise, I think, to treat the Lushai as something of a special case.

The entire Naga, Chin and Lushai hills area is more heavily populated than
the Kachin Triangle area. In the Chin Hills, we begin with conditions something like those of Leach's zones B and C. Population density approaches its
maximum among the Naga groups who are surpassed only by the Wa. Although it is impossible at this point to make any definite statements, I think

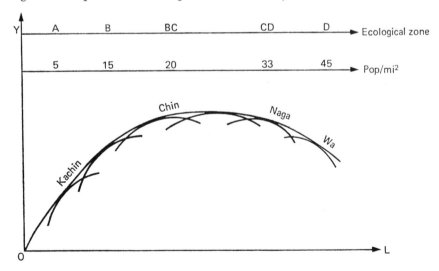

A. Primary forest predominates
B. Secondary forest predominates
C. Lighter secondary forest, scrub grassland
D. Grassland predominates

we might have a case for the following kind of evolution of the process of production.

In terms of long run input/output ratios, the Kachin of the Triangle region have the most productive economy. The Chin still have an expanding economy, but at a much slower rate, and afterwards, things get much worse. The Chin Hills may have been more heavily populated at one time and there are reports of a great deal of grassland in some areas (Lehman 1963:9). Lehman indicates that there was a population explosion in the Chin Hills as early as the sixteenth century (Lehman 1963:22), and there is evidence that Chin expansion has been in progress for a much longer time than that of the Kachin. While, on the whole, the Chin economy appears to be a rather successful adaptation to changing economic conditions, there are parts of the central hills, especially in Falam district, where land shortage is a critical problem. Thus, in spite of all adjustments, there is good reason to believe that the marginal yield on labor gets progressively worse as we move from Kachin to Wa.

Topological Transformation

The degradation of the conditions of production imposes a new set of constraints on the former system of social reproduction. If we take the low density Kachin formation as a starting point, I believe that we can show how a number of structural transformations will generate the basic properties of Chin and Naga formations.

The evolution of the production function described by the graph involves two major contradictions. The first, and most important, results from the reduction in the growth rate of surplus output. It is this change which comes into conflict with the demand for surplus generated by the relations of production and causes the breakdown in the expanding *gumsa* system. In terms of the long cycle however, it means increasing difficulty in getting the entire process started, i.e., a slow growth rate. It also means increased affinal competition at the expense of the vertical exchange structure which may disappear altogether in some cases. It is the affinal exchange system which permits the development of ranking on which the segmentary hierarchy is founded, so it is natural that the last development in *gumsa* evolution should be the first to disappear in devolution. But the conflicts between affines work themselves out in an entirely new set of circumstances which result from the de-verticalization of the lineage structure. This transformation, which I call topological for reasons that will be obvious, is produced by the contradictions of an expanding territorial system in conditions of increasing density. Earlier we discussed territorial growth and showed how it was linked to the expansionist political economy of the domain and was not just a mechanism to maintain a low population density. The expansionist tendency is reinforced by declining fertility and high demands on yield so that sooner or later conflict between local groups destroys supralocal organization and leads to the concentration of population in large aggregates, mostly for the purposes of defense.

The effect of population concentration on the lineage structure is critical, and it is a principal determinant of the other Chin and Naga transformations. The Kachin exchange and production unit is the local lineage. It contains no more than five families or so and has no difficulty in turning distant kin into affines. The main reason for this is that genealogically distant kin are also spatially distant. The village is small, migration and fissioning are very rapid processes, and the sphere of relevant alliances is always defined by locality. That is, affinal hierarchy is established at home first and then later abroad, and since the same process is going on in each village, the number of lineal competitors decreases at each level. Thus, outside of the local line, there is very little in the way of a larger lineage segment. Consequently,

>classificatory 'brothers and sisters' who are in *lawu lahta* status frequently marry.« (Leach 1954:138).

In a situation of developing rank, it is relatively easy to get rid of non-inheriting sibling lines, and they may eventually become wife-takers of the original *uma* branch. What happens now if we bring all these dispersed lines together in a single large village?

The result is that the lineage quite simply gets larger. If local lines cannot easily fission and send soon-to-be-forgotten branches off to other localities, then minimal segments are bound to collect. The result is that minimal, minor, major and maximal segmentation come to have a reality in which descent is quite clearly recognized by all. It is, in Fried's terms, a reinforcement of demonstrable descent. This seriously narrows the manoeuverability of the former local lineage which has now become a minor lineage within a larger structure which has taken over some of its former functions. In any case we have now to deal with a new kind of unit, one which structurally precedes and therefore blocks the development of the hierarchical clan that among the Kachin, could only emerge as a result of »endogamy« at all levels above that of the local lineage.

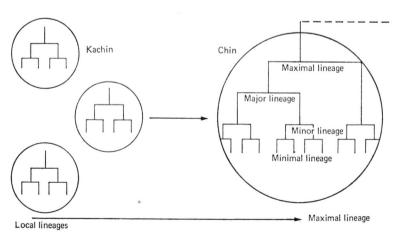

Local lineages   Maximal lineage

I have chosen to call the above transformation »topological« because it can best be understood as a »compaction« of a prior dispersed set of loosely linked units into a tighter formation by the sole operation of agglomeration. No new relationships have been added, no new elements. All that has happened is that a widely ramified genealogical space with great possibilities of fission has been brought together into a single closed geographical space where such fission is much more difficult at any but the lowest levels.

All the major properties of Chin and Naga development flow from this lineage transformation as well as the already well developed contradictions that exist in affinal ranking. We begin by discussing the Central Chin who represent the first stage in this process.

The Central Chin are usually thought of as roughly equivalent to the Kachin and numerous comparisons have tended to support this analogy. The most common similarities cited are, marriage, bridewealth, feasting and alliance ranking. While there is no doubt that there are certain invariant properties that persist in both groups, I would suggest that there are also major transformational changes that cannot be overlooked in a larger evolutionary context. Following is a concise statement of what appear to be the most important structural differences.

a) Small villages concentrate into larger village forms. Hamlets become quarters in the larger unit. The Chin word, *veng*, means either »hamlet« or »quarter.« This is clear evidence of the topological nature of the transformation.

b) We have seen that the local line and small village of the Kachin have been expanded into a larger village with a very wide demonstrable descent group. The named levels of segmentation suggested by Lehman are, minimal, minor, major, maximal and clan. The minimal lineage is the household, the basic unit of production. The minor lineage is made up of several minimal lines and is equivalent in size but not function to Leach's local lineage. It is the unit of alliance and status rank. The major

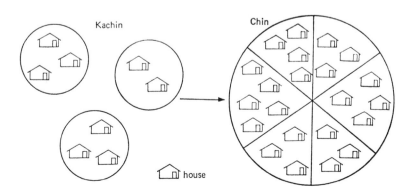

lineage is a group of temporarily equal minor lineages that may act as a political unit. It is also the fundamental (i.e., absolute minimal) unit of exogamy, not the minor lineage as among the Kachin. The major lineage can be the main land holding unit, but the minimal line usually has this function. The maximal segment might best be interpreted as the village level representative of the clan. Maximal lineages of aristocratic families are very important in that they are the segmentary level containing the ranked major lineages that contend for leadership. The clan contains several maximal lines, usually of different localities that compete for paramountcy. We note, however, that such competition is restricted to aristocratic lines and that there is a pre-existent distinction between aristocratic and commoner clans, the latter based, as we shall see, on principals very different than those found in Kachin society. Beyond this distinction, however, the relations between higher order segmentary units are extremely unstable. This is in large part due to a contradiction between the production and exchange functions of the minimal and minor lineage and the land control and rank functions of the major and maximal segments.

c) Asiatic property, i.e., by claims of ancestry in the local spirit hierarchy, is all but gone. On the contrary, land has become a transferable item in brideprice.

»The effective holders of farm plots in almost all cases are again individual households, and in most villages, only a few families own the bulk of the land.« (Lehman 1963:77).[1]

Land title brings with it a very important political power, since owners have a theoretical right to distribute plots the way they please. A large landowner is also able to make his personal plots as large as he likes each year. He need not follow the rule that a plot must be used several years in succession before going fallow, and he can, if desired, open a new field every year. Land rent is usually only a token sum, but sharecropping on the owner's personal fields occasionally occurs. All this expresses the absorption of land into the horizontal exchange structure.

There are some very significant transitional cases in the northern areas of the Chin Hills, where the chief did not allow the accumulation of land titles in the affinal exchange network.

»In the autocratic group, hereditary titles are restricted to *one per field,* the balance going to the headmen for redistribution, but in the democratic group, no such restriction exists.« (Stevenson 1968:90).

The chief's claim to title in Zahao as in some northern groups like the

---

[1] Lehman is referring to the groups we have called Central Chin which he studied and which, unlike earlier authors, he classes with the groups further north, emphasizing in this way the broad contrast with the egalitarian groups in the Southern Chin Hills.

Siyin and Sokte does not seem to be based on ritual position. It is simply »lordship of the soil«. It is noteworthy that in these areas where there are *single* chiefs, and where local organization approaches what we might call a minor Kachin type domain, *the villages are much smaller* than in Falam or Haka (see chart, page 226). These chiefs also collect »a hind leg or, in some cases, both, of any wild animal killed in the chase« (Stevenson 1968:40). Other tribute is nominal, and there does not seem to have been any corvée on the chief's land. In the above quotation, the distinction autocratic/democratic in clearly a misnomer, since hereditary rank exists in both systems. The real issue is the presence or absence of a segmentary hierarchy as the determinant of rights over land.

d) Where the vertical property structure disappears and is replaced by the alliance-exchange structure, the former system of political control must also disappear. Thus, among the Central Chin tribes, it is rare to find a paramount chief, and there is nothing approaching the conical domain hierarchies of the Kachin area. As Lehman observes with respect to the Kachin:

> »No parallel to this paramount right in land exists for the Northern Chin Hills.« (Lehman 1963:132).

The affinal exchange structure dominates the entire circulation process, and the cycle whereby wealth is converted by feasting into prestige and then validated by marriage exchanges, is linked, not to claiming a position in the segmentary hierarchy, but to the accumulation of land titles and wife-taking followers. In any one powerful village like Haka, there are two or more competing chiefs, each with control over substantial numbers at home and in other villages. But there is no single chiefly position and the competition, though restricted economically is open indefinitely to the chosen few.

e) Inheritance among all the Northern and Central Chin shows a marked devolution of ultimogeniture into more or less complex systems in which eldest or youngest son, or more often both, divide the main property. However, it appears to be usual to take care of all sons in one way or another. The body-pairing system, »*ro co*«, is a good example of this. Here, a first division is made equally between eldest and youngest son, then between next eldest and next youngest and so on. The specified function of this form of inheritance is the

> »prevention of too large an accumulation of property in the hands of one branch of a family.« (Stevenson 1968:168).

It is also common for segments of the same major lineage to hold land jointly.

> »This is to prevent lineage segmentation from taking effect too rapidly within politically powerful lineages.« (Lehman 1963:79).

The practices have the contrary effect of the strict, if contended, ultimogeniture of the Kachin. Instead of restricting control and authority to the smallest possible unit, there is a tendency to spread things out among sibling lines. This, of course, can only lessen the possibility of the evolution of neat hierarchies. It results in more or less equal, if competing, wealthy houses.

f) Among Kachin *gumsa* groups, the supernatural world is highly ordered. It is, further, a direct ancestral extension of the social world and plays a crucial part in the economic affairs of the domain. Lineage ancestors merge with the spirit world in a single segmentary hierarchy which provides a means of communication with the forces that control prosperity. The Chin spirit hierarchy is not nearly so clear. There is a supreme spirit who does seem to receive offerings at higher feasts of merit, but who gets no communal sacrifices. Bareigts reports for Hnaring (Lautu) that there are three village spirits whose origin is unclear although he suggests that they might be ancestors of the whole group. Communal sacrifices are performed in a sacred area inside the village and are directed by village priests. It would appear that the Kachin hierarchical spirit world has more or less collapsed. All the Chin categories of *nats* correspond to those of the Kachin, but they are not organized in terms of the same conical principles.

g) Leach suggests that the Kachin *manau* feasts are similar to feasts of merit among the Chin and Naga (Leach 1954:119). While there are

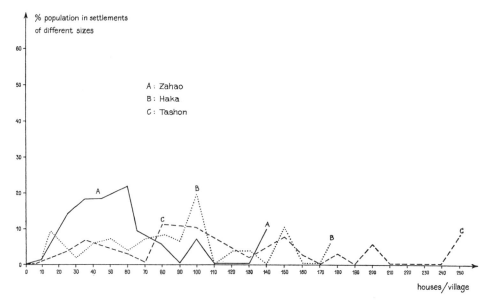

indeed similarities, the differences are perhaps more important. *Manao* feasts appear to be directly related to the specifics of *gumsa* structure. They are above all *community feasts* in which the giver represents the larger community before the spirit world in an attempt to bring on increased prosperity. Feasts of merit, on the other hand, seem to be primarily competitive affinal potlatches as Rosman and Rubel have suggested (Rosman and Rubel n.d.). That is, they are primarily part of the horizontal exchange system, which must necessarily be the case since, as we have seen, the vertical system has all but vanished. Feasts of merit do involve offerings to higher village spirits who are not, however, genealogically related, but this is in no way a community feast. Its major benefits are an elevation of status, the right to raise one's daughter's brideprice and, after a given number (variable) of feasts, the right to sit on the village council. The series of feasts is of variable length and probably depends on the local availability of resources, but there are almost always a number of competing individuals engaged in the cycle. From all appearances, the feast of merit system is somewhere between *gumlao* and *gumsa*, that is, in the continual process of establishing affinal rank. But there is a definite hierarchization, and the giving of feasts is important since it defines a certain aristocracy implied in the term »*bawi-lam*«, »the way to attaining *bawi* (aristocratic) status.« (Lehman 1963:178).

An interesting aspect of the feast of merit is the distribution itself. There seems to be a specific attempt not only to raise one's relative rank with regard to wife-givers, but also with regard to one's own clan.

> »The characteristic difference in the reciprocities between patrilineal male relatives and the others named are that, excepting the Khualdar, the former do not help at feasts.« (Stevenson 1968:143).

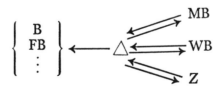

The giver of a feast of merit is competing for the leadership of his lineage and clan. His patrilineal kin reciprocate later, by helping with his affinal payments.

What should be clear in all this is the fact that the feast of merit is primarily an attempt to dominate one's kinship network although this implies that one gains status in the village as a whole.

While the Kachin local lineage is a single independent status unit that need only be concerned with affinal rank, the Chin minimal unit is burdened with a large number of patrilineal kin who must also be subordinated, not by turning them into affines, although this can occur to some degree, but primarily by means of feasts of merit which establish one's position in the clan as well as in the affinal network. In any case, a much larger portion of the total available surplus is being used to maintain relative kinship rank than among the Kachin.

>These feasts ... are the cornerstone of Chin economic structure. The largest portion of the Chin surplus resources are utilized through this channel.« (Stevenson 1968:137).

h) Slavery exists among the Central and Northern Chin, but it appears to be mostly debt slavery. In the past there were slave raids, but the influx of slaves does not appear to have had anything of the magnitude of the Kachin operation. The large majority captured may have been the result of warfare with other Chin groups. Nevertheless, debt slavery seems to predominate and the proportion of such slaves in any village approaches an average of fifty percent. Below are Bareigts' figures for Hnaring (Bareigts 1969).

	Families	%
Noble	58	19
Commoner	70	23
Slaves	178	59

The existence of such large numbers of slaves is quite understandable for reasons we have already discussed. Among the Chin, the accumulation of debts is especially accentuated by the increased emphasis on affinal obligations, and the possibility of accumulating land titles. In those areas where land titles are most readily negotiable and can be bought and sold at will (apparently a recent development), the proportion of slaves may reach 85% of the population (Stevenson 1968:179).

But slaves are not centrally controlled, and many nobles have more slaves than their local headmen. Here again, rather than being concentrated, wealth is distributed among a number of high ranking lineages.

As we have said, slaves are no more than commoners in debt who give up their independent lineage status to become low ranking members of noble households, at least temporarily. Most slaves appear to be exterior, i.e., having their own houses. On marriage, a master must build a house for his slave as well as paying his brideprice. Contrary to the Kachin, the Chin *tefa* system does not appear to be the basis of an extraction of surplus from a specific class of the population. The word »slave« is used for a much wider range of debt relations and *tefa* who are not actually living in their master's houses are not subject to anything like the tribute and corvée required of Kachin *ngong mayam*.

The Chin system is characterized by an extreme development of inter-lineage competition, an attempt to assert and maintain affinal rank, but also to achieve leadership within the maximal lineage and clan. Especially within an aristocratic maximal lineage, there is a great deal of competition for leadership between major branches. While, theoretically, there is ranking at this level, this is not necessarily the actual situation simply because there are no clear ways of establishing paramount rule.

»Within Haka Town the heads of Sangpi and Sangte (maximal lineages of Zathang Clan) were equally chiefs on account of their external realms, and Sangpi and Sangte occupied different settlement wards and so could be said to have different realms even within Haka itself. No one actually ruled over Haka as a whole.« (Lehman 1963:115).

Political rank is built by transforming surplus into prestige, prestige into brideprice, land titles and thus followers. It is reinforced by making strategic alliances with other lineages engaged in the same process. A headman is necessarily someone who has a large number of land titles, a great deal of wealth (implied), and is able to make good marriages. His position enables him to receive something similar to the tribute and corvée of the Kachin Chief. Since he owns a great deal of land and has enormous personal plots, he will ask a number of commoner families to work for him. He is entitled to two baskets of millet from his dependents at the opening of every fifth swidden (i.e., not very often), and if he is a chief over subject villages (conquered) he can receive an annual tribute. Lehman distinguishes a chief from a headman only in terms of the presence or absence of an external realm of authority. External control is the result of either war or marriage. In the first case a substantial tribute is taken, in the second, only that due a wealthy aristocrat. There are no domains in the Kachin sense. A chief may be lord over other villages, but this is either in his status as wife-giver or ruler by conquest. It is significant that, unlike the Kachin, the powerful chiefs are always the leaders of the largest villages; they are great military leaders.

This is a different kind of system than that of the Kachin. Most rank relationships are individual. There is nothing so clear and distinctive as a local segmentary hierarchy with lineage heads, village headmen, domain chiefs and a paramount. The headman or chief bases his authority on a personal following of wife-takers and those who work his land (also his wife-takers). This is an individualized set of relations, the result of the total dominance of the affinal relationship at the level of exchange of wealth and the acquisition of status. But within the more or less exogamous segmentary lineage, ranking is very difficult to establish. A symptom of this is the existence of both individual status rank and class rank, the latter being inherent in the clan. This results in wealthy commoners who are by status rank *bawi* (noble) although unable to escape the class rank of their clan.

>This would amount to the establishment of a new clan, and so far we have found no instances of such a thing.« (Lehman 1963:113).

There is a theoretical possibility that a powerful and wealthy minimal lineage can manipulate its genealogy, that it can strategically eliminate old connections and create new ones. But this is a very difficult task in a system where descent is usually demonstrable and clan affiliation known to all.

Among the Kachin where genealogical memory loses its collateral function outside the local line, these problems are practically non-existent. A powerful local lineage can usually subdue a potential competitor sibling line by making it *dama*. The maximal lineage among the Kachin is highly endogamous. The chiefs of a single clan or maximal lineage frequently marry in a circle. This kind of thing does not occur among the Chin where the maximal lineage *tends* to remain exogamous unless there is a marked rank difference between its major segments. Intermarriage does create new minor, major and maximal lines among the Chin, but affinal politics of this sort is more restricted than among the Kachin, and one cannot as readily turn kin into affines.

The youngest son of a Kachin *duwa* does not inherit part or even all of a given number of land titles and affinal followers. He inherits a position in a segmentary hierarchy. There is only one such position defined by the absolute identity of territorial and genealogical segmentation. Thus, there is only one village, one domain, one territory, none of which can be subdivided. There is no real land title among the Kachin. There is, rather, supremacy over the community and its land which is determined by a monopoly over a ritual hierarchy. No such position exists among the Central Chin and headmen and chiefs derive their authority exclusively from the horizontal exchange system.

>The power of autocratic headmen as of chiefs was derived from their position as preferred wife-givers and land-owners.« (Lehman 1963:145).

Structural Dominance of Horizontal Exchange

The formation of Kachin *gumsa* results from the transformation of wealth into rank and rank into a hierarchical position within the segmentary structure of the village and domain. In the Chin system, hierarchy is the result of direct control over individual lineages and, most important, over the land they cultivate. This is only possible because land has become incorporated into the affinal or horizontal exchange. Because of the extension and dominance of the horizontal system, the community is more or less fragmented into numerous headmen and their personal followers. The unity of the community as a ritual entity headed by a single lineage is replaced by a division of functions. In the Chin village, religion, i.e., ritual attempts to bring on prosperity, is primarily the affair of priests. Control over land and followers is not the result of ritually based authority; it is a direct implication of the exchange process itself.

The transformation of the local lineage into a segmentary clan has a critical effect on the structure of alliances and on the economy of the minimal and minor segment, the production-exchange unit that in Kachin society is a basic precondition of affinal ranking.

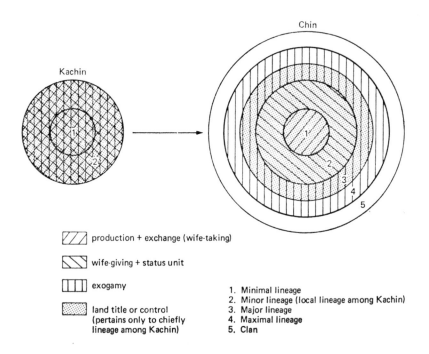

production + exchange (wife-taking)

wife-giving + status unit

exogamy

land title or control
(pertains only to chiefly
lineage among Kachin)

1. Minimal lineage
2. Minor lineage (local lineage among Kachin)
3. Major lineage
4. Maximal lineage
5. Clan

In the above diagram I have tried to show the major differences between Kachin and Chin lineage organization. Among the Kachin, all the functions except production itself are combined in the local lineage. Among the Chin there is more of a fragmentation of the different levels. The distribution of the functions are, of course, variable, as is the degree of segmentation, but I have tried to show them in their maximal extension in order to underline emergent incompatibilities between the different levels. In both groups, minimal lineage segmentation is very rapid, but judging by the description in Lehman, the Chin minimal line, more than the Kachin equivalent, appears to be an independent *wife-taking* unit, whereas the minor lineage is the unit of status. The latter is consequently concerned with the regulation of *wife-giving*, or rather, since it is homogenous with regard to prestige, it is chosen as if it were a single entity by other wife-taking lineages. The result, even at the primary level of segmentation, is that there is a conflict between the status of the minor lineage and the independent alliance strategies of the minimal segments. Among the

Kachin, on the contrary, it appears as though the local lineage is both a wife-taking and wife-giving entity, a single alliance unit.

The major lineage level is the absolute limit of exogamy, but it is uncommon for people to marry within the limits of the maximal lineage. While the minimal lineage is the usual holder of land title, it is possible for as large a group as the major lineage to jointly own landed property. Finally, political authority is often exercised at the level of the maximal segment, especially in noble clans.

This differentiation within the segmentary structure makes total dominance virtually impossible. Since the minimal segment can collect land titles, a political-economic dominance can be achieved inside the maximal lineage. But such authority is temporary, because in inheritance there is a dispersion of property titles in such a way that they cannot be increasingly accumulated by any one branch. Assuming that the minor lineage acts as a single political-economic unit (i.e., according to our »political economy of the local lineage« model), it can achieve affinal rank with respect to a great many other minor lineages, but it cannot turn its sibling lineages into affines of lower status. Thus, there is a persistent status indeterminacy at the major lineage level. This applies equally to the maximal lineage where a number of segments compete for paramount status, but where exogamy makes this extremely difficult. Maximal lineage endogamy can, of course, occur, but it certainly does not appear to be the rule. In the most powerful villages where there are several strong chiefs each with his external realm, there is little evidence of an attempt at internal affinal ranking. As opposed to the Kachin, the Chin system appears to be overburdened with siblings at the very start. The Kachin *duwa* only begins to amass such unwanted contenders after he is already established as paramount. In Kachin society, everything is geared to the rapid expulsion of blood kin and their transformation into possible affines. While it is possible for a Haka Chin to marry into his own patriline, it is reported to be quite rare. In any case, where it does occur it is usually recognized as endogamy and the lineage must be legally split. This problem does not arise for the Kachin.

The emergent contradiction in the fusion of local lines into a segmentary clan is that between the political-economic functions of the production-exchange unit (minor lineage at most) and the new extended exogamy which prevents internal ranking and inhibits the political maneuverability of the formerly independent local lineage. Further, the development and strengthening of maximal and clan levels, makes new demands on the minimal unit in the form of increasing and extended patrilineal obligations. While Lehman appears to be correct in insisting that the Central Chin has a segmentary lineage organization, it is not hard to understand how Leach and others have been misled by certain facts to believe the contrary. (Lehman 1963:106; Leach 1957). While the smaller lineage segments do in fact establish their own fairly independent sets of alliances, and while the affinal network of the minimal lineage maps increasingly less well into the exchange networks at higher levels of the clan (i.e., degree of affinal overlap varies inversely with collateral proximity), there is undoubtedly a tendency for a certain pressure to be exerted by the maximal segment on the political and thus marital affairs of lower levels. Recognition of this tendency is crucial for an evolutionary analysis, since as we move to the Naga it becomes dominant while the lower segmentary levels disappear altogether. Bareigts, who seems to make the same mistake as Leach with respect to internal segmentation, does give some valuable information concerning maximal lineage (clan for Bareigts) strength in Hnaring. The Lautu maximal segment appears to have a political unity not described for the Haka (Bareigts 1969, Chap. 2). He indicates that it has control over land, houses, property and even marriages. The maximal lineage does not own land as a unit, nor does it have a single leader, but it is described as having a kind of clan interest in all of the activities of its members. This is expressed in the activities of the clan council which deals more or less democratically with the affairs of the group.

A final consequence of the disparity between the alliance function of the minimal unit and the political functions of the clan is the problem of reversal of alliances at higher levels of segmentation.

»Let us suppose that there is a major segment A to which I am wife-taker and then I give a daughter in marriage to the line A1 (my effective affinal relationships having been with A2). A1 and A2 will undoubtedly cease to take *arsa* together thereafter. Moreover, I must at once pay compensation to A2 since I have violated a prohibition against reversing the direction of an affinal relationship.« (Lehman 1963:120).

Here, as opposed to the Kachin, affinal categories are extended beyond the actual lineage of the wife-giver to a number of collaterals; all those who share in a particular part of brideprice (*arsa*).[1] But at the maximal lineage level, reciprocity can in fact occur. As long as the *arsa* component of the brideprice is not shared by B1 and B2, then for all practical purposes, there is restricted exchange between maximal lineages.

This is a very significant step in the evolution toward Naga type structures. Maximal lineage reciprocity is probably still rather rare among the Chin and may well vary with the corporate strength of the clan. It is difficult to ascertain its effects, but it must certainly pose a problem with regard to ranking,

[1] *Arsa* is an extremely important component, consisting of chicken meat, of brideprice that is distributed to all members of the wife-giving group.

since if restricted exchange occurs over any length of time, the lineages involved must either fission or drastically reduce the transitive aspect of ranking.
Bareigts implies that reciprocal alliances of the kind described here can co-
exist at the maximal level and that the lineage is simply split for the purposes
of marriage. Reciprocity of this kind may not be that important in a system
where the main unit of status and rank is the minor lineage and where the
major lineage is a relatively independent political entity, but where the internal ranking of the clan is weak this can come to look like a system of restricted
exchange. On a global level it might be similar to the Garo where asymmetrical alliance between closely related lines fades into bilateral exchange at
more distant levels. The major difference here might be nothing more than a
matter of the ranking (as a process) of segments and the stress put on the
minimal and minor lineages as the only relevant units. The reciprocity among
maximal lineages or clans is indicative of a certain ambiguity in the rank
structure itself. While it might, on the one hand, imply the existence of rank
differences within the maximal lineage, it might also reflect on the affinal
status of the exchange units themselves. That is, $A1 \rightarrow B \rightarrow A2$ might imply
$A1 > A2$, but if A2 is a powerful major lineage in its own right it might also
imply that $B = A1$. In any case, it could certainly put the whole rank structure
in doubt. An outlet is provided for this kind of conflict in the form of lineage
fission, but the fact that the conflict arises points to a basic contradiction between the growing strength of the clan and the affinal exchange system.

Expansion and Conflict in the Horizontal Exchange System

Leach (1957) has argued that the extreme elaboration of brideprice payments
among the Lakher[1] (as among the Chin) is related to their relative ease of
divorce as compared to the more moderate Jinghpaw Kachin (Leach 1957). He
has recently restated his position,
> »Which links this 'development of prestations' to the legal permissability
> of divorce, and thus discriminates between Lakher, Haka and Gauri on
> the one hand and Jinghpaw on the other.« (Leach 1969).

Lehman, is his review of Leach's review of Levi-Strauss (above) criticizes the
insufficiencies of this position and gives a more satisfactory analysis. He suggests, contrary to Leach, that elaborate bridewealth payments are intimately
connected to the degree
> »to which high descent-group rank is ambiguously defined at law, as both
> necessarily hereditary and achievable through the giving of 'feasts of
> merit,' and by the contracting of advantageous marriage alliances with
> payments at previously unprecedented marriage prices.« (Lehman 1969:
> 124).

He goes on to assert that,
> »It is precisely in the context of this ambiguity in the means for justifying

[1]) The Lakher are closely related neighbors to the Chin.

claims to aristocratic status and the attendant instability of political relationships involving rank, that divorce is made easy.« (Lehman 1969:124). Lehman's analysis coincides exactly with what we would expect. The entire economic flow of surplus is directed toward the maintenance of affinal rank. But this appears to be the case for a reason exactly opposite to that suggested by Leach. The Haka and Lakher are not more stratified than ordinary Jinghpaw. If this were the case then the elaborate brideprice would be unnecessary. On the contrary, the expansion and extension of these payments is linked to the increasing difficulty of establishing and maintaining affinal rank. This explanation is also implied by Lehman.

When Leach's comparative analysis is interpreted from an evolutionary perspective, we find that the development of affinal tension follows our long-term production function quite closely. The Jinghpaw Kachin, of the Triangle, have the least elaborate payments and the lowest divorce rate. A woman once married becomes the property of the *dama* lineage. The Gauri (Kachin), of the Sinlum (Sinpraw) area, have the same system of payments, but the strain between *mayu* and *dama* is increased. Gauri girls don't go to live with their husbands immediately but remain at home for a number of years where they enjoy complete sexual freedom. Divorce is rare but possible upon return of the brideprice. Among Central Chin groups, the brideprice is much more elaborate. Not only does the WF receive payment, but also WMB, i.e., wife-givers' wife-giver, and the price is extremely inflated. Divorce is relatively easy and part of the brideprice, that paid to WMB, may be kept.

An explanation suggests itself for this increasing affinal conflict, for what Lehman refers to more explicitly as ambiguity in claims to rank positions. As available surplus decreases or even increases at a slower rate, the maintenance of affinal rank becomes more of a strain on the exchanging units, and debts take on a much greater importance. We have suggested that Jinghpaw, Gauri and Central Chin represent a descending order of productivity or availability of resources. This progression (or regression) corresponds to the collapse of the vertical exchange structure and the emergent dominance of horizontal exchange as the sole determinant of status. The extension of payments to WMB is an attempt to make the most out of the ranking process. But it is only an attempt, because the system continues to be openly competitive and absolute rank is never clearly established. The strains in affinal relations are maximized by the existence of segmentary clans. The individual minimal line must validate its rank not just to a single wife-giver or wife-taker, but to a wide range of collaterals whose status may not be affected by the marriage. Furthermore, one has to assert one's rank within the major and maximal lineage of one's own clan. It is necessary in such circumstances to invest a great deal in the horizontal exchange networks if anything like a dominant position is to be achieved.

Gumsa/Gumlao

Leach suggests in several places that the *gumsa/gumlao* variation of the Kachin is analogous to autocratic/democratic variation among the Chin and Naga (Lehman 1963:140–1). Lehman has suggested, at least for the Central Chin, that this difference is one between class rank and status rank. The first is purely hereditary while the second is the result of accumulated wealth. But he insists that,

> »status rank is no more than a weaker from of class rank.« (Lehman 1963: 145).

I would take this argument one step further. There are no true *gumlao* societies in the Central Chin Hills because the basis of rank has been shifted from one of ritual position to one of land ownership. But this also implies that there are no true *gumsa* societies here. The only groups which approach *gumsa* organization are the Zahao and the northern groups where land title is more or less monopolized by one lineage and where lesser rights exist by virtue of one's position within the territorical segmentary hierarchy. But we have said that these regimes seem to feel the need to make an explicit attempt to prevent the transfer and accumulation of titles, and this is surely evidence of a conflict between the two forms of property.

The so-called democratic villages of the Central Chin were often centers of great power. Tashon, for example, which ruled a very wide area, had no single chief but was headed by an elected council »who were presumably all aristocrats.« (Lehman 1963:141). Thus, the democratic villages were only democratic within one level. This would be equivalent to a number of *gumsa* chiefs marrying in a circle. No single aristocratic headman dominated Tashon village. Rather, each had his own realm and his own followers within and beyond the village. The only difference between Haka and Tashon is that the latter had more chiefs, that its realm »was even less consolidated than that of Haka.« (Lehman 1963:146).

> »The power of the leading families were equal and so each family held the others in check. They apparently cooperated in council, but no single network of alliance and affinity could build up autocratic powers.« (Lehman 1963:147).

The degree of autocracy varies inversely with the number of chiefly families, aristocrats who can maintain a larger following. Thus, the absence of paramount rank among the Chin is equivalent to the modus vivendi reached by competing *gumsa* chiefs which results in a marriage circle. I argued earlier that the difference between *gumsa* and *gumlao* was structurally one of degree and not kind. If this be the case, then the democratic Central Chin are far more autocratic than the small *gumlao* communities of the Kachin. The difference is crucial. In a true *gumlao* community, all hereditary rank is denied which implies that all lineages are more or less on an equal footing. Among the Chin this is impossible because of the intervention of a stronger form of property. One is an aristocrat primarily because of the possession of land titles. Land is determinant here because it necessarily implies that there are subordinate lineages to rent it. Thus, while on the surface, the Chin system appears to be *gumlao* since there are only big-men competing for prestige and no explicitly hereditary hierarchy of positions, the fact that land can be accumulated and not just status creates a new kind of aristocracy. There may be no cultural recognition of differentiation on the basis of ownership, but this new form of property does indeed function within the older social categories. If an individual owns half of the village lands and passes the titles on to his son, this is *de facto* aristocracy. A *gumlao* rebellion does not address itself to this problem at all. As a result, Central Chin society varies between more or less hierarchy at the highest levels of aristocracy, but the whole system rests on the continued existence of the aristocratic/commoner distinction. The only society which lacks hereditary rank altogether is Matupi Chin to the south and it is significant that land titles cannot be accumulated over time here. This is prevented by what appears to be a stronger maximal lineage and clan organization.

Supralocal organization where it does occur, and it appears to be very unstable at all times, is not entirely like that of a *gumsa* domain. Warfare plays a very important part in the establishment of larger realms and local segmentation plays a relatively minor role. The chief of a realm receives tribute from subjugated villages, token rent from land titles in other villages, and the normal payment due to an aristocratic wife-giver. All the channels in which wealth circulates are the result of individual affinal links or warfare. It appears that whole villages are subordinate only when they have been conquered. Otherwise all payments are between individual allies. In the Kachin domain, supralocal organization is not individualistic and headmen of villages and village clusters are linked in an inclusive hierarchy. This cannot occur among the Chin unless a very wealthy aristocrat succeeds in »buying up« all the land in a village.

It should be clear then, that Chin hierarchy is based on different principles than that of the Kachin. But these principles are the product of the increasing dominance of the horizontal exchange system. Among the Kachin, control over land is based on claims on the segmentary structure. Among the Chin, political rank is based on control over land. I take the latter to represent a kind of proto-feudal tendency. It is similar in some ways to Marx's Germanic Mode in which land titles are individually owned but negotiable and thus where concentration of property is the basis of hierarchy (Marx 1964:75–82, Gurevich 1972). The Chin system (like the Triangle Kachin) never develops beyond ranking, however, due to the limits of productivity. This is expressed in the emerging contradiction between the independent individual exchange unit and the increasing size and strength of the maximal lineage and clan.

Further Devolution

As we move in the direction of the Naga and Wa, the tendencies that were shown to exist for the Chin become much stronger. I do not intend here to discuss the very wide variation that exists, but merely to outline some of the major devolutionary trends.

Population density increases to an average of 33/mi² in the Naga Hills. The villages become much larger than they are among the Chin. Angami villages average 450 houses; Lhota villages, 293 houses; Ao villages, 578 houses; Rengma, 420 houses (Allen 1905). There appears to be real land shortage in much or even most of the territory. The Naga Hills gazetteer reports that in those areas where the Angami practice irrigated terracing, there is little jungle to be seen (Allen 1905). There appears to be little forest in most of the territory except in valleys (uninhabitable) and on steepest hillsides.

Availability of land varies from region to region and village to village. Some Lhota who have a good deal of land seem to follow a cultivation-fallow cycle of 1/10, but this is rare. Land is usually cultivated for at least two years running and then fallowed for five, seven, ten, or twelve years, i.e., as long as possible. Among the Marring Naga, however, the land shortage is so acute that fallow is virtually non-existent. Their swiddens are,

>covered with an elaborate system of herring bone drains to prevent the rains from washing all the surface soil from the slopes.« (Allen 1905:30).

The village is the largest political unit. There are no supralocal realms at all. In fact, more often than not, political integration reaches its maximum below the village level. The village section or *khel* is usually the dominant organizational unit, and they are often complete political and economic entities in themselves. In certain Angami villages, the section is fortified and there is every indication that intravillage disputes often lead to warfare among the various *khel*.

The minimal and minor lineage loses much of its importance and even its identity. The clan is generally the unit of exogamy although there are examples of endogamy in the largest clans. Among the Konyak, Lhota and Angami, exogamy is extended beyond the clan to include groups of clans (phratries), or entire village sections. This emergence of larger clan units is critical, as we have shown, for the political and economic independence of the smaller lineage segments which may lose all their former functions.

The Sema Naga are in many ways closer to the Chin than any of the other groups and they make an interesting comparison. Clans are not as important here as in other Naga groups.

>The basis of Sema society is the village (*apfu, agana*), or part of a village (*asah*).« (Hutton 1921a:121).

Village sections are suposedly under the control of a chief whose power stems from the fact that he is a landowner. It is probably best to qualify this. It seems likely that the formation of a village section is no more than the formation of a headman-plus-following. Smaller villages have a single chief, but large villages have several. The actual structure of the village polity is not quite clear in the ethnography. The category *mughemi* appears to be applicable to any non-chiefs. But it is also used to designate a kind of debt bondage in which a man unable to pay brideprice asks a chief to provide him with a wife in exchange for labor service on the chief's land. Wealth can be converted into land titles, however, as among the Chin, and this appears to be the economic cornerstone of Sema hierarchy.

> »Persons are often found with well recognized rights to a few days labor in their fields who are no longer, or who never were recognized as having any claim on the chieftainship.« (Hutton 1921a:149).

Hutton is not specific as to the nature of claims to chieftainship outside of land control, but there is one trend in Sema society that appears to serve as the basis for a real chiefly claim over village land. This is the fact that the Sema are still expanding, which implies the formation of new small settlements. Chiefs have a policy, when possible, of sending their eldest sons off with a segment of the dependent families to found a new village, and there appears to be a tradition that a village founder has title to all the land. In this way, just as among the northern (not central) Chin there are numbers of relatively small villages with single chiefs. But where expansion slows down, where brothers cannot be sent off, property begins to be dispersed within the clan. This second tendency is the stronger of the two in Sema society, judging by the distribution of land within the village. Sema ethnography is especially valuable here because it gives us an insight into the possible transition from an original Kachin type structure to the present Central Chin and Naga system. The progression seems to run like this:

1) impossibility of expansion – growth of village
2) collection of brothers within the chiefly line
3) division of village land – »democratization« of inheritance rules
4) progressive individualization of land title
5) land title becomes negotiable
6) new possibility of accumulation

This transition might account for the difference between Zahao, Sokte and Siyin Chin land tenure and that of the Central Hills. The Sema appear to have something of both the chiefly claim and the secondary accumulation, but it would be very difficult to distinguish the two since once land and followers are amassed, the chiefly claim will be accepted by the community. Sema chiefs do not have any of the local or supralocal power of their Chin equivalents. They have a much smaller economic base to work on, a less productive technology. The claims they can make on their followers are not as great as those of the Chin, and there is, above all, the growing contradiction between the clan and the individual lineage. As population pressure is greater, the clan is forced together in a more decisive way. This is evident in Sema inheritance rules.

a) If a man has no sons, land goes to brothers, cousins, etc., to *collaterals of the same generation.*
b) Land inherited by sons *is not divided* during that generation, but must wait for grandchildren who then *divide it equally.*

With such a system of inheritance, it is practically impossible to keep land titles within a lineage of narrow span. All property, no matter how acquired, must eventually be dispersed throughout the larger clan. In a recent article, Hutton makes clear that Sema are not nearly as *gumsa* as one might believe from his earlier description.

>The authority of a Sema chief is quickly sapped when he can no longer shed off his brothers and sons to found new villages with retainers of their own.« (Hutton 1965:23).

We might well conclude from this that with increasing population density, the Sema, who were at the time of description expanding eastward, might in time come to look like the Angami. Naga groups that have not been able to expand have become quite egalitarian in most respects. Here, the clan takes on a much more central role in the management of land and internal politics. The Ao have a tradition that all chiefs came from a single clan, but they are not themselves hierarchically organized. This is to be expected. Ranking is established by the action of independent minor or minimal lineages that are capable of concentrating wealth in their own hands. With the strengthening of clan structure, the lineage ultimately disappears and segmentary structure gives way to the egalitarian clan.

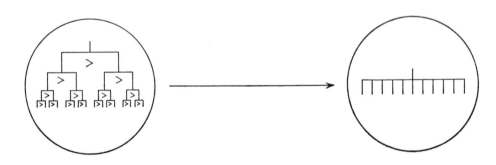

Among the Lhota, the clan is the major land-owner and individuals can only hold land within the confines of the larger unit. That is, if there are no heirs, the land reverts to the clan for eventual redistribution. The Angami, who are often singled out for their private property rights in terraced fields are no different from the Sema in this respect. Land titles are transferable, but they are inherited equally so that property tends to be continually redistributed within the larger clan.

With the increased size of the lineal unit, political manoeuvre becomes very difficult. The feast of merit cycle still exists and is a means to prestige, but it cannot be transformed into ranked affinal relations. There are wealthy men in every village, but their wealth is dispersed in inheritance and the most that can be achieved is a large measure of influence within a single generation.

There are very often clan and even village section headmen, but their status is not usually hereditary.

The Naga have gone much further than the Chin with respect to the even distribution of political and economic functions in the wider patrilineal group. Here, the horizontal exchange structure begins to be dominated by the expanded clan. This is reflected in the re-emergence of restricted exchange. Levi-Strauss has made an excellent analysis of the way asymmetrical and symmetrical tendencies are combined in Naga alliance systems (Levi-Strauss 1967: Chap. 7). We have seen how the growth of restricted exchange among the Chin could come into contradiction with the attempt to establish rank. Among the Naga the contradiction is solved in favor of equality, for it is no longer a question of independent exchange units. The unit of exogamy is the clan, and since there is no possibility of maintaining asymmetrically ranked relations, there is a tendency to revert to bilaterality. Most Naga groups permit both patrilateral and matrilateral cross-cousin marriage. But since the classificatory kin group is very large, exchange is almost always reciprocal at the clan level (i.e., simultaneously patri- and matrilateral). This is all reflected in the various combinations of threes and twos in the hierarchy of exogamous units. The Lhota have three phratries of nine clans each, usually grouped into villages of two *khelu*. The Angami have two *khelu*, the Memi have three, one of which is of theoretically lower status. The Angami have gone farthest in the direction of »dualism« and they have been interpreted as having a moiety system. It is interesting, however, that in their mythical representation of the sibling ancestors of the sections a definite ranking emerges.

»Of the two ancestors of Angamis, Thevo, who emerged the first, was the ancestor of Kepezoma, who are entitled by virtue of his priority to a precedence in eating over the descendents of the younger Thekrono. The Kepepfuma, however, claim that Thekrono was really the elder of the two, but that Thevo outwitted him in the matter of precedence by arrogating to himself priority of birth and proceding to eat first on the strength of it without giving Thekrono an opportunity to assert his right.« (Hutton 1921b:112).

Hutton reports that the moieties are no longer exogamous and that the dualist system is breaking down. The myth may be taken to reflect the possible disruption in former affinal reciprocity, but it might also represent an earlier stage of ranked clans. Aristocrats and commoners form a dual division of clans among the Chin and it is rather typical to represent such vertical divisions in terms of the senior/junior rank of mythical ancestors. The word *khelu* which refers today to the largest exogamous unit among the Naga, ordinarily means »generation.«

Gumsa/Gumlao

Most descriptions of Naga tribes stress that former exogamous groupings are on the point of becoming endogamous or vice versa. Among the Lhota, some clans remain exogamous, others are split into intermarrying pairs that are ranked in terms of the elder/younger distinction. Hutton cites the example of the Sema who declared that his ancestors were not really from his named clan and that consequently he could from then on marry endogamously. He lost his head shortly thereafter in a feud with a neighboring village, evidently as divine punishment for his outrageous act. (Hutton 1921a:130).

Stories like the one described above reflect the conflict, especially in Sema society, between the clan and the smaller lineage segments. Hutton, Mills and other authorities assumed that there is a tendency for the clan to dissolve into smaller segmentary units, but there is just as much evidence that the contrary is occuring. In fact it is difficult to determine the direction of development in most cases. I would suggest, however, that there is a kind of fluctuation or oscillation between fusion and fission and that this is related to the contradictory tendencies of ranking and clan unity in conditions of high population density and degraded environment.

The Sema appear to be at the end of a period of expansion in which a hierarchical structure was able to develop, at least at the local level, by the continual establishment of relatively small villages. With increasing density this became impossible and the system began to turn in on itself. The Sema prefer matrilateral cross-cousin marriage. FZD marriage is permitted but it is considered to be sterile, and, in fact, in the politico-economic sense it is sterile. It prevents the emergence of extensive exchange networks and blocks the development of ranking. It greatly limits the political and economic choices of exchange units by creating reciprocal obligations to give and take from the same set of kin.

The Lhota, on the other hand, who resemble the Angami in many ways, have just gone through a period of rapid expansion by war. In their northward movement, they expelled a large portion of the Ao tribe from the area they were then occupying (Hutton 1921b:363). Their technological conditions of social reproduction were significantly altered as a result.

»The fact that Lhotas do not suffer from shortage of land as the Semas and Angamis do, also helps to produce this peaceful state of affairs.« (Mills 1922:96).

This would imply that the Lhota, having successfully expanded are at the beginning of a new cycle. There is some evidence for this. To begin with, marriage regulations are quite strictly asymmetrical. A man cannot marry his FZD, but he is *expected* to marry a girl of his mother's clan, i.e., a classificatory MBD.

»There is no fine for not doing so, but his mother's clan are likely to take offence.« (Mills 1922:95).

Unlike other Nagas, the Lhota indulge a great deal in the practice of polygyny. Furthermore, they have the most elaborate brideprice arrangements which include not only the mother's clan but also that of the WMB, i.e., wifegivers of wife-givers (as among the Chin). This seems to be evidence for the beginning of a new attempt at ranking and a general expansion of the economy.

War plays an important part in this cycle, since it creates the preconditions for new economic expansion. It is not a negative feedback mechanism, as suggested by Vayda for the Naga, in which man/land ratios are readjusted to maintain a prior balance (Vayda 1971). On the contrary, war is the result of the imbalance caused by an expansionist economic system. The Lhota, who appear to be starting a new cycle of growth, do not attempt to regulate their population size. On the contrary, they value children very highly, and maximum fertility is a cultural goal. Territorial expansion does not readjust man/land ratios for any but the expanding group. Former occupants are quite simply expelled by force and they undoubtedly end up on worse land with a higher density. Except in the utterly tautological sense, that warfare recreates the conditions for new warfare, the negative feedback analysis completely misses the point. Furthermore, and this is fundamental here, this system (*gumsa/gumlao* plus warlike expansion) does *not* reproduce itself over time. Our whole analysis has been an attempt to show precisely that as density increases, the kind of expansion undertaken by the Lhota becomes much more difficult, and the system may degenerate into a continuous state of war as is apparently the case among the Wa. It is at this stage that headhunting takes on full significance. The taking of human life is extremely rare among the Kachin, somewhat less rare among the Chin, and quite common among the Naga. The Kachin make a tremendous effort to import large numbers of slaves. The Chin also take slaves, but not, it seems, on the same scale. The Sema have no slaves and most other Naga groups have few or none except for those that are produced internally by debt bondage. Captives are killed rather than transformed into new laborers. As we move from the Kachin to the Naga, the function of military activity becomes less a search for labor and more a search for land.

Structural Inversion: The Sacred Founder

I have been arguing that while there is a moderate amount of expansion in some parts of Naga Land, increased population density makes the cycle much more difficult to carry on. Most of the Nagas are *gumlao* and it is unlikely that they could ever again get beyond this point in the cycle. The Eastern Angami supply an interesting and somewhat morbid structural response to this state of affairs.

In these villages, which are all democratic, there is an official called the Tevo who represents the »sacred founder's kin«.

> »He is the mediator between the community and the supernatural world, the personification of the village in its relation to the forces pervading nature and human life.« (von Furer-Haimendorf and Mills 1936:923).

This could easily be mistaken for a description of a Kachin *duwa*. It is precisely that kind of power to which the Sema chief has no access. That is, while the Sema chief-founder is purely secular, the Kachin chief is the mediator between the community and the higher powers. The Sema and Angami, unlike the Kachin, split the two functions in such a way as to weaken both of them.

> »Whereas among the Semas the founder and his descendents are the secular chiefs and rulers of the village, among the intensely democratic Angami, the kin of the founder is without temporal authority.« (von Furer-Haimendorf and Mills 1936:923).

While the Tevo is, in a sense, a reincarnation of the »asiatic« mode chief, representative of the higher unity of the community that we found developing among the Kachin, his actual situation is quite the inverse of the Kachin *duwa*. The following list should demonstrate this:

a) It is strictly forbidden to borrow anything from a Tevo's house – to »steal« from him means exile from the village.

b) The Tevo cannot borrow rice on the usual village condition of repayment after the next harvest, for this would imply the eventual removal of grain from his house which is strictly forbidden.

c) A Tevo may not touch thatching grass. If he did, »the crops would be light and soon finished.« (von Furer-Haimendorf and Mills 1936:925).

d) When the Tevo returns from the fields, he must never enter the village empty handed; he must carry at least firewood.

e) Cooking pots must never be left empty – this holds for all eastern Angami, but especially the Tevo.

f) For the first seven harvests (four years), the Tevo must not eat any of the meat given to him in his official capacity.

g) During this period, he must refrain from sexual intercourse.

h) He may not partake in any of the usual fertility and »prosperity« sacrifices and ceremonies, at reaping sowing, and for rain-making.

All of the social relations of the Tevo are symmetrical inversions of the usual generosity required of a chief. Similarly, all his relations with the supernatural and natural world are purely negative. This is coupled with rituals of abundance, but in conditions of obvious scarcity. This structural inversion, seems in some ways to be an attempt to negate the long term process which gave rise to scarcity. It is a negation of the function of giving, a negation of the principles of economic and demographic expansion and a total inversion of the ritual of prosperity. One no longer offers an enormous feast to invoke the power of the spirits for future prosperity. On the contrary, one refrains from acts of conspicuous consumption and the display of wealth in order that the harvest will not be destroyed. The political equality of these societies is founded upon the ritual negation of everything that brought about the degradation of the conditions of production.

Everything we have said about the *gumsa/gumlao* cycle, the increase in warfare and headhunting and finally, this structural inversion, demonstrates sufficiently well that the Naga are not emerging from a former dualistic moiety and clan structure into an expanding segmentary lineage system. On the contrary, things seem to be going in the opposite direction. They would have to be, given the overall degeneration of the economic base. Dualism is more likely to be a recent development which might be taken as a kind of final acceptance of the impossibility of the previous system. Levi-Strauss, approaching the analysis of Naga societies from a different point of view, comes to very similar devolutionary conclusions.

»On peut parfaitement concevoir que sur la base d'une vieille organisation clanique, certains clans se soient transformés en lignées féodales unies entre elles par une structure d'échange generalisé, tandis que les autres auraient continué à fonctionner dans l'ombre et dans les campagnes lointains, selon une formule reciproque. *Quitte pour l'échange restreint, à reprendre la première place quand le système féodal atteint sa periode de crise, dont certaines coutumes Naga attestent assez l'apparition.*« (Levi-Strauss 1967:324) (my underline).

Headhunting, the Wa, End of the Road

Headhunting exists among all the Nagas. It is also sporadically practiced by some Chin, but it is not so systematic an activity as among the former group. Mills, in an interesting paper on the ethics of headhunting describes two common rationalizations for the activity (Mills n.d.). The first is that it provides the hunter with slaves in the next world. Among the Sema one must get a certain number of heads to claim the prestige needed to make a good marriage. This is in itself an interesting attempt at population control, but there is a more general ritual significance which serves as the ideological basis for the practice. It is the head which contains the »soul-force« of a man, and when captured, this force is added to that of the village community which is thought of as a kind of reservoir. Soul-force appears to be the key to village prosperity. Captured heads are mounted as trophies under the village sacred tree, the functional equivalent to the Kachin *numshang*, that is, the place where communication is made with the spirit world. In all cases, headhunting is a self-perpetuating activity and there are a number of omens in the ritual preparation of captured heads which are interpreted as meaning more heads in the future. Unlike the Chin who may occasionally take a head in battle, the Naga have more or less institutionalized the sport. It is only among the Rengma that headhunting is explicitly linked to the productivity of the crops, but this is implied for all of the other groups by the notion of soul-force. (Mills 1937:161).

Headhunting is a further structural inversion of the Kachin system. The Kachin treat the extra-domain world as a source of human labor to be drawn upon whenever possible. The practice of headhunting is the reverse of this. It keeps people away, or by doing away with them physically, transforms them into a spiritual force to provide a badly needed increase in crop yield. The notion of providing slaves in the next world is similarly a negation of keeping slaves in this world. The distribution of these two rationalizations as reported by Mills is an excellent indicator of the direction of evolution which we have suggested.

	slaves in next world	village prosperity
Kuki[1])	+	—
Naga	+	+
Wa	—	+

As the economic base becomes increasingly degraded, the first thing given up is slavery, i.e., the most obvious attempt to recruit outside labor. Potential slaves in this world are converted into slaves in the next world, and the former master, gives up rank status which would result from increased output, replacing it with a kind of spiritual wealth in the hereafter. Eventually, the denial of the expansionist character of the system becomes less important, and the problem of village survival takes precedence. Finally, among the Wa, slaves are completely forgotten about and headhunting is linked exclusively to the harvest.

The Wa

There is comparatively little information on the social structure of the Wa, but as their headhunting has drawn a great deal of attention, much has been written about them. Among the so-called Wild Wa, headhunting appears to be a regular part of the agricultural year. It has a season, March through April, just before sowing, and is well integrated into the ritual cycle. Heads may not be taken inside the village, and it is considered »unneighborly and slothful« (Scott and Hardiman 1900: Pt. I, Vol. 1:500) to take heads from villages on the same ridge. Rather, it is said that heads taken from the greatest geographical distance have the best effect on crop yield. The mounting of the trophies on poles in an avenue of trees outside the village is accompanied by a sacrifice and a feast if possible. These village groves are, significantly, the only trees to be found on the otherwise bare hills. While heads should be taken from a distance, they are not generally taken outside of Wa country. This is apparently because the result of headhunting, keeping people scarce, only is meaningful within the political-economic confines of Wa agriculture.

As expansion is a local phenomenon, we should expect to find the most extreme conflict between those who are just far enough apart so that they no longer consider themselves neighbors. It is the territory which is contiguous to the local group that is most in demand, a situation which is bound to affect the strategy of political and military alliances in the larger territory. The Wa policy is reflected in the maxim,

»next ridge enemy, next ridge but one, friend.« (Harvey 1933:84).

[1]) Mills appears to refer to all Kuki groups, Lushai, Old Kuki, as well as Chin.

The elaborate agricultural ritual and sacrifices of the Kachin, the cult of prosperity in which many animals were slaughtered and distributed, is replaced here by the hunting of human victims, but for the same ritual purposes. In other groups, wealthy men keep animal heads as trophies, as exterior symbols of their prestige and service (feasting) to the community. For the Wa, human heads replace those of animals with no change in ritual function. But the whole system is now working in reverse. Before, increased population was linked to increased prosperity. Now, depopulation is linked to survival.[1])

The Wa states are very densely populated with a mean of 43/mi². But in the areas of most intense headhunting it gets as high as 49/mi². Furthermore, the Wa country is entirely surrounded by a political and demographic barrier af Shan and Chinese states, so that expansion is virtually impossible. Below is a list of these states.

Burma Side	Density	China Side	Density
N. Hsenwi	41/mi²	Mongting	40/mi²
S. Hsenwi	37/mi²	Kengma	37/mi²
W. Manglon	35/mi²	Mongmong	36/mi²
E. Manglon	?	Monlem	33/mi²
Kokang	41/mi²	Monyims	34/mi²

While none of the states are more densely populated than those of the Wa, they are politically powerful and often linked to national powers. Wa who emigrated in the past have all become more or less assimilated. There is a continuum of Tame Wa groups, beginning with those on the border of Wa country proper to those who have become buddhist and are integrated into the surrounding states.

There appears to be a very interesting relationship between interior, head-hunting, and exterior, tribute taking, Wa. The exterior Wa seem to have subjected some of their Lahu neighbors and they receive a regular tribute. They are referred to as »soft« by Wa of the interior, Kawa, who are constantly at war with them, usually successfully. There appears to be a regular replacement of Lawa by expanding Kawa groups at the periphery of Wa country. But their newly acquired privileges transform the Kawa into Lawa, and the expansion process continues (Barton 1929:63–4).

It seems that the process of becoming »soft« consists mainly in the dispersal of settlement and a weakening of the village military organization that is so important in the interior. They resemble, in a remote way, the description of

[1]) I stress here that this is a question of ideology. The effectiveness of headhunting as a population control mechanism is extremely questionable. It certainly cannot be said to have controlled density in the Wa state. More important is the ritual link between the activity of headhunting and fertility. While this may be not explicitly expressed it is implied by the undeniable link between decapitation, depopulation and the notion of crop fertility.

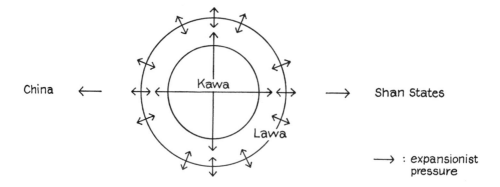

the tribute taking Kachin (from Shan) of Leach's zones B and C. While disunity is the common state of affairs, some Lawa have molded themselves into loose supralocal polities,

> »Whose federations often merge into effective leadership only, however, to break up again by inheritance or rebellion.« (Barton 1929:64).

The variation in village size among the Wa is, as among the Naga, a confirmation of the developmental sequence we have outlined. It is reported that in areas of fiercest headhunting, the villages are relatively small but very close together.

> »These tribes are very much divided against themselves and the villages though perhaps more heavily stockaded ... are much smaller.« (Barton 1929:66).

It stands to reason that when independent villages are packed into a small area, the chances of boundary disputes are multiplied geometrically. Further west, the situation has evolved toward the larger village.

> »The biggest village here would hardly be much larger than Mengting (250 houses) whereas further west they would be up to two or three times the size of Mengting (say therefore, 500 to 700 houses).« (Barton 1929:66).

There is practically no information on the internal structure of these independent villages, but what few remarks I have found may give some idea of their internal and external political relations. Villages have chiefs who appear to be primarily war chiefs. Such centralization of authority during periods of warfare exist for the Nagas as well, (Mills 1922:96) and if the Wa have more stable leadership, it is due to their continual state of war. There are occasional federations of villages for the purpose of doing battle, and these are often under powerful war leaders. But even great chiefs,

> »exercise influence rather than jurisdiction, for even in their own village there is nothing to distinguish him outwardly from other villagers ... some of the nearest villages deny his authority.« (Scott 1893 in Harvey 1933).

As the result of incessant warfare, the largest villages can sometimes get tribute from smaller neighbors that they have conquered, but this appears to be a very unstable situation, and the tribute may be nothing more than a token peace offering. Where supralocal relations do exist they are the result of competition for land that may be fiercer than that existing in the Naga Hills. It is reported, nevertheless, that powerful Angami Naga villages in the densest areas sometimes took tribute from their neighbors. In any case there is no real supralocal polity to speak of, and all relations of this sort are temporary accords between independent units.

The village itself is a vertible fortress with a very thick rampart surrounded by a deep ditch. The only entrance to the village is a long and narrow tunnel through which access would be practically impossible for a large group of attackers.

Things may have been very different in the past. There is evidence of a more developed political organization with paramount chiefs. In Panglong, there are very old and famous silver mines that were formerly worked by the Chinese, but the Wa who controlled the area are known to have taken tribute. Whatever conditions were formerly, the Wa of today live in a totally degraded habitat. They are described as working very hard to make a living off the land. There is virtually nothing but grassland in the area and hillsides are usually completely cultivated. The main crops are buckwheat, millet and maize. Some rice is grown at lower altitudes. A more recent innovation is the large scale cultivation of opium for market. This seems to require a very heavy labor input and in many areas it has replaced staple crops. Opium growers are usually the victims of Shan middlemen and are almost always in debt. In areas where the soil, because of better slopes and relative underuse, is in better condition, opium is not grown, but is replaced by ordinary food crops (Harvey 1933:92). Finally, it appears that crop failures are quite common and talk of famine is very frequent. This is especially true of the groups that have adopted intensive opium cultivation.

There are in many villages large circular barrows, whose circumference is sometimes as much as 400 feet and whose functions and origins are not precisely indicated. From the description they appear to resemble the Angami sitting circles, burial mounds of the founder ancestors. These are used for village ceremonies and meetings and they seem to be similar to the circular platforms that are used by the Kachin for their *manao* ceremonial feasts and the dancing that accompanies them. Some Wa informants said that the stone axes, swords, beads and human remains found in the barrow belonged to a »bygone race of giants«. (Harvey 1933:115). The mounds are strewn with great boulders, and it is said that this is,

> »Where giant Wa ancestors after they had been fighting among themselves rested and their blood fell in big drops which became stones. It is the custom for passers by to lay a leaf or stone on one of the stones, at the same time wishing for money, cattle, paddy and repayment of debts.« (Draye nid. in Harvey 1933:14).

Summary

In this section I have attempted to show how a number of societies distributed in space might be understood in terms of a temporal model. This can be dangerous to the extent that particular local histories are not taken into account. My purpose, however, has not been to account for any one society in its entirety, but for a number of common structures that can, I think, be abstracted from their particular cultural contexts. It is, moreover, perfectly legitimate to interpret the distribution of these societies in a purely structural manner. That is, we might simply treat Kachin, Chin, Naga and Wa as a system of transformations in which an invariant set of elements is recombined and modified as the result of external techno-economic constraints. But this would be missing a very important element in the analysis. Whether these societies are linked historically or not, and they most certainly aren't, it is possible to show theoretically how one might get from one to the other. The simple transformational model assumes that the distribution of constraints (population density, techno-environment) are independent of the social system. In the more comprehensive perspective of the social formation, there are no such independent variables, for it is the operation of the system through time which causes the critical changes in its own conditions of reproduction. Thus, the model implies that the Wa and Naga must have passed through earlier stages similar to those of the Chin and Kachin.

The most important variable in the devolutionary process is the growth of population density and attendant degradation of the environment. But population growth is a dependent variable, dependent on the properties of the social relations of production, i.e., specifically the high demand for surplus and labor. I have suggested that the individualization of property begins with the accumulation of brothers and the consequent division of land into separate holdings. This destroys the former »asiatic« structure in which landed property as an alienable object did not exist. The ability to divide land implies the existence of individual rights. The horizontal exchange system, finally, incorporates land titles and the vertical structure all but disappears. But this increase in population pressure and the development of individual lineage property or even private property *does not* lead to stratification as some theories would have it. (Fried 1967: Chap. 5; Harner 1970; Carneiro 1970). On the contrary, it leads ultimately to egalitarian, permanently *gumlao* society. The population pressure theory of evolution entirely omits the central material variable, production. Stratification only exists where it *can* exist. A dense population may indeed indulge in a great deal of warfare, but it does not lead to class structure unless a surplus can be produced to support the structure. Further, if one does not suppose that force is the sole operator in this hypothetical process, the economic question becomes more complex. The rate of surplus production must be sufficient to cover the rate of increase in demand without intensifying internal social contradictions.

On the other hand, as we shall see in the next section, the chances for state formation seem highest in the low density systems, if the technology can be made more productive so as to support continued expansion of the *gumsa* system without the intersystemic contradictions which usually cause its collapse. In this way growing population is incorporated into the developing state rather than blocking its evolution. The final product is, of course, high density states, but high density is a condition which develops as a result of state formation rather than being its cause.

II. Evolution: The Asiatic State – Some Suggestions

In *Political Systems in Highland Burma*, Leach speaks about a fluctuation between *gumsa* and Shan forms of organization. All of his evidence indicates that this tends to occur where there is a substantial increase in available wealth, or in our terms, surplus, at the disposal of the chief. According to Leach, the fluctuation is based on imitation by Kachin of existing Shan forms. In fact, his entire explanation for the *gumlao/gumsa* cycle is that petty chiefs who try to make themselves into Shan princes usually find that they have lost the support of their kin and thus, the basis of their power. The arguments developed here lead in a different direction, one closer to Leach's earlier thesis (Leach 1946). Specifically it focuses on the transformation that takes place in tribal society when the technological base becomes more productive, i.e., when there is a substantial increase in potential surplus. This in fact consists in the removal of the main limiting factor in *gumsa* development. The question to which we address ourselves here is the nature and results of this transformation of an entire social formation.

From the start, we must be sure not to confuse this with Leach's notion of »becoming Shan«, which, because based on outward appearance, covers a number of totally unrelated developments. For example, if a small band of Kachins moves into a Shan valley by force, dominates the population and takes over official positions formerly held by Shans, this falls into the notion of »becoming Shan«. Likewise, if a Kachin chief has personal control over outside resources such as trade, he can become a Shan prince.[1] Neither of these cases is af any importance for us here, since they do not represent an evolution of one structure toward another. A Kachin becoming a Shan and a Kachin system becoming a Shan system are two quite unrelated processes. In fact, the first is not a process in any meaningful way. It is quite simply a case of a change in identity, a borrowing of cultural traits. It is unfortunate that Leach who emphasizes the importance of dealing with structures rather than cultural content seems to make no distinction here.

[1] I am referring here to the assimilation of Shan culture by a powerful Kachin chief and his integration into a larger Shan domain. Such »princes« are no more than wealthy Kachin chiefs. This should not be confused with the transformation of *gumsa* structure that might occur when trade becomes an integral part of the Kachin economy.

From the very start, we have tried to show how *gumsa* development is an internal process that has nothing to do with the presence or absence of Shan influence. Maran has confirmed this in his distinction between the traditional *gumchying gumsa* of the Triangle who have not been influenced by the Shan and *gumsa* Kachin of the valleys who have more or less become Shan. Even here I would stress that what is important in this kind of analysis is not the fact of being Shan, but the structural changes involved. It is not necessary to become Shan in order to evolve in the direction of the state.

Kachin type systems have evolved into state formations independently of Shan influence. The best example is Manipur, originally a Naga group that descended into a very fertile valley as early as the ninth or tenth century and evolved into a powerful state. Another example might be the Shan sub-state of Möng Si which is inhabited mostly by Kachin. Historically, of course, all of the states of the area may be descended from Kachin type systems. The Shans, Burmese, and Chinese have all evolved from earlier tribal forms. This, at least, is a working assumption of most anthropologists and historians. The question that must be answered is how. But to answer it we cannot simply look at the transition process described by Leach which is closer to acculturation than to evolution.

Now that we have made clear the object of our analysis, we must face the fact that it is very difficult to study, mostly because of the lack of historical data. This would not be so much of a problem if the state forms had been more or less isolated, but this is not the case. We know virtually nothing about the pre-buddhist Palaung state of Tawngpeng, nor is there any available information on pre-hindu Manipur. As most of these societies have had further developments *as states* there are innumerable difficulties that arise in trying to abstract earlier from later forms of organization. The problem of abstraction and reconstruction would require a work in itself. All that can be done here is to develop some of the theoretical implications of the earlier Kachin model with a different kind of production function and to suggest some of the ways in which these implications are manifested in the available data.

The Evolution and Dominance of the Vertical Exchange Structure

The difference between devolution and evolution is a difference between two kinds of dominant structures, two kinds of relations of production. We have already seen how in the long cycle, the vertical structure disappears very early and the horizontal structure becomes totally dominant. If, on the other hand, we move our original system to a different sort of production function, one which has relatively long term increasing returns and very high absolute yields, verticalization becomes dominant and the horizontal-affinal system becomes a secondary structure in an emergent state formation. This state has particular characteristics which have been referred to in discussions of the »asiatic« mode. The dominant Kachin property form which we have discussed serves as the basis for the development of an »asiatic« state. I believe that it is possible to show how the properties of the vertical structure can give rise quite naturally to that specific form of state structure and that it is not, therefore, necessarily an external result of conquest, although warfare may play an important part in the process of transformation.

How does the vertical structure become dominant? How does it supplant the formerly dominant horizontal structure? These questions can be answered by examining the changing functions of these two structures in a *gumsa* system that has managed to continue expanding beyond its normal limits.

Gumsa hierarchy is established by a process of affinal ranking in which positions are maintained by the act of exchange itself. That is, in order to maintain one's position in the rank structure one must maintain an asymmetrical relation with one's subordinates. Verticalization which is an outgrowth of this process, works against its very basis. Position within the conical *gumsa* domain is not a question of affinal status, but one of claims on a ritual hierarchy. In the Kachin domain two forms of social rank are in conflict with one another. Neither the vertical nor the affinal structure can achieve dominance. A *duwa* must be a wife-giver as well if he is to keep his position. Everything changes, however, if the vertical structure assumes complete dominance, if rank is totally independent of affinal status. This requires a higher degree of mystification than previously existed, for the *duwa* will now owe his position *entirely* to his descent from and close connection with the supernatural deities. We have seen that the justification for tribute to a chief is that he fulfills the very important ritual-economic function of maintaining prosperity through his sacrifices. The redistributive aspects of the *manao* feast are intimately tied to the ritual function. But feasting is also a means of validation, a means of maintaining status, and if the Kachin chief is to remain powerful he must redistribute. But if the vertical structure is firmly established, if there is no question but that the chief is in fact closely related to the gods, if he is accepted as representing the entire community, then there is no longer any need for him to prove his status by feasting.

To be more explicit, the only difference between a *gumsa* domain and a state form is that in the former, position is determined by exchange whereas in the latter, position is defined independently of it. It is, to oversimplify, determined by religious position.[1]) But the relations which come to dominate in the state form are already present in the religious structure of the »tribe«. We have already shown how the ritual and production aspects of Kachin economy cannot be separated. They form a single vertical system. Sacrifice is made to the *nats* (spirits) who in return maintain or increase the fertility of the soil and the general prosperity of the community. This is a system of ritual tribute, pure and simple. There is no redistribution of offerings by the spirits. The return is

---

[1]) See Conclusion I of Chapter VII. When the distribution of labor input and output is determined by relations whose content is »religious« this does not mean that such relations are ideological but that the religious relations function as relations of production.

in the form of maintaining the conditions of production. The Kachin makes offerings to a segmentary hierarchy of *nats*. He has no direct access to the highest *nats* but can only reach them through the mediation of lesser *nats*. The progression is something like this,

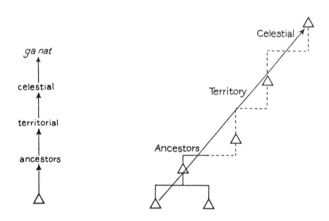

The function of each lesser *nat* is to go to the next higher *nat* and finally to persuade the supreme deities to do their job which is, economically, to reinforce the same system by making it possible to offer better sacrifices the following year.

In the Kachin system, the *nats* are the real proprietors of the land, if such a thing as property can be said to exist. In any case, they receive tribute (sacrifice) only because of their function in the religious-economic cycle of reproduction. Here, then, is the root of the vertical/horizontal opposition. Man's relation to nature is one of dependence on the supernatural. One pays tribute to the *nats* in return for a continued good yield. The relations between men are of a different order, however, since there is, at first, no such dependency, but rather reciprocity. Prestige varies directly with generosity and one can maintain status only by continually reinforcing the asymmetry of generosity, the inverse of the tribute relation. How do the tables get turned? Somehow, the status generated in the exchange process must be transformed into a position in the vertical ritual system. But the internal logic of the segmentary structure enables this transformation to occur quite naturally.

1) A wealthy lineage head, A, who can afford to give great feasts to the entire village can only do so because he has good harvests.
2) But the way in which one gets good harvests is by sacrificing to the local and celestial *nats*. That is, wealth is not the product of labor and control over others' labor, but the »work of the gods«.
3) If A is successful, it must be because he has more influence with the *nats*.
4) But influence can only be the result of a closer genealogical relationship.

5) Therefore, A must be more closely related to the local *nats*, which is where the chain of communication begins.

6) The claim that A's lineage is the same as that of the local *nat*, and that his ancestor is, therefore, the territorial deity, is perfectly natural.

A's promotion to headman, or to chief is, in terms of this logic, due to his privileged genealogical position and not to his wealth. In other words, *the Kachin religious structure is an inverted representation of reality.* If all wealth is god given, then the wealthy must be closer to the gods. The whole economic process is viewed as if it were the work of the spirit world. Marx seems again to have had the key to the situation.

> »In reality, appropriation by means of the process of labor takes place under these preconditions, which are not the product of labor, but appear as its natural or divine preconditions.« (Marx 1964:69).

As the local *nat* is identified with the ancestor of the whole community, the chiefly lineage comes to represent that community as a whole, and being closest to the deities, he has greatest control over the prosperity of the group. He takes tribute from he community because of his position in the larger segmentary structure. He becomes the lowest level of mediation between the community and the highest spirits.

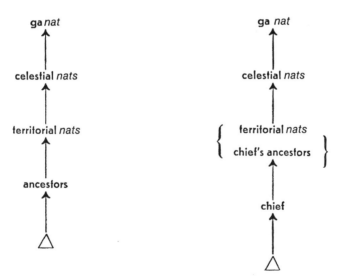

A feast-giving, thigh-eating chief is involved in two relations simultaneously. He receives tribute and corvée because of his ritual position and his function in the reproductive cycle. But he remains a feast giver, although of a different sort. He begins as a distributor and ends as a redistributor, and although this latter act is commonly represented as chiefly generosity, it amounts to using the community's labor to enhance his own status. The act of redistribution only appears to be reciprocal on the surface, but it is based on an underlying asymmetrical economic relationship, since the chief, entitled to labor at the most important times of the year is in a very important way exploiting the potential surplus of the group. Further development of the vertical structure brings with it a decline in feast-giving activity. This is only because the chief comes to be more like an ancestor, more of a deity. This is accompanied by further claims on the genealogical hierarchy. The Kachin *duwa* is descended from the domain *nat* who is affinally related to the *madai nat*. The Shan *sawbwa* and Burmese prince are the direct descendants of the highest deities. *Instead of representative of the community to the gods, he becomes the representative of the gods to the community.* This transition accomplished, he has only one social function left, to ensure general prosperity, which requires nothing in the way of redistribution since he is, after all, maintaining the entire economic system by means of his ritual.

Once paramount authority is vertically established, independently of the horizontal exchange system, everything is changed. All positions become anchored in their relationship to the royal line. The royal lineage is the only absolutely defined political, religious and economic position in the state and all other positions can only be defined with reference to it. This new political fact, the absolute determination of status by segmentary position, totally destroys the basis of the former horizontal system, for now, in order to find a place in the hierarchy one must become affiliated with what is already established. The headman in Kachin owes his rank primarily to the wealth – prestige cycle in his own community. In the state he owes his rank to the recognition by the central authority.

Marriage alliance is no longer an economic exchange in which rank is asserted. All ranks are predetermined and marriage can only serve the secondary function of linkage to centers of power. Among the Shan, there is no hypogamy since it is no longer necessary to establish status in this fashion. On the contrary, women may move up the hierarchy as tribute; secondary wives or concubines. That Leach assumes this to be in opposition to Kachin custom is something of an exaggeration (Leach 1954:218–19). A Kachin chief may take a secondary wife or concubine of lower status. This kind of marriage is simply the expression of accepted status superiority of the »wife-taker«. Thus, Kachin secondary marriage is a kind of embryo form of the tribute wife-giving of the Shan. In general, in a system of pre-defined rank or class, marriage can only serve to cement alliance between equals or allegiance from inferiors.

I would venture to say, however, that Shan society does not represent a direct development out of the *gumsa* system, but a much later development. A better example might be pre-Han China, especially the so-called feudal states. Here we find, in western Chou society, that,

> »Dukes possessing the same name as the royal house were addressed by the King as paternal uncles; dukes with other surnames were addressed as maternal uncles.« (Hsu 1965:3).

The full fledged Shan states such as the early kingdom of Nan Chao represent a much more developed system in which kinship has been broken and replaced by a more strictly bureaucratic mode of appointment. But the above example is very close indeed to a Kachin domain, a kind of ambilateral conical clan, where rank is determined independently of exchange. We note, however, that the use of such kinship terms did not necessarily imply an actual genealogical tie. It was, at least to some extent, simply a way of representing a system of ranked lineages, but this time in an already developed class structure. Ancient Chinese society might be taken as a kind of mid-point between the Kachin system and the full-fledged bureaucratic state of the Shan and Burmese.

The emergent state is a supralocal organization in which positions are not determined locally, but by the larger polity. In later evolution, all political offices are defined externally. Everyone from ministers to governors to headmen are »sent down« by the state. In this way the village community is reduced to little more than a unit of production. It tends to close in on itself. Most Shan villages are highly endogamous. The village is no longer a total field of political economy, but a subordinate part of a larger structure. It has become a peasant community.

The political and economic relations which characterize the »asiatic« state are not created *ex nihilo.* They are the result of the direct transformation of tribal society in which a formerly secondary relation becomes dominant. The ritual relation between man and the supernatural (including ancestors) becomes the dominant relation between rulers and their subjects (see diagram next page).

The »asiatic« state is an elaboration of the vertical structure to a maximal extent. It is founded on absolute control, in theory, over land. This is not property in the sense of a transferable item. It is rather, a total identification of the ruling lineage with its territory and the supernatural forces that see to its prosperity. All other rights to land are mediated either by kinship or, in later developments, by royal grant.

In its early stages, the »asiatic« state is a direct evolution of a former kinship based society. It is the growth of a conical clan structure in the context of local hierarchy. It is a community based system in which there are villages, village clusters, domains, sub-states and states, all levels of increasing inclusiveness. The only feudal resemblance is agriculture, political hierarchy and the appropriation of surplus by one class. But these criteria might apply to any agricultural state. If one defined feudalism as generally as that one would end up with a European and an Asiatic variety, but from an evolutionary standpoint this would be meaningless. Unlike the »asiatic« formation, feudal relations develop, from the very start, outside of kinship and as a replacement for it (Bloch 1961).

The development of Kachin type systems in the direction of the state is only possible in an expanding economy with increasing or constant returns to scale. This means that the economic base must be changed radically in order to absorb

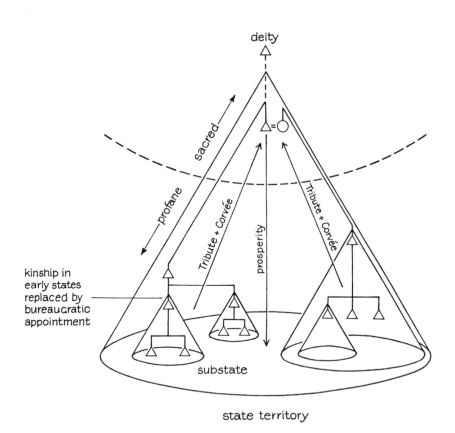

more labor without loss of productivity. Our preceding discussion, dealing exclusively with the transformation of structures, may have seemed too peaceful. This is not intended. The expanding Kachin system is a labor-hungry, territory-grabbing economy and there is no question but that warfare and conquest are instrumental in the formation of larger states. But the role of warfare is predetermined by the expansionist nature of the economic system. The history of the Northern Shan states is one of war, consolidation, fission and then war again. It is certain that conquest led from small states to larger states, but it is doubtful whether there was any more than a change in size involved. The point I am trying to make here is that war, assumed by some to be the cause (as the result of population pressure) of state formation, is in itself neutral. The formation of the state can only be correctly understood in terms of the transformation of previously existing structures. Conquest of territory or importation of labor may make such a transformation possible, but it does not tell us anything about the outcome of structural change. On the contrary, it is the internal dynamic of the social system which can tell us when and where war and conquest will occur.

There is a good deal of evidence that Kachin type systems do tend to evolve into state forms where the economic conditions are so altered as to make continued expansion possible. The state of Möng Si was almost entirely Kachin in population. It contained 100 Kachin, 20 Shan and 15 Palaung villages, a population of about 12,000. The political organization of the state was like that of an expanded domain. It was headed by a Kachin *myosa*[1]) who resided in the state capital, a village of only 30 houses. The paramount chief or *sawbwa* (a Shan name), headed several sub-domains each of which is ruled by a *duwa*, »a relative of the *myosa*«. (Scott and Hardiman: Pt. II. Vol. II:477). There is, unfortunately, little information relating to the history of Möng Si, but it may have begun as an exploiter of trade routes. The state remained a very active trade center.

»There is a good deal of trade in opium, rice and lac, and Chinese caravans visit the möng every year and bring pans, cauldrons, coarse cotton
cloth, carpets and the like. Formerly, they had to pay heavy tolls to the
Kachin chiefs through whose territory they had to pass.« (Scott and Hardiman: Pt. II, Vol. II:477).

In any case, the formation of a stable state most likely depended not on trade but on the shift to plains agriculture. The capital of the state,

»is situated in a beautiful oval valley about six miles long and three miles
wide, forming a large and fertile paddy plain with smaller valleys running into it from all sides.« (Scott and Hardiman: Pt. II, Vol. II:477).

Unfortunately, it is very difficult to use such a case an an example of evolution because a great deal is collapsed into a short time span. When the Kachin move into Shan valleys they move into a Shan buddhist environment. Möng Si is a sub-domain of the larger state of North Hsenwi. It is difficult to tell its age, but much of its internal structure is adopted from the already existent larger state. It is significant, however, that major structural characteristics of the Kachin domain and the Shan *möng* are practically identical so that little change would be necessary. It is important, however, that district heads are still called *duwa* and that they are all relatives of the paramount. It is quite probable that the formation of this state was a consolidation of a previous confederation of domain chiefs on the basis of a permanently expanded economy. The class structure was probably like that of other Shan states. A certain amount of surplus was channeled into the buddhist establishment and the construction of pagodas.

»There is a fine *pongyi kaung* with a group of pagodas.« (Scott and
Hardiman: Pt. II, Vol. II:477).

It is quite certain that the head of state and his entourage were supported by the taxes they took.

---

[1]) *Myosa* is a Burmese word for district governor – literally »district eater«. The concept accurately reflects the fact that the domain head does not own his territory but is appointed by a
central authority.

It must be stressed here that the majority of the state is Kachin and that the class structure is a Kachin class structure. Leach questions the probability of this kind of development.

»He cannot accept women from his Shan adherents without prejudice to his position as a Kachin, he cannot go on giving women to his Kachin adherents (his *dama*) without prejudice to his status as a Shan prince. Or, to put it another way, the Kachin can 'become a Shan' without loss of status but his commoner Kachin followers cannot. Therefore, in becoming a Shan, the Kachin chief tends to isolate himself from the roots of his power, he offends against the principles of *mayu-dama* reciprocity and encourages the development of *gumlao* revolutionary tendencies.« (Leach 1954:223).

Leach further states that the only way an »over-successful« chief can maintain his position is »with the aid of external authority« (Leach 1954:224). But this argument is entirely contradicted by the facts of Möng Si, where it appears that a paramount chief »became Shan« while keeping his affinal ties with subordinates, where Kachin followers took to wet rice, and where external support was without a doubt minimal. Möng Si was perhaps the strongest substate in Hsenwi, and it survived the long and bitter struggles for power that occurred in the nineteenth century, during which time the Kachin chiefs had no external aid and were, in fact, the principal supporters of the ousted prince Hseng Naw Hpa who was in no position to help them maintain their power. The only conclusion possible is that Kachin domains can indeed become Shan states and without external support, if they make the transition to wet rice.

A very interesting case of transition is Assam of the early nineteenth century. Here, things were not so Shan oriented, and while the British reversed the transformaion by freeing »slaves« there is little doubt that the Kachin here were in the process of state formation. Leach's unpublished thesis contains an excellent analysis of the available data (Leach 1946). The Kachin who moved west fom the Triangle area came upon the valleys and plains of Assam. A group of them became attached to the Ahom state, but the process of development of a Kachin state seems evident from a number of sources. Chiefs of the Tsasen clan were settled in Hukawng and along the Tayun, Dihing and Tenga Pani rivers in northwest Assam, theoretically in the territory of the Assamese state but evidentally quite independent.

Earlier we showed how slavery was an integral part of the expansion of a *gumsa* system. The limitations of the economy set limits on the importation of slaves and the increased population density led to breakdown in the *gumsa* system. In the Assamese plains, this process was more successful, simply because diminishing returns were no problem. It is not absolutely clear how the plains communities were established. Sometimes already existing communities were conquered. Often a number of communities were settled together and the Kachin (Singhpo) achieved dominance through their relations with the paramount powers. A more interesting phenomenon, and probably the crucial one here, is the practice of slave raiding into the hills or into other plains communities. There are reports of depopulation throughout this area, and relations of this sort may have been the fundamental mechanism in establishing a labor base. We have already stated that these were not slaves in the ordinary sense of the word, since they tended to become integrated into the Kachin community. But the community structure itself may have been in transition. According to Leach, the structure of the plains communities was similar to the Kachin domain. Here, however, there were numbers of *mayam* sattelite villages. The composition of this lower class is quite interesting. Its members are called *Dunias*.

> »The Dooaneahs are descendents of Burmese or Singhpo fathers and Assamese women, captured in predatory irruptions and kept as slaves. Assamese males also carried off into slavery, are from the loss of caste, by their connections with the Singhpos and the adoption of Singhpo habits, denominated Dooaneahs.« (Butler 1847:126).

But the identity of this class is not so clear and a later observer remarks,

> »*Itonias* – or *Dhoanniahs* as Brodie calls them although I believe they are really an offshoot of the Singhpos.« (Butler 1874 in Leach 1946:453).

Leach has shown in his analysis that these groups were not *mayam* in the ordinary sense, but more probably in the process of becoming commoners, albeit, commoners of a different sort. Thousands of so-called slaves were released by the British during the 19th century and the economy of northeast Assam was crippled. Three thousand out of the ten thousand inhabitants of Hukawng were supposedly slaves. However confused the criteria for deciding just who were slaves, there can be no doubt about the existence of a very large dependent population. If these dependent villages had, as they apparently did, the status of exterior slaves (*ngong mayam*), they formed, it can be said, a real exploited class.

Leach points out that the release of the slaves coincided with the start of Assam tea manufacture (Leach 1946:471). In any case, a community that was on the way to becoming a small state was permanently destroyed.

> »From that time there had been a gradual falling off in power and influence of all the Singhpo chiefs of the Nao and Boree Dihing frontier, the remaing Assamese and other dependents leaving them as opportunity offered until many chiefs who before possessed hundreds to cultivate their lands were left without means of subsistence.« (Hannay 1847:44).

But the developing class structure is evident in the data on village organization.

> »The stockade is circular in form with a strong breastwork behind. The houses are built in a circle facing outwards while there is a smaller stockade in the center where the chief has his houses.« (Vetch 1873:279).

Leach remarks that this village plan is an illustration of the principle of core lineage plus appendages (Leach 1946:471), but the normal Kachin village which is ideologically of such a form, does not have any spatial marking of core and outsiders. It is more probable that the distinction in class was being made as clear as possible by the organization of space. The same plan characterizes many east and southeast Asian cities and towns. The capital of Manipur, Imphal, was no more than a royal palace and stockade surrounded by a very large collection of closely packed villages.

It is again very difficult to reconstruct the internal organization of the Tsasen domains with any precision, but the general process of transformation seems to be that implied in our model of *gumsa* society. With a new technological base, the principals of *gumsa* organization could work themselves out to their fullest. Slaves could be imported at a much greater rate with no economic barriers to contend with. In the fertile valleys of Assam the potential surplus that could be appropriated was nothing short of enormous. Even if productivity remained the same, and it was probably much greater, the absolute surplus would be much larger simply because density and thus intensity of culvation was greater. More land was put into cultivation by more people with no diminishing returns. Further, the use of plough and oxen reduced the labor cost of output in a very important way.

> »In short, the argument is that if the British had not appeared on the scene 1825, then the Singhpos and their Dooaneah followers would have coalesced into a single ritual and political structure and would have come to form elements of one or more »states« organized on Shan lines.« (Leach 1946:481).

The best demonstration that things were in fact moving in that direction is the fact that the Tsasen chiefs unlike other chiefly Kachin clans, had no Madai *nat* ritual, thus no great redistributive feasts. (Leach 1946:482). The nature of their ritual-economic activities is not known, but it appears that a movement away from redistribution was occurring.

In all these relatively recent examples there is a great deal of interference. The fact that Kachin developments which have only been partially recorded take place in the context of already existing states and state religions, makes it difficult to elicit the underlying structural changes which are often quickly skewed by outside influence. In order to grasp the possibilities of evolution it is better, I think, to take examples from the more distant past in which these societies can be examined in »purer« conditions.

The states of pre-Han China belong to what is commonly known as the feudal period of Chinese history. We have seen, however, that on the basis of some evidence, there might be significant resemblance between these early states and Kachin structure. Hsu, who accepts the feudal classification is careful to qualify it.

> »At this point we can see the distinctive features of Chinese feudalism; its counterpart in Western Europe, according to Marc Bloch, differed significantly because the feudal ties developed when those of kinship proved inadequate.« (Hsu 1965:3).

But why is the word »feudal« applied to such different situations? One cannot help but think that what is meant here is quite simply the notion of a landed aristocracy. But, in fact, »feudalism« refers to a particular system of property rights in which personal tenure is *exchanged* for labor service (rent). The asiatic mode cannot be construed in such a way. Tribute and corvée are not part of an exchange of rights and duties between landlords and individual peasants. They are owed to the ruler in his function as representative of the community and maintainer of prosperity.

The pre-Han state is similar to a greatly expanded Kachin domain, or rather a large number of domains organized and controlled by a prince (or king) who resides in a capital of »great domain«.[1]) Ultimate authority is apparently based on a monopoly over the agricultural deity who ensures fertility. The deity is not a separate higher entity, but ancestor of the royal family. The chiefs or lords of sub-states and domains are, like the junior branches of a Kachin *mung*, excluded from the highest cult ritual.

»Des les débuts, il a du être necessaire de diviser les terres en exploitations separées confiées à divers membres de la famille sous la direction du Prince qui commandait seul la propriété religieuse marquée par le culte d'un dieu du Sol propre. Au Prince appartenait le droit d'appeler les vassaux aux armes, de réunir les troupes et de les passer en revue devant le tertre du dieu du Sol . . . De là l'existence de deux classes de Seigneurs, les Princes, revêtus de fonctions sacrées, et les simples Seigneurs, leurs vassaux.« (Maspero 1967:7).

---

[1]) Since writing this section, I have come to think of the progression from Shang through Eastern Chou and the Warring States period as more differential than appears here. Unfortunately, it is difficult to sort out which social structural traits belong to which period, but I think that the model developed here would apply best to the Shang. By late Shang and early Western Chou there seems to be significant structural change within the aristocracy, especially in the use of prestige articles to maintain alliance relations. The so-called feudalism of the Chou, especially, may best be construed as a period when noble rank is determined less by the segmentary structure and more by the exchange of valuables, where the maintenance of power depends not only on monopoly over the deities but also over valuable prestige goods, associated at first with ceremonial displays but later given away selectively to enforce the loyalty of the nobility. Bodde (1956) sees a break between Shang and Chou on the basis of the Chou form of investiture whereby nobles, in return for the usual tribute and favors, received, at the royal Chou temple, a number of gifts such as bronze vessels, weapons, chariots etc. which we can interpret as prestige goods. This kind of relationship is apparently linked to marital alliances so that matrilateral links might be the form taken by the major political relations in the kingdom. Maspero (1950) stresses the difference between this kind of political relation which seems to exist between statelets or domains in the Chou period and an older form of segmentary patrilineal hierarchy which governs intra-domain organization. In the Chou period there appears to be a re-emergence of exchange relations and the development of an economy based on the control of prestige good production and distribution. This might still be considered to be a development which occurs within the »asiatic« structure and which does not alter the basic relations of production.

Political and economic control is maintained by exclusion from ritual office, which amounts to exclusion from control over social reproduction. This is accomplished by strict primogenture. Younger brothers and ministers are granted their own domains but no ritual power.

>»Au temps des Tcheou Occidentaux, les premiers constituaient des domaines privés en faveur de leurs cadets ou d'officiers de la maison, à qui ils donnaient des terres sans dieu du Sol particulier et, par conséquent en se réservant les droits religieux et politiques.« (Maspero 1967:7).

The entire structure is held together by kinship, either segmentary, or affinal in the case of unrelated officiers and ministers.

>»All of these families were either descended from the ducal house or connected with it by marital ties.« (Hsu 1965:7).

Furthermore, all rank positions in the state hierarchy are determined or rationalized by genealogical connections.

>»Just as the younger sons of dukes established branch families of high-grade ministers, so the younger sons of these ministers established branch families of low-grade ministers and *shih*[1]), who served the ministers roughly as the ministers served the dukes.« (Hsu 1965:7).

All this is a striking parallel to the structure of a Kachin domain, but on a much grander scale with numerous distinct levels of nobility. And the parallel carries over into local organization as well. At the lowest level, the individual domain is quite small, consisting of no more than 600 families distributed in a number of hamlets (Maspero 1967:9). The local lord simply lives in one of these hamlets. His residence, a kind of local court, is at the center of the village. It contains a reception hall, a place of public and private ritual, quarters for family, servants, noble functionaries, etc. The chiefly residence is surrounded by houses of the officers of the domain and then those of the peasants and artisans attached to the domain. This general local organization is similar to the dispersed pattern of the Kachin and the lord's compound might well be taken as a further development of the concentric pattern described for the Singhpo villages of Assam.

Economically, however, there are some important developments. The artisans, who in Kachin society are dispersed and not pure specialists are here organized centrally as a separate class. This *does not* represent a technological innovation. The Kachin as well as other tribal groups we have discussed have blacksmiths, they make their own cloth, baskets, weapons, instruments of production, etc., and it is very often the case that a village or individual will specialize in some particular trade. But, there is no clear and simple division of labor. The blacksmith is also an agriculturalist, and most of the crafts are part time activities. The only difference is one of organization and a significant change in the relations of production. Artisans are now non-agricultural; they are supported by inceased agricultural production. More significant than the

---

[1]) *Shih* is a scribe.

centralization of small scale industry is the great proliferation of noble functionaries. Every domain has its intendant, authorized to plan and organize the work cycle on the farms. Every intendant has a right-hand man in charge of seeing that his orders are carried out. There is a director of corvée activities, a director of servants and military personnel, a director of artisans, a director of commerce, etc. The only significant economic effect of this administrative class is the intensification of exploitation. There may well have been attempts to reorganize both agricultural and artisanal activities for higher productivity, but this took place largely within the same level of technological development and cannot be said to constitute a change in technological base. In any case, it is quite evident that such reorganization as did occur was carried out in order to extort larger surpluses, most of which must have gone to support the very managerial class that organized such exploitation.[1] The king has officers for every conceivable activity, and there can be no question about the top-heaviness of these over-administered states. They are, in essence, aristocratic bureaucracies, but they emerge directly from the previous tribal structure. It would be nothing short of naive to claim that these bureaucracies were necessary for the operation of the productive process. On the contrary, they indicate, first a partial neutralization of the intrinsic tendency of the kinship structure to fission, and second a development of a real class structure. The assignment of named functions to all positions in the segmentary hierarchy gives the former kinship network a permanence that it did not formerly possess. A noble's status no longer derives entirely from his genealogical connection with the King, but is defined independently by his special role in the »family company«. But this implies an expansion of the aristocratic class in a way which is impossible in the Kachin system, where there are only two functions, headman and chief.[2] In the *gumsa* system, all aristocratic lineages which do not hold local minor chief or headman posts are functionally no different than commoners. Their only claim is genealogical and it is difficult to maintain. In the pre-Han state, junior lines are all assigned to some role in the organized bureaucracy. Thus, their relative status is anchored to the extent that their lower kinship rank is doubled by a secondary but »necessary« function in the larger decision making machinery of administration. In consequence, the shedding of junior lines which characterized Kachin society no longer takes place and *the exploitation of the community by a single lineage is expanded into class exploitation.*

[1] A recent article tends to support this view, claiming that the evolution of the Chinese state »was based not on technology but on the fruit of human toil taken away from the many and given to the few. One can only conclude that the urban revolution was a revolution of the social system, and that civilization was its by-product«. (Chang 1974:11).

[2] There is, however, some evidence that non-inheriting chiefly lines among the Triangle Kachin can be assigned pseudo-managerial or judicial positions that entitle them to a portion of the total surplus of the domain (Maran La Raw, personal communication). This could be the germ of the bureaucratisation that is fully developed in the Chinese states.

How would Wittfogel explain the existence of such bureaucracies in pre-hydraulic China? Contrary to his functional-causal hypothesis, it seems quite clear that the great bureaucracies of the empires are no more than expanded versions of an already established tendency which, in turn, can only be explained in terms of the internal dynamics of pre-existent social forms. Technological change merely establishes the pre-conditions in which these tendencies can work themselves out.

Religion plays a central role in the pre-Han state. Just as among the Kachin, it is directly involved in the process of production. It is *not* simply a reflection of social relations of production, but is an integral part of them. The basic properties of the religious system are exactly like those of the Kachin. Ancestors are deified and can be traced back, in the case of aristocrats, to the beginning of time. There is no clear distinction between the social world and the supernatural realm. The latter is not a reflection, but a *continuation* of the former.

>Dans la société antique, l'element fondamental de l'organization tant laïque que religieuse était la seigneurie. Dans la seigneurie la société laïque reposait sur deux bases: le groupe familial et la possession de la terre seigneuriale; parallèlement la religion reposait sur deux cultes; celui des ancêtres et celui du dieu du sol.« (Maspero 1967:17).

But the two parallel cults become one at the top of the social hierarchy. »Les ancêtres étaient la famille divinisée: le dieu du Sol etait la seigneurie divinisée.« (Maspero 1967:17).

As in *gumsa* society, control over people is directly linked to the monopoly of the supernatural world. The king has direct access to those celestial beings that provide for his people's well being. Other nobles have similar powers to a greater or lesser degree, depending on their genealogical ties to the ruler. Thus, in theory at least, the distribution of ranks is mediated by the ruler himself. Political, like spiritual authority flows through the conical clan structure from the gods to the king, then to princes and finally to petty aristocrats.

»Chaque famille noble avait ainsi ses ancêtres protecteurs dont les puissances correspondait à celle de la famille elle même et dont la protection s'étendait, non seulement sur les descendants, mais sur tous ceux qui dépendait d'eux, sujets, serviteurs, animaux, domaines, champs et maisons.« (Maspero 1967:18).

The main economic function of the ruler is the maintenance of prosperity. He is involved in all phases of the agricultural cycle by means of ritual offerings to his ancestors who control fertility. The deity is an agricultural spirit, the ruler of millet, and it is only the king who has effective control over him. In fact, while all other administrative functions are distributed among the ministers, the king remains the only person capable of communicating with the supreme powers. Thus, the authority of a ruler is not based, as in feudalism, on land title, but on his religious-economic role in the reproduction of the society.

»De jure sovereignty was associated with the religious function.« (Hsu 1965:21).

The pre-Han state appears in all its essentials to be a larger more elaborate version of the Kachin domain, and it is not unreasonable to link the two in an evolutionary sequence. The ancient Chinese states were, however, very verticalized versions of the Kachin system. The dominant organizational principle was not affinal rank, but segmentary position. All authority was distributed through the conical network and emanated from one source, the king, senior lineage of the entire state.

»Since a noble owed his status to the charisma his clan had inherited from these ancestors, it was only reasonable that the ruler, who represented the main branch of the clan, had inherited more of the holy nature than a lesser member.« (Hsu 1965:21).

The state capital was a domain like any other, only larger, containing palaces and temples and a number of public buildings. Royal administration was just like the governing of the domain. All the principles remain the same, they merely include larger numbers of villages and levels of administration.

The structure we have described is equivalent to Marx's »asiatic« state. It can be said to have evolved from an earlier tribal form similar to that of the Kachin. It is impossible here to separate the evolution of class dominance from that of the state since the two are part of the same evolving structure. In the strictly organizational sense, it might even be said that the state form precedes stratification. The Kachin domain is in most respects analogous to a state formation. It is a hierarchical order in which a paramount ruler at least nominally controls the entire territory and its inhabitants. The Kachin formation is not a class structure, or if so, only to a very minimal degree since only the chief's family can be said to be in an exploitative position. But this position is itself predicated on the monopoly of a ritual required for the reproduction of the whole group, domain or state. The form of control is first established within a ranked society, but it permits the development of class stratification. In this way, the segmentary state can be said to have preceded the emergence of class structure. Now, in fact, the administrative officials of pre-Han society are at the same time the upper class, the aristocracy supported by agricultural and artisinal surplus labor. Thus, there is absolute identity between state organization and stratification. The class structure develops within the former kinship structure. It does not destroy it, but is, rather, sanctioned by it. This is because the tribal-kinship system is itself a state in miniature. At every level, from the smallest domain to the kingdom, the nobility has the same ritual function which serves as the means and the rationalization for control and exploitation. Interestingly enough, there seems to have still been ritual redistribution in the early states (Maspero 1967:25), but it existed simultaneously with the extraction of a surplus large enough to support an extensive pseudo-managerial nobility. There is no contradiction here. As we have shown, tribute and corvée

are not given on the understanding that they will be returned. The redistributive aspect of the economy becomes less important as the vertical ideology
is strengthened. Surplus is appropriated by a class that is considered necessary
to the production process. The Kachin chief appropriates his surplus for the
same reasons, but he is bound by a horizontal exchange system as well, since
his status is only maintained by feasting. The existence of a former redistributive stage in pre-Han (early Shang) states does demonstrate, however, the
critical importance of the ability to produce a large absolute surplus. This
would seem to be the major technological requirement for the transformation
of tribe to »asiatic state«, since it permits class structure to develop while the
redistributive function still remains as a secondary phenomenon.

The ritual claims on the deities are greatly strengthened in the »asiatic« state,
and there is evidence that increasing verticalization creates a rupture between
the aristocracy and the peasant or commoner class. The Kachin chief is directly
descended from the founder of the Kachin race who is affinally related to a
celestial spirit, son of the supreme deity. The Chou imperial house has moved
further up the hierarchy and is directly descended from the supreme deity.

»The first birth of our people
was from Chiang Yuan
How did she give birth to our people
She had presented a pure offering and sacrificed
That her child bareness might be taken away
She then trod on a toe-print made by Ti (supreme deity)
And was moved
In the large place where she rested
She became pregnant: she dwelt retired
She gave birth to and nourished (a son)
Who was Hou Chi (chief agricultural deity)« (Hsu 1965:16).

The transition from the Kachin system entails a strengthening of the ties to
the celestial powers.

This transformation suggests an increasing concentration of ritual power.
At the same time there appears to be a definite rupture between the ritual of
the nobility and that of the common people. The latter have their sacred ancestors, but they are not traced back to celestial powers. Thus, only the nobility,
in varying degrees, has the crucial access to the forces that ensure prosperity.
Among the Kachin, the situation is similar, but commoners are still connected
with secondary celestial spirits. Furthermore, the *ga nat* sacrifice, i.e., to the
highest deity, is still to some degree a village or domain function and it is performed at the *numshang* which belongs to the community at large. In the Chou
and Shang states, however, monopolization by the royal house is complete and
all communal sacrifices are in the royal compound.

Briefly, then, the »asiatic« state evolves directly out of previous Kachin type
structures. The basic relationships remain similar, but they are stretched
to fit the emergent class system. The increase in absolute potential sur-

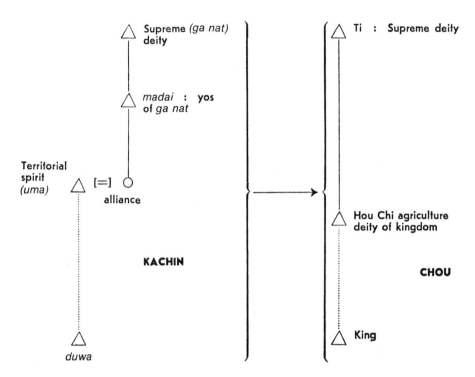

plus is utilized to expand the aristocracy into a dominant class, but in terms of the same ritual-economic structures. Control over nature is strictly monopolized and genealogical connections with the celestial powers are restricted to aristocracy. Within the aristocracy, all authority is mediated by kinship links to the royal lineage, but positions are further reinforced and stabilized by making them functional parts of a large bureaucracy. Redistribution necessarily becomes a secondary phenomenon, since it is no longer important for the maintenance of rank. A fixed amount of land is cultivated for the nobility and redistribution only occurs with secondary surplus, left over after the reproductive needs of both classes are seen to. It is a kind of secondary prestige function which proves the efficiency of the nobility in their role as providers of plenty.

The formation of the lower class results from mechanisms which already operate in the tribal system. Slaves are captured as well as generated internally, and the two categories tend to be integrated as a single class. The extensive turbulence caused by raiding, debt slavery and the like tends to loosen the bonds of kinship among commoner lineages whose ancestors disappear along with their identity as independent political and economic units.

The particular determinant characteristic of the asiatic state is that political authority, ritual authority, and appropriation of surplus are all anchored to a single vertical structure (see next page). All nobility is defined by a genealogical relation to the royal family, and the royal family sanctions its power in terms of its descent from the highest gods. This is a sacred hierarchy, not as a simple reflection of secular organization, but as a ritual-economic unity. Things have gone further than the simple tribal ranking system. The lower ranks have become a lower class and are increasingly excluded from communication with the supernatural forces upon which they depend for their livelihood.

The »asiatic« state is the end product of *gumsa* evolution. It is the development of class and state structure on a kinship base, but on a base that has been completely verticalized so that all transactions, all economic flows, are determined, not by contract, not by exchange, but by segmentary position. *Gumlao*, *gumsa* and the »asiatic« state thus form a kind of structural continuum. Rank is first established by the horizontal exchange system. It is then ratified by claims on the supernatural world, and finally, with an expansion of absolute surplus, the hierarchy becomes a fixed entity, and economic flow is coordinated by the hierarchy rather than hierarchy emerging out of the economic flow. But the weaknesses of *gumsa* organization remain. The accumulation of aristocratic lines makes the system very top heavy and the power of the sovereign tends to be eroded. Property is of a very weak sort. While »in theory the Chou king personally owned every square inch of the empire« (Hsu 1965:110) this was not ownership in the sense of feudal or capitalist property. It was, just as in

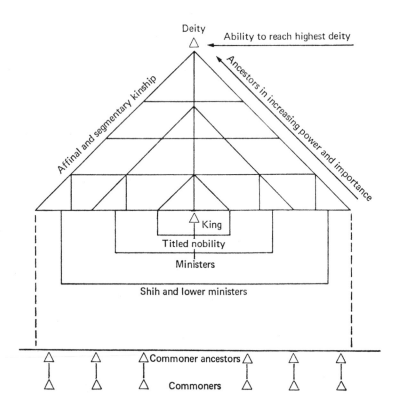

the tribe, control sanctioned by relationship to the deities. Marx speaks of the »legal absence of property« and this is confirmed by the empirical analyses of Hsu.

> »It is therefore misleading to think that the Chinese concept of ownership was the same as the modern judicial idea of ownership. What seems to have mattered was the actual control of a given piece of land.« (Hsu 1965: 110).

But this control is defined in terms of ritual-economic function. Consequently, just as in *gumsa* society, if wealth can be accumulated to a disproportionate degree within the state, the chances of fission are very great. The entire pre-Han period is characterized by constant inter and intra state warfare. In a segmentary state, each segment is potentially a state in itself.

> »En conséquence, l'historie de l'époque des Tcheou fut faite de guerres incessantes, d'une lutte ininterrompue pour l'hégémonie de principautés, demi-états despotiques.« (Tokei 1957:170).

But the new state forms that emerged from the wars were made up less of blood relations and more of appointed ministers who could be controlled by the royalty since they owed their position, not to an undeniable genealogical connection but to the will of the king. The old aristocratic bureaucracy was an outgrowth of the royalty and connected to it by a system of kinship ranking. The new bureaucracy was a distinct class. It was related to the king only by wealth and functional role and tended increasingly to usurp the privileges of the old nobility. Tokei, discussing late Chou development speaks of,

> »La tendence bureaucratisante de l'Etat 'asiatique,' tendence que se manifeste, plus ou moins, à l'encontre des conditions premières naturelles (noblesse, etc.).« (Tokei 1967:170).

The state form that emerges from the wars has thus broken through the constraints of segmentary kinship, and verticalization is taken to its absolute extreme, in that royalty is now qualitatively separated from the bureaucratic aristocracy. But a whole new series of contradictions is involved in this transition. The breakdown of hereditary »asiatic« aristocracy opens the door to new horizontal exchanges. Property titles are divided, commercial capital emerges, and land becomes concentrated in the wealthy families that emerge from the wars. The ensuing history is one of conflict between asiatic and feudal tendencies, between centralization and peripheral accumulation of wealth and power. The cycles of expansion and fragmentation are analogous to the *gumsa/gumlao* cycle, but on a higher level of organization. True *gumlao* tendencies make their appearance only in the periodic peasant revolts, and they are linked as in Kachin society to overexpansion and diminishing returns. But the more general fusion and fission characteristic of Chinese history is of a different nature, corresponding to cycles of accumulation of private or feudal property within the state leading to fission and then later recentralization. It is a conflict between individually owned alienable (horizontal) property and the dominant »asiatic« mode (vertical) which tends to make everything over to the state, a state, however, which is not simply an apparatus for the regulation of inter-group conflict in the upper class, but a class in itself.

The evolution of asiatic state forms was not confined to China but occured in most of Southeast Asia. The development of the Laotic state from earlier Thai tribal structures seems to follow the same path.

> »Ces sociétés thai sont, caracterisées par des structures étatiques primitives, dominées par de minorités aristocratiques. Le chef suprême de la famille dirigeante, les *cam* (l'or) s'appelle Cao Phem Cam. *Il est le médiateur entre la divinité et le reste de la société donne au printemps le premier coup de pioche propitiatoire,* reçoit un impôt en nature et en barres d'argent, a droit à des corvées. *C'est à dire que le travail et les impôts destinés à la communauté se confondent avec le travail et les impôts destinés à l'individu personnifiant l'Etat et les forces vives de la communauté.«* (Manivanna 1969:311) (my underline).

Contrary to what is usually assumed, I would tend to think that the »asiatic« state proper, characterizes only the early stages of evolution from the prior ranked tribal structures. The great »oriental despotic« empires are much more complex organizations which contain a number of conflicting »modes of production«. The classical Chinese state contains state as well as various kinds of private landed property. The original asiatic states were uniform in this respect, but we can point to conflicting vertical and horizontal tendencies even at the earlier tribal stage. However, what remain conflicting tendencies in the ranked society, become conflicting forms of organization, of property, in the fully developed state. *Gumsa/gumlao* variation takes place within a single »asiatic« property form, but the kind of fluctuation characteristic of the large states is more an oscillation between Chin and Kachin forms of property. In other words, in the classical state, we are dealing with fully materialized tendencies competing for control of the same object, land. The asiatic society envisaged by Marx as developing right out of tribal society is thus limited to these early states, based on a single vertical relation of production. Later developments are such that »asiatic« property is complemented by other forms. In many cases, however, the »asiatic« form is dominant and these states are also »asiatic« social formations. In a few cases, »asiatic« property may even have been maintained to the exclusion of all others. This appears to have been true for the Mauryian empire of Kautilya. But generally, it is very difficult to maintain this simple property relation other than by a very strict control over subordinate elements in the aristocracy, by constantly absorbing potentially fissioning nobles into the state bureaucracy. If despotism and absolutism are developed to a high degree in these states, it is principally in reaction to the intrinsic weakness of »asiatic« property, its legal non-existence.

Summary

In this section I have suggested a possible development of »asiatic« state forms out of pre-existent *gumsa*-type structures. I have attempted to clarify the way in which the class system develops on already established kinship forms whose content, so to speak, is significantly altered in the process. The gradual dominance of the vertical exchange system is the outcome of tendencies which are already present in the »tribal« social formation, tendencies which need only be freed by removing the constraints of hill swidden technology.

Throughout this and the preceding chapters we have been critical of mechanical materialist approaches. Our aim, in this book, has been to restore and contribute to the more realistic materialism which Marx developed in his most serious theoretical works. One can be a materialist without being a technological determinist – the two positions have little to do with one another. The assertion of the ultimate reducibility of the properties of social behavior to the properties of lower order biological systems and even to the statistical mechanical properties of matter[1]) is of a different order than the claim that social forms can be reduced to technological forms. We have tried to show that the latter approach is continually falsified by the data, that techno-ecological conditions do not generate social structures and that a more consistent approach using the notion of social formation can yield more interesting results. One can, after all, be both a determinist and a materialist without being a vulgar materialist.

It is with this in mind that I now address myself to some of the problems of determination which have been raised here.

Conclusion I

Evolution, Mystification and Ideological Bias

The first responce of the cultural materialist to this analysis will undoubtedly be, »emic« or worse, »eclectic«!! Why? Because religion is only a sanction for already existing states of affairs. My analysis has consisted in showing how control over people and appropriation of their surplus is linked to control over communal deities whose magical function is to bring prosperity. The evidence is quite clear for Kachin society that claims to political ritual office precede or imply authority over the community and not vice versa. Is this nonsense? Can people be so mystified into the acceptance of emergent stratification? The answer is apparently yes! Further, it should only seem strange to those materialists who are themselves caught up in the ideology of the capitalist system. A number of examples come to mind. In what sense, for instance, should an

---

[1]) Reducibility does not imply that we can easily deduce the properties of living organisms from statistical mechanics but only that the most general laws can be combined with specific conditions to account for higher orders of complexity. However, the properties of higher order systems, while theoretically deducible from those of their constituent systems, are not identical with them. We can explain the structure of chemical compounds in terms of the more general properties of simpler elements, but the latter still have *different* properties from the former. Reducibility must not be confused with identity.

ancestor cult be more ideological than a bank account? Or is money somehow more real than god? Marx's answer was that capitalism is a »religion of everyday life« and that religion in some societies can provide the central relation of production, i.e., control over the process of social reproduction. »Asiatic« property or non-property, control by virtue of descent from the divinity is no more fictitious than the so-called legal ownership of capitalist society. Property for Marx,

> »is merely a conscious attitude to the conditions of production as to one's own – an attitude established by the community for the individual, proclaimed and guaranteed as law.« (Marx 1964:92).

What could be more »emic,« more fictitious, more ideological than property itself. Yet it determines the very form of exploitation. The definition of stratification as »differential access to basic resources« (Fried 1967: Chap. 5) is not a material one (in the mechanical materialist sense). Rather, it is intimately linked to the mystification of those »excluded«. Differential access is the result and not the cause of property relations. To think the contrary is to follow Dühring into the »force theory of history« (Engels 1969:190–220) in which property is camouflage for the police force or army that first established »differential access«. On the contrary it is mystification that plays the critical role in the evolution and maintenance of social systems.

Access to material goods in capitalism is by means of liquid capital, an entirely fictitious good, a fetish, in Marxist terms, that represents a social relation as a relation between objects. In the period of the breakdown of Western European feudalism, merchants who had accumulated large amounts of liquid capital were able to buy things such as labor power which previously were not for sale. How could an individual be faced with the alternative of starvation or working for a salary? The necessity wasn't material in the vulgar sense, but due to the existence and necessary acceptance of a form of value and therefore of a specific relation of production.[1]) The only material givens are x machines or fields capable of Y output and a population n. After technological constraints are accounted for, the rest: who is to work and who is not to work, how output is to be divided, etc. is determined by social forms which are not in themselves technological phenomena. What appears as necessary in daily life is the *immediate expression* of the misrepresentation, the mystification of social relations of production.

Fried, in his very interesting book on political evolution, accepts property as a means of restricting access to land and other essential productive resources (Fried 1967: Chap. 5). He also accepts the legal superiority of prior residence as a means of restriction. Such means of restriction are not independent but are seen as the result of increasing population pressure. But what is left totally in

---

[1]) All of this occurs, of course, in conditions where, for the producer, the question of the reorganisation of the social totality never arises, but only the question, how to survive in given »material« i.e. social circumstances.

the dark is the nature of property itself. One has the impression that the author accepts the material reality of such claims to control. But if such is the case, then it is equally reasonable to accept claims on territorial deities.

The cultural materialist layer-cake approach to society, with technology on the bottom and a topping of social and ideological superstructures is no more than the ideological representation of our own society when content is confused with function. It is somehow assumed that the higher one ascends on the cake, the more imaginary the entities become. Marx's division of the social formation into infrastructure and superstructure may seem similar at first, but it is, unlike the mechanical materialist caricature, based on strictly functional and not absolute cultural distinctions. Let me be more precise about this. The social formation is conceived of as a structure in which the elements of infra- and superstructure are linked in a single process of social reproduction. An infrastructural element such as relations of production is defined by its place in the reproduction of society, *not by some intrinsic cultural property*. This implies that *any* cultural unit can play a role in the immediate functioning of the economy. In the cultural materialist framework, religion is by definition part of the ideology, a reflection of something else which is more real. In the Marxist framework, all fictitious entities are equal. Thus, ritual monopoly can be as important in production as any form of direct property. That things are not seen this way by radical empiricists is only an indication of the degree to which they remain victims of capitalist ideology. In the last analysis, however, legality and sanctity are perfectly equivalent in their unreality.

There is another important point which is related to the preceding remarks. It appears that much of the argument about differential access as the cause of stratification is rather misguided. It is an attempt to find some tangible object on which to hang the evolutionary process. But the argument is back to front. What is given, what is truly material in class society, is differential access, not to resources, but to social product. This, in turn, is expressed by one form of property or another. Now Fried assumes that if one group is burdened with reproducing both itself and another group, the latter must somehow have »gotten hold« of the forces of production. But we are not told how this comes about. Evolution is conspicuously absent from *The Evolution of Political Society*. This is due to an exclusive focus on static forms and little or no interest in the dynamics of the social economy.

To be purely materialistic once again, *stratification is not equivalent to differential access to basic resources*. On the contrary, the latter is an *ideological misrepresentation* of a material fact which consists only in the appropriation over time of the surplus of one group by another, or more specifically, the reproduction of two social classes by the labor of one class. Thus, Fried's definition is, in essence, a mere abstraction of the notion of legal property. »You work *MY* land in *exchange* for a *RENT* which enables me to do no work at all.« »MY«, »exchange«, »RENT«, here, all express a particular form of class exploitation which, materially, reads simply »you work enough land to support both me and yourself« – *All the rest is mystification though not ideology since the fetishized social form determines the fact of surplus appropriation by non-producers.*

There are three possible theoretical positions with regard to evolution implied by this discussion, only one of which appears to make sense. The first is that all class society is the result of superstratification, i.e., conquest by a minority (?) (Duhring, possibly Carneiro). The second, functionalist theory, is that stratification is necessary to work some new technology (Wittfogel), or is somehow technically more efficient (Harris, 1963; Davis and More, 1945). The marxist position is that the development of class exploitation is rooted in the internal evolution of a fetishized form of social relations in new conditions of reproduction. Fried's approach must lead either to the position that property is a material reality, or to the theory that the means of production are simply taken over forcefully by a minority.

In this section I have tried to account for the transition from ranked to class society in terms of the dynamic properties of the former. I have tried to demonstrate how, in techno-economic conditions which permit continued expansion of surplus, a *gumsa* system, based on the conversion of affinal rank into segmentary rank by means of ritual dominance, could be transformed into an »asiatic« state similar to the pre-Han systems. The transformation involves, is even based on, the elaboration of a previously existing mystification, which enables lineages to take on especially sacred functions in the most crucial ritual of the group. In a religion whose exclusive concern is production, control over the deities implies control over the producers. It is the fact that the tribal community represents the world upside-down which permits privileged lineages to assume control of the society. In a sense, then, there is differential access to basic resources. But the resources are supernatural forces and not land. One might be tempted as an enlightened empiricist, to caricaturize the situation in the following way, to make it seem more »down to earth«: The celestial *nats* are »fertilizers« owned by the royal house or chiefly lineage. Commoners simply pay rent for access to this necessary magical capital addition to their labor. This, of course, is a gross distortion of the relations of production. There is no rent, no exchange. Tribute and corvée are for the support of a class that fulfills a function that is thought to be absolutely necessary for the prosperity of the whole society. There may be redistributive feasts, but the economy is not redistributive in the sense of reciprocity. Furthermore, redistribution is not a necessary element in the system, since surplus is not appropriated on the understanding that it will be returned. Sacrificial feasts that *are* given serve to reinforce the spiritual power of the ruler, not to maintain his class position. It is significant that the great feasts of the Shang period disappear in the later Chou dynasty where such orgies were considered the mark of the former state's decadence.

Conclusion II

Residence and Evolution: Mystification or Materialism

Two materialist analyses of Leach's work, by Fried (1967) and de Heusch (1971), have come to practically identical conclusions regarding the development of *gumsa* organization. Both, I think, are misled by their own materialist interpretations of what are in fact Kachin ideological categories. The fundamental error is rooted in the misconstrual of the following statement from Leach:

> »Some affinal links are associated with land tenure while others are not, but it always is the latter which are the most enduring. The basis of *dama* inferiority seems to lie in the fact that when *mayu* and *dama* are members of one territorial unit, the *dama* must have by implication broken the normal rule of patrilocal residence. The fact that *dama* are settled alongside their *mayu* implies that the founder of the *dama* (lineage) must have settled matrilocally with his father-in-law, and it is thus a token of inferior status.« (Leach 1954:83).

It is not my intention to discuss de Heusch's analysis which is in most ways excellent, especially with regard to its exposition and criticism of Leach's oscillatory »explanation«. His own interpretation of *gumsa* development is taken directly from the passage cited above. Where *mayu/dama* is combined with matrilocality it produces a real *gumsa* type ranking. The following transition is implied.

1. At first there are only *gumlao* communities – groups of lineages that have collective control over their village lands. Here *mayu/dama* relations are egalitarian and without economic effect.
2. With the introduction of immigrant lines, the same *mayu/dama* relation takes on new significance:

$$Mayu: \quad A \xrightarrow[\text{land}]{\text{women}} B \quad Dama$$

$$\xleftarrow{\hspace{2cm}}$$
$$\text{brideprice} = \text{rent}$$

According to de Heusch the critical factor is »l'alienation foncière« (de Heusch 1971:117) which permits the growth of differential brideprice and lineage ranking. A lineage that settles with its *mayu* becomes a tenant as well as a wife-taker to the latter.

But this argument contradicts the facts as presented by Leach. In a *gumlao* community there is no lineage »property«. In fact, as I have tried to show, *madu* rights of sovereignty do not correspond to anything like the feudal or private property notion implied by de Heusch's analysis. A *gumlao* community »owns« its land in common although there may be permanent individual use rights. Therefore, it does not appear feasible that an incoming *dama* lineage could become a tenant to a resident *mayu* lineage; i.e., there can be no transfer of title which did not exist in the first place. Furthermore, we have shown that a *gumsa* system has no equivalent to rent – an exchange of land for a payment in surplus product or labor. Kachin tribute is »asiatic« and not »feudal.«

A more serious error in this analysis is that it makes the virtually impossible assumption that the transition from *gumlao* to *gumsa* depends on the majority of lineages changing from patrilocal to matrilocal residence while a minority of »core« lineages stays home. This is patently absurd. It reduces the evolution of ranking to a kind of game of musical chairs in which everyone changes places and then, suddenly, hierarchy appears.

Fried's argument is like that of de Heusch, but he goes on to tie the change in residence pattern to increasing population density which might, if geographically variable, cause migration from more to less populated areas. This is, again, completely contradicted by the facts. The areas of highest *gumsa* development are those with the lowest densities (5/mi^2). Matrilocal residence is not the result of population pressure. In a *gumsa* community there is only one chiefly lineage but extensive ranking. The entire concept of *mayu/dama* tenancy is contradicted by the fact that all the land is »owned« by a single lineage. If we were to treat de Heusch and Fried's analyses seriously, we would be led to assume that there were only two hereditary rank classes one of which was limited to a single lineage. But this is simply not the case. Rank is *not* determined by land title in the Kachin system. On the contrary, the one land title that does exist is controlled by means of segmentary position in an emergent hierarchy which is itself generated by the internal dynamics of the economic system.

The error in the above interpretations is more profound than it seems at first glance. It is as if the only way that political and economic subordination can be envisaged is in terms of private property in the means of production or its abstract equivalent, differential access to basic resources. To accept the Kachin category of prior settlement as a sufficient or even minimal explanation for political and economic differentiation is to accept an ideology totally uncritically, perhaps because it vaguely corresponds to a capitalist »reality« which is conceived as the only possible basis for such a development. Prior settlement leads to prior rights, i.e., private (lineage) property – a seemingly sound basis on which to transform the purely ideological *mayu/dama* kinship system into something more »solid.« But if, as we have said, feudal property is no less unreal than kinship, the whole thing is open to question.

> »The fact that *dama* are settled alongside of *mayu* implies that the founder of the *dama* lineage must have settled matrilocally.« (Leach 1954:83).

The word »implies« here does not mean that matrilocal residence is a prerequisite for true ranking. Rather,

> »The formal seniority of the *mayu* to the *dama* in such cases provides the basis for claim to prior land title.« (Leach 1954:83).

Here is the key to the problem. Claims to land title are the result of ranking and not vice versa. Prior settlement is the ideological expression of segmentary rank which develops on the basis of the *mayu/dama* system. The chiefly line which has sole claim to land does so because it is directly descended from the territorial *nat*, ancestor of the local lineages. Thus, the internal properties of the verticalization process imply, logically, the equivalence of land rights, segmentary superiority and *mayu* superiority.

1. Rank, established affinally, implies that *mayu* is always in a position of relative superiority.
2. *Uma* rank, descent from the *mung nat* implies:
   (a) ritual superiority
   (b) that the chiefly lineage is the nearest relative of the community founder.
3. The combination of *mayu* plus eldest or founder-lineage status implies prior land title with regard to *dama* who are by implication later settlers and junior lines.

Thus, *gumsa* ranking which results from the combined functioning of vertical and horizontal exchange structures can be represented ideologically in terms of prior land title. But this is truly a secondary representation and not the basis of *gumsa* development.

The acceptance at face value of an ideology because it corresponds to what appears to be a materially based relation in our own society is the worst kind of error. *The ultimate idealism is to treat the ideological as if it were material.* It must be stressed again that, in a marxist approach, the distinction between infra and superstructure is functional and not a matter of cultural content. If property relations are material operators in capitalist society, this is not because they are *intrinsically* infrastructural, but because of the way they actually function in capitalist reproduction. In Kachin society, however, neither prior residence nor land title functions as a relation of production. Both are, functionally, ideological; i.e., they represent, in a transfigured way, the results of the operation of the infrastructure.

CHAPTER VIII

Conclusion

Implications of the Marxist Model

The present analysis has consisted in an attempt to explain the distribution of a number of societies in time and space by means of a single model of social reproduction. The model itself is a sub-category of a general theory stated at the very beginning of this thesis, one which has very definite implications for the way we can think about social formations and their evolution.

Synchrony and Diachrony

The pervasive dichotomy between historical and synchronic explanation is the result of the empiricist abstraction and institutionalization of the category »time.« The distinction is, however, quite absurd. There are no historical laws as such. As all history is the history of ... it is impossible to speak of principles and forces which are somehow outside of the object of study without recourse to metaphysics. The laws of history are identical with the laws of social forms. Evolution is the result of the internal development of social systems, not something that happens between »stages«.

Marx, in *Capital*, made the first and perhaps the only notable attempt to understand the mechanisms of historical movement in terms of the structural properties of a single social system. This amounted, not to a search for »laws of history« but for the »laws of motion« of a particular mode of production. Marx's focus on the internal properties of social reproduction transcends the false dichotomy prevalent among anthropologists of both »idealist« and »materialist« persuasions. Even among evolutionists, social systems are envisaged as fixed entities; structural wholes, yes, but structured in the Radcliffe-Brownian sense, in terms of stable behavioral relations between observable elements. In sum, there has never been an attempt to explain the transition from one evolutionary stage to another in terms of internal dynamics. Evolutionary »explanation« has consisted primarily in the lining up of empirical or abstract empirical types (band, chiefdom, state etc.) in a relative chronology. Vulgar materialist hypotheses are an immediate outgrowth of this empiricism in which the correlation between types of society and types of technology or levels of population density are simple mindedly converted into causal statements. The problem of transformation is forgotten and replaced by an exogenous independent variable whose development appears as the immediate cause of a designated evolutionary type. This approach thoroughly mystifies the issue of social change. Thus, even among evolutionary theorists, the social formation is conceived of as static so that the causes of transition from one stage to another must be relegated to exterior mechanisms.

Contrary to this view is the marxist notion of social reproduction which neutralizes the distinction between historical and functional processes by utilizing a model that incorporates the time element. The internal properties of a social system determine whether or not it will reproduce itself in exactly the same way and in exactly the same conditions.

The intuitive if superficial characterization of »primitive« societies as »cold« as opposed to »hot« societies corresponds to the marxist distinction between simple and expanded reproduction. The marxist notion, however, is quite specific and could only sanction the use of the term »cold« for societies that reproduce themselves in identical conditions of production over time. In such cases, long and short term properties are exactly the same. It is probable that »primitive« societies, like the Kachin, are not nearly so »cold« as they appear in ethnographical accounts. On the contrary, it is more probably the ethnographic descriptions that are »cold.« While social relations are often adequately described as static phenomena, the description can never be complete without including the economic flow whose properties determine the long term development of the system. Static representations, of course, are just as common in the analyses of so-called »hot« societies where, in fact, the historical dimension may only be present because the experience of it is quite direct. Further, as invariant structures (in the behaviorist sense) seem to be more difficult to discover in modern capitalist societies (due to the total disregard for the nature of the specifically capitalist relations of production), there has been a global dichotomization of social forms into those that are static, structured, »cold«, as opposed to those that are dynamic, unstructured and »hot« (Sartre 1963). This dichotomization is more evidence of the ideology to which we referred in the introduction.

Leach's oscillatory hypothesis is a case in point. Faced with two forms of political-economic structure, one »egalitarian,« another hierarchical, both within the same basic kinship system and technology, he postulates that both forms tend toward their opposites in such a way that *gumsa/gumlao* variation follows a fixed cycle. Leach's analysis of the Kachin has been blocked by his own empiricism since he first published on the subject. In 1951, for example, there is not the slightest indication that *gumsa* and *gumlao* might be linked historically. On the contrary, the entire explanation hinges on the association of matrilateral cross-cousin marriage with a system of ranked lineages; i.e. that the unilateral properties of the marriage relationship are best able to express the rank differences between local lineages. This hypothesis is *totally* false in relation to the Kachin material. That it has never been formally rejected can only be attributed to the unscientific context within which anthropologists think and work. In *Political Systems* (1954) we are told that matrilateral marriage occurs in both ranked and egalitarian forms. Leach's discovery that the two types are historically related has, finally, become reified into his oscillatory hypothesis (1969).

It should be quite evident that Leach is trapped by his unwillingness to make truly explanatory statements about his evidence. His hypotheses do little more than recapitulate or correlate parts of the existing data. Armed with a purely empirical notion of social structure he finds a number of coexistent elements which can only be »explained« in terms of themselves. Asymmetrical exchange, ranked lineages, tribute, corvée etc. make up one polar type. Asymmetrical exchange, egalitarian polity etc. make up another. In the earlier argument (1951) it is simply postulated that the ranked system is functionally related to generalized exchange. In the latter, the two political forms are joined in a cyclical model which simply reiterates actual historical variation. In both cases we are confronted, not with explanation, but with redescription. The status of »explanatory model« must be denied for »hypotheses« which contain no information other than that already present in the data. Leach's notion of oscillation says no more than that *gumlao* and *gumsa* variants tend to replace one another over time. This, in turn, is no more than a historical fact.

While Leach seems to assume that his model is truly explanatory, he does attempt to go further than that, to offer reasons for the oscillatcry nature of Kachin systems. It is here that he is weakest. Among the factors thought to determine *gumsa* development are:
1) the asymmetry of the *mayu/dama* relation itself (1954:221) – apparently an idea borrowed from Levi-Strauss.
2) exterior political and economic circumstances (1954:212).
3) imitation of Shan princes (1954:213).

The factor which leads to *gumlao* rebellion is simply the tendency of powerful *gumsa* chiefs to repudiate their kin obligations (1954: 203).

These factors are never linked in a systematic way. Nor are they explored in any real depth. All of the factors except the first are phenomenal and not structural. But even the first, which might be shown to have specific long term implications for the development of hierarchy, is treated as a merely static behavioral relationship.

>»The asymmetry of the *mayu-dama* relationship is, as it were, inconsistent with the dogma of status equality between lineages which dominates *gumlao* theory.« (Leach 1954:211).

Leach seems to be implying here that there is somehow an overt conflict between the status inequality of *mayu/dama* relations and *gumlao* political ideology. He does this in spite of the fact that there is ample evidence of societies which are, in fact, asymmetrical and yet have stable *gumlao* systems (Southern Chin, Old Kuki). In order to »explain« the *gumlao-gumsa* transition, he must assume that the *mayu/dama* relationship of *gumsa* society is already present *in exactly that form* in *gumlao* society, and ranking can only emerge as the result of an overt conflict between the abstract ideas of rank and equality. Thus, the one factor which might be said to have dynamic consequences for Kachin evolution is reduced to a simple static asymmetry. Leach's suggestions do not help us to understand the transition from *gumlao* to *gumsa*. The change would have to be an immediate and qualitative shift, a direct and forceful claim to rank and authority. His account of *gumlao* revolts is better simply because he is not faced with a transition like that from *gumlao* to *gumsa*, but a breakdown in existing social relations, the immediate result of the contradiction between rank and kin obligations. But he is totally unable to tell us why these strains build up in the system. The picture he gives is simply one in which a power hungry chief repudiates the kin ties which are the basis of his power.

Leach's »explanations« all reduce to actual visible phenomena, behavioral relations, or, at most, to the »systems of ethics« (1954:292) which serve as reference points for behavior. For the empiricist, »structure« refers to observable social institutions, relations or categories. He is, thus, faced with an impasse; the necessity of explaining data in terms of itself. The marxist (and structuralist) approach, on the contrary, focuses on the invisible *structural properties* of visible social processes. The dynamic properties of economic flows in Kachin systems are not observable, but can be said to *account for* a number of observable phenomena.

In Leach's framework it is impossible to understand how one can get from an egalitarian to a hierarchical form other than by simply »doing it,« by imposing rank differences on former egalitarian relations. In our framework, we have tried to show how the properties of the functioning of Kachin society cause the transition from *gumlao* to *gumsa*, and how the inter-systemic contradiction in the system causes its breakdown. Leach's *gumlao/gumsa* oscillation is the result of the functioning of a system of expanded reproduction in conditions of long term demographic stability. Major transformations occur when the conditions of production are changed, either by increasing density in the same techno-environment (devolution) or by removing the constraints of the hill swidden system. In either case we are faced with the same social system, but where internally determined tendencies are faced with new possibilities or impossibilities of development.

The categorical distinction between synchrony and diachrony is, as we have seen, thoroughly reinforced by the institutional dichotomy between ethnography and history. If descriptions are »cold« and »explanation« must always be reducible to the observable, then there is no way of avoiding the reification of the synchronic/diachronic distinction. Our own analysis of social reproduction is an attempt to transcend that false distinction. The properties of a social system, which can always be described synchronically, determine its evolutionary path. Consequently, the category »synchrony« can only be applied to those (hypothetical) societies that are truly »cold«, i.e., that reproduce themselves in identical conditions of production.

Transformational Models of Evolutionary Processes

The model we have used has two major components, one which accounts for structural variation and another which determines the limit conditions of variation and development of a particular structure. The object of analysis, the social formation, contains a number of distinct levels which are articulated with one another in terms of a set of intersystemic constraints and are dominated by a particular set of relations of production whose internal properties determine the direction of development of the social formation within the bounds set by those constraints. The interplay of internal variation, structural dominance, and intersystemic contradiction generates the multilinear development of the social formation.

We have shown how the Kachin system of social relations is structured in such a way that it tends to become increasingly hierarchical with time. In certain conditions, the very functioning of this system alters the productive base in such a way that the political structure becomes impossible to maintain. There is a collapse of vertical »asiatic« structures and a reinforcement of horizontal structures. In other conditions, by simply moving the Kachin system into fertile plains, we change the productive base in such a way that the *gumsa* tendencies are able to work themselves out to their fullest extent. On flat and fertile soils, conditions of production are significantly changed even for the same slash-and-burn technology. As the soil is far deeper than that of the hillsides, there is less loss of fertility. Nor is there any danger of soil run-off. Further, the flat terrain makes a larger percentage of the total land area available for cultivation. Productivity is higher, as is the population density permitted by the flat surface. Thus, the absolute surplus is multiplied many times and *gumsa* development is not blocked by the normal limitations of hill agriculture.

In any case, the transformations which occur are the direct result of the internal properties of a preceding system. The evolving conditions of production determine only the limits and not the direction of structural variation. But a complete analysis must consider two axes, one which accounts for changes in reproductive conditions and another which accounts for structural possibilities. The marxist framework transcends the superficial incompatibilities between multilinear (Steward 1955) and general (White 1959) evolution. A simple multilinear approach to our data would simply correlate Naga, Chin and Kachin social structures with their particular local ecologies and perhaps show the adaptive relations between them. A mechanical materialist might further obscure such superficial analysis by assuming that the individual social forms were »caused« by their environments. The generalist would, of course, have no way of handling such variation, but might see the broad similarities of the variants and be inclined to somehow group them in terms of a particular technological stage of development. In our approach, variation is not a particular adaptation to a specific environment. It is the result of the reproduction of a system in changing conditions of production where, as with the

Kachin, these conditions may be altered by the functioning of the system itself. In any case, the *source* of variation is always the social system. The only difference between general and specific evolution is the level of analysis. The former is concerned with the fundamental properties of a mode of reproduction; i.e., with the most general characteristics of the system and the constraints of production which determine its outer limits of variation. The latter (specific evolution) focuses on the internal variation which takes place within those limits. Both of the levels are fully integrated into the marxist model which, as we have seen, generates local variation and explains the process of major evolutionary changes in terms of the dialectical relation between internally determined developmental tendencies and the intersystemic relations between forces and relations of production.

I have attempted to show that a structural-marxist model[1]) is capable of explaining historical transformations which cannot, I think, be accounted for in other approaches. Any theoretical analysis always poses more questions than it answers, and there are a great many things that are implied about the societies analyzed which are not, in fact, part of the available data. New materials would certainly be needed to test many of our hypotheses. This is not, however, a situation to be avoided, but rather, one to be welcomed. If theories did not ask for more data, there would be no development in our understanding of the world. Truth would not advance if there were no falsification.

»All science would be superfluous if the outward appearance and the essence of things directly coincided.« (Marx 1967; vol. III:96).

---

[1]) This »structural marxism« is clearly unlike that of the Althusserian school.

Abbreviations

A.A.:	American Anthropologist
B.E.F.E.O.:	Bulletin de l'Ecole Française d'Extreme-Orient
Bijdragen:	Bijdragen tot de Taal-, Land- en Volkenkunde
C.A.:	Current Anthropology
C.E.R.M.:	Centre d'Etudes et de Recherches Marxistes
F.A.O.:	Food and Agriculture Organization (United Nations)
H.J.A.S.:	Harvard Journal of Asian Studies
H.R.A.F.:	Human Relations Area Files
J.A.S.B.:	Journal of the Asiatic Society of Bengal
J.B.R.S.:	Journal of the Burma Research Society
J.R.A.I.:	Journal of the Royal Anthropological Institute
P.U.F.:	Presses Universitaires de France
R.A.I.:	Royal Anthropological Institute
Recherches Internationales:	Recherches Internationales à la lumière du marxisme
S.W.J.A.:	Southwest Journal of Anthropology

Bibliography

Ainslie, Lieut.
1893   *Tour Through the Trans-Salween Shan States,* Rangoon

Ali, S. M.
1964   *History of Chittagong,* Dacca

Allen, B. C.
1905   *Assam District Gazetteer: Naga Hills and Manipur* Vols. A and B, Shillong
1906   *Assam District Gazetter: Jaintia Hills, The Garo Hills and the Lushai Hills,* Shillong

Anderson, J.
1871   *A Report of the Expedition to Western Yunnan Via Bhamo,* Calcutta
1875   »Papers connected with the development of trade between British Burma and Western China and with the mission to Yunnan«, *Parliamentary Papers,* no. 56

Badgley, W. F.
1873   »The Lusheis«, Indian Antiquary, 2

Bareigts, A.
1969   *Les Lautu*, Memoire de Diplôme: Ecole Pratique des Hautes Etudes, Paris

Barnard, J. T. O.
1925   »The History of Putao«, J.B.R.S., 15
1934   *A Handbook of the Rawang Dialect of the Nung Language*, Rangoon

Barnes, J. A.
1967   »Inquest on the Murngin«, Occasional Papers R.A.I.

Barrau, J.
1958   »Subsistance Agriculture in Melanesia«, Bernice Bishop Museum, Bulletin 219

Barton, R.
1929   *Wa Diary*, Rangoon

Bayfield, G. T.
1835   »Historical Review of the Relations between the British Government in India and the Empire of Ava from the Earliest Date on Record to the Present Year«, Appendix to Pemberton (1835), Calcutta
1873   »Narrative of a Journey from Ava to the Frontier of Assam and Back Performed between December and May 1837 Under the Orders of Colonel Burney ...«, in *Selection of Papers regarding the Hill Tracts between Assam and Burma and on the Upper Brahmaputra*, Calcutta

Belshaw, C.
1967   »Theoretical Problems in Economic Anthropology«, in Freedman, M. (ed.) *Social Organization*, Chicago

Benedict, P.
1941   *Kinship in Southeast Asia*, unpublished Ph.D. Thesis, Harvard University, Cambridge

Bernot, L.
1965   »Levirat et sororat en Asie du Sud-Est«, L'Homme, 5
1967   *Les Cak*, Centre Nationale de Recherche Scientifique, Paris
1967   *Les Paysans arakanais du Pakistan Oriental*, 2 Vols. Mouton, Paris

Berthe, L.
1965   »Ainés et cadets; l'alliance et la hierarchie chez les Baduj«, L'Homme, 5

Bessaignet, P.
   1958   »Tribesmen of the Chittagong Hill Tracts«, Asiatic Society of Pakistan, 1

Bettelheim, C.
   1959   »Variations du taux de profit et accroissement de la productivité du travail«, Economie Appliquée, 1
   1964   »Le surplus économique«, in *Planification et croissance accélérée*, Maspero, Paris
   1970   *Calcul Economique et formes de propriété*, Paris

Bich, N. L.
   1967   »Le mode de production asiatique dans l'histoire du Vietnam«, in Recherches Internationales, Paris

Blaut, H. M.
   1960   »The Nature and Effects of Shifting Agriculture«, in *Symposium on the Impact of Man on Humid Tropics Vegetation*, U.N.E.S.C.O.

Boulbet, J.
   1966   »Le miir,« BEFEO

Bose, J. R.
   1934a   »Religion of the Aimol Kuki«, Man in India, 14
   1934b   »Social Organization of the Aimol Kukis«, Journal of the Dept. of Letters, University of Calcutta, Vol. 25
   1934c   »The Marrings of Manipur«, Calcutta Review, April
   1934d   »Dual Organization in Assam«, Journal of Dept. of Letters, University of Calcutta, Vol. 25
   1937a   »Marriage Classes among the Chirus of Assam«, Man, Vol. 37, 189
   1937b   »The Origin of Tri-Clan Marriage Classes in Assam«, Man, Vol. 37

Boserup, E.
   1965   *The Conditions of Agricultural Growth*, Chicago

Brown, R.
   1874   *Statistical Account of the Native State of Manipur and the Hill Territory*, Calcutta

Bryce, J. A.
   1893   »The Chin and Kachin Tribes«, Asiatic Review, 5, 10

Buchanan, F. R.
   1820   »An account of Assam with Some Notes Concerning the Neighboring Territories«, Annals of Oriental Literature, Vol. 1

1821	»An Account of a Map of the Country North From Ava«

Burling, R.
1958	»Garo Cross-Cousin Marriage«, Man
1960	»An Incipient Caste Organization in the Garo Hills«, Man in India, 40
1963	*Rengsanggri*, University of Pennsylvania, Philadelphia

Burma
1892–94	*Northeast Frontier Report*
1889	*Report on the Operations on the Frontiers of Upper Burma*

Butler, J. (Maj.)
1847	*A Sketch of Assam with Some Account of the Hill Tribes*

Butler, J. (Capt.)
1874	*Report on the Exploration Survey of the Naga Hills*, Shillong
1875	»Rough Notes on the Angami Nagas and their Language«, JASB, 44

Carey, B. and *Tuck H.*
1896	*The Chin Hills: A History of the People, Our Dealings with Them, Their Customs and Manners*, Rangoon

Carneiro, R.
1960	»Slash and Burn Agriculture« in Wallace (ed.), *Man and Culture*, Philadelphia
1970	»A Theory of the Origin of the State«, Science 169

Carrapiett, W. J. S.
1929	*The Katchin Tribes of Burma*, Rangoon

Chagnon, N.
1963	»The cultural ecology of shifting (pioneering) cultivation among the Yanonami Indians«, Proceedings of the Eighth International Congress of Anthropological and Ethnological Sciences, Vol. 3, p. 249, Tokyo

Chambers, D. A.
1899	*Handbook of the Lusei Country*, Calcutta

Chang, K. C.
1974	»Urbanism and the king in ancient China«, *World Archaeology*, Vol. 6, London

Chang, Y. T.
1944	»Anthropological Features of the Shans of Southwest Yunnan«, Man. 55

Chayanov, A. V.
1966	*The Theory of Peasant Economy*, Homewood

Ch'en Tsung-hsiang
   1947   »The Dual System and the Clans of the Li-Su Shui-t'ien
                          Tribes«, Monumenta Sinica, 12

Clark, C. and Haswell, M.
   1966   *The Economics of Subsistence Agriculture*, New York

Cochrane, W.
   1915   *The Shans*, Rangoon

Condominas, G.
   1953   »L'Indochine; le milieu, les sociétés indochinoises, in Le-
                          roi-Gourhan et Poirier, eds. *Ethnologie de l'Union Fran-
                          çaise, Paris*

Conklin, H.
   1957   *Hanunoo Agriculture in the Phillipénes*, F.A.O., Rome
   1961   »The Study of Shifting Agriculture«, Current Anthropo-
                          logy, 2

Coryton, J.
   1875   »Trade Routes between British Burma and Western Chi-
                          na«, Journal of the Royal Geographical Society, 45

Couchman, G. N. H.
   1892   *Report on the Kachin Hills Northeast of Bhamo–1891–92*,
                          Rangoon

Dalton, E. T.
   1872   *Descriptive Ethnology of Bengal*, Calcutta

Dalton, G.
   1968   »A note of Clarification on Economic Surplus«, A.A. 62
   1969   »Theoretical Issues in Economic Anthropology«, C.A. 10,1

Das, T.
   1945   *The Purums*, Calcutta

Dasgupta, P. C.
   1935   »A Note on the Kom«, Journal of the Departement of
                          Letters, University of Calcutta, 26

Davis, A.
   1894   *Gazetteer of the North Lushei Hills*, Shillong

Dawson, G. W.
   1912   *Burma Gazetteer: Bhamo District*, Rangoon

Divitcioglu, S.
   1967   »Essai de modeles économiques à partir du mode de pro-
                          duction asiatique«, in Recherches Internationales, Paris

Duckham, A. and *Masefield, G.*
 1970 *Farming Systems of the World,* London

Dumond, D. E.
 1961 »Swidden Agriculture and the Rise of Maya Civilization«, SWJA 17

Dumont, L.
 1966 »Descent or Intermarriage? A Relational View of the Australian Kinship Systems«, SWJA 22

Durrenberger, E. P.
 n.d. »Notes on the Historical and Sociological Context of the Lisu Political System«, Unpublished m.s., Chiengmai

Engels, F.
 1963 *The Origin of the Family Private Property and the State,* International, New York
 1969 *Anti-Dühring,* Progress, Moscow

Enriquez, C. M.
 1923 *A Burmese Arcady,* London

Feng, H. & *Shryock*
 1938 »The Historical Origins of the Lolo«, HJAS 3,2

Firth, R.
 1961 *History and Traditions of Tikopia,* Polynesian Society, Memoir 33, Wellington
 1963 *We the Tikopia,* Boston

Fisher, C. A.
 1964 *Southeast Asia – A Social, Economic and Political Geography,* London

Forrest, G. W.
 1908 »Journey on the Upper Salween«, Geographical Journal 32

Fried, M.
 1957 »Classification of Corporate Unilineal Descent Groups«, JRAI 87
 1967 *The Evolution of Political Society,* New York

Fryer, G. E.
 1875 »On the Khyeng People of the Sandoway District«, JASB

Furer-Haimendorf, C. von
 1938 »The Morung System of the Konyak Naga«, JRAI 68
 1939 *The Naked Nagas,* London
 1969 *The Konyak Nagas,* New York

Furer-Haimendorf, C. von and *Mills, J.*
1936   »The Sacred Founder's Kin Among the Eastern Angami Nagas«, Anthropos 31

Geddes, W. R.
1960   »The Human Background«, in *Symposium on the Impact of Man on Humid Tropics Vegetation*, UNESCO

Gernet, J.
1970   *La Chine Ancienne*, Paris

Gilhodes, C.
1908   »Mythologie et religion des Katchins«, Anthropos, 3
1909   »Mythologie et religion des Katchins«, Anthropos, 4
1910   »La Culture materielle des Katchins, Anthropos, 5
1911a   »Mythologie et religion des Katchins«, Anthropos, 6
1911b   »Naissance et enfance chez les Katchins«, Anthropos, 6
1918   »Marriage et condition de la femme chez les Katchins«, Anthropos, 14
1917–18 »Mort et funérailles chez les Katchins«, Anthropos, 12–13
1919–20 »Mort et funérailles chez les Katchins«, Anthropos, 14–15

Geertz, C.
1968   *Agricultural Involution*, Los Angeles

Georgescu-Roegen, N.
1960   »Economic Theory and Agrarian Economics«, Oxford Economic Papers

Godden, C. M.
1898   »On the Naga and Other Frontier Tribes«, JRAI, 26

Godelier, M.
1965   »Objet et méthode de l'anthropologie économique«, L'Homme, 5
1966a   »Système, structure et contradiction dans *Le Capital*«, Temps Modernes, 246
1966b   *Rationalité et irrationalité en économie*. Maspero, Paris
1967   »La Notion de mode de production asiatique et les schemas marxistes d'evolution des societés«, in Garaudy (ed.) *Sur le mode de production asiatique*, CERM, Paris
1969   »La pensée de Marx et d'Engels aujourd'hui et les recherches de demain«, La Pensée, 143
1970a   »Fétichisme, religion et théorie générale de l'idéologie chez Marx«, Annali del'Institute Giangiacomo Feltrinelli
1970b   »Economie marchande, fetichisme, magie et science selon Marx dans *le Capital*«, Nouvelle Revue de Psychoanalyse, 2

1971a	»Salt Currency and the Circulation of Commodities Among the Baruya of New Guinea«, in Dalton (ed.) *Studies in Economic Anthropology*, America Anthropological Assn. Washington.
1971b	»Qu'est-ce que definir une formation économique et sociale? L'exemple des Incas«, La Pensée, 159

Goswami, B.
1960a	»System of Bride Price in Lushai«, Journal of Social Research
1960b	»The Kinship System of the Lushai«, Bulletin of the Anthropological Survey of India

Goswami and Majumdar
1968	»Garo Marriage«, Man in India, 48

Gourou, P.
1953	*L'Asie*, Hachette, Paris
1968	»Problèmes de régression des techniques chez les Marma des Chittagong Hill Tracts«, L'Homme, 8

Granet, M.
1953	*Etudes Sociologiques sur la Chine*, Paris

Gray, E.
1894	»Diary of a Journey to the Borkhamti and the Sources of the Irrawaddy, 1893«, Govt. of India Foreign Affairs Proceedings, 7–15

Grant-Brown, R.
1913	*Burma Gazetteer: Upper Chindwin District*, Rangoon

Green, J. H.
1934	*The Tribes of Upper Burma North of 24° Latitude and their Classification*, m.s. dissertation, Cambridge University

Gurdon, P.
1914	*The Khasis*, London

Gurevich, A.
1972	*»Individual and Society in the Barbarian States«*, Pts. I and II, in Soviet Anthropology and Archaeology, spring, summer

Hall, D. G. E.
1955	*History of Southeast Asia*, London
1964	*Atlas of Southeast Asia*, London

Hannay, S. F.
   1847   »Sketch of the Singphos or Kakhyens of Burmah, the
                   Position of this Tribe as Regards Bhamo and the Inland
                   Trade of the Irrawaddy with Yunnan and their Connec-
                   tion with the Northeastern Frontier of Assam«, Calcutta

Hanson, O.
   1906   *The Kachins,* Rangoon

Harner, M.
   1970   »Population Pressure and the Social Evolution of Agricul-
                   turalists«, SWJA, 26

Harris, M.
   1959   »The Economy Has No Surplus?«, A.A. 61
   1963   »The Classification of Stratified Groups«, Pan American
                   Union, Washington

Harvey, G. E.
   1933   *Wa Precis,* Rangoon

Head, W. R.
   1917   *Handbook on Haka Chin Custom,* Rangoon

Henry, A.
   1903   »Lolos and Other Tribes of West China«, JRAI, 33

Hertz, W. A.
   1912   *Burma Gazetteer: Myitkyina District,* Rangoon

Heusch, L. de
   1971   »Signes, réciprocité et marxisme«, in *Pourquoi l'épouser,*
                   Gallimard, Paris

Ho, R.
   1960   »Physical Geography of the Indo-Australian Tropics«,
                   in *Symposium on the Impact of Man on Humid Tropics
                   Vegetation,* UNESCO

Hodson, T. C.
   1901   »The Native Tribes of Manipur«, JRAI, 31
   1902   »Headhunting Among the Hill Tribes of Assam«, Folk-
                   lore, 20
   1908   *The Meitheis,* Nutt, London
   1911   *The Naga Tribes of Manipur,* London
   1921   »The Garo and Khasi Marriage Systems Contrasted«,
                   Man in India, 1

Hoe, Tan Chein
   1956   One hundred years of forestry in Burma, in *The Burmese
                   Forester,* Vol. VI, Rangoon

Hsu, Cho Yun
    1965   *Ancient China in Transition,* Stanford

Huke, R. I.
    1954   *Economic Geography of a North Burma Kachin Village,*
                    Hanover
    1965   *Rainfall in Burma,* Hanover

Hutton, J. H.
    1921a   *The Sema Nagas,* MacMillan, London
    1921b   *The Angami Nagas,* MacMillan, London
    1929   *Diaries of Two Tours in the Unadministered Area East of
                    the Naga Hills,* Memoir, Asiatic Society of Bengal
    1949   »A Brief Comparison Between the Economics of Dry and
                    Irrigated Cultivation in the Naga Hills«, Advancement of
                    Science, 2:21
    1965   »The Mixed Culture of the Naga Tribes«, JRAI 95, Pt. I

Izikowitz, K.
    1951   *Lamet: Hill Peasants in French Indochina,* Göteborg

Jones, D.
    1967   *Cultural Variation Among Six Lahu Villages in Northern
                    Thailand,* Unpublished Ph. D. dissertation, Cornell Uni-
                    versity, Ithaca

Jordan, M.
    1958–59   »L'Animisme des Chins«, Bulletin de la Societé des Mis-
                    sions Etrangers de Paris, Hong Kong, several issues

Judd, L. C.
    1964   »Dry Rice Cultivation in North Thailand«, Southeast Asia
                    Program: Data Paper no. 52, Cornell
    1969   »The Agricultural Economy of the Hill Thai«, in *Tribes-
                    men and Peasants in Nothern Thailand,* Proceedings:
                    First Symposium of the Tribal Research Center, Chiang
                    Mai

Kirchoff, P.
    1968   »The Principles of Clanship in Human Society«, in Fried
                    (ed.) *Readings in Anthropology* Vol. II, Crowell, N.Y.

Kauffman, H. E.
    1938   »Die Fallen der Thadou-Kuki in Assam«, in Zeitschrift
                    Für Ethnologie, 70:1
    1956   »Les Mégalithes de la région Mro«, International Con-
                    gress of Anthropological and Ethnological Sciences, Phi-
                    ladelphia

Ko, T. S.
1892   »Chin and Kachin Tribes on the Borderland of Burma«,
             Asiatic Review

Kosminski, E.
1963   »Evolution des formes de rente féodale en Angleterre du
             XIe au XVe siècle«, in Recherches Internationales, 37

Kunstadter, P.
1965   *The Lua? (Lawa)*, Princeton Center for International
             Studies: Research Monograph no. 21
1966   »Residential and Social Organization of the Lawa of
             Northern Thailand«, SWJA, 22
1967 (ed.)   *Southeast Asian Tribes, Minorities and Nations*, Prince-
             ton

La Raw, Maran
1967a   »Toward a Basis for Understanding the Minorities of
             Burma«, in Kunstadter (ed.) *Southeast Asian Tribes, Mi-
             norities and Nations*, Princeton
1967b   »Notes on the Algebra of Interacting Human Groups«,
             m.s. unpublished

Latter, B.
1846   »Note on Some Hill Tribes on the Koladyne River«,
             JASB, 15

Lattimore, O.
1962a (1940) *Inner Asian Frontiers of China*, Beacon, Boston
1962b   *Studies in Frontier History*, Mouton, The Hague

Le Than Khoi
1959   *Histoire de l'Asie du Sud-Est*, P.U.F., Paris
1964   *L'Economie de l'Asie du Sud-Est*, P.U.F., Paris

Leach, E. R.
1945   »Jinghpaw Kinship Terminology«, JRAI, 45
1946   *Cultural Change with Special Reference to the Hill Tri-
             bes of Burma and Assam.* Unpublished Ph.D. Disserta-
             tion, University of London
1949   »Some Aspects of Dry Rice Cultivation in North Burma
             and British Borneo«, Advancement of Science, 6:21
1951   »The Structural Implications of Matrilateral Cross-Cou-
             sin Marriage«, JRAI, 51, also in *Rethinking Anthropo-
             logy*, 1961
1957a   »Aspects of Bridewealth and Marriage Stability Among
             Kachin and Lakher«, Man, 57, also in *Rethinking An-
             thropology*
1957b   »On Asymmetrical Marriage Rules«, A.A. 59

1958	»Concerning Trobriand Clans and the Kinship Category Tabu«, in Goody (ed.) *The Developmental Cycle in Domestic Groups,* Cambridge
1960	»Descent Filiation and Affinity«, Man, Jan.
1962	*Rethinking Anthropology,* L.S.E. London
1963	»Alliance and Descent Among the Lakher«, Ethnos 28
1967	»The Language of Kachin Kinship«, in Freedman, M. (ed.) *Social Organization,* Chicago
1969	»Kachin and Haka Chin«, A Rejoinder to Levi-Strauss, Man 69

Lebar, E. (ed.)

1964	*Ethnic Groups of Mainland Southeast Asia,* HRAF, New Haven

Lehman, F. K.

1963	*The Structure of Chin Society,* Illinois Studies in Anthropology no. 3, Urbana
1969	»On Chin and Kachin Marriage Regulations«, Man, 69

Levi-Strauss, C.

1953a	»Kinship Systems of Three Chittagong Hill Tribes«, SWJA, 8
1953b	»Miscellaneous Notes on the Kuki«, Man, 51
1958	*Anthropologie Structurale,* Plon, Paris
1960a	»La Structure et la forme«, Cahiers de l'Institut des sciences économiques appliquées
1960b	»On Manipulated Sociological Models«, Bijdragen 116
1962a	*Le Totemisme Aujourd'hui,* P.U.F., Paris
1962b	*La Pensée sauvage,* Plon, Paris
1965	»The Future of Kinship Studies«, Proceedings RAI
1967 (1949)	*Les Structures élémentaires de la Parenté,* Mouton, Paris
1971	*L'Homme Nu,* Plon, Paris

Lewin, G.

1967	»The Problem of Social Formations in Chinese History«, Marxism Today, Jan.

Lewin, H.

1869	*The Hill Tracts of Chittagong and the Dwellers Therein,* Calcutta

Löffler, L.

1960	»Patrilateral Lineation in Transition«, Ethnos, 25
1964	»Prescriptive Matrilateral Marriage: A Fallacy«, SWJA 20
1966	»L'Alliance asymétrique chez les Mru«, L'Homme 6:3

Lowis, C. C.
1906   »A note on the Palaungs of Hsipaw and Tawngpeng«,
                    Ethnographical Survey of India, Vol. 1, Rangoon

1919   »Tribes of Burma«, Ethnographical Survey of India, Vol.
                    4, Rangoon

Luce, G. H.
1931   »A Note on the People of Burma in the Twelfth and
                    Thirteenth Century A.D.« Census of India Vol. II, pt. 1:
                    Appendix F
1940   »Economic Life of the Early Burman«, JBRS 30

Luce, G. H. and *Pe Maung Tin*
1939   »Burma Down to the Fall of Pagan«, JBRS 29

Mac Rae, J.
1801   »Account of the Kookies ..«, Asiatick Researches 7

Manivanna, K.
1969   »Aspects socio-économiques du Laos médiéval«, in Gar-
                    audy (ed.) *Sur le mode de production asiatique,* CERM:
                    Paris

Mark, L. L.
1967   »Patrilateral Cross-Cousin Marriage among the Magpie
                    Miao«, A.A. 69

Marshall, H.
1922   *The Karen People of Burma,* Ohio University

Marx, K.
1964   *Pre-Capitalist Economic Formations,* International, New
                    York
1967   *Capital.* Three Volumes, Progress, Moscow
1968   *Theories of Surplus Value.* Two Volumes, Progress, Mos-
                    cow
1970   *Fondements de la critique de l'économie politique,* An-
                    thropos, Paris

Masefield, G. B.
1970   *A Handbook of Tropical Agriculture,* Oxford

Maspero, H.
1965   *La Chine Antique,* P.U.F., Paris
1967   *Histoire et Institutions de la Chine Ancienne,* P.U.F.,
                    Paris

Mauss, M.
1970/71   *Oeuvres Complètes.* Three Volumes, Minuit, Paris

Maybury-Lewis
    1960   »The Analysis of Dual Organizations«, Bijdragen 116
    1965   »Prescriptive Marriages Systems«, SWJA 21
    1967   »The Murngin Moral«, Transactions: N.Y. Academy of Sciences, Ser. II, 29

McCall, A. G.
    1949   *Lushai Chrysalis*, Luzac, London

Miles, D.
    1969   »Shifting Agriculture; Threats and Prospects«, *Tribesmen and Peasants*, Chiang Mai

Milne, L.
    1924   *Home of an Eastern Clan*, Oxford

Milne and *Cochrane, W.*
    1910   *Shans at Home*, Murray, London

Mills, J. P.
    1922   *The Lhota Nagas*, London
    1926   *The Ao Nagas*, London
    1931   »The Bete Kukis of North Cachar«, also »The Khelma Kukis« in Census of India, Assam, Vol. III; pt. I, Appendix B
    1937   *The Rengma Nagas*, London
    1939   »The Effect of Ritual Upon Industries and Art in the Naga Hills«, Congrès International des Sciences Anthropologiques. London; Proceedings. Referred to in unpublished form in this thesis

Nakane, C.
    1958   »Cross-Cousin Marriage among the Garo of Assam«, Man, 58
    1968   *Garo and Khasi*, Mouton, Paris

Needham, R.
    1958   »Structural Analysis of the Purum«, A.A. 60
    1959   »Vaiphei Social Structure«, SWJA 15
    1960a   »Alliance and Classification among the Lamet«, Sociologus 10
    1960b   »Chawte Social Structure«, A.A. 62
    1960c   »A Structural Analysis of Aimol Society«, Bijdragen 116
    1961   »Notes on the Analysis of Asymmetrical Alliance«, Bijdragen 117
    1962   *Structure and Sentiment*, Chicago
    1963   »Symmetry and Asymmetry in Prescriptive Alliance«, Bijdragen 119
    1966   »Age Category and Descent«, Bijdragen 122

Neufville, J. B.
1828   »On the Geography and Population of Assam«, Asiatick Researches, 16

Orans, M.
1966   »Surplus«, Human Organization, 25

Pa Lian Uk
1968   *The Chin Customary Law of Inheritance and Succession as Practiced among the Chins of Haka Area.* Unpublished L.L.B. Thesis, University of Rangoon

Parliamentary Papers
1839   *Tea Cultivation in India,* no. 39, London

Parry, N. E.
1931   »On the Flowering of Bamboos«, Journal of the Bombay Natural History Society, Vol. 34
1932   *The Lakhers,* MacMillan, *London*

Parry, W.
1894   »Report on a Twelve Days Tour in the Country Northeast of Kindat«, Rangoon

Pearson, H.
1957   »The Economy Has No Surplus«, in Polanyi et.al. *Trade and Market in the Early Empires,* Glencoe

Peebles, E. C.
1892   »Report on the Irrawaddy Column; 1891–2«, Rangoon

Pemberton, R. B.
1835   *Report on the Eastern Frontier of India,* Calcutta

Pelzer, K.
1967   »Man's Role in Changing the Landscape of Southeast Asia«, Journal of Asian Studies, 27

Pitchford, U. C.
1937   »The Wild Wa States and Lake Nawngkhio«, Geographical Journal, 90

Pokora, T.
1967   »La Chine a-t-elle connu une société esclavagiste«, Recherches Internationales

Reid, A. S.
1893   *Chin-Lushei Land,* Calcutta

Rosman, A. and *Rubel, P.*
n.d.   »The Potlatch Model in Societies with Generalized Ex-
                    change«. Unpublished m.s.
1971   *Feasting With Mine Enemy*, Columbia: New York

Ruhemann, B.
1948   »Relationship Terms of Some Hill Tribes of Burma and
                    Assam«, SWJA, 4

Sachs, I.
1965   »Le Concept de surplus économique«, L'Homme, 5
1967   »Nouvelle phase de la discussion« (asiatic mode), Recher-
                    ches Internationales

Sahlins, M.
1958   *Social Stratification in Polynesia*, University of Washing-
                    ton
1963   »Poor Man, Rich Man, Big Man, Chief«, Comparative
                    Studies in Society and History
1965a   »On the Sociology of Primitive Exchange«, in Banton (ed.)
                    The Relevance of Models for Social Anthropology, Lon-
                    don.
1965b   »Exchange Value and the Diplomacy of Primitive Tra-
                    de«, Proceedings of the American Ethnological Society,
                    University of Washington
1968   *Tribesmen;* Prentice-Hall, N.J.
1971   »The Intensity of Domestic Production in Primitive So-
                    cieties«, in Dalton (ed.) *Studies in Economic Anthropo-
                    logy*, Washington, D.C.
1972   *Stone Age Economics*, Chicago

Sao, S. M.
1965   *The Shan States and British Annexation*, Southeast Asia
                    Program: Data Paper 57, Cornell University, Ithaca

Sartre, J. P.
1963   *Critique de la raison dialectique*, Paris

Scott, J. G.
1916   »The Red Karens«, Journal of the Central Asian Society,
                    Vol. 3:2 and 3

Scott and *Hardiman, J. P.*
1900   *Gazetteer of Upper Burma and the Shan States*, three vo-
                    lumes, Rangoon

Shakespear, J.
1909   »Kuki-Lushei Clans«, JRAI, 12

1912	*The Lushei Kuki Clans,* MacMillan, London

Shakespear, L. W.
| 1914 | *History of Upper Burma, Upper Assam and the North-east Frontier,* MacMillan, London |

Shapiro, W.
| 1969 | »Semi-Moiety Organization and Mother-in-Law Bestowal in Northeast Arnhem Land«, Man, 4 |

Shaw, W.
| 1929 | »Notes on the Thadou Kukis«, JASB |

Sladen, E. B.
| 1868 | »Official Narrative of the Expedition to Explore the Trade Route to China via Bhamo«, Parliamentary Papers no. 51, London |
| 1871 | »Exploration via the Irrawaddy and Bhamo to South Western China«, Proceedings, Royal Geographical Society, 15 |

Smith, W. C.
| 1925 | *The Ao Naga Tribe of Assam,* MacMillan, London |

Spencer, J. E.
| 1968 | *Shifting Agriculture in Southeast Asia,* Berkeley |

Stack, E.
| 1908 | *The Mikirs,* MacMillan, London |

Stamp, L. D.
| 1924 | »Notes on the Vegetation of Burma«, Geographical Journal, 64 |
| 1967 | *Asia,* Methuen, London |

Steiner, F.
| 1957 | »Towards a Classification of Labor«, Sociologus, 7 |

Stevenson, H. N. C.
1937a	»Feasting and Meat Division among the Zahao Chins«, JRAI 67
1937b	»Religion and Sacrifices of the Zahao Chins«, Man, 37
1937c	»Land Tenure in the Central Chin Hills«, Man, 37
1938	»Some Social Effects of the Religion and Sacrifices of the Zahao Chins«, JBRS, 33
1968 (1943)	*The Economics of the Central Chin Tribes,* Gregg

Terray, I.
| 1969 | *Le Marxisme devant les sociétés primitives,* Maspero, Paris |

Tokei, F.
    1967   »Le Mode de production asiatique en Chine«, in Recherches Internationales

Vayda, A.
    1961a   »A Re-examination of Northwest Coast Economic Systems«, Transactions of the N.Y. Academy of Sciences, Ser. II Vol. 23
    1961b   »Expansion and Warfare among Swidden Agriculturalists«, A.A. 63
    1968   »Hypotheses about the Functions of War«, in Harris Fried and Murphy (ed.) *War*, New York
    1971   »Phases in the Process of War and Peace among the Marings of New Guinea«, Oceania, Sept.

Vetch, H.
    1873 (1842)   »Report of a Visit by Captain Vetch to the Singhpo and Naga Frontier of Luckimpore«, in Selection of Papers regarding the Hill Tracts between Assam and Burma and on the Upper Brahmaputra, Calcutta

Walker, J. J.
    1892   »Expedition among the Kachin Tribes of the Northeast Frontier of Upper Burma«, Proceedings of the Royal Geographical Society, 14

Webster, C. and *Wilson, P.*
    1966   *Agriculture in the Tropics*, Longmans, London

White, L.
    1959   *The evolution of Culture*, McGraw-Hill, New York

Williams, C. and *Joseph, K.*
    1970   *Climate, Soil and Crop Production in the Humid Tropics*, Oxford

Wittfogel, K.
    1957   *Oriental Despotism*, New Haven

Young, O. G.
    1962   *The Hill Tribes of Northern Thailand*, Bangkok

Appendix

Religion as Economy and Economy as Religion. (Ethnos 1 - 4. 1975)

> »I should even like to assume that the feast of the ancestors and all connected with it is the driving force in the entire economic and social life of the Lamet.« (Izikowitz 1951:332)

K. G. Izikowitz was perhaps the first social anthropologist who attempted to envisage the different levels of a social formation as constituting a structural unity in a way that allowed him to transcend the ethnocentric notions that abound in most anthropological theory concerning the relation between social relations and religion. Instead of directly applying cultural distinctions drawn from our own society, Izikowitz discovered, on the contrary, that religious activities could be the very motor of the socio-economic life of some societies. The majority of English and American anthropologists have tended to regard religion as a reflection of a somehow more concrete social reality so that ancestors, for example, are mere symbols of prestige to be manipulated as representations of relative status which must have been established by other means. This basically Weberian position, in which religious symbols must, by definition, have a merely ideological function of legitimation or demonstration has, I think, been a serious obstacle to the analysis of the structure of a wide range of tribal systems.

Implicit in this functionalism is the lack of distinction between cultural categories and material functions so that it is assumed as a matter of course that supernatural spirits must, by definition, be reflections of some more real categories, that they can have no material function in economic life.

In the following discussion I will try to develop Izikowitz' lead and outline very briefly what appears to be a specific cultural structure, which accounts for the dominant place of religion in economic life and which integrates the supernatural world with that of living lineages and organizes the material processes of reproduction in a kind of tribal society that is quite widespread in Southeast Asia. The significance of the analysis will be seen, I think, when comparing different cultural structures as wholes so that the function of religion can be comprehended as a variable dependent on the larger structure and where economic functions are mystified by social forms which can only be understood in terms of their cultural specificity.

As I have analyzed the Kachin economy in relation to kinship and religion elsewhere (1972, 1975), I shall take that society as an example of a structure which appears to have wider application. The Kachin category system unites the following relations in terms of a single structure:

1) the relation between the world of the living and that of the ancestors and supernatural powers
2) the structure of age ranking
3) the structure of affinal ranking

Kachin kinship space contains two axes, horizontal and vertical, both of which are reflected in the terminology which is a variant of Omaha. The vertical axis defines a continuum of relative age, linking the members of a living local patriline to a chain of ancestors that ascend ultimately to the highest spirits that control prosperity and fertility. As these spirits are defined similarly for all groups, it is possible to envisage the structure as a single segmentary hierarchy linking all lineages to one another through common ancestry. The highest spirits are not different in kind from ancestors but are merely more distant lineage founders. In fact, local territorial spirits are the nearest common ancestors that link all the lineages of a village or village cluster to higher segmentary levels. Nature is thus organized along the same lines as society. But to conclude that this results from the simple ideological act of projection would be to overlook the fact that the way in which society acts on nature and thus on itself is determined by this organization. The horizontal relation defining affinal connections between local lineages is similarly inflected in such a way that lateral distance becomes equated with vertical distance. Leach and Levi-Strauss have both analysed the structure of generalized exchange among the Kachin. All that need concern us here is the fact of patriliny and the superiority of wife-givers (*mayu*) over wife-takers (*dama*). This is clearly manifested in the kin terminology by the merging of age (descent) categories with affinal categories.

> »Thus, the *mayu* of the *mayu* are classed as grandparents, the *dama* of the *mayu* are classed as brothers, the *dama* of the *dama* are classed as grandchildren.« (Leach 1961:82)

This classification applies not only to real relatives but across the whole field of social relations, since all non-relatives are treated »much as if they were

20 Friedman

remote relatives of ego's own clan« (Leach 1961:82). Thus, if we envisage the teminology as a series of relative age rows and lineage columns, the bottom row merges with the extreme left column and the top row with the extreme right column. Generally, as genealogical distance increases, affinal seniority becomes identical with patrilineal seniority. It would, I think, be incorrect to see this as the expression of some kind of ambiguity in the distinction between affinal and lineal categories as this is only true for our own classifications. Rather, it would be more accurate to say that genealogical categories are defined not only with respect to descent and alliance but also with respect to genealogical distance.

In another work (1972; 1975) I have tried to characterize the nature of Kachin social economy in terms of the articulation of two structures, horizontal and vertical, which correspond to the preceding description of the kinship terminology. That is, horizontal relations are those determined by the alliance and exchange system while vertical relations are organized around the relation of lineages to their own and to community ancestors.

In the schema on page 47, economic flows are channeled in two directions. Local surpluses are converted into prestige by feasting the local village and, later, increasingly wider groups. The specific nature of this vertical relation is, as we shall see, crucial in the definition of the larger political units that emerge in Kachin evolution. The prestige gained in feasting is converted into relative social rank in the sphere of affinal relations by raising the brideprice for lineage daughters. The vertical and horizontal aspects of the circulation process are linked in a positive feedback relationship that generates increasing rank differentiation over time. Here I am not so much concerned with actual mechanisms of this process, which I have described elsewhere (1972), as with their cultural specificity.

The social value of a local group is first determined by the ability to produce a surplus which can be distributed to the larger community. This social value, which we have called prestige, belongs to all members of the group and is transmitted to daughters. The latter, who are alienated in the exchange process, are merely the embodiment of the superior value of the wife-giver to subordinate (by definition) wife-taker, who, by accepting the alliance and paying the stipulated brideprice, exchanges real wealth for a kinship connection to the source of wealth.[1] But the source of wealth is not a mere fund of real goods. Rather, it is in its turn a social relation through its own ancestors to local spirits and through them to the highest deities, who are the only ultimate source of prosperity. In other words, wealth must not be conceived as a collection of alienable objects with intrinsic value. On the contrary, the woman given in marriage is not a wealth object, but represents the social value of her lineage. As such, exchange is not a simple transfer of valuables, but consists primarily in the establishing of a genealogical link to the supernatural forces that make the accumulation and distribution of surplus possible. Wealth, then, is not a tangible mass of goods but the ability to produce wealth, an ability which can only be defined in terms of a specific relation to the supernatural. Since value cannot be separated from the producers of value, it cannot be associated with a given amount of real wealth. Value can only be social value, the attribute of a group which, therefore, can only be communicated to other groups by the transfer of its members. The superiority of wife-givers and the patrilineal character of the local group are in this way inextricably linked to a single larger cycle of social reproduction in which prestige generated at a point of production is transferred as higher status by the giving of wives.

The cultural content of prestige is similarly defined in terms of relations to the supernatural. Prestige gained by feasting and age-rank are equivalent phenomena. As wealth can only be given by the spirits who are no more than distant ancestors, the amassed surplus of wealthy lines must be the result of closer genealogical ties (i.e. influence) to such higher powers. Since local spirits are by definition simply more distant ancestors, prestige consists in the identification of the local group as an »older« segment. We must be careful to separate the notion of prestige, our own concept, from the social form which it has in Kachin society, as relative distance from a local spirit, ancestor-founder of a larger group. In this respect it is important to note that the definition of chief (*duwa*) is simply the nearest descendant of the territorial spirit so that the properties that define the chiefdom are already contained in the general structure of Kachin social organization.

Now, in fact, the concentration of prestige and its conversion into affinal and age-rank is part of a process of expansion in which control over labor is accumulated by the internal generation of debt (and debt slaves) through inflation of brideprice and other payments and, more important, through the incorporation of captive slaves into the prestigious lineages. This, in turn, increases the ability of these lineages to accelerate their production and feasting activity and to extend their alliances in such a way that ranking expands territorially as well as vertically. But the form of this accumulation of control over labor and the distribution of its product are determined by the structures described above. The conversion of surplus into rank differentiation takes the form of the establishment of a genealogical hierarchy where prestige is measured by kinship distance from a territorial spirit and where affinal subordinates are defined by their lower age-rank, so that their ancestors can be defined as patrilineal junior siblings of their superior wife-givers. The form taken by the chiefdom is that of a conical clan where rank is defined exclusively in terms of genealogical distance. Chiefs are not new cultural elements in *gumsa* (ranked) society but emerge because of the way the accumulation process is structured, i.e. in terms of a relation between production, distribution and the world of ancestral spirits.

There is, then, a coherent relation between alliance and descent insofar as the latter might be said to encompass (in Dumont's sense) the former. The establishment of a relation to the supernatural through ancestors is transmitted or extended to subordinates by means of alliance. Thus, it is possible to reach the ancestors either vertically or horizontally. It is the latter relation which is the basis of ranking, but its very content is such that it appears immediately as if it were the former. That is, what we know to be an economic exchange between lineages is organized by a cultural structure which identifies that relation as the forging of connections to a common ancestor spirit who appears to make the economic transaction possible.

Now, as we have seen above, there is no question but that from the material standpoint, the Kachin system requires certain kinds of external relations. The extension of alliance relations is identical with political expansion, and there is a necessary accumulation of captive slaves to meet the demands for surplus generated internally. It is unlikely that the Kachin system could ever have developed large chiefdoms on the basis of internal production and accumulation alone. Certainly, the demand for prestige which, as we have shown elsewhere (1972), tends to accelerate, is much greater than any increase than could be forthcoming from a single closed population. However, the social form of this expansion and growth is such that there is no social distinction between internal and external because the exchange relation is itself an internal relation. It is for this reason that Maru, Lashi and other groups can so easily »become Kachin«. It is only with Shan and Lisu that such development cannot occur since these systems are dominated by different structures. In such circumstances, and aside from the direct incorporation of individuals, the Kachin system must utilize other ideological means for recognizing alliance relations.[2] Generally, the exchange relation does not maintain an ideological opposition between groups but incessantly incorporates them into a larger political and religious entity. Interiorization is the dominant cultural operator of Kachin expansion.

From the point of view we are advancing here, a number of other aspects of the systems appears in a new light. We rely on recent papers by Löffler (1968) and Woodward (m.s. 1974), which compare the religious organization of a number of Southeast Asian hill tribes. Kachin, Chin and Naga groups all maintain affinal type relations with their ancestors. Feasts are a means of maintaining the »alliance« with the sky world which is seen as a *superior* ally. That patrilineal ancestors can be treated as affinal relatives to whom one must behave as to superior wife-givers clearly indicates the way in which alliance relations are incorporated into descent relations, at least for Kachin. But the structure of the supernatural varies significantly from Kachin to Chin and Naga groups. Elsewhere we have tried to show how the latter could be seen as involuted transformations of the former, where the basis of verticalization has been destroyed. In the resultant structure, ancestors are linked only to demonstrable descent groups and there is no further link between these ancestors and the higher spirits. The ancestral world is no longer part of a functional hierarchy and becomes merely the land of the dead, which is a reflection of this world where all the same social relations are enacted. In fact, in many Naga societies, a number of heavens are postulated in lieu of the Kachin ancestral hierarchy – this being deducible from the fact that ancestors too must have a sky world to which sacrifices can be made.

Among the Kachin there is only one land of the dead that is in the sky. The highest spirits, the sky and earth deities (often joined), are both situated in the sky. If the latter has the whole earth as his domain, he always dwells in the heavens. Similarly, ancestors and spirits as a single categorical unit are both superior »wife-givers«. Among the Naga there is a great deal of ambiguity on this point. For many there are two lands of the dead, one in the sky, superior ally, and one in or below the earth, inferior ally. It is often said that good, i.e. wealthy, people go to the sky world after death while the poor descend into the earth. The Kachin, it would seem, view the universe as a single domain of the highest spirits so that the living and dead are not seen as two unitary groups in alliance. Instead, the living are incorporated into the world of the ancestors as an act of political subordination. The Naga, on the other hand, having lost the vertical economic relation, generalize the affinal structure in such a way that the living come to represent a lineage which must have both wife-givers and wife-takers. The supernatural alliance, like its earthly counterpart, is a conflictual relation in which sky people are not necessarily benefactors but powerful affines that have to be pleased in order to continue to be socially and economically successful, i.e. to maintain peace with the forces of nature. The Naga universe cannot be described as a segmentary hierarchy but only as an alliance network. This situation seems to result from increasing intensification and population density–itself caused by the expansionist nature of the economy –which has two irreversible effects. First, the environment is degraded so that declining productivity no longer permits the accumulation of surplus demanded by a Kachin type economy. It becomes much more difficult to establish affinal superiority on the basis of ever increasing feasting activity. More crucial is the structural transformation provoked by increasing density directly. The latter leads to increasing warfare and the formation of large defensive villages. The formation of Kachin type conical domains depends on the ability to send off all sons but one to establish new settlements in an act of lineage fission and then to reintegrate them in a regional *mayu-dama* hierarchy.

Among Chin, but especially Naga, groups such expansion is blocked so that local exogamous clans develop. In such cases the local lineage production and exchange unit no longer corresponds to the exogamous unit. The accumulation of sibling lineages implies that land must be divided in inheritance, that it can enter, as other inheritable wealth objects (cattle, valuables) into the horizontal exchange network. This latter development destroys the very basis of the Kachin system where land remains indivisible and where rank and power depend entirely on a relation to the supernatural. Furthermore, the very existence of large exogamous clans implies that local lineages cannot convert their patrilineal relatives into inferior allies so that there is a large block of relatives that is removed from the sphere of affinal competition and among whom no clear ranking can be established. In the emergent larger exogamous unit, in which descent is clearly demonstrable, the local lines cannot manipulate their relations to distant ancestors so that status differences can no longer be based on the identification of one's ancestors with territorial deities. As the exchange unit is the minimal lineage and not the clan as a whole, the wife-giver/wife-taker asymmetrical alliance cannot be extended to other patrilineal relatives in the respective clans. These collateral lines maintain their own, largely independent, alliance strategies. As the minimal unit already has well defined segmentary relations to all other units in its clan, the affinal relation cannot be turned into a new segmentary relation (el/yo) based on higher order relations between ancestors since this would be in flat contradiction to the already existing demonstrable descent relations. In this way the cycle of conversion of alliance rank into conical (vertical) rank is broken by the elimination of the relation between lineage hierarchy, ancestors and territorial deities.

Everything in the Kachin system goes up because all alliances consist of the establishment of a vertical relation. As such, all ancestors are in the sky world. The Kachin (gumsa) explain their origin in terms of descent from the heavens. For the Naga, however, origins are often more complex, and distance in space may take precedence over vertical genealogies. The land of the dead is not necessarily straight up or down. It is often associated with a specific horizontal direction. The horizontal alliance relations are not skewed to merge with higher generations and are quite independent of the vertical axis. Thus the dead can as easily be located to the East or West as in the sky or earth.

The crucial structural differences between Kachin and Naga type systems can be further clarified by comparing their modes of relation to the external world. The Naga are headhunters. The Kachin are slave raiders. For the Naga, the taking of heads is equivalent to stealing the ancestors of one's enemies. Heads are converted into pseudo-ancestors for one's own group. The Naga are known for their intensive warfare as well as for their lack of political hierarchy. They practice swidden agriculture in a throroughly degraded area that has become so, as we have said, through increasing population density in a technology that is incapable of supporting such a development. The Naga »devolution« occurs because the expansionist tendencies of the economy are blocked by the impossibility of territorial growth. The Kachin, on the other hand, represent the successfully expanding form of the same system. They take slaves as well as create politically subordinate wife-takers. The ideological expression of their relation to subordinate non-Kachin is especially revealing. It is said that they can only reach the land of the dead by having a Kachin as their political superior, for only the latter knows the true road to that land. Upon arrival, the Kachin guide becomes a »pseudo-ancestor« of the subordinate's lineage.[3] Thus, the Kachin incorporate living people as social inferiors, as if they were of a lower generation (slaves are treated much as if they were permanent children), whereas the Naga take heads and convert them into higher generation catogeries in an attempt to create ancestors.[4]

The Kachin structure seems to be characterized by a focus on local productivity. Means of circulation such as cattle and foreign and local valuables are subordinated to the production-feast cycle. It appears that they cannot be accumulated independently but rather that they can only be used to symbolize prestige gained in feasting. In the process of gaining control over labor, which is determined by the connection between feasting and affinal exchange, the possession of prestige goods is a dependent variable. All forms of accumulation in this system are subordinated to the capacity to give feasts, to demonstrate the supernatural power of one's lineage, to bring prosperity. Chin and Naga have the same basic structure but there the link between alliance and the production-feast cycle has been severed. Thus, while an attempt is still made to dominate other groups through the giving of feasts, the mechanisms by which prestige can be transformed into absolute vertical rank are not present so that only the strictly competitive wife-giver/wife-taker relation remains. While exchange is now a much more independent phenomenon, it still functions to establish prestige resulting from the production of agricultural surpluses which continue to be associated with the benevolence of supernatural spirits.

I might suggest here that there are other systems in which the horizontal relation is not so inextricably bound up with the vertical relation. This is the case where the accumulation of wealth such as prestige goods is independent of the agricultural feast cycle. In such systems, which appear to be widespread in Indonesia, Melanesia and Africa, there is, as among the Naga, no clear link between alliance relations and the supernatural. In fact, they are rather opposed to one another. Wife-givers often represent ritual power while wife-takers represent political and »economic« power, and it is often the latter who are superior in rank. It is important to note in this respect that a strong matrilineal or bilineal tendency is present in these societies so that affinal relations between »production« units are reified into descent relations. The function of descent in the »other« line here may be to gain access to circulating wealth which cannot be produced by the local kin unit and/or the labor force that it dominates. In such systems exchange is directly a question of the circulation of some form of wealth. Prestige depends immediately on the control of prestige goods rather than such control emerging and symbolizing the prestige gained by a demonstration of the »productivity« of a local group. Affinal alliance does not establish a genealogical connection to a supernatural source of production, but on the contrary forges relations between sources of the accumulation of moveable wealth and units who have no direct access to such wealth. As such,the horizontal relation is sufficient to establish dominance in an absolute way. The circulation of one kind of goods is a means of control over labor and dominates the other economic processes so that the ritual power embedded in the connection between the productivity of the earth (labor) and the supernatural is set off against the power resulting directly from the possession of prestige goods. Ancestors are no longer exclusively located in the heavens, but are seen as historical personages who come from outside the local area bringing with them the wealth object that are now monopolized by their descendants. Where this is not made explicit, it is still often the case that ancestors, especially those of high status, are seen as external people who established political dominance over authochtones while becoming their affines. This is a common phenomenon in many parts of Indonesia, Oceania and Africa where prestige goods accumulation is a dominant economic form.

While it might appear that some form of areal trade system is the determinant factor in these systems, this is not necessarily the case. The Siassi traders of New Guinea, for example, who are important middle men in an extensive trade network, seem to be quite similar to the patrilineal type systems described earlier in this paper in spite of the fact that they are often in possession of large quantities of ceremonial goods, many of which they themselves produce for exchange. It does not appear, however, that the Siassi have an autonomous prestige goods sector of their own. Rather, all their wealth goods are converted into pigs and food to be used in a purely big-man type feasting economy. The Siassi, as well as a number of other island traders (Young 1972), engage in a specific type of exchange which seems to be associated with patriliny while other groups such as those of the Trobriands, Rossell Island, or Manus, who appear to have a special prestige goods sector, are matrilineal or bilineal. In these latter systems there is a class of wealth objects (shells, dogs' teeth, arm bands etc.) that bear a specific relation to all other produced goods. They circulate widely between high status individuals and they serve, as extremely valuable objects, to attract dependents as well as the whole gamut of agricultural and other products that are exchanged for the privilege of having some access to the source of those objects. The possession of such highly valued goods is prestige in itself, and the latter need not be demonstrated by other means. Furthermore, since it is possession which is crucial here, the giving of wives to non-possessors can serve no function. On the contrary, women will be married up in order to gain access to the goods, and the matrilineal tie will be a means of creating a permanent institutional link to such goods. In exchange for such access, the now inferior wife-givers become the dependent economic supporters of their wife-taker (e.g. *urigubu* among the Trobrianders), which permits the latter to give great feasts and engage more intensively in interregional competitive trade expeditions.

In these societies the place of ritual is very different from that of the Kachin or Naga since power is no longer exclusively linked to the ability to produce a local surplus. While in the prestige good dominated systems of Indonesia and Melanesia there is a clear ideological relation between agricultural success, which remains crucial for the demonstration and maintenance of relative status, and the power of one's ancestors, this activity is now dependent upon the primary control over prestige goods which are obtained independently of the production-feast cycle. In the Kachin system, production is converted into prestige which is then converted into dependent labor through affinal exchange. Prestige goods enter the process as expressive variables which symbolize the already attained prestige of the feast-giver and which may be monopolized as purely sumptuary markers of status. In the prestige good system, the starting point is the valuables themselves, which are converted directly into dependent labor and then into feasts which symbolize the already established power of the rich man. In the former system the religion is a central element in the organization of the economy (all exchange, as well as feasting, is organized in terms of a relation to the supernatural powers) and prestige goods are superstructural symbols. In the latter system prestige goods are the dominant economic operator while the religious feast takes on a more ideological function. Yet, are the prestige goods intrinsically more secular than the spirits that are so instrumental in Kachin economy? After all, such goods are more or less sacred; they have their personal mythical histories, and they are associated with a power like that of the supernatural forces. While it is, of course, true that we have more or less definite notions about the cultural characteristics of religion, we should be prepared to accept the possibility that religious categories can have directly economic functions just as »wealth objects« can be but mere ideological symbols. In terms of cultural content we can easily distinguish between religion and money, but in terms of their functioning in material reproduction we have to ask a new set of questions. The way categories are connected in larger systems is more significant in understanding a social system than an analysis that assumes that, as in our own society, the supernatural is always »ideology« and money always »economic«.

In our analysis of the Kachin system we saw how relations to the supernatural were crucial determinants in the functioning of the economy. Among
the Chin and Naga the system was transformed in a way that made the ancestral structure of the supernatural a mere ideology while the religious feast
remained a dominant element in economy. Finally, in the case of Indonesian
and Melanesian prestige good systems we had an example where the religious
feast was itself an ideological phenomenon expressing the power resulting
directly from the possession of wealth objects.

In none of these cases can an understanding of any of the elements or cultural categories be attained without analyzing the significant larger totality of
which they are a part. We might in fact suggest that the correspondence between patriliny and superior wife-givers and matriliny and superior wife-
takers is a determinate aspect of different social forms of reproduction, different processes of accumulation, different kinds of relation between production and circulation.[5] Types of alliance and descent relations might better be
understood not as isolated institutional phenomena but as parts of larger economic cycles.

The categories economy, religion, social structure, are not obvious enough
in their meaning to enable us to analyze any society. I have tried here to show
that the specificity of the social organization of production and reproduction
cross-cuts boundaries that have traditionally been drawn between supposedly
discrete levels in all societies. If a relation to the supernatural can be called
religious in content, then we must still contend with the fact that it can determine in large measure, and in a systematic way, the goals of production and
distribution. But this is not enough, for if religion is an essential infrastructural element, it is itself but part of a larger cultural structure which organizes
affinal relations as well as relations to the supernatural. It is this structure
which defines the nature of ritual activity, dominates the internal functioning
of the economy and determines the direction of evolution of the social formation. There is no culturally defined economy, nor is there a culturally defined
religion. As institutional categories these belong only to our own and perhaps
a few other kinds of society. If we are to explain the functioning and evolution
of social systems, it is necessary to discover the specificity of their internal
structures. We must accept from the start that the structure which organizes
material production and reproduction may also organize other activities in a
way that no *cultural* distinction can be drawn between the economic and the
non-economic.

By insisting on a clear distinction between cultural form and material function we can avoid the problem which has confronted structural marxists as
well as functionalists and structuralists. Thus, Godelier, who was the first to

suggest the distinction (1966:91–93), has often been inconsistent in following through its implications, retreating to a more Althusserian position where, for example, ideology is an internal element of the relations of production.

> »Cette croyance en l'efficacité surnaturelle de l'Inca croyance partagée par la paysannerie dominée comme par la classe dominante, constituait non pas seulement une idéologie légitimant après coup les rapports de production, mais *une part de l'armature interne de ces rapports de production.*« (Godelier, 1973b:117–118)

Thus, in those societies where the economic position of an upper class appears to be defined in terms of religious criteria, the religion, which is by definition ideology is simultaneously internal to the infrastructure. But if ideology is defined functionally, as a relation to an already determined economy, it can only be misleading to assume that the former can be part of the latter. Such confusion can only be the outcome of defining »instances« such as economy and ideology as abstract forms of cultural institutions. It is precisely this kind of confusion that has led Althusserians to account for the fact that a »non-economic« instance can dominate production in terms of the structural causality of the economy. This position has left them open to such anti-materialist critics as Baudrillard (1973), who can simply claim that if pre-capitalist societies do not have the categories »economy«, »ideology«, »politics«, etc., then we cannot use such categories in our analysis. Godelier states, for example, that in primitive society,

> »les rapports productifs n'apparaissent pas comme séparés des rapports sociaux, politiques, religieux, parentaux ...« (Godelier 1973a)

as in our own society. Baudrillard replies that if relations of production do not have any independent existence, it is wrong to impose our own marxist categories on them, to create distinctions which simply do not exist for those societies (1973:58). But his argument is reasonable only if we assume that relations of production are institutional categories like kinship, religion, etc. It is the failure to distinguish orders of reality that enables the cultural relativist position to dominate. If a society has not the category »economy«, then it has no economy! The marxist is correct, I think, to object to such a position, but he may have no good argument against it. Some marxists, following the example of Lukacs, have, in opposing vulgar materialism, adopted the relativist position that historical materialism is merely the »self-knowledge« of capitalist society and not clearly applicable to other systems that do not have the same cultural categories. For,

>in such societies economic life did not yet possess that independence, that cohesion and dominance, nor did it have the sense of setting its own goals and being its own master which we associate with capitalist societies.« (Lukacs 1971:238)

The structural marxists who would oppose this cannot do so unless they make clear that »economy«, »ideology«, etc. are not institutions to be more or less embedded in other institutions, but material functions of social reproduction. To say that religion functions as economy is not to say that ideology can be infrastructural but that a cultural structure which is for us ideological, because of its place in capitalist reproduction, is infrastructural in another society. The notion of disembeddedness of the economy is, in this framework, only the statement that the cultural form that organizes economic processes is structurally separated from cultural forms that organize other functions. Economic relations are not transparent in our society because we have a cultural form corresponding directly to economic activity. On the contrary, if we do not differentiate the cultural form from the material process that it dominates, we can never understand how, in our own society, the economy can still be a »religion of everyday life« (Marx 1966:238).

Notes

[1]) The relations referred to here are those established in the process of ranking. When groups, such as lineages of distantly related chiefs, are of similar »social value« – a situation which is necessarily unstable – the affinal relation cannot incorporate lower into higher groups.

[2]) In such cases, alliance never becomes descent and the groups involved remain as separate parties to the exchange. Where Kachin chiefs do accept subordination by alliance to larger states, this may imply the adoption of the dominant state's religion, an attempt to raise one's status by incorporation into an admittedly superior society. Wife-giving only establishes a vertical relation within the Kachin system where differential prestige already exists.

[3]) This may account for the apparent ethnic homogeneity of the *gusma* as opposed to the *gumlao* areas.

[4]) An intermediate and probably transitional form of this ideology also occurs in which the heads taken become slaves to their captors in the afterworld. It is found primarily among Kuki-Chin groups.

[5]) We note in this respect that Crow systems are opposite to Omaha variants of the Kachin type in that wife-takers are senior rather than junior in terms of relative age categories: wife-takers = father's group, wife-givers = son's group.

References

BAUDRILLARD, J. 1973. *Le miroir de la production.* Paris.

FRIEDMAN, J. 1974. *The Place of Fetishism and the Problem of Materialist Interpretations. Critique of Anthropology,* 1.

– 1975. Tribes States and Transformations in Bloch, (ed.) *Marxist Analyses in Social Anthropology,* London.

GODELIER, M. 1973 a. L'Anthropologie économique in Copans (ed.) *L'Anthropologie, science des sociétés primitives?* Paris.

– 1973 b. *Horizon, trajets marxistes en anthropologie.* Paris.

HARDING, T. 1967. *Voyagers of the Vitiaz Strait.* Seattle.

HUTTON, J. H. 1921. *The Sema Nagas.* London.

– 1921. *The Angami Nagas.* London.

IZIKOWITZ, K. G. 1951. *Lamet: Hill Peasants in French Indochina.* Göteborg.

LEACH, E. R. 1954. *Political Systems of Highland Burma.* London.

– 1961. *Rethinking Anthropology.* London.

– 1967. The Language of Kachin Kinship in M. Freedman (ed.) *Social Organization.* Chicago.

LEHMAN, F. K. 1963. *The Structure of Chin Society.* Urbana.

LEVI-STRAUSS, C. 1967. *Les structures élémentaires de la parenté.* Paris.

LÖFFLER, L. G. 1968: Beast, Bird and Fish: An Essay in Southeast Asian Symbolism in *Folk Religion and World View in the Southwest Pacific.* Tokyo.

LUKACS, G. 1971. *History and Class Consciousness.* Cambridge.

MALINOWSKI, B. 1961. *Argonauts of the Western Pacific.* New York.

MARX, K. 1966. *Capital.* III. Moscow.

MEAD, M. 1930. *The Social Organization of Manua.* Bernice Bishop Museum Bulletin, No. 76.

MILLS, J. P. 1922. *The Lhota Nagas.* London.

– 1926. *The Ao Nagas.* London.

POWELL, H. A. 1960. *Competitive leadership in Trobriand political organization. J. R. A. I.* 90.

– 1969. Genealogy, residence and Kinship in Kiriwina. *Man,* 4.

– 1969. Territory, Hierarchy and Kinship in Kiriwina. *Man,* 4.

SCHWARTZ, T. 1963. Systems of Areal Integration: Some Considerations Based on the Admirality Islands of Northern Melanesia. *Anthropological Forum,* 1.

UBEROI, S. 1962. *Politics of the Kula Ring.* Manchester.

WOODWARD, M. 1974. *Asymmetric Exchange in the Religious and Social Organization of the Hill Tribes of Assam and Burma.* m.s.

YOUNG, M. 1972. *Fighting With Food.* London.

Appendix II

Generalized Change, Theocracy, and the Opium Trade [*Critique of Anthropology* 7:15–31, 1987]

After the publication of Nugent's "Closed Systems and Contradiction: The Kachin in and out of History" (*Man* 17, 1982) and the ensuing exchange between himself and Leach (1983), I felt that further discussion might only confuse the issues even more than Leach had proceeded to do by avoiding the main arguments. Since the reproduction of Nugent's thesis in Wolf's magnum opus (1982), with pretensions to a new approach with which I have myself been associated, I have changed my mind. Beyond the problems involved in the historical material itself, is what I feel is the inadmissible vulgarization to which the global approach is submitted and the consequently low theoretical level to which Nugent manages to plummet his analysis. I hope to correct this in the following sketch, not by means of Leachian slander, but by taking Nugent's propositions seriously enough to warrant a principled critique.

Nugent appears to present his approach to Kachin material as an application, strangely implicit, of a world system perspective, or perhaps what is generally referred to in American anthropology as a "political economy" framework. This entails placing the Kachin in a larger geographic and historical perspective and considering the way in which Kachin economic relations to the larger regional and world economies has determined their particular history and even their political organization. I find it curious, to say the least, that he should suggest this as a new perspective when he had access to my book which in its introduction to the original thesis (1972) explicitly presents a "global systemic" framework for an interpretation of the Kachin and Kachin-type local systems. In discussion (1979:10–15), I argue that the Kachin historically occupy a position in the larger system that I refer to as independent-expansionist or predatory. Unlike the usual peripheral zones of larger centers of civilization, predatory structures are independent insofar as the maintenance of their internal organization does not depend on their integration in a larger reproductive process.

> Expansionist tribal structures—predatory structures. These are structures containing internal cycles of accumulation and that expand against both center/periphery structures and dependent structures (specialist producers and trade specialists), exploiting the flow of

wealth in the larger system by extortion. They often expand into small states, sometimes into larger "barbarian" empires—especially in periods of decline of the centers on whom they feed. Examples of such structures are found in northern Southeast Asia, Yunnan, Central Asia, etc. Such structures tend to become dependent on their ability to exploit other sectors of the system when they expand into states and empires insofar as they must maintain increasingly elaborate military machines, political alliances, and a greatly elaborated court life.' (Friedman 1979:13)

In contrast to such internally reproductive structures, peripheral structures are those whose internal reproductive organization is directly integrated into larger regional cycles, thus whose very existence depends on their external relations. Thus, the Tai "feudal" statelets, tributary to Angkor, appear to have been organized as prestige-good systems where chiefly or princely position depended upon the monopoly of export/import and whose particular kinship structure might be understood as a product of the flows of people and valuables that are derivative of such monopolistic relations (Condominas 1976).

I also argued quite explicitly that predatory structures might become transformed into peripheral structures in changing conditions in the larger field of the global system and that the reverse process might also be a possibility (1979:14). In the body of the book itself I refer to and discuss the way that some groups had become specialized in particular kinds of production or control over trade routes (nothing new of course) and how this specialization could be related to the maintenance of *gumsa* type of organization and even to its transformation into Buddhist-based state forms—i.e. no longer *gumsa* nor even traditional Kachin (a problem that Nugent entirely overlooks).

Nugent's presentation, thus, represents nothing new to me, nor, I suppose to Leach. But in his pretensions to a world systemic historical understanding, it is quite extraordinary that he does not refer to my own theoretical perspective which clearly aims to articulate local and global processes. Perhaps this is due to the fact that, in spite of claims to the contrary, Nugent's perspective on the Kachin is both a-theoretical and a-structural. It is because of this that his "explanation" of the emergence of the category of *gumlao* seems such an inadequate substitute for any of the already existing discussions.

Historical Correlation Versus Structural Analysis
Nugent's argument is quite simply that the existence of Kachin chiefdoms (*gumsa*) was a function of the regional trade system linking Upper Burma and China in which the Kachin participated as producers of opium and jade, and as "protectors" of trade routes. Opium production is singled out as the most important factor in the *gumsa* economy. The increasing instability of the area beginning with the Panthay rebellion in the 1850s led to a virtual breakdown in the trade, undermining the basis of chiefly authority, and precipitating, fi-

nally, a series of *gumlao* revolts and the establishment of a *gumlao*-egalitarian polity, which had *never* existed previously. This political decline was reinforced by British intervention and annexation, which prevented the Kachin from engaging in their usual trading and opium-producing activities. Thus, in the Triangle region, north of the administered area until the 1920s, *gumsa* hierarchy began to appear soon after the re-establishment of peace, a development that was hindered by the British presence further south.

The "theory" behind this periodization of Kachin history is simply (quite simply indeed) that trade causes political hierarchy, its disappearance the collapse of hierarchy. No attempt is made to even suggest what the relation might be between trade and social structure: Who might control the trade or the production of trade goods; how the goods might circulate internally. If, for example, chiefs are known to possess opium-producing slaves, this does not account for the existence of chiefs in the first place, nor for the fact that intensive trading and opium growing are primarily associated not with *gumsa* but with *gumlao* Kachin (Maran La Raw 1967:138–9).

Now to begin with, it is generally acknowledged that the Kachin of the Eastern Hills (Sinlum and Sadon areas) were engaged in trade and especially "protection" upon which I have argued, the maintenance of *gumsa* organization depended in the nineteenth century. The disruption of the Burma-China trade certainly affected the domains along the southern routes through Sadon and Sinlum, but it is arguable that the real blow to the political system was the British prevention of Kachin taxation of the trade. My argument was that the revenues of trade could be invested in the heavy demands for feasting and inflated costs of circulation required to uphold *gumsa* hierarchy in an area that was so depleted agriculturally as to be inadequate to such purposes. In other words, a *previously established* chiefly polity could be maintained by a kind of petty imperialism. There is, however, no evidence that *gumsa* structures ever developed on the basis of exclusive lineage rights to opium-producing land. While opium cash cropping has apparently increased significantly in this century, associated in fact with the spread of *gumlao* organization, the nineteenth century *gumsa* domains were primarily dependent on their military control over the trade routes.

If there is evidence of large-scale opium cultivation among the Kachin (Singpho) of Assam in the 1830s, something that cannot be clearly ascertained, as demonstrated by the exchange between Leach and Nugent, this still absolutely begs the whole question of the relation between chiefly structure and opium production. Nugent refers to Bayfield (1873) in his argument for the existence of large-scale opium production in the Hukawng Valley (no reference is made to the Singpho-Kachin semi-states further west in Assam). This officer describes the generalized production of opium in "carefully fenced in" village plantations. It is clear that there is opium here, but it does not seem likely that the scale of "plantation" suggested by Nugent would be "carefully fenced in." More curious is the fact that another early report (Hannay 1837) makes no reference to the so-called opium trade adduced by Nugent.

> The only traffic of any consequence carried on in this valley is with
> the amber which the Singphos sell to a few Chinese, Chinese Shans,
> and Chinese Singphos, who find their way here annually. (Pemberton
> in Hannay 1837:271)

It would appear that opium was among the commodities purchased in exchange,
and only one commodity among others:

> The Chinese sometimes pay in silver for the amber, but they also
> bring them warm jackets, carpets, straw hats, copper pots, and opium,
> which they give in exchange for it. (Hannay 1837:271)

To claim, as Nugent does in reference to Kachin purchase of opium from the
Chinese, that this is a mere question of seasonality seems patently ridiculous.
After all, his one source from the period in question, Bayfield, was there in the
same "off-season" as Hannay. It seems, furthermore, quite absurd that a re-
connaissance expedition of the type undertaken by Hannay should have been
so casual as to have been entirely ignorant of so important a cash crop for British interests, especially if it were grown on a significant scale.

Some of the most stratified of the Singpho inhabited the plains area of Assam
northwest of the Hukawng Valley. Nugent does not discuss these groups with
reference to the opium economy. We know from the earliest reports that these
Kachin had thousands of Assamese slaves later freed by the British for their
tea plantations. The economy of the Ahom state of Assam, to which the Singpho
were vassal, was quite developed and there was a great deal of trade. Nowhere
is it stated that opium was the mainstay of the region, although it is surely the
case that opium was produced in the eighteenth and nineteenth centuries.
What can be said is that after the British had crippled the Kachin political
economy in Assam there are reports of "immoderate addiction to opium" (Butler
1847 in Elwin 1959:399) in the midst of widespread political decadence and
increasing impoverishment.

Nugent uses the material from this area to argue that the "repudiation of
gumsa obligations" was a function of British intervention and not part of an
internally generated cycle. No one, to be sure, denies the course of events
here. But the decline of the Assamese Kachin polities has nothing to do with a
gumlao revolt. Not only is there not a single reference to such a revolt, but the
later descriptions of the area continue to describe a stratified society, albeit in
a state of dissolution. Leach's early argument (1946:481) was that the Kachin
of this area were well on their way to state formation before the British liber-
ated the enslaved basis of their development. I used the same material to demonstrate the capacity of the Kachin system to develop in the direction of a
state-class organization in favorable condition of expansion. I even suggested
that the Assamese Kachin had deviated significantly from the traditional *gumsa*

model (Friedman 1979:262). All of this militates against Nugent's interpretation. The fact that no *gumlao* revolt occurred in this area is, furthermore, directly contradictory to Nugent's simple no trade = no chiefs thesis.

The entirety of the historical material upon which Nugent's thesis is based comes from two periods in two areas; the first from the Hukawng-Assam border area in the 1830s and '40s and the second from the Eastern Hills region in the 1880s and onward. Virtually no reference is made to the classical homeland of the Kachin chiefdom, the famous Triangle region between the *Mali Hka* and *Nmai Hka* rivers. Evidence of neither commercial opium production nor the control of trade routes is to be found for this region. Its great *gumchying gumsa* domains were very hierarchical and possessed a great many slaves. They also experienced a classical *gumlao* movement in the nineteenth century and were by all accounts on their way back to a *gumsa* structure early in this century.

Nugent attempts, but only by implication, to argue that the Triangle Kachin were opium cash croppers. His argument is based on references to Yunnan in general in the nineteenth century. He thus feels safe in stating that this famous *gumlao* revolt resulted from the breakdown in the China-Burma trade and that the revival of *gumsa* was possible because the Triangle Kachin, beyond the bounds of British administration, "continued to collect tolls from trading caravans" (Nugent 1982:523). This argument is doubly false! The singular reason is simply that the Triangle Kachin do not appear to have had any direct access to the trade routes in question, all of which were in the hands of the Eastern Kachin, the Gauri and Atsi clans. This would imply that neither the disruption of the trade routes nor their reinstatement could affect the *gumchying* polities in a direct way. No one, of course, is denying that the Triangle Kachin had access to opium, especially in the late nineteenth century, but its presumed centrality to the local political economy is simply contradicted by the facts. In his scramble to summon evidence for large scale opium production in the Triangle, Nugent makes use of MacGregor and Sandeman who refer to the use of opium as money. MacGregor, who visited Hkamti Long, which is, moreover, northwest of the Triangle, in 1886, also describes the Kachin relation to opium as a clear case of buying and not of selling:

> The Hkamtis said that sometimes a trading party went to China, that the journey took them one month and eight days, that they had to cross in boats two big rivers . . . The traders bought opium in China at the rate of 10s6d a pound, but they said it was not so good as the Assam opium, which they could obtain after a journey which only took them half the time it did to go to China. The opium of Assam cost them, however, about 30s a pound. (MacGregor, Maj. C. 1887:34)

The very fact that opium was used as a means of circulation would seem to imply that it was relatively scarce and not, as suggested by Nugent, a major product. In any case the Kachin and Shan of Hkamti Long ought not to be lumped together with the chiefly domains of the Triangle. Now it is, of course, probably that the Triangle chiefs received tradegoods from the East in exchange for titles, since it is known that the trading chiefs of the Gauri and Atsi attached themselves to the Triangle Shadan Tu lineage (Friedman 1979:112; Leach 1946:565). But in the absence of any sign of major opium production in the area, the Kachin of the Triangle can only be considered as counter-evidence for Nugent's argument.

Finally, even the Eastern Hills region bordering on China, which was the most heavily and increasingly involved region in opium production from the middle of the nineteenth century, does not appear to have operated on a scale like that implied by Nugent. Walker (1892) places opium production in the following perspective.

> A good deal of opium is grown locally, nearly every village having its little patch of poppy cultivation; but the local output does not nearly meet the demand, and a great deal if not the bulk of the opium is bought sometimes from passing Chinese traders, but more frequently the Kachins make a little trip across the frontier and purchase the article for themselves at one of the Chinese outlying villages. (Walker 1892:168)

More generally, the overall picture for the region associates a progressively widening opium production throughout the latter nineteenth and twentieth centuries to a situation exactly opposite to that suggested by Nugent. Those areas that have come to rely almost exclusively on opium have tended to become or maintain a *gumlao*, or at least a *gumrawng gumsa* organization; a kind of *gumsa* system that,

> Acknowledges no hereditary paramount chief, and where a claim to chieftainship must be justified ritually as well as in terms of capable leadership . . . whose chiefs generally become powerless figureheads. (Maran La Raw 1967:139)

This contrast between more or less "democratic" opium growers in a heavy trading zone and "autocratic" or perhaps theocratic agriculturalists without such connections is completely contrary to Nugent's entire model. But then, the group usually singled out as the most illustrious of opium specialists in the region in the early part of this century are the "egalitarian" headhunting Wa of the Burma-China border.

Internal Cycles and External Determinants

Let me try and place the previous discussion in perspective. Nugent argues, sometimes explicitly, sometimes covertly, that there is no such thing as a *gumsa/*

gumlao cycle and, on the contrary, that *gumlao* is the historical product of a nineteenth-century breakdown of a Burma-China trade featuring opium that was previously organized in a stable system. Even if Nugent's general argument made sense, his understanding of the history of Burma-China relations ought to have convinced him that the northeast border area has been a constant scene of turbulence and instability and that for centuries before the 1850 Panthay rebellion, armies from both the Burmese and Chinese sides traversed the Kachin Hills. Such turbulence ought to be argument enough for the probable oscillation between *gumlao* and *gumsa* forms of organization in the past. Thus, even if one were to accept Nugent's argument concerning the relation between trade and hierarchy, the history of the Kachin might still be argued to be cyclical. For more serious reasons, however, Nugent's propositions must be rejected. Because there is no demonstrable connection, theoretically or otherwise, between trade and/or opium production and *gumsa* in the first half of the nineteenth century, because opium cash cropping and even increasing trade intensity are tendentially associated with declining *gumsa* and because the one area, the Triangle, where both access to trade routes and cash cropping are at a minimum, is designated as the traditional home of *gumchying gumsa* polity; because of all this and more, Nugent's "model" must be discarded. In the absence of a theoretical analysis of the relation between trade, opium, and chiefly power, and in the presence of empirical correlations that positively falsify his assumptions, the only support that can be mustered for this barest of hypotheses is the several statements confirming the existence of Kachin-owned slaves (presumably chiefly) that produced opium. But in the absence of any theory to the contrary, it is logical to assume that monopolizing trade routes and producing opium for sale, just as producing jade and amber, were the things that *already established chiefs* did in the proper circumstances. In so far as these activities enabled them to further increase their prestige and status within the defined structure of the Kachin system, they clearly maintained and even promoted the expansion of *gumsa* relations, no more no less. Nowhere is there the slightest indication that such activities were the foundation of the emergence of *gumsa* polity.

Finally, the cycles purported by most to exist for the Kachin are also present among a number of other groups, such as the Naga and Chin, who occupy very different geo-political positions is the larger region. The advantage of the model of internal cycles of autocracy and democracy is that it is independent of the specific historical phenomena to which Nugent is entirely bound. The existence of such political cycles over a wide region, with and without trade, is evidence enough against an external factor argument.

It should also be reiterated, since Nugent is clearly unaware of the existence of structural differences, that many of the so-called *gumsa* Kachin may have been organized more like Shan states, or, as I argued for Assam, like theocratic or "asiatic" states. This would imply that the concept *gumsa* cannot properly be applied to them, as both their internal structure and dynamic properties are significantly different.

In sum, the argument against Nugent is that:

1. Opium production and other forms of commerce may have helped to maintain, and even in some cases expand, *gumsa* organization where it already existed, but there is absolutely no evidence that such organization ever originated on such a base.

2. On the contrary, the available evidence indicates that opium production and high levels of trade intensity are related not to development but to a decline in *gumsa* hierarchy.

3. The Triangle region, which is the home of the traditional paramount chiefs of the *gumchying gumsa* domains, is the area least associated (if at all) with border trade and opium production.

4. Many of the Kachin cited as *gumsa* by Nugent, such as the Singpho of Assam, the Jade Mine district Kachin, etc., appear to have been organized in more state-like forms, or, as in the case of the Jade Mine chiefs, on the lines of a family company, so that the category *gumsa* may not even be applicable. In fact, it might be argued that, in some cases, the specialization in a trade good could be responsible for the transformation of *gumsa* domains into small states entirely reproduced via the larger market. It is significant that those areas where *gumsa* had been transformed into other kinds of state or class structures did not experience *gumlao* revolt in the nineteenth century. All these phenomena militate against Nugent's interpretation.

5. The cyclical phenomenon that Nugent has tried to explain away is not limited to the Kachin but occurs over a very wide area among groups faced with external conditions that are incommensurable with those assumed to exist for the Kachin.

As an alternative to simple-minded correlations we shall, in the following, sketch a reconstruction of the relations between the internal dynamic of the Kachin system and the larger regional processes within which it was contained.

1. Kachin political forms cannot simply be divided into the opposed types, *gumsa/gumlao*. Nor are these two polar types equivalent to chiefly versus egalitarian society. To begin with, there are, according to Maran La Raw (1967b), three distinct kinds of Kachin chiefship. *Gumchying gumsa*, to which we have referred, occurs exclusively in the Triangle region. This is the "traditional" theocratic organization based on fixed inheritance of office. *Gumrawng gumsa*, the "proud and free" chiefship, occurs mainly in the Eastern Hills region and is associated with the Burma-China trade route area. *Gumrawng* chiefs are characterized as "antihereditary" insofar as they do not accept the legitimacy of hereditary claims to office, which must be ritually demonstrated by every claimant. *Gumrawng* chiefs are associated with the rejection of subordination to chiefs of "higher" status, i.e., the *gumchying* chiefs of the Triangle to whom they may have been attached in the past. They are, then, *gumsa* but not hereditary, and they seem to fit into the more or less fragmentary picture of the Eastern Hills domains in the latter part of the nineteenth century. *Gumlao* chiefs are a rather

special case since they are not antihereditary, but simply nonhereditary, and owe their positions to an act of subordination to other *gumsa* chiefs. This is also a phenomenon localized to the Eastern Hills area, preponderant in opium-growing zones where commercial wealth might be used in an attempt to build local followings via political alliance-subordination to "real" chiefs. The existence of such chiefs might appear to be a contradiction in terms. The ambivalence of their position is captured in the translation "republican chiefs." *Gumlao* chiefs are doubly dependent, first on the sponsorship of a *gumsa* chief and second on the recognition of a local population that may at any time have them removed. True *gumlao* is, by definition, a community without any alliance relation to a *gumsa* polity. A truly independent *gumlao* community is, thus, necessarily chiefless, since *gumlao* chiefship is no more than a function of such a dependency relation.

Finally, there are *gumsa* polities settled in larger Shan domains that are not to be considered thoroughly Kachin in terms of their internal structure insofar as their chiefly positions are fixed by administrative fiat and are not the result of any internal process of differentiation. *Gumsa* chiefs in the Shan States are part of a larger administrative organization and not an emergent institution at the local level.

These political types are, furthermore, as we have argued (1979), transformationally related to one another. *Gumchying* can become *gumrawng*, *gumlao* can become *gumsa*, *gumrawng* might even conceivably become *gumchying*. In no case can we accept the oversimplified dichotomization suggested by Nugent since it overlooks some of the most essential structural variations observable in the historical and ethnographic material.

Another important point, referred to above, is that the nineteenth-century Tsasen chiefdoms of the Hukawng Valley and Assam were probably not, as Nugent assumes, examples of typical *gumsa* organization. On the contrary, it would appear that these chiefdoms were significantly transformed in the direction of state-class formation (Friedman 1979:260–262; Leach 1946:481–2). The significant decline of the major chiefly redistributive ritual (of the *madai nat*), in conditions where the resource base had shifted to intensive agriculture and/or mining, indicated the emergence of an altered process of social reproduction in these areas. But then, I argued for a number of variant developments from trade-route imperialism to specialized production within a larger regional economy, that might have important transformative effects upon the internal *gumsa* dynamic, effects that might account for the Shan-state–like character of certain Kachin domains (1979:191–195; 257–260).

2. The nomenclature of the *gumsa/gumlao* cycle might well be considered incorrect insofar as *gumlao* concerns the question of legitimacy and not of hierarchy as such. In this sense, Nugent's proposal that *gumsa* is traditional while *gumlaw* (in the sense of egalitarian) is a recent historical product is contradicted by the clear evidence of political oscillation, not only among the nineteenth- and twentieth-century Kachin but among the Naga and Chin, who

appear to have comparable cycles of expansion and contraction.

Nugent criticizes Leach's evidence for the Hukawng Valley in the last century to the effect that:

> The Singphos have no acknowledged chief. Each Tsanbwa is the independent head of his own village. (Bayfield 1873:222)

Nugent's answer to this is simply that *gumsa*, by definition, refers to the existence of chiefs and not to the size of their domains. But, in terms of our enumeration and discussion of Kachin political types, such an argument misses the point. First, chiefship is not identical to *gumsa*. There are *gumlao* chiefs. Second, the existence of single village chiefs is a strong indication of the political fragmentation typical of *gumlao*, or at least of *gumrawng*, organization. If our aim is to characterize the various states of Kachin society, large unified domains versus fragmented village organization, paramount chieftaincies versus democratic or "republican" elected headmen, then whether or not people refer to one another as *gumlao* may not be entirely relevant. That is, if *gumlao* refers to a mid-nineteenth-century movement against the inheritance of chiefly title (Maran La Raw, personal communication), then it need not have any direct bearing on the essentially different process of the cyclical expansion and collapse of chiefly hierarchy. It is certainly conceivable that the word *gumlao* might well have altered its meaning over time. Neufville (1828) claims that the word refers to Kachin slaves, and it might be argued that the original meaning of the term was similar to the notion of communities dependent upon powerful chiefly neighbors who become their wife-givers. This, in any case, would be congruent with Maran La Raw's definition of *gumlao* chiefship. If the internal mechanisms of exchange and accumulation of status which we posit to be general for Kachin society are accepted, then the social differentiation that must occur in *gumlao* society in combination with the external alliance-submission to more powerful *gumsa* chiefs ought logically to lead to the establishment of *gumlao* chiefship. Now it is conceivable that the kind of *gumlao* movement suggested by Maran La Raw consists in the repudiation of the dependency upon *gumsa* chiefs that may have characterized an increasingly wealthy *gumlao* chiefly class. Such an argument may be partially correct, but it can only become intelligible in light of the argument that I shall present below.

3. Our model of *gumsa* developments envisages the conversion of agricultural surpluses, via feasts, into prestige, affinal rank, and finally segmentary rank, all of which is dependent upon a rapid accumulation of slaves and a process of agricultural intensification in conditions unsuitable to such intensification. The outcome is periodic crisis and a breakdown of the process of accumulation, i.e., "*gumlao*" revolts. In my argument, this essentially internal accumulation cycle was variously articulated with larger regional processes. In the Eastern Hills, the Kachin chiefs became dependent upon control over the trade routes in order to maintain their *gumsa* organization. Consequently, any

disturbance in the trade ought to have led to a more *gumlao* situation, i.e., political fragmentation, since the local economy had no resources to fall back upon in order to maintain the *gumsa* requirements of feasting and exchange.

According, again, to Maran La Raw, the origins of the *gumlao* movement are related not to the decline but to the increase in trade in the Eastern Hills. The key to understanding this phenomenon lies at the intersection of the internally driven expansion of *gumsa* domains and the regional economy. The basic means of domain extension is the emigration of elder sons (noninheriting) with a segment of the local population to clear new areas. The process is ritually rather complicated (see below) and requires that the son first forfeit his chiefly status and then give a series of large-scale feasts over a seven-year period, pay an enormous brideprice, greater than any in "living memory," all under the sponsorship of an established *gumchying* chief. At the end of the period, the "candidate" gives a great feast to which the sponsor is invited. He is finally granted full title as a *gumchying gumsa* chief. This process implies both territorial expansion and an extraordinarily high rate of inflation, both of which are indicated in the model that I have suggested (1975:79). It also reveals the locus of contradiction in the expansion process itself. A *gumyu* pretender to chiefship can only maintain himself in such a position so long as he has the resource base to continue feasting throughout the period of his candidature. If domains expand into areas where such resources are not easily obtainable, there are bound to be conflicts. In such cases, a situation where there is a high ratio of *gumyu* to *gumchying* chiefs can easily become a *gumlao* crisis. There is reason to believe that this may have been the case in the Duleng area of the northern Triangle (Friedman 1979:178–179). This is the kind of process that I took to be the classical model of Kachin cyclical expansion. The high ratio referred to above would presumably be the result of the difficulty encountered by pretenders in completing their candidacies. A similarly skewed ratio would tend to emerge in the Eastern Hills, but this time for opposite reason. From the structure of the alliances and genealogies it can be ascertained that the Eastern Kachin were subordinate elder son or *dama* lineages to the great *gumchying* chiefs of the Triangle. Here the large and easily accessible wealth of the trade routes must have created the conditions for intensive decentralized competition among a growing number of potential chiefs and put heavy inflationary pressure on the entire system. Now, *gumlao* philosophy is based on the repudiation of the legitimacy of *gumchying* imposed ratifications of chiefly status, in other words a repudiation of the tributary links to the Triangle.

Given the lack of precise historical data, I would suggest two possible interpretations of the *gumlao* phenomenon. According to Maran La Raw, *gumlao* is a direct product of the increase of attainable wealth in the Eastern Hills. The increasing density of trade entailed a more fragmented accumulation of wealth, more regional competition for status, more "chiefs" and a destabilization of domain hierarchies—a generally *gumrawng* state of affairs. The *gumlao* movement, according to Maran La Raw, was a "philosophical" rebellion against the claims of hereditary chiefship, not of chiefship in general. This would appear to be a logical outcome of the trade-induced flood of *arrivistes*. But however much the increased commerce might have corroded the traditional chiefly hierarchy, the dislocation of the trade routes and the consequent disruption of accumulation would still have had drastic effects on whatever other process was underway. Thus, the violent overthrow of chiefly hierarchy referred to in the British reports is one where the existence of chiefs is simply not tolerated, and where egalitarianism would appear to be the norm. Now, if what anthropologists and colonial officers have called *gumlao* is not the same as Maran La Raw's definition, this is probably due to the changing historical context:

> *Gumlao 1*: increased political fragmentation due to access to trade routes and opium production for cash. *Gumlao* "chiefs," *gumlao magam* (republican chiefs) are nonhereditary and regionally powerless, but they can be quite rich.

> *Gumlao 2*: the collapse of accumulation processes in either agricultural or trade-based zones; it is characterized by the absence of chiefs—the establishment of powerless headmen (*akyi*) in their place and the absence of a larger regional economy and polity.

The introduction of opium in a *gumlao 2* situation, and perhaps even a *gumlao 1* situation, is bound to have "egalitarian" effects. The reason is simply that there is a tendency for everyone to be able to cultivate this cash crop, to accumulate cash that is convertible into prestige, and thus to undermine the conditions of existence of hierarchy which is dependent on the increasing monopolization of the distributable wealth in society.

My earlier interpretation of Eastern Hills history was that the area was essentially *gumrawng* at the start of this century. The previous existence of a *gumlao 1* or *2* movement not withstanding, it would appear that this region, where trade-route imperialism was essential for *gumsa* organization, was converted via British intervention into an increasingly *gumlao* opium-based economy. While the British might have been able to prevent the Kachin from taxing trade routes, they could not prevent opium production.

> Although the British made a number of efforts at abolishing opium cultivation in the Shan States, geography, ethnography, and politics ultimately defeated them. (McCoy & Adams 1972:70)

The reasons for this are pretty clear:

> The British were hardly eager to spend vast sums of money administering these enormous territories, and so, in exchange for the right to build railways and control foreign policy, they recognized the

sawbwa's traditional powers and prerogatives . . . doomed their future efforts at the eradicating opium cultivation in northeastern Burma. The *sabwas* received a considerable portion of the tribal opium harvest as tribute, and opium exports to Thailand and Lower Burma represented an important part of their personal income. (McCoy & Adams 1972:71)

The unstable transition between the former trade route imperialism and the present opium dependency which occurred in the latter part of the past century corresponds to the emergence of *gumrawng gumsa*, where many potential chiefs make largely unsuccessful claims to paramountcy.

Another correlation worth considering is that opium production occurs primarily in areas of high population density and relatively high levels of ecological depletion, i.e., in areas where cash cropping may have become a necessity for survival. The Eastern Kachin Hills and the Yunnan borderland, as well as the Wa country, are all severely overintensified zones. The "egalitarian" Wa, as well as the *gumlao* Kachin, are clearly associated with opium in precisely these regions. Whether opium is a significant source of wealth is unclear, but all reports indicate that the proceeds of opium sales are (or were) the monopoly of middleman traders. Opium, then, is not so much a resource for the establishment of hierarchy as a cash crop of last resort for increasingly impoverished and declining polities. As I stated for the egalitarian, head-hunting Wa, opium growers were invariably in debt to Shan middlemen, and wherever ecological conditions were somewhat better, there was a tendency to grow food crops instead of opium (Friedman 1979:249; Harvey 1933:92).

Conclusion

I have tried here to raise the level of a previous exchange between Nugent and Leach to one more adequate to a journal of serious intellectual pretensions. Nugent's truly simple-minded argument was never really answered in any way by Leach, who merely scanned his old notes to find empirical counter-evidence for Nugent's totally inadequate "model," permitting the latter to do the same ad infinitum. Did they or did they not have large plantations in X in 1830? How shall we interpret the reports of X, Y, and Z regarding the existence of *gumlao* in the early literature? Why did Leach write one thing in 1946 and the opposite thing in 1983? How can Leach be questioned about the history of the Kachin when he has read *all* the published and unpublished data and, like Baron Munchausen, *vos dere Charlie*? While Leach's list of "facts" about opium does make sense it is altogether inadequate as a "demolition," "formal" or otherwise, of Nugent, since instead of presenting a counter-argument we are reduced in the end to comparing quotations. It is not difficult to demonstrate the inconsistency of Nugent's argument with the commonly available empirical material. It can, as I have tried to show, be falsified. But Leach is not interested in the argument—which is beneath his contempt. He is only concerned to ridicule the lack of Nugent's expertise. This, of course, is nothing new for Leach, who has always tended to argue by dismissal on general grounds (so-and-so never did fieldwork, so-and-so has no mathematical background, so-and-so is not an anthropologist). Thus, Lévi-Strauss is interesting but really doesn't know the material. Maran La Raw (student of Chomsky) is a mere Kachin schoolteacher and not to be believed. The numerous missionaries who inhabited the Kachin Hills for most of their lives cannot be trusted since they had no anthropological training. Is this the same expert who presumably lost his field notes before writing his thesis, who has virtually totally contradicted himself with respect to the basic structures and mechanisms of Kachin society several times since his thesis (clearly his best work)? It would appear so. But then, this is the same Leach who has recently characterized Gluckman as an anthropologist whose South African "Russian-Jewish" background led him to "an irrational devotion to stable systems in general" (Leach 1984:20). It is Gluckman, of course, alone among the "functionalists" who speaks of hypertrophy and of "steady change of magnitudes within and between institutions until there is a sudden and radical transformation of form" (1968:232), the same anthropologist who brilliantly criticized *Political Systems of Highland Burma* for functionalizing history and turning contradictions into a model of equilibrium (oscillating), in a mysteriously unpublished review article! All of this inconsequence, self-contradiction, and admitted "arrogance and prejudice" (Leach 1984:21), on the part of one of the anthropological knights of the Empire does not do much for the discipline. I, for one, have nothing against polemic, but there was a time when a certain amount of intellectual argument was an absolute requirement. Even Leach was an active participant and major contributor to such debate (Leach 1961).

I have tried to show in my discussion that Nugent's hypothesis concerning variations in Kachin political structure is theoretically inadequate and clearly falsifiable if one makes use of the existing data in a systematic fashion. I have, further, tried to provide a more satisfactory model to account for the way in which the articulation between the Kachin system and larger global processes might account for the historical phenomena to which Nugent has addressed himself. In the introduction to Friedman (1979), I have even sketched a global model that might account for both the distribution and maintenance of Kachin-type structures in larger systems.

I consider the emergence of a global framework in anthropology to be of utmost import (Ekholm & Friedman 1980) for the future of the field. But this requires a theoretical elaboration that is more structurally sensitive and sophisticated than the kinds of correlation that satisfy Nugent and other "political economists" (Ekholm & Friedman 1984). If I have maintained a serious tone throughout this discussion, it is because previous rampage by Leach so obscured the problem as to render it unrecognizable.

References

Bayfield, G. T.
   1873   "Narrative of a Journey from Ava to the Frontier of Assam and Back, Performed between December 1836 and May 1837 under the Orders of Colonel Burney...," in *Selection of Papers*, 134–244.

Butler, J.
   1837   *A Sketch of Assam with Some Account of the Hill Tribes, by an Officer*, London.

Condominas, G.
   1967   "Essai sur l'evolution du systeme politique thai," *Ethnos*, 1–4.

Ekholm, K. & Friedman, J.
   1980   "Towards a Global Anthropology," in Blusse, L., Wesseling, G. D. & Winius, G. D., (eds.), *History and Underdevelopment*. Leiden.
   1985   New Introduction to (1980), in *Critique of Anthropology*, 97–119.

Elwin, V. (ed)
   1959   *India's North-Eastern Frontier*, London.

Friedman, J.
   1979   *System, Structure and Contradiction in the Evolution of 'Asiatic' Social Formations*. Copenhagen.

Gluckman, M.
   1968   "The Utility of the Equilibrium Model in the Study of Social Change," *American Anthropologist*, 70.

Hannay, S. F.
   1837   "Abstract of the Journal of a Route Travelled by Captain S. F. Hannay in 1835–36 from the Capital of Ava to the Amber Mines of the Hukawng Valley on the South Eastern Frontier of Assam," *Trans. As. Soc. Bengal*, 6 April.

Harvey, G. E.
   1933   *Wa Precis*, Rangoon.

Leach, E. R.
  1946   *Cultural Change with Special Reference to the Hill Tribes of Burma and Assam*. Unpublished Ph.D. dissertation, University of London.
  1951   "The Structural Implications of Matrilateral Cross-Cousin Marriage," *JRAI*, 51.
  1954   *Political Systems of Highland Burma*. London.
  1961   *Rethinking Anthropology*. London.
  1969   "Kachin and Haka Chin: A Rejoinder to Levi-Strauss," *Man*, 69.
  1983   "Imaginary Kachins," *Man*, 18.

Levi-Strauss, C.
  1967   *Les structures elementaires de la parente*, Paris.

MacGregor, C. R.
  1887   "Journal of the Expedition under Colonel Woodthorpe from Upper Assam to the Irrawadi," *Proc. R. Geogr. Soc.*, 9.

Maran La Raw
  1967a   "Toward a Basis for Understanding the Minorities of Burma," in Kunstadter (ed.), *Southeast Asian Tribes, Minorities and Nations*. Princeton.
  1967b   *Notes on the Algebra of Interacting Human Groups*. Manuscript.

McCoy, A. W.
  1972   *The Politics of Heroin in Southeast Asia*, New York.

Neufville, J. B.
  1828   "On the Geography and Population of Assam," *As. Res.*, 16.

Nugent, D.
  1982   "Closed Systems and Contradiction: The Kachin in and out of History," *Man*, 17.
  1983   Reply to Leach, *Man*, 18.

Walker, J. J.
  1892   Expeditions among the Kachin Tribes of the North East Frontier of Upper Burma Compiled by General J. J. Walker from the Reports of Lieut. Elliot . . . ," *Proc. R. Geogr. Soc.*, 14, 3.

Wolfe, E.
  1982   *Europe and the People Without a History*, Berkeley.